Introduction to Biblical Christian Education

Edited by

WERNER C. GRAENDORF

❧ ❧ ❧
❧ ❧ ❧

MOODY PRESS

CHICAGO

Library of Congress Cataloging in Publication Data

Main entry under title:
Introduction to Biblical Christian education.
    Includes bibliographies.
    1. Christian education. I. Graendorf, Werner C.
BV1471.2.I57   207   81-1608
ISBN 0-8024-4128-9

Second Printing, 1981

Contents

Part I
UNDERSTANDING BIBLICAL CHRISTIAN EDUCATION

Part II
CHRISTIAN EDUCATION AS A DYNAMIC PROCESS

Part III

THE PERSON IN CHRISTIAN EDUCATION

Part IV

THE FAMILY IN CHRISTIAN EDUCATION

Part V

ORGANIZING THE CHURCH FOR CHRISTIAN EDUCATION

Part VI

THE SCHOOL IN CHRISTIAN EDUCATION

Direction

THIS VOLUME on contemporary ministry represents two simple but deeply pervasive convictions. One is that the fullest development of God's people, both as individual believers and as productive members of the Christian fellowship, demands a viable Christian education ministry.

The correlated conviction is that such ministry must find its essential heart and direction in the Word of God.

This, then, is a volume of practical guidance in contemporary Christian education, clearly viewed in biblical perspective. It is concerned with today's believer—his family, and his church—and the biblical faith he seeks to build and share.

The writing participants in this volume represent a broad spectrum of evangelical Christian educators. Some are established as key church thinkers, others are in process. Each has a unique contribution.

Our prayer is that what has been compiled will strengthen individual faith and ministry, as well as deepen the vitality of Christ's work everywhere.

WERNER C. GRAENDORF, Ph.D.

About the Book

HERE IS A SOLID, contemporary textbook on the basics of evangelical Christian education. It continues the pattern initiated by the 1964 J. Edward Hakes volume on education,* which has been used extensively as an introductory Christian education text.

The thirty chapters of the present volume provide a substantial overview of the Christian education field. Although the primary focus remains on the church, the survey includes biblical education related to such other concerns as the Christian school, inner city ministry, and education on the mission field.

As a symposium of thirty-four educational writers, the book represents an invigorating cross section, both geographically and vocationally, of evangelical educational thought. Contributors range from businessmen and pastors to college presidents and teaching wives. The majority, of course, are practicing educators.

The material has been arranged to lend itself readily to classroom instruction, as well as to casual reading and reference use. The thirty subjects covered are grouped under seven major categories, each representing a major area of educational concern.

The three chapters of the introductory unit focus, appropriately, on the *biblical basis* of evangelical Christian education.

The second unit, of five chapters, considers the *dynamic forces* involved in Christian teaching, including such topics as personal Bible study and the work of the Holy Spirit in education. The unit editor of this grouping, as well as for the following two units, was Dr. Robert E. Clark.

A third unit was given to the *understanding of the learner,* viewed consecutively as child, youth, and adult. A fourth unit considers the critical area of education and the *family*.

Moving from the learner and his family, the fifth grouping considers the believer's church and its educational thrust. This unit was guided by unit editor Dr. Doris Freese.

The *school* as an educational ministry was developed in the sixth unit, with Allyn Sloat serving as editor for this, as well as for the last unit. The final unit provides perspective on such *special concerns* as the parachurch ministry, special education, the inner city, and the mission field.

The chapters may be studied in units or used individually. Each has in the table of contents an introductory outline that indicates the chapter content, and all include a set of suggestions for further study. Most of the chapters also list biographical resources.

*J. Edward Hakes, ed., *An Introduction to Evangelical Christian Education* (Chicago: Moody, 1964).

Part I

UNDERSTANDING CHRISTIAN EDUCATION

THE CHRISTIAN'S ABILITY to effectively use Christian education has an essential base in the clear understanding of what Christian education really is. Such understanding begins with its biblical nature and recognizes the major influence it has, not only in the Christian's personal life, but in the life of his family, his church, and his community.

That is the thrust of the three chapters of this opening unit, for, as the first chapter points out, Christian education is considerably more than simply an educational program. It demands understanding as a basic biblical ministry, and we are here introduced to the subject of *biblical* Christian education. The first chapter goes further to provide the foundational orientation for the book.

The evangelical Christian seeks to build his life and his service on the teachings of the Word of God. In chapter 2 he is challenged to examine for himself the biblical foundation of Christian education ministry.

As Christians we are part of the family called the Body of Christ—believers of all ages. What those believers have done about Christian education in the past is an important part of our understanding of how God has worked through His people throughout history. Chapter 3 provides us with that part of our educational foundation.

1

The Challenge of Biblical Christian Education

WERNER C. GRAENDORF

THE EVANGELICAL CHURCH of the 1980s is a church of unprecedented opportunity for meaningful ministry.

It has available the communication tools and materials of a revolutionary space age. It has a fresh climate of respectability for its terms and concepts. It can use an infallible but contemporary language Bible, and it recognizes anew the ongoing work of the Holy Spirit.

It is hoped that the church of the 1980s will also recognize anew and use productively one of its most potent and sometimes neglected tools—its educational ministry.

Like education in general, Christian education has at times had an uncertain sound. A denominational church leader, for example, writing for a national survey on church ministry for the eighties, sensed "an amazing confusion about what is Christian education."[1]

How unfortunate. For here is the means that Christ willed to His people for their strength and growth and ministry. Here, indeed, is the heart of discipleship—the making of learners—as Jesus so dynamically demonstrated in His own Spirit-empowered teaching.

As concerned believers and churches we cannot ignore our biblical educational ministry.

The educational process that each of us comes through in life shapes what we believe, what we value, and what we are able to accomplish. Where that process is haphazard, weak, or aborted, it is usually reflected in the quality of life. Certainly, education in itself is no guarantee of effectiveness or success. But the Spirit-empowered understanding and outliving of Bible-based teaching is a considerable assurance. That is our challenge as parents, pastors, and educators.

WERNER C. GRAENDORF, Ph.D., is professor of Christian education, Moody Bible Institute, Chicago, Illinois.

The remaining decades of this century are pivotal for education. Secular educators such as John Holt and Ivan Illich have written about the de-schooling of society. Others speak of the failure of American education.[2] There are extensive experimentations and deep uncertainties.

What about Christian education? What is the educational challenge for the church as it seeks to equip productive believers in this decade? There are basic educational challenges to consider:

- The biblical understanding of our Christian faith—really knowing what we believe
- The experiential development of life as a Christian—Christian living as an everyday experience
- The intergenerational growth of the Christian family—having a truly Christian home
- The moral development of our children—preparation for living in an increasingly amoral culture
- Our meaningful impact as Christians on contemporary society—touching people for Christ.

Focal in the outworking of each of those is a meaningful teaching ministry. Take the growth of the Christian family as an example. We are talking about the educational involvement of providing a biblical understanding of marriage and family; of training for effective sharing of parental faith and standards with children; of meaningful family worship; of family communication and recreation; of parent-teen relationships.

Those are critical concerns of educational effort as it impinges on today's Christian family. Into that comes the use of such educational means as the teaching seminar, the young couples' Bible class, the resource center of quality audiovisual and reading materials, and the encouragement of informal sharing-learning experiences. There is a concern for productive discipleship on the family level.

The program indicated is more than a routine Sunday school class. We are considering *ministry*, a reflection of a biblical understanding of education. Indeed, it is the thrust of this chapter (and the book) that such a biblical approach to Christian education points us to a powerful instrument intended by God for Christian life and ministry in our day.

It is clearly in such a context that Howard Hendricks of Dallas Theological Seminary wrote: "Christian education is not optional . . . it is essential."[3]

Biblical education provides authoritative principles on which to build. Secure in its biblical grounding, it cannot be boxed into inflexible forms and is free to use contemporary means for ministry.

Let us take an example. An educational assumption of the ministry for the 1980s survey referred to previously was that the Sunday school has outlived its usefulness.[4] For those who understand Christian education only in terms of its forms such as the Sunday school, the assumption can well be a threatening declaration. Or it can be a challenging opportunity to evaluate biblical ministry.

To be ultimately effective, the church's educational ministry must be defined in terms of its authoritative, integral meaning rather than in terms of its agencies or forms.

Although the book itself is a development of that approach, there are some foundational considerations to guide us.

CHRISTIAN EDUCATION AS *Biblical*

The first consideration is that we are talking about *biblical* Christian education, the educational approach that has its roots in God's dealings with His people from back in Genesis (Gen. 18). It is the education used by Christ in the development of His disciples (Matt. 5), and it is the emphasis credited to the apostle Paul for his eighteen months at Corinth (Acts 18). It is, therefore, an educational approach that looks to the biblical record for both its origin and its relevance.

Drawing its foundations from the Scriptures, biblical Christian education makes no apology for its theological orientation. C. B. Eavey has expressed it: "To gain true understanding of Christian education . . . one must also have a correct conception of the nature of Christianity."[5]

Interestingly, the 1978 Abingdon Press survey text of Christian (religious) education noted, "Today, the relationship between theology and education is somewhat more mystifying to representatives of both fields."[6] Yet, that relationship was quite clear to educator Paul Vieth, who wrote in an earlier survey, *The Church and Christian Education:* "Christian education can find its purpose, content, and method only in the nature of Christianity (theology)."[7] As biblical, the education we are discussing finds its orientation in God and looks to His Word for an understanding of its meaning and place.

CHRISTIAN EDUCATION AS *Education*

Biblical Christian education must be understood as true education. Note that education itself is not a school or school form, although much education takes place in a building or organized program identified as a school.

The general dictionary definition of education points to "a teaching-learning process." Significantly, biblical education also uses the terms *teaching* and *learning*. In that foundational educational passage in Deuteronomy 4, for example, "learn" and "teach" appear together in God's educational instructions to Moses (v. 10).

Again, in Paul's education-oriented chapter 3 of 2 Timothy, he refers specifically to learning and teaching in discussing Timothy's Christian education experience (vv. 10-15). The terms clearly reflect biblical education.

Especially critical in the interpretation of this education is, of course, our understanding of the term "learning." The approach of a behaviorist educational psychologist such as B. F. Skinner would be to define it in terms of conditioned change in a stimulus-response setting.[8] Biblical usage, however, encourages the concept of growth or development, as Cornelius Jaarsma in his *Human Development, Teaching and Learning* points toward,[9] and Gestalt-oriented (cognitive-field) psychologists such as Jerome Bruner favor.[10]

From a biblical perspective, Paul in Colossians, for example, associated education with completeness or maturity (1:28) and related instruction to being built up and established (2:7). Peter in his writings spoke of knowledge and use of the Word of God in terms of growth (1 Pet. 2:2). Luke described Jesus' progress mentally and socially as growth ("the Child continued to grow," 2:40).*

Biblical education then, can be said to be concerned with the *growth* of individuals in a bona fide educational effort. Yet, it is a distinctive type of growth that results from a distinctive type of education. We need to examine that distinction.

CHRISTIAN EDUCATION AS *Christian*

Lois LeBar titled her pioneering work on evangelical education appropriately, *Education That Is Christian.*

The teaching-learning process we are discussing, although it represents recognizable education, must be viewed within the framework of the added dimension of its Christian orientation.

What actually makes education Christian? There are external factors that are sometimes accepted as identification. Frank E. Gaebelein, for example, in *The Pattern of God's Truth,* notes the daily chapel services, Bible department, and student activities of a Christian nature that might be considered the marks of a Christian school. Yet those in themselves, as he points out, do not make that school's education Christian.[11] There is a deeper consideration.

Certainly in Christian education the person of Jesus Christ is at the focus, as the term *Christian*—"Christlike"—itself already implies. But there is still a broader concept that, while including the Christ-centeredness, provides a total perspective.

Look again at the Scripture references that were noted in the section on

*The scholarly development of an evangelical theory of learning is a continuing need.

biblical orientation. In the Deuteronomy passage the distinctive of that education seems unmistakable. The teaching-learning process was entwined about and focused on the revealed Word of God. The teaching was of the statutes, judgments, commandments, law, and words of "the LORD your God" (Deut. 4:1-10). It was a specific content that was not to be changed (v. 2). Old Testament education concerned the Word of God.

The distinctive in 2 Timothy 3 is just as clear. The focus of Timothy's educational experience was on "the sacred writings. . . . Scripture is inspired by God" (2 Tim. 3:14-16).

In his discussion of Christian education philosophy, Gaebelein has stated it well: "Is there, then, a watershed, a continental divide, as it were, that separates a consistent Christian philosophy of education from all forms of eclecticism? The answer is a clear affirmative. The great divide is nothing less than the authority of the Bible and its acceptance as normative. . . . a thoroughly Christian view of education must not only be based upon Scripture; it must also stand under it."[12]

Another evangelical writer adds the definitive note that "without the Bible as the foundation and core . . . there can be no true Christian education."[13] And LeBar's chapter on authority and creativity in *Education That Is Christian* points out well the relationship of such reliance on divine authority with the challenge for Christian initiative and creativity.[14]

Therefore, the education we are talking about finds its essential authority in the biblical record—the record of God's setting forth in written form His purpose and plan for man. It also draws its definition and operational orientation from that same record. Its Christian nature is, in essence, Bible-based education.

But education that is Christian has one other qualification. As Jesus taught during His personal ministry, He added a special distinctive. It is an invigorating addition, for it moves Christian education beyond the limits of any purely human endeavor. It is expressed most concisely in John 14: "But the Helper, the Holy Spirit, whom the Father will send in My name, He will teach you all things" (v. 26). An essential part of Christian education is the empowering of the Holy Spirit, the One who indwells the believer.

In his fine study on the work of the Holy Spirit in Christian education, Roy Zuck makes it clear:

> The Holy Spirit, working through the Word of God, is the spiritual dynamic for Christian living. If the Holy Spirit is not at work through the teacher and through the written Word of God, then Christian education remains virtually ineffective and is little different from secular teaching. . . .

The presence of God's Holy Spirit in teaching takes Christian education beyond mere programming, methodology, and techniques. The Spirit's work in education makes it a divine, supernatural ministry.[15]

CHRISTIAN EDUCATION DEFINED

	CHRISTIAN EDUCATION IS—
Descriptive	A Bible-based Holy Spirit-empowered (Christ-centered) Teaching-Learning process

Functional	That seeks
	    To *guide* individuals at all levels of growth
	        Through contemporary teaching means
	        Toward knowing and experiencing God's purpose
	            and plan
	            Through Christ
	            In every aspect of living, and
	    To *equip* them for effective ministry,

Philosophic	With the overall focus
	    On Christ the Master Educator's Example and
	        Command to make Mature Disciples.*

Fig. 1.1

There are three aspects of this definition of Christian education. First of all is the simple, *descriptive* identification. In it we define *learning* as personal development toward maturity, and *teaching* as providing for and encouraging effective learning.

However, to adequately understand Christian education, there needs to also be a *functional* delineation of the basic description. For example, where we understand learning as personal development, our educational process becomes concerned with *individuals*, as was also the ministry of Christ (e.g., the call of Philip, John 1:43).

Where teaching is focused, as in our definition, on being a provider and encourager (facilitator), the instructor becomes a *guide*. The example of Jesus here is the expressive picture of the shepherd (John 10).

Bible-based education in operation calls for doing (experiencing, applying) as well as knowing (Deut. 4:1; Luke 6:46-49).

The reader is challenged to discover for himself the biblical foundations

*Developed in the author's course in Contemporary Christian Education at Moody Bible Institute, 1976.

that undergird the remaining functional aspects of equipping individuals for effective ministry.

Finally, in seriously coming to grips with the meaning of Christian education, there is the aspect of purpose, sometimes identified as *philosophy*. Here we summarize Christian education as a teaching-learning process with the overall focus (purpose) on Christ the master educator's example and command to make disciples (Matt. 28:19-20).

In this philosophical aspect of Christian education is perhaps its most significant meaning. Two contrasting "classroom" incidents will serve to illustrate.

The first incident took place in a classroom at the University of Southern California. The instructor asked the eleven students of the class what they wanted ultimately to accomplish as educators. Three of the men in the course—Education and Value Theory—were superintendents of California school districts. The others were advanced graduate students in education.

As one of those eleven students, I remember well the responses. There were two major patterns: financial security and vocational prestige, with a polite bow toward social uplift.

There were also eleven students (disciples) in the second incident. It took place on a mountainside near the Sea of Galilee in Palestine. The instructor there, too, spoke of educational purpose to His "class" that day.

"Go therefore," He said, "and make disciples . . . teaching them. . . ." Behind those words of Jesus the master teacher, as recorded by one of the eleven, were more than three years of educational example. Before Him on the mountainside sat the ultimate result of His effort—eleven disciples, whom He now sent out to also teach for discipleship, the developing of mature followers of Jesus Christ.

In his study on discipleship, Dwight Pentecost gives us this picture:

> Throughout His ministry Jesus Christ was occupied with making disciples. His ministry was devoted to teaching and training men that these men might be His disciples. From among those who called themselves disciples of the Pharisees and from among others who called themselves disciples of John, and from those who called themselves disciples of Moses, our Lord called men to be disciples of Jesus Christ. His earthly life was invested in these men that they might be His disciples and that they might do the work of a disciple.[16]

The educational implications of teaching for discipleship are far-reaching. Among the most significant is that discipleship education is carried on as much by example as by verbalization; demonstration as compared to telling. Jesus' direction to His disciples (the root word for disciple is *pupil*) was "follow me," and the pupils learned from their Teacher's daily example in every aspect of living.

In that context, the educational significance of the Christian family and the Christian camp becomes tremendously impressive. Likewise, in each Christian education ministry the choice and training of the leadership assumes crucial discipling importance.

In an electronics age of growing impersonalization, often reflected in church work, the one-to-one emphasis of discipleship points toward teaching concern for individuals. The example of Christ in His ministry with individual disciples and the work of Paul with Timothy provide a first-century pattern for that type of education.

It is interesting to note that one of the major concerns of secular education in recent years has been individualized instruction.[17]

There is also growing interest in some areas of secular educational psychology on modeling theory. The studies and principles developed by such researchers as Albert Bandura, professor of psychology at Stanford University, have affinity to discipleship principles.[18]

We have surveyed the essential nature and meaning of Christian education. It will be helpful to also reinforce its validity for contemporary ministry.

CHRISTIAN EDUCATION AS CONTEMPORARY

As one stands on the Mount of Beatitudes in Palestinian Galilee, there is a nostalgic sense of educational history. For there, overlooking the Sea of Galilee, is the traditional site of Jesus' teaching as recorded in Matthew 5. Here the master teacher carried on the ministry we now term "Christian education."

But there is also contemporary realism. For as one raises one's eyes from the mount to the other side of the Sea of Galilee, there appear the Golan Heights, grim reminders of Middle Eastern war and international tensions.

Christian education in the contemporary scene—does it fit today?

There is an answer. It is clear and positive, an answer that the evangelical believer will find encouraging as well as challenging in three areas.

First, the assumption that it is biblical Christian education makes such education imperative. The person who acknowledges the biblical record as valid will find there the *biblical command* to teach.

The already-noted Deuteronomy passage on education, for example, makes the divine directive explicit, as Moses explains in 4:5: "See, I have taught you statutes and judgments just as the LORD my God commanded me."

The Great Commission of Jesus is also an imperative: "Go therefore and make disciples . . . teaching them" (Matt. 28:19-20). Paul's directions to Timothy are specific: "Prescribe and teach these things" (1 Tim. 4:11). For one who takes time to study the Scripture record, the communication of the Christian faith by educational means becomes a clear directive.

The evangelical educator James Murch expressed it emphatically: "Christian education is one of the chief functions of the Church. Since its beginnings education has played an indispensably vital role in its welfare and advance. The basic aims, content and techniques of Christian education have remained the same throughout nearly two thousand years but approaches, forms and programs have changed with changing times. In this crucial period in the history of the world it is imperative that Christian-education leaders face the situation and take appropriate action."[19]

Christian education is indeed not optional.

Second, the biblical teaching directive was accepted by the Christian community in the past, as the pages of *history* amply substantiate.

The record of the early church in Acts notes that the followers of Jesus Christ, daily in the Temple and from house to house "kept right on teaching and preaching Jesus as the Christ" (5:42), and the history of the Christian church from then on is replete with educators and their educational impact. Kendig Cully introduces his volume *Basic Writings in Christian Education* with this note: "From the first century to the present, the church has had to be concerned with the teaching aspects of its corporate existence. That it has taken this responsibility seriously is evident from the abundance of material from practically every century testifying to a concern with the what and how of education."[20] The subsequent listing of educational writings by such church leaders as Chrysostom, Augustine, Luther, Calvin, Comenius, and twenty-five others is indicative of the historical status of education.

The critical place of Christian education in the development of America is well known. Eavey summarizes: "From the time America was settled until 1787, the year the Constitutional Convention met, life in general and education in particular were prevailingly Christian."[21] (That pioneering colonial textbook *The New England Primer* provides a remarkable perspective here.)

It is not difficult to assess historically the positive effect on church ministry of responding to the biblical injunction for teaching. Nor can one fail to recognize the neglect of Christian education in low periods of church vitality, such as the Middle Ages represent.

Clearly, history adds strong encouragement for the place of Christian education in the productive ministry of the evangelical church.

Finally, there must be recognition that the divine imperative for Christian education has a solid, pragmatic base in *the nature of the educational process* itself. Beyond biblical command and historical encouragement, Christian education makes good sense.

As one considers the educational process, some factors become apparent that point up the divine wisdom in establishing teaching along with preaching as the foundation for effective Christian life and ministry. Although they in no way question the validity of the ministry of proclamation (preaching), these educational factors point to some distinctive values.

1. Whereas preaching normally concerns adults, teaching provides communication potential for *every age level,* as well as for varied stages of spiritual development. The educational approach can bring the Christian message to the level of the four-year-old. It can likewise gear to the needs of the new Christian, while providing mature teaching for the advanced believer. If the church is to minister to all ages and to all levels of Christian need and growth, Christian education is indispensable.

2. Moreover, the teaching medium provides us with the channel for *passing on the content and meaning of our faith and heritage* to each generation. The church recognized early the need for a membership that understood both the content and the implications of the gospel. The catechumenal schools of the very early centuries developed a persecution-absorbing, dynamic Christianity.

J. Stanley Glen writes in *The Recovery of the Teaching Ministry:*

> The teaching ministry is the one ministry which when taken seriously assumes the responsibility of communicating the truth at the human level and in human form. It insists that the substance of the Bible and of its faith, including the substance of the great confessions of the church, are essentially intelligible and must be communicated from one generation to another if the church is to be the church and men and women are to hear the word of God. This means that the teaching ministry is the guardian of what may be regarded in the best sense as the tradition of the church.[22]

3. Further, the nature of education permits *direct interaction* and the healthy stimulus of group dynamics. Effective teaching encourages student participation and the sharing of knowledge and experience. Prerequisite here, of course, is the adaptability of Christian education to small groups composed of peers or those with common interests.

4. The creative use of the teaching process provides a *wide range of communication tools and agencies.* Here modern teaching methods and technological advancements offer enrichment and amplification in the presentation of the biblical message to an electronics-oriented generation.

5. In terms of agencies, the *varied forms of Christian education* offer an

extensive and exciting choice for productive outreach and ministry. The multi-faceted Christian camp, Christian day school, sturdy Sunday school, home Bible class, children's church, and the whole realm of Christian higher education—all are educational channels for contemporary Christian impact.

Once the integral meaning of Christian education is rightly understood, and its scriptural purpose is clearly established, there is virtually unlimited potential for meaningful outreach and development.

6. We have considered especially local church education. But there is also the extensive area of *training for service and vocation* represented by Christian higher education. Here is the Bible institute, the Bible college, the Christian liberal arts college and university, and the theological seminary—a whole field of Christian education in itself.

7. Finally, as gripping as any consideration, the biblical definition of Christian education in terms of *discipleship* projects it thoroughly into contemporary relevancy. We note again the individualization in such ministry, the modeling challenge, and the related characteristics of such educational philosophy that make it fully relevant for the character and needs of contemporary culture.

As a ministry drawing on Bible authority and operating in Holy Spirit empowering, contemporary Christian education offers the alert Christian and the person-oriented church a solid approach to some of the basic concerns of Christianity, as noted in the beginning of the chapter. Here is indeed one of God's choicest tools for the life and work of His people.

But effective Christian education carries with it a basic challenge. A discipleship-oriented education calls for example. Paul the apostle spelled it out in his word to the students at Corinth: "Be imitators of me, just as I also am of Christ" (1 Cor. 11:1). Again, he reminded his pupil Timothy, ". . . teach these things . . . show yourself an example . . ." (1 Tim. 4:11-12). That is not a call for perfection. It is a call for growing Christians, seeking spiritual maturity as they teach and lead.

The challenge of contemporary Christian education, then, is for teachers and leaders who are willing to give themselves by life and preparation to discipleship teaching. It asks for concern for the individual student. It calls for creativeness in methods and forms. It draws strength from pastors and churchmen with educational vision. It aims for quality.

The potential of such education? As an instrument under God's approval and direction, rightly understood and used, guided by men and women of discipling dedication and stature—who can limit its impact for the cause of Jesus Christ in this decade?

FOR FURTHER STUDY

1. On the basis of further research, prepare to lead a discussion on one of the five points listed in this chapter (e.g., Christian Education as biblical).
2. Prepare an analysis of a specific local church's educational strengths and weaknesses.
3. Using a standard secular textbook on education (e.g., on principles of teaching), take some of the major areas and indicate how they relate or do not relate to Christian education.
4. Do an in-depth biblical study of the definition of Christian education given in this chapter.
5. Apply a discipleship approach to an educational ministry with the mentally retarded. (See also chapter 16.)
6. On the basis of the chapter, do a comparative study of God-centered education and man-centered education.
7. Show specifically how a quality ministry of Christian education would effect one of the five concerns listed at the first part of the chapter (e.g., the biblical understanding of our faith).

NOTES

1. Charles A. Hammond, "Church Ministry in the 80s," *Theology and News Notes* (Fuller Theological Seminary), vol. 26, no. 2 (June 1979): 13.
2. Frank E. Armbruster, "Why American Education Is Failing," *Reader's Digest,* January 1978, pp. 106-9.
3. Howard G. Hendricks, in Foreword to *Spiritual Power in Your Teaching,* by Roy B. Zuck, rev. ed. (Chicago: Moody, 1972).
4. Hammond, p. 13.
5. C. B. Eavey, *History of Christian Education* (Chicago: Moody, 1964), p. 11. Note also Introduction to Lawrence O. Richards, *A Theology of Christian Education* (Grand Rapids: Zondervan, 1975).
6. Sara Little, cited in Marvin J. Taylor, ed., *Foundations for Christian Education in an Era of Change* (Nashville: Abingdon, 1976), p. 35.
7. Paul H. Vieth, *The Church and Christian Education* (St. Louis: Bethany, 1947), p. 44.
8. B. F. Skinner, *Beyond Freedom and Dignity* (New York: Random, Bantam/Vintage, 1971), indicates some possible implications of this approach. For learning theory in general see Ernest R. Hilgard and Gordon H. Bower, *Theories of Learning* (New York: Meredith, 1966), and Morris L. Bigge, *Learning Theory for Teachers* (New York: Harper & Row, 1971).
9. Cornelius Jaarsma, *Human Development, Learning and Teaching* (Grand Rapids: Eerdmans, 1961), pp. 72-74.
10. Jerome S. Bruner, *The Process of Education* (New York: Random, Vintage, 1960), especially chap. 4.
11. Frank E. Gaebelein, *The Pattern of God's Truth* (Chicago: Moody, 1968), p. 16.
12. Frank E. Gaebelein, cited in J. E. Hakes, ed., *An Introduction to Evangelical Christian Education* (Chicago: Moody, 1964), p. 41.
13. Roy B. Zuck, *Spiritual Power in Your Teaching,* rev. ed. (Chicago: Moody, 1972), p. 5.
14. Lois E. LeBar, *Education That Is Christian* (Westwood, N.J.: Revell, 1958), chap. 7.
15. Zuck, pp. 18, 161.
16. J. Dwight Pentecost, *Design for Discipleship* (Grand Rapids: Zondervan, 1971), p. 13. For further study on discipleship, the growing list of available literature

would be well prefaced by A. B. Bruce's *The Training of the Twelve* (1901; reprint ed., Grand Rapids: Kregel, 1971).

17. Note Nelson B. Henry, ed., *Individualizing Instruction* (Chicago: National Society for the Study of Education, 1962); also Ronald C. Doll, ed., *Individualizing Instruction* (Washington, D.C.: Association for Supervision and Curriculum Development, 1964).
18. See, for example, the chapter "Learning Through Imitation of a Model," in Norman E. Hankins, *Psychology for Contemporary Education* (Columbus, Ohio: Merrill, 1973).
19. James D. Murch, *Teach or Perish!* (Grand Rapids: Eerdmans, 1961), pp. 1-2.
20. Kendig B. Cully, ed., *Basic Writings in Christian Education* (Philadelphia: Westminster, 1960), p. 9.
21. Eavey, p. 305. See also Edwin H. Rian, *Christianity and American Education* (San Antonio, Tex.: Naylor, 1949).
22. J. Stanley Glen, *The Recovery of the Teaching Ministry* (Philadelphia: Westminster, 1960), pp. 25-26.

SUGGESTED READING

Bigge, Morris L. *Learning Theories for Teachers.* New York: Harper & Row, 1971. A basic text on the subject.

Bruner, Jerome S. *The Process of Education.* New York: Random, Vintage, 1960. Represents Bruner's perceptive interpretation of an in-depth conference on education that he chaired in 1959. He has been professor of psychology at Harvard University.

Cully, Kendig Brubaker, ed. *Basic Writings in Christian Education.* Philadelphia: Westminster, 1960. Interesting and helpful historical compilation of educational writing by 30 educators from all periods.

Doll, Ronald C., ed. *Individualizing Instruction.* Washington, D.C.: Association for Supervision and Curriculum Development, 1964. A basic compilation of educational thinking on individualization. Especially helpful are the contributions by editor Doll.

*Eavey, C. B. *History of Christian Education.* Chicago: Moody, 1964. Evangelical coverage of people and movements in Christian education from Jewish roots through the 1950s.

Engel, James F. and Norton, H. Wilbert. *What's Gone Wrong with the Harvest?* Grand Rapids: Zondervan, 1975. An analysis of present church life, with suggested strategy for ministry.

*Gaebelein, Frank E. *The Pattern of God's Truth.* Chicago: Moody, 1968. An extremely valuable contribution on applied Christian education philosophy.

Glen, J. Stanley. *The Recovary of the Teaching Ministry.* Philadelphia: Westminster, 1960. A sometimes cutting analysis of weaknesses in the church's educational ministry. Somewhat in the vein of James Smart's 1954 *Teaching Ministry of the Church.*

*Hakes, J. Edward, ed. *An Introduction to Evangelical Christian Education.* Chicago: Moody, 1964. Predecessor of this volume. Still has much useful Christian educational material.

Hankins, Norman E. *Psychology for Contemporary Education.* Columbus, Ohio: Merrill, 1973. A rather good volume on secular educational psychology.

Henry, Nelson B., ed. *Individualizing Instruction.* Chicago: The National
   Society for the Study of Education, 1962. A good symposium on foundational
   material for individualizing teaching.
Hilgard, Ernest R. and Bower, Gordon H. *Theories of Learning.* New York:
   Meredith, 1966. A basic text on the subject.
Jaarsma, Cornelius. *Human Development, Learning and Teaching.* Grand Rap-
   ids: Eerdmans, 1961. One of the few evangelical texts on educational psy-
   chology; by the former professor of education at Calvin College, Michigan.
*LeBar, Lois E. *Education That Is Christian.* Westwood, N.J.: Revell, 1958.
   Good, practical insights on Christian education. Still used for courses on
   Christian education philosophy.
*Murch, James DeForest. *Teach or Perish!* Grand Rapids: Eerdmans, 1961.
   Incisive, challenging call for contemporary Christian education ministry by
   the key leader in the development of the National Sunday School Association,
   former seminary Christian education professor, and National Association of
   Evangelicals magazine editor.
Pentecost, J. Dwight. *Design for Discipleship.* Grand Rapids: Zondervan,
   1971. Well presented study on discipleship by Dallas Theological Seminary
   professor.
Rian, Edwin H. *Christianity and American Education.* San Antonio, Tex.:
   Naylor, 1949. An analysis of American education in a religious, historical
   context. Extensive bibliography.
Richards, Lawrence O. *A Theology of Christian Education.* Grand Rapids:
   Zondervan, 1975. An attempt to build an educational model on theological
   implications.
Schaeffer, Francis A. *The Church at the End of the Twentieth Century.* Down-
   ers Grove, Ill.: Inter-Varsity, 1970. A study of the contemporary church in
   the usual incisive Schaeffer style.
Skinner, B. F. *Beyond Freedom and Dignity.* New York: Random, Bantam/
   Vintage, 1971. Often called the most influential psychologist of our time,
   greatly affecting contemporary education.
Taylor, Marvin J., ed. *Foundations for Christian Education in an Era of Change.*
   Nashville: Abingdon, 1976. This is the current Abingdon Press survey vol-
   ume on Christian (religious) education. Of special interest is evangelical
   Edward Hayes' chapter "Evangelicalism and Christian Education."
Trumbull, H. Clay. *Yale Lectures on the Sunday School.* Philadelphia: John
   D. Wattles, 1888. A classic study on the Sunday School.
Vieth, Paul H., ed. *The Church and Christian Education.* St. Louis: Bethany,
   1947. A well-presented volume representing a study on the status of Chris-
   tian education in the mid 1940s by the International Council of Religious
   Education. Surprisingly relevant.
*Zuck, Roy B. *Spiritual Power in Your Teaching.* Rev. ed. Chicago: Moody,
   1972. Formerly titled *The Holy Spirit in Your Teaching,* this is a definitive
   study on the Holy Spirit in Christian education.

*Especially recommended.

2

The Biblical Foundations of Christian Education

EDWARD L. HAYES

CHRISTIAN EDUCATION, as noted in the first chapter, arises from the fertile soil of the Bible. The biblical revelation of God's dealing with His covenant people Israel and the examples of Jesus and His apostles form the seedbed for what we know today as Christian education. We look to the biblical record for both its origin and form. Its purposes, methods, and institutional expressions are rooted in the Scriptures.

All that the expression "Christian education" implies in our contemporary world must somehow be subjected to the scrutiny of the explicit and implicit teachings of the Scriptures. This in no way limits the church, dictating an exact reproduction of primitive style. Rather, the biblical wellspring of principles and examples is seen as vital to the creation, perpetuation, and renewal of Christian education endeavors.

Viewing the Bible as God's living word can recharge Christian education at its base. Foundational to a vital church ministry is a vital and authoritative theology. Such a theology does not spring from an existential base devoid of absolutes and certainties, but from revelatory truth. Contrary to some modern thinking, such a theology need not be viewed as wooden, lifeless, and culture-bound. The view that the Scriptures are the authoritative Word from God rather than stifling the human spirit opens windows to answers that free mankind to become all that God intended in His creative process. A basic presupposition for the evangelical Christian educator, then, is an authoritative Word.

The teaching function of the church flows from the Bible. It does not ignore the contemporary setting and the developmental needs of the learner, but it finds its roots in the Word of God. Sara Little wrote sev-

---

EDWARD L. HAYES, Ph.D., formerly academic dean and professor of Christian education, Conservative Baptist Theological Seminary, Denver, Colorado, is now executive director of the Mt. Hermon Association in California.

eral decades ago that Christian education is to be "a servant and not a master of revelation."[1] That vantage point is particularly important in developing an educational stance and style. The primary focus is not on mankind, but on God. The human factor is by no means ignored, but it is not the point of beginning. What we think about God indicates what we do about education. What we think about God, however, depends upon what we think about the Scriptures.

Process theology, espoused by Randolph Crump Miller and others as useful to Christian education, cannot provide an anchor of truth. Only a shifting relativism emerges from that theology. Its proponents are to be admired for attempting a holistic stance toward education, but they have cut the moorings. They have deserted revelatory truth, or, at best, they have redefined revelation in human terms. Such absence of divine transcendence leaves theology and education to human definition. But to the evangelical, the Bible functions as the primary source and the only inerrant criterion of truth.

The direction of our educational stance is plain. It lies in a return to a central principle of education—namely, that of going to original sources. We must teach the Bible itself. We must return to the Bible, which has made every renewal movement in Protestantism possible. Evangelicalism does well to take heed to the swinging pendulums of time, noting their correctives to imbalanced practice. But a shifting theology will correct nothing. Only the Scriptures will provide a rudder through crisis and, at the same time, chart a course to remedy the ills of society. "To lose the Bible," writes Carl Henry, "is to lose everything."[2]

JEWISH EDUCATIONAL ROOTS

The roots of Christian education run deep into the soil of Judaism. It should not seem strange that the church claims a Judaic heritage—the New Testament church was founded by Jews; the New Testament was written by Jews, with the exception of Luke, and the Bible of the early church was the Hebrew Scriptures of the Old Testament. Stuart Rosenberg calls Christians to "rediscover roots that are Semitic."[3]

Hebrew origins of Christian education have been amply chronicled by William Barclay[4] and Lewis Joseph Sherrill.[5] Certain dominant threads make up the fabric of the rise of teaching in Hebrew history. And Hebrew history, we need not be reminded, is largely Bible history. From earliest times the Hebrews were called "the People of the Book."[6]

God, to the Hebrew, was manifest both in history and in the law. Profoundly convinced of God's leading through His covenant relationship with Israel, the Hebrews faithfully taught the young so "that they should put their confidence in God, and not forget the works of God, but keep

His commandments" (Psalm 78:7). To the Hebrew the concept that God was teacher emerged from the nature of God Himself. He was creator, covenantor, and sustainer. His will and wisdom were to be sought and cherished. Thus priest, prophet, king, sage, and scribe were all viewed as interpreters in one way or another of the grand drama of the Lord in history and in revelation.

One passage has become imbedded in Hebrew consciousness more deeply than any other. The instruction of the Shema contained in Deuteronomy 6:4-9 set the agenda for the home and the nation. So great was instruction in the eyes of God's chosen people that they equated it with life. "Take hold of instruction; do not let go. Guard her; for she is your life," wrote the sage (Prov. 4:13).

The religious rites of the Hebrew people were occasions for pedagogy. Household ritual provoked wonder, reverence, and joy, as well as questions (see Deut. 6:20). The Passover, particularly, kindled a reminder of the past. The Sabbath, the feast days, and the bar mitzvah were all part of a living liturgy that impressed a theology on the minds of the simple as well as the great.

Through the bitter years of exile, Judaism survived because of an ingrained respect for education. What the Tabernacle in the wilderness and the Temple in Jerusalem were to the devout, the synagogue became to the Jew in exile. Although its exact rise is obscure, the synagogue probably emerged in Babylon. Both Josephus and Philo carry the synagogue back to the time of Moses. It developed as one of those rare educational institutions that corresponds with the nature of the faith it represents.

The principal purpose of the synagogue was teaching. Barclay writes, "It is necessary clearly to remember that the Synagogue was very much more a place of teaching than the modern Church. The object of the Synagogue Sabbath services was not public worship in the narrower sense of the term; it was not devotion; it was religious instruction."[7] It was the center where the law was explained, expounded, and applied.

Postbiblical Judaism was later to build on that Old Testament foundation. The importance of teaching in the Old Testament may also be seen in the various words used to describe the communication of God's works and word to mankind. Hebrew words dealing with the concept of education, like Near Eastern thought in general, portray vivid word pictures. Selected words illustrate the emergence of an educational style.

The Hebrew word *hanak*, "to educate" or "to train," comes from a root word meaning to dedicate or consecrate. This verb is used in Proverbs 22:6: "Train up a child in the way he should go, even when he is old he will not depart from it." The education of a child from the Hebrew perspective was viewed as an act of consecration. More than worship, how-

ever, is prompted by *hanak*. It properly means "to rub the palate or gums."
Here, in this simple word used to convey the notion of teaching, is a world
of pictures. When a child began to be instructed in the Torah, the Hebrew
law, honey and sweet cakes were used as incentive. Thus the psalmist
refers to the law as sweeter than honey (Psalm 119:103) and Ezekiel the
prophet, upon eating the scroll, exclaimed, "It was as sweet as honey in
my mouth" (Ezek. 3:3).

The most common word translated "teach" in the Old Testament is
lamath, which means "to stimulate, to exercise in." It conjures up the idea
of an animal's being placed in a yoke for learning. Another form of the
same word is used to describe an ox goad. Israel is referred to by the
prophet Hosea as a "trained heifer" (Hos. 10:11).

Other words richly portray teaching as separating issues and ideas,
sharpening or pricking learners, and shepherding. But the richest of the
words for teaching is the one from which we get the word *Torah* itself. It
is derived from a word meaning "to shoot, throw, or cast." Instruction is
viewed as direction from God. The law of God may be seen as that body
of teaching "cast forth" by the Spirit of God. Thus, the law itself was
viewed by the Hebrew people as the substance of their teaching, a light
and a guide to life. Christian education does not deny the roots of its
Hebrew heritage. With the dawning of a new age, the epoch of Christian
tradition built firmly upon the law and the prophets. New Testament
teaching did not emerge in a vacuum. Its context was the long history of
a rich teaching style. It is to that new era that we now give attention.

EDUCATION IN THE NEW TESTAMENT

Christianity takes its educational cues from a cluster of sources. The
example and teachings of Jesus, the apostolic preaching and writings, and
the embryonic style revealed in the biblical record of early Christian worship and fellowship primarily form the base of New Testament education.

Christian teaching finds its impetus, as well, in the etymological context of pregnant Greek words that articulate the teaching function. In
several dominant words that recur frequently we are able to infer a content, a style, and a context in which education is to take place.

Furthermore, the nature of the church, its mission and ministry in the
world, as revealed in the Scriptures, provides a framework for educational
action. Such a biblical theology is too broad a subject to treat extensively
in this chapter, but it must be taken into account if we are to devise a
comprehensive statement on the nature of New Testament education.

JESUS THE MASTER TEACHER

Christian education had its beginning with Jesus. This is not to ignore the past, but Jesus brought unique freshness to the teaching task. He came from God, and He taught God's message as one having authority. Jesus was a teacher. He used teaching as the chief vehicle of communication. Charles Benton Eavey has stated it well: "Teaching was His chief business. He was often a healer, sometimes a worker of miracles, frequently a preacher, but always a teacher."[8]

Chapter 4, "Christ the Master Teacher", deals with this subject in more detail, but let it be said that the educational dimension of the gospel record has provoked considerable writing. Much of the research and writing represents an attempt to view Jesus' teaching through the eyes of twentieth-century educational psychology. Even the classic work of Herman Harrell Horne, published first in 1922,[9] revealed the tone and tinting of an emerging school of religious educational thought. This assessment is not meant to discourage educational investigation into the teaching methods Jesus employed, but one must always be reminded that our categorizations, perceptions, and conclusions, in large measure, are biased by our contemporary understanding of education.

An example of that kind of attempt to make Jesus the man for all seasons is Richardson's *The Christ of the Classroom*. At the peak of early twentieth-century religious education fervor he wrote, "A study of Jesus Christ's mastery, as a teacher, may be made by noting the chief characteristics of competency in teaching, as defined by the science of education."[10] Such a science of education has, of course, been defined and redefined many times over during the past five decades.

What serves as a caution for the study of Jesus' educational techniques must serve as a caution for educational study anywhere in the New Testament. It is both safe and profitable to pay attention to the biblical data without inferring too much by way of dogma in method. We claim dogma in faith for sure, but not dogma in methodology.

THE APOSTOLIC TRADITION

We dare not underestimate the powerful thrust of the Great Commission and its teaching directive upon the apostles. Pentecost turned timid followers into bold preacher-teachers. Those who responded to Peter's message that day continued steadfastly in the apostles' teaching (Acts 2:42). And it is noted that daily in the Temple and in houses the apostles kept on teaching and preaching Jesus Christ (Acts 5:42).

It is helpful to visualize the New Testament materials as forming three great emphases. To be a teacher in the New Testament sense embodies the call to faith, the explanation of the faith, and elaboration on the moral and spiritual implications of the life of faith.

Apostolic preaching formed the core of action, calling men and women to repentance. Emphasis was upon the death, resurrection, and exaltation of Jesus. Paul in his preaching developed those faith-forming themes, but emphasized another dimension—Christ as preexistent agent of creation and reconciler of all things to Himself by His death on the cross.

Faith formation, faith explanation, and moral development are seen in the apostolic tradition. The ease with which the terms *preach* and *teach* are used to convey the corpus of God's truth and the curriculum of godly living attests to the fact that the teaching was no peripheral function in primitive Christianity.

EARLY CHRISTIAN WORSHIP AND TEACHING

Very little is known of the primitive church style of meeting together. We usually have to rely upon the material from the postbiblical period to give insight into the corporate behavior of Christians in worship, fellowship, and learning. Several themes, however, can be developed from the New Testament data, revealing the central importance of education in the life of the early church.

In the Acts of the Apostles we learn that the persistent behavior of Christians involved the apostles' teaching, koinonia, prayers, observance of the Lord's Supper, and compassionate caring, first to the saints, and then toward all others. As Christianity moved outward to the larger Roman world it became necessary to emphasize family, primarily parental, responsibility in teaching. New converts from paganism could not be counted upon to know and respect the traditional Jewish roots of family education so central to the Old Testament era. Furthermore, the pastoral epistles, particularly, outline ministerial duties and church responsibilities in regard to the educative task.

The Timothy letters include Pauline directives to teach the Word. Timothy is exhorted not to neglect the gift that was in him (1 Tim. 4:14) and to stir up the gift of God (2 Tim. 1:6). A strong case can be built that the gift of teaching was in Paul's mind. The tone of the two letters and the frequent reference to teaching give strong indication of the deep concern of an aging apostle for the perpetuation of the faith through a teaching ministry of the Word.

Six general themes, which emphasize the importance of teaching, occur in the two letters. (1) Teaching is viewed as essential for the proper handling of the inspired Word (2 Tim. 2:14-15; 3:16-17). (2) Teaching is necessary for soundness in faith (1 Tim. 4:6, 11, 16; 6:3-5; 2 Tim. 4:3). (3) Teaching is also viewed as useful for the establishment of harmonious households (1 Tim. 6:1-2). (4) The ability to teach is a requirement of pastors and other spiritual leaders (1 Tim. 3:2; 2 Tim. 2:24). (5) Furthermore, teaching is seen to be an essential corollary to Bible reading, exhortation, and preaching (1 Tim. 4:13; 2 Tim. 4:2). (6) Finally, teaching is presented by Paul as vital to the perpetuation of the faith (2 Tim. 2:2).

In the Titus epistle Paul gives similar instruction regarding teaching. Sound teaching is the retardant to error in the body of believers and the means of persuasion in the world (Titus 1:9; 2:12). Teaching is the effective vehicle of establishing order in the household (Titus 2:1-10), and sound teaching is the means of emphasizing the example of believers as a pattern of good works before non-Christians (Titus 2:7, 10).

The intense concern for communal sharing in primitive Christianity grew out of the Christian call to a life of discipleship. No mere recitation of creed, even one as lofty as the early affirmation of Christ's lordship, could build up the saints. It was the corporate togetherness that edified. Always the Word was central. Even music was viewed as pedagogical. The life and work of the early church, as revealed in Scripture, revolved in large measure around teaching. Yet, there was always a compelling impetus outward from the assembly of saints to the surrounding world.

THE CHILD AND THE CHURCH

Christian education has properly emphasized the significance of childhood. Within the New Testament much is revealed about the centrality of the child in church concern. "There is no gospel picture dearer to most people," writes Barclay, "than the picture of Jesus setting the child in the midst or taking him in His arms."[11] Children's work is not to be despised. Our Lord's rebuke of the disciples, His example of setting children in the midst of them, and His comparison of the simplicity and openness of a child to receiving the kingdom of God set an agenda for church education (cf. Matt. 19:13; Mark 10:13; Luke 18:15). God is willing to care for children with guardian angels (Matt. 18:10). Christ's teaching is clear that the Christian duty to the child is absolutely binding. To receive a child is to receive none other than Jesus Himself (Mark 9:36; Luke 9:48). The child is the very pattern of the kingdom. Unless a person becomes as a child there is no entrance to God's spiritual kingdom.

Beyond the gospels, the New Testament teaching on children is meager, but it provides essential directives for church and family education. Children must obey parents (Eph. 6:1); fathers must not overdiscipline to the point of discouragement and rebellion (Eph. 6:4; Col. 3:21). Spiritual leaders must rule their own households well (1 Tim. 3:4, 12; Titus 1:6), and parents have an absolute duty to provide for their children (2 Cor. 12:14). Barclay concludes that the New Testament knows nothing about an exact curriculum of religious education in the churches for children, nor does it speak about schools.

"The New Testament is certain," he writes, "that the only training which really matters is given within the home, and that there are no teachers so effective for good or evil as parents are."[12] Finally, the New Testament reveals, by example, the mature faith of Timothy whose godly mother and grandmother faithfully taught him the Word of God, which was able to make him wise unto salvation (2 Tim. 3:15).

IMPORTANT NEW TESTAMENT EDUCATIONAL WORDS

Throughout the New Testament a variety of words are used to convey educational meanings. Ten of those are included here for study and research.

Didasko. This is the most common word in the New Testament for teaching. Roughly two-thirds of its occurrences are in the gospels and the first part of Acts. Paul rarely uses the word. In its noun form it is translated "doctrine" in the King James Version (Acts 2:42; 2 Tim. 3:16).

Didaskolos. This word for teacher is often used of Jesus and of other Christian teachers including Paul (1 Tim. 2:7). An entire category of gifted Christian workers bore this title (1 Cor. 12:28; Eph. 4:11).

Paideuo. One of the richest Greek terms, this word means "to give guidance and training." The verb comes from a noun that means "little child." It is used of parental teaching (Eph. 6:4) and of the value of the inspired Word (2 Tim. 3:16).

Katecheo. This is a rare word used only by Luke (Luke 1:4; Acts 18:25; 21:21) and Paul (Rom. 2:18; 1 Cor. 14:19; Gal. 6:6). We get our words *catechism* and *catechumen* (learner) from it.

Noutheteo. Literally this word means "to shape the mind" and is translated "admonish" in the King James Version (1 Cor. 4:14; 10:11; Eph. 6:4; Col. 3:16).

Matheteuo. Here is the important New Testament word for "to disciple," with the noun form usually occuring most in the Bible. It occurs only in the gospels and the Acts of the Apostles.

Oikodomeo. Used in the context of spiritual growth and maturity, this word means "to edify" or literally "to build up" (1 Cor. 3:9; 8:1; 1 Thess. 5:11; 1 Pet. 2:5).

Paratithemi. This word means "to set before" or "to place beside." Paul uses this word in 1 Timothy 1:18 and 2 Timothy 2:2, translated "commit."

Ektithemi. Used only in Acts 11:4, 18:26, and 28:23, this word means "to explain facts in logical order" or, as it is translated, "to expound."

Hodegeo. Our final New Testament word carries with it the sense of leading, guiding, or showing the way. Judas was referred to in Acts 1:16 as a guide to those who took Jesus captive. The Holy Spirit is called a guide in John 16:13. The Ethiopian needed one to guide him into the meaning of the Isaiah text (Acts 8:31), the Pharisees are called blind guides to the blind (Matt. 15:14; 23:16, 24), and Christ shall one day lead saints to experience the living waters of eternal life (Rev. 7:17).

This rich list of New Testament words needs to be explored within the various contexts. The words imply content to be taught, actions to be engaged in, and, in some cases, nuances of methodologies.

A NEW TESTAMENT THEOLOGY OF CHRISTIAN EDUCATION

The value of evangelical Christian education will rise or fall on the soundness of its theological foundations. Yet, few have attempted integration of the theological disciplines with the educative process.

Where does one begin to construct a biblical theology of education? Pioneer religious educator Paul Vieth, in *The Church and Christian Education,* declared, "Christian education can find its purpose, content, and method only in the nature of Christianity."[13] He was writing in a context of the new religious education endeavors, which were finding their moorings in secular humanism and psychology rather than revelation. His assessment still provides a challenge for theological formulation.

To begin with, our conception of truth determines our pedagogy. It is the epistemological question that is fundamental. Here evangelicals sink their anchor deeply into revelatory truths and hold tenaciously to a literal biblicism. God is viewed as the center of education, as He is viewed as the center of truth. Authority resides in God, and all truth, if it be truth, is seen as divine truth. Problems of biblical literalism are handled forthrightly. There is no plea for a wooden literalism that fails to distinguish between what is symbolical and poetical, doctrinal and practical, historical and epochal. While the human element is recognized, the Bible is accepted as infallible—that is, totally trustworthy and authoritative in all matters of faith and practice.

The authority of the Scripture, viewed as divinely revealed, in no way precludes investigation. The encounter of divine truth and human experience is cherished, although a dynamic view of revelation is rejected. The Word does not become God's Word in experience. It is already the Word of God. Objective truth stands as mentor and judge of the human experience.

Thus, as previously noted, evangelical Christian education rejects the idea that process theology is useful in formulating educational foundations. From the process theology vantage point, theology is valuable only when it is viewed as relational. Randolph Crump Miller, chief exponent of process theology in educational theory, speaks of the goals of attitude, relationships, content, and personal morality, but he hopes "that many will see fit to work out a system of beliefs consonant with empirical and process theology."[14]

Evangelical rejection of process theology does not negate creativity and the importance of relationships. A number of evangelical Christian education scholars have addressed those issues, all from the vantage point of orthodox faith. Lawrence O. Richards, in *A Theology of Christian Education*, uses relationship as his central motif.[15] Lois LeBar, in *Focus on People in Church Education*, emphasizes the human dimension,[16] and the Lutheran educator Allan Hart Jahsmann, in *Power Beyond Words*, investigates the nonverbal elements of our faith.[17] Another evangelical, Martha Leypoldt, in *Learning Is Change*, places heavy emphasis upon the dynamic quality of life-changing faith.[18] Each of those authors seeks to bring the correctives that Miller desires, yet on the basis of orthodox biblical theology.

Evangelical educators seek an adequate method to fit an adequate theology. God must be at the center. Authority must rest in the Scriptures. Jesus is seen as reconciler and mediator, the Holy Spirit as tutor and guide. Both teacher and learner are open for truth. Each person must internalize God's truth and be accountable for changing human character to conform to godliness. Building relationships that edify in the corporate body of Christians is valued, even essential. The church is to be engaged in vocal public witness to the gospel, and compassionate social action is not to be seen as incongruous to faith. Christian hope, based upon the reality of Christ's resurrection, ascension, and imminent return to earth, brings about a purified ethic and affects how we govern our ways and how we relate to governmental authority. Those and other motifs are building blocks for a theology of education.

Developed within the context of a biblical view of the human soul, the abject sinfulness of mankind, the necessity of divine atonement, the need for personal salvation, and the creative genius of the learner who shares, even residually, the image of God, those blocks provide a framework for evangelical educational action.

CONCLUSION

This chapter has attempted to set forth some convictions evangelicals have about the biblical basis of Christian education, its roots in both the Old and New Testaments, and its relationship to Christian theology. The author agrees with J. Stanley Glen as he issued a call for a recovery of the teaching ministry in our churches:

> The teaching ministry is the one ministry which when taken seriously assumes the responsibility of communicating the truth at the human level and in human form. It insists that the substance of the Bible and of its faith, including the substance of the great confessions of the church, are essentially intelligible and must be communicated from one generation to

another if the church is to be the church and men and women are to hear the word of God. This means that the teaching ministry is the guardian of what may be regarded in the best sense as the tradition of the church.[19]

FOR FURTHER STUDY

1. Investigate the Jewish educational style from the postexilic period to the time of Jesus. What education would Jesus have been given as a child?
2. Using the Hebrew and Greek words noted in this chapter, prepare a research study of those words in their biblical contexts.
3. Develop a concise definition and outline of the apostle Paul's teaching style through an inductive study of the epistles to the Galatians, Ephesians, and Colossians.
4. Form a panel to discuss the author's assumptions in the section "A New Testament Theology of Christian Education."
5. What is process theology, and how does it conflict with biblical theology?

NOTES

1. Sara Little, *The Role of the Bible in Contemporary Christian Education* (Richmond, Va.: John Knox, 1961), p. 175.
2. Carl F. H. Henry, "Restoring the Whole Word," in *The Religious Education We Need*, ed. James Michael Lee (Mishawaka, Ind.: Religious Education, 1977), p. 65.
3. Stuart E. Rosenberg, *Judaism* (Glen Rock, N.J.: Paulist, 1966), p. 16.
4. William Barclay, *Educational Ideals of the Ancient World* (Grand Rapids: Baker, 1974).
5. Lewis Joseph Sherrill, *The Rise of Christian Education* (New York: Macmillan, 1953).
6. For a concise treatment of the Judaic heritage and a Christian concept of learning, see Marvin R. Wilson, "The Jewish Concept of Learning: A Christian Appreciation," *Christian Scholar's Review* 5(1976): 350-63.
7. Barclay, p. 24.
8. C. B. Eavey, *History of Christian Education* (Chicago: Moody, 1964), p. 78.
9. Herman H. Horne, *Jesus the Master Teacher* (New York: Association, 1922).
10. Norman E. Richardson, *The Christ of the Classroom: How to Teach Evangelical Christianity* (New York: Macmillan, 1931), p. 3.
11. Barclay, p. 234.
12. Ibid., p. 236.
13. Paul H. Vieth, *The Church and Christian Education* (St. Louis: Bethany, 1947), p. 44.
14. Randolph C. Miller, "Continuity and Contrast in the Future," in *The Religious Education We Need*, ed. James Michael Lee (Mishawaka, Ind.: Religious Education, 1977), p. 50.
15. Lawrence O. Richards, *A Theology of Christian Education* (Grand Rapids: Zondervan, 1975).
16. Lois E. LeBar, *Focus on People in Church Education* (Westwood, N.J.: Revell, 1968).
17. Allan H. Jahsmann, *Power Beyond Words* (St. Louis: Concordia, 1969).
18. Martha Leypoldt, *Learning Is Change* (Valley Forge, Pa.: Judson, 1971).
19. J. Stanley Glen, *The Recovery of the Teaching Ministry* (Philadelphia: Westminster, 1960), pp. 25-26.

3

Christian Education in Historical Perspective

CLIFFORD V. ANDERSON

AN ADEQUATE UNDERSTANDING of present Christian education includes an appreciation of how God has worked through education in the past.

Beginning with the teaching emphasis of the Hebrew people, the education picture includes some of the outstanding leaders and historical events of the Christian church.

BIBLICAL BEGINNINGS

EDUCATION IN HEBREW HISTORY

The oral and written traditions of the Hebrew people tell of a God who called into existence, guided, and entered into covenant with a people. He brought them into a land where He provided laws for their relationships to their fellowmen. He provided rituals and leadership to enable them to approach God, determine His will, and learn to worship the Holy One. In the events associated with the Exodus a nation was formed and trained. Moses, the nation-builder and law-giver, laid out the arrangements that governed and guided them. Joseph, centuries before the giving of the commandments at Horeb, had lived in accordance with those laws.

God's revelation of His will for man came at different times, through a variety of means. Priests taught the law and ministered at the altar of sacrifice. Prophets discerned and spoke the Word of God, and called the nation to repentance. Sages meditated upon life and shaped a wisdom literature that guided the conduct of young and old. Poets and musicians sung of the hand of God in the lives of men and extolled His virtues. Judges and kings ruled with a sense of stewardship under God.

CLIFFORD V. ANDERSON, Ed.D., is professor of education and associate dean of Bethel Theological Seminary West in San Diego, California.

Many emphases in Christian education are rooted in those Hebrew origins. There were no formal schools before the exile, with the unique exception of the schools of the prophets (2 Kings 2:3, 5, 7; 6:1). Community life was the setting for learning. Socialization and instruction occurred spontaneously and in response to teachable moments that arose when questions were asked. National observances affected the lives of all persons. Processions, costumes, odors, feasting, fasting, rites, touching objects, singing, Sabbath observance, and the Tabernacle all were part of community life and contributed to both adult and childhood education.

Children participated in the activities of the home. History and law were communicated by parents as well as by leaders in the community. Parents were challenged to learn in response to their own questions and those of their children. The conduct of children was controlled, and respect for parents was expected. The calendar with its special holy days of Passover, Tabernacles, Pentecost, Day of Atonement, and later Purim broke into the routines of life with a reminder that God had acted in history and provided for mankind. The weekly Sabbath observance called the nation to an identity as the people of God.

The exile of the Jewish nation created an identity crisis. Some of the dispersed simply merged into the culture of the areas where they settled. Others resisted accommodation and increased their efforts to teach the Word of God, and a new institution appeared. The synagogue as a meeting place emerged to provide for education and worship. Every village had such a place, and some cities had several. The reading, translation, and explanation of Scripture were the focal activities. Although not all could journey to the Temple when it was rebuilt, the Word of God could be heard and understood at the synagogues.

Although learning in the home continued, Hebrew education, already enhanced by the synagogue service, was further assisted through the introduction of formal schools. The success of and need for those elementary schools were evidenced in a Jewish ordinance of A.D. 64, which called for elementary schools in each district and town. Classrooms were usually close to a synagogue. Study consisted of explanations and traditions related to the Scriptures and customs of the people.

Women were not sent to school, but they were taught through the instruction and socialization that occurred in the home and community.

Lewis Joseph Sherrill summarized Judaism's education: "The education, when complete, has its three channels of home, synagogue, and school system, and Judaism keeps all of these as long as is humanly possible. But when the worst comes, it can do without the formal schools, and it can even do without the synagogue; for the whole religion in essence passes from one generation to the next through the household."[1]

EDUCATION AND JESUS CHRIST

In the fullness of time, Jesus the Christ was born into a humble Jewish home. The gospels provide some detail on His home life, but they mainly record His adult life and teaching. We assume that Jesus was educated in the traditional ways available to Jewish youth where He lived. Informal instruction in the home, community life with its calendar of special days, visits to Jerusalem and the Temple, the synagogue and its school in Nazareth, and learning a trade were all among His educational experiences. When He followed His calling into public ministry He was known as a teacher. He gathered disciples and placed primary attention upon them, although He did not ignore the masses.

The content of Christ's teaching, the communication skills He employed, and His personal teaching characteristics have earned for Him the recognition of the world as a foremost teacher. Christians confess He is also the world's Savior and Lord. The drama that Scripture portrays is of a God who speaks and acts redemptively in history, and who did so powerfully in Jesus Christ, the master teacher.

The First Thousand Years

THE GREAT ADVANCE

The resurrection appearances and ascension of Jesus brought His disciples from despair to a sense of destiny. The kingdom of God was breaking in upon them! As foretold by Jesus, the Holy Spirit had come and empowered the believers for witness. Hated by the Jews and oppressed by the Romans, believers found comfort in the Holy Spirit and in the fellowship of other believers. Those with material resources shared with others less fortunate. They taught the gospel and interpreted the Scriptures by studying the Old Testament and recalling the teachings of Jesus.

After coming together for teaching and prayer, believers scattered to share the good news and minister to others. They gathered in the Temple and went from house to house, engaged in their gladsome activity of exhortation and teaching. When persecution came they prayed for one another and for boldness to witness. Strengthened by their association with one another, they returned to the streets and spoke with any who would listen.

Accused of filling Jerusalem with their teaching, they ignored threats and confessed that they must obey God rather than men. Persecution drove them outward. Thus the effort to destroy the church led to a missionary extension that insured its existence. Rank and file believers gossiped the good news and earned the description of "followers of the Way," "Christians," and "those who have turned the world upside down."

When the Christians assembled there was more than one communicator (1 Cor. 14:26). Spiritual music was encouraged (Col. 3:16). Women were co-workers in gospel work, and their status was raised through instructions given to husbands to love their wives as Christ loved the church (Eph. 5:25). Children were to be treated with consideration and nurtured in the Lord. Slaves and masters were reminded that they both had a master in heaven.

Churches met in homes, and leadership was appointed to provide for the ongoing care of the group. Members were reminded to honor elders who governed effectively and worked hard at preaching and teaching (1 Tim. 5:17). A young pastor was encouraged in public reading of Scripture, exhortation, and teaching (1 Tim. 4:13). Christians, in going from place to place, often resorted to the local synagogue, place of prayer, or marketplace to share Christ with Jews and God-fearing Gentiles. At Ephesus, Paul left the synagogue when Jewish resistance continued, and for two years he taught daily in the school of Tyrannus (Acts 19:9-10).

The early church commended itself and its message by a combination of factors. Kenneth Scott Latourette notes:

> Better than its rivals, Christianity gave to the Graeco-Roman world what so many were craving from a religion. To those wishing immortality it pointed to the historic Jesus, risen from the dead, and to the promise that those who believed in him would share with him in glorified, eternal life. To those demanding high morality it offered standards beyond the full attainment of men and the power to grow toward them. To those craving fellowship it presented a community of worship and of mutual aid, with care for the poor, the infirm, and the aged. To those who, distrustful of reason, longed for a faith sanctioned by immemorial antiquity, it pointed to the long record preserved in what it termed the Old Testament, going back to Moses and beyond him and pointing forward to Christ. To those demanding intellectual satisfaction it could present literature prepared by some of the ablest minds of the day.[2]

Socialization has been a powerful method of education in the church. The informal associations of believers and the regular meetings of the church provided settings for teaching, worship, and fellowship. Teaching and life-style were influenced through active involvement in witnessing, caring, praying, giving, loving, and forgiving. The symbols of baptism and the Lord's Supper taught the realities of the new life in Christ. Home life was touched by the changes wrought in family members by the power of the gospel. Respect for each member of the family was cultivated. A growing body of literature provided accounts of the life and teachings of Jesus, and letters from leaders refuted error and unfolded truth.

Integration with the Word of God in the Old Testament and ethics for daily life were also concerns of the writers. Life-style, literature, and leadership were chief concerns of the early church—in its teaching ministry to the "called out" community, and in the world it was reaching for Christ.

As first-generation Christians passed on, there was left for future generations a body of literature that later was recognized as the authentic canon of the Holy Scripture known as the New Testament. The gospels and epistles gave historical credibility to the critical events in the church's history, and they were the basis for the church's message. Those God-inspired documents shaped the life-style of the church and of the individual believers, and great concern was expressed for correct doctrine (teaching) (Luke 1:1-4; John 20:30-31; Acts 1:1-3; Rom. 1:1-7; 1 Tim. 1:3-7, 6:20-21; 2 Tim. 1:8-14, 3:14-17, 4:1-5).

Leaders such as Clement, bishop of Rome; Ignatius, bishop of Antioch; Justin, Irenaeus, Tertullian, Clement of Alexandria, Origen, Cyprian, Athanasius, and Augustine combatted heresy, encouraged faithfulness, and explained the faith and practices of the church to those within and outside.

Leadership in the early church was shared by gifted members of the Body of Christ. Members with spiritual gifts such as prophecy, teaching, wisdom, tongues, interpreting, healing, and helping actively shared in the ministries of the church. As time passed, greater care was taken to set apart competent leadership in the church, and believers were strongly encouraged to submit to and respect their leaders. Key center churches and their leaders in Jerusalem, Antioch, Alexandria, and Rome received greater respect. In time Rome came to be first among equals and then the chief church. Constantinople became the center of the Eastern church and was chief rival to Rome.

Training became a mandatory activity in the early church as great numbers of converts were attracted to its fellowship. The courage of believers willing to die for their faith, the moral tone of the Christian community, the love of the brethren for each other, the living challenge to Graeco-Roman philosophy, and the testimony of rank and file believers, led the Roman government to oppose, persecute, tolerate, and eventually accept the faith of the followers of Jesus.

Catechumenal training arose to insure that those embracing Christianity understood the faith and were committed to the life-style expected of believers. Inquirers in the catechizing instruction classes were carefully taught, and only when they had proved competent in belief and life was baptism given. Ethics was clearly emphasized, often in the form of contrasting ways of light and darkness. This form of adult education reached its peak in development between A.D. 325 and 450.

The catechumenate declined when it came to be widely expected that children should be baptized in infancy and when pagans, lacking Christian motivation, were commanded by law to go to church. Origen, a great teacher who died in A.D. 254, warned catechumens that though Simon Magus of Acts 8 was washed with the water of baptism, he had not been washed unto salvation. "Mark, catechumens, and listen, and, as a result of these warnings, prepare yourself before baptism. . . . He who is washed unto salvation receives both water and the Holy Spirit."[3] Cyril of Jerusalem (A.D. 310-386) warned the candidate for baptism in his introductory lecture, ". . . If you just continue in your evil disposition, I have cleared myself by telling you, but you cannot expect to receive God's grace. For though the water will receive you, the Holy Spirit will not. . . ."[4]

During those early centuries laymen demonstrated the doctrine of the priesthood of believers. They entered into decision-making, participated in worship, discussed theology, and were involved participants in outreach.

More thorough instruction than that available to the catechumen became available through the institution of the catechetical school. In those schools, principally of Alexandria, Antioch, Edessa, and Nisibis, the learning of the world was examined and rejected or integrated with the Christian teaching. Clement, called the first great Christian scholar, was a teacher in Alexandria in A.D. 190. Origen, his student, served there from 202-231, and no subject of study was forbidden in his classroom. Many of the leaders of Christendom were touched by the catechetical schools, but the schools were also feared by the church because heretical teachings were sometimes in vogue.

In addition to the catechumenal classes in the churches and catechetical schools in certain cities, some schools were conducted in the key (cathedral) churches of regions. There were also monastic schools, for monasticism had appeared as a protest against the church's too-easy peace with the world. Heretical groups sprang up, objecting to some condition in the church or promoting some teaching that had been neglected by the church. Those groups challenged the church to doctrinal preciseness as expressed in the creeds. Well-read laymen challenged positions taken by the church that appeared to conflict with their interpretation of Scripture.[5]

THE DARK AGES

The fifth century saw the sack of Rome by the barbarians of north and northeast Europe. The seventh to the tenth centuries saw the Muslim Arabs advancing in the Eastern empire and North Africa.

During that time the growing influence of the bishops brought the church under their power. The absence of scholarship that had previously been found in catechetical schools, along with the closing of secular schools, resulted in a decay in the education of clergy. That affected teaching given to the laity. Instruction was replaced by ritual. The lamp of learning flickered except for monastic and cathedral schools, which preserved some semblance of literacy and instruction and maintained libraries. Because of that situation, the Roman papacy (chief bishop) increased in power, claiming authority over both church and state. Monastic orders carried on the tradition of the life of devotion and of service. Mystics sought for the vision of God beyond the ordinary trappings of the ritual of the church.

Teaching in the church was largely done through the ritual mass with its symbolism in worship. Drama was used later in that period to depict the key events in the life of Christ. Sometimes priests as well as the people were illiterate. The majority of the laity had little knowledge of the meaning of the gospel. Architecture and art communicated some messages to those who pondered their meanings. The home, of course, had its influence, but with ritual-bound theology and baptismal regeneration in infancy accepted by many, there was less reason to teach Christianity in the home. As with the church in general, those were dark times for Christian education.

THE SECOND THOUSAND YEARS

PRE-REFORMATION DEVELOPMENTS

As the second millennium of Christian history began, there were forces at work that would in time reform the church. Crusades to free sacred sites in the Middle East from the heathen or to convert heretical peoples contributed to exposing new or long forgotten ideas and technology. Scholasticism, as a philosophical system exploring the relation between reason and faith, reached its high point in Thomas Aquinas in the thirteenth century. The universities in the thirteenth and fourteenth centuries took up the work of preserving and extending learning that in previous centuries had been promoted by various emperors, churchmen, cathedral schools, and monastic orders. They arose as guilds of teachers, often associated with cathedrals, offered studies in theology, law, and similar fields. The Renaissance glorified learning; the Greek classics and the Scriptures were rediscovered, translated, and studied by schoolmen, and began to penetrate society.

Meanwhile, the "heretical" sects such as the Waldenses and Brethren of the Common Life, in reaction to the evils in the church, formed communities of believers. Preaching and teaching the Word of God, they sought a life of obedience to revealed truth as well as an authentic relationship to God.

New monastic orders were making their appearance. Francis of Assisi received God's call to preach and live the simple life in 1209. The Franciscan order was a direct result. Dominic was an older contemporary of Francis, and the Dominicans were dedicated to teaching and scholarship as well as preaching. In some places "heresies" were being destroyed through the Inquisition or an armed crusade.

As always, there were also sincere people of God with educational vision. Gerald Groote (1340-1384), for example, opened his home to seekers who shunned worldliness and sought to live a life of devotion centered on the teaching of the Bible. They aided in the revival of learning and started other communities in the Low Countries and Germany. The Brethren of the Common Life, as they were known, were mystics albeit practical in their disciplines of life.

Erasmus, a leading humanist of the Renaissance, earnestly desired the reform of the church. John Wycliffe, who died in 1384, translated the Bible into English and sent out itinerant preachers known as Lollards to reach and teach the masses. John Hus, professor and preacher in Bohemia, was excommunicated and burned at the stake in 1415. Savanarola of Florence preached repentance and transformed the city, but because of his persistent criticisms of evils in the church was excommunicated and later killed in 1498.

Lewis Joseph Sherrill offers this basic observation of the period from about 450 to the Reformation:

> Christian education is colored at virtually every point by the emphasis laid on sacramental conceptions of the grace of God. However great the values that can be claimed, and they *are* great, the full story is seen only when it is also asked, what did the conception of grace eliminate from education, and thereby eliminate from personal and social life? Again we suggest that the middle ages themselves, as they were, contain the materials for the answer: clergy and people indelibly religious, profoundly reverent in many respects, dependent on priests for safety now and for destiny hereafter, often rebellious, knowing they were enslaved, but profoundly ignorant of those simple Christian conceptions that would set them free, and therefore increasingly ready to turn and rend the religious thing that bore them down.[6]

It is apparent that bad or inadequate theology weakens Christian education and thereby conceals the gospel. Sacraments without instruction become superstition. If people achieve "salvation" through ritual, however symbolic of reality it may be, education loses its God-ordained purpose in the church or home.

Methods of religious communication in the Middle Ages, in addition to symbolism picked up by participants and observers of the rituals, included

paintings, sculpture, stained-glass windows, religious plays, the oral word
of the preacher, stations of the cross (a walk through the events of Christ's
suffering), and hymns.

THE PROTESTANT AND CATHOLIC REFORMATIONS

Events that transpire in history develop out of a combination of conditions and persons in which God is at work.

Martin Luther (1483-1546) heard in his family the Ten Commandments,
the Creed, the Lord's Prayer, and that pardon comes from the free grace
of God. Thomas M. Lindsay reminds us that the roots of the Reformation
were found in the instruction given by the pious parents, the hymns and
prayers of the church, and sermons of revivalist preachers.[7]

As a student, Luther read the Scriptures, commentaries, and devotional
works. His early doubt and struggle gave way to assurance as the truth
"the just shall live by faith" gripped him. On October 31, 1517, he posted
ninety-five theses he was prepared to debate. In them he challenged the
sale of indulgences to Germans in order to pay for construction of church
buildings in Rome. He criticized the concept of indulgences, since merit
could not be stored up and transferred to others with ability to pay a price.
The newly-developed printing press carried those courageous sentiments
far beyond Luther's original purpose and thrust him into a controversy
that eventually drove Luther to the conclusion that Scripture alone was
authoritative.

In 1520 his *Open Letter to the Christian Nobility of the German Nation
Concerning the Reform of the Christian Estate*, the *Babylonian Captivity
of the Church*, and *Freedom of the Christian Man* brought a number of
issues into focus.[8]

The tenets of Protestantism were being clarified: justification by faith
alone, the priesthood of all believers, the authority of the Word of God
as contained in the Scriptures, and the right and duty of each believer to
interpret the Scriptures.[9]

Luther's contributions included a new liturgy, the importance of the
sermon as a teaching tool, religious literature for children and adults, use
of the common language in church, congregational participation in song,
the tract, and the notion of compulsory education under the state in which
the Scriptures are prominent.[10] His translation of the Bible helped to
standardize the German language. Emphasizing the home and the laity,
he helped bring Christianity to the masses.

The Reformed Churches appeared simultaneously with Lutheranism.
Huldreich Zwingli (1484-1531) and John Calvin (1509-1564) were early
leaders.[11] The Reformed churchmen differed from other branches of the
Reformation in several ways but were united in basic affirmations related

to salvation, Scripture, and the priesthood of believers. Calvin stimulated popular education and sought to build an ideal community in Geneva through cooperative church and state efforts.

Restoration to the pattern of the early church was the theme of the Anabaptists of the Reformation. They were more pessimistic regarding the world and optimistic regarding the church. The church was a gathered community of believers, not a territorial assembly. Church and state should be separate, and more radical ethics of pacifism, abstinence from alcohol, withdrawal from public life, humility, and other life-style matters were of critical importance. In spite of excesses that discredited some of them, radical Christians provided a stimulus to the established church in places where they were allowed to exist.

In the Roman Catholic aspects of the Reformation, Ignatius Loyola (c. 1491-1556) took a different approach than Luther in his struggle for identity and peace with God. Devoted to Rome, he established a new monastic order. The Society of Jesus was under the control of the pope and gave itself to the instruction of children and the ignorant in Christian doctrine.[12] H. Clay Trumbull, in the Lyman Beecher Lectures at Yale in 1888, credits that order with a more effective use of education with the young, thereby arresting the progress of the Protestant Reformation.[13] The Council of Trent, which met from time to time between 1545 and 1563, initiated reforms such as preparing a catechism for the young, providing for education for the priesthood in colleges and seminaries, defining dogma, and overhauling its administrative machinery.

Francis Xavier (1506-1582), a disciple of Loyola, is said in ten years "to have planted the cross in fifty-two different kingdoms, preached through nine thousand miles of territory and baptized over one million persons."[14] Although that assessment apparently stretches the truth, the impact of that Roman Catholic missionary-educator was immense.

Community life, literature, learning, and leadership played an important part in many manifestations of the Reformation. The Word of God was powerfully presented in sermons, tracts, hymns, and catechisms. Popular education received further impetus in Calvinistic Netherlands when the Synod of Dort in 1619 decreed that civil authorities have the duty to provide schools for all boys and girls. John Amos Comenius (1592-1670), a bishop among the Moravian Brethren, contributed to the broad movement and counseled leaders in several nations on common schools. His *Great Didactic*, published in 1657, urged teaching everything to everyone. Called the first modern educator, some of Comenius's principles of instruction are still accepted.

The Thirty Year War of 1618-48 was a debilitating struggle over religious and political authority. The terms of peace fixed boundaries, required toleration of the Reformed and Lutherans, and granted permission to those of faiths other than that of their rulers to worship as they wished and educate their children in their faith.[15]

A religious awakening followed the years of war. Pietism was its most striking feature. A personal knowledge of Christ, practical Christian living resulting in good works, separation from worldliness, and evangelistic zeal characterized that movement. Philip Jacob Spener (1635-1705) as a pastor, through sermon and catechesis, stressed instruction. He and others gathered in homes for discussion of sermons, study of the Word of God, and prayers. A Spener sermon in 1669 spoke of conducting private meetings for the cultivation of holiness. "How much good it would do if good friends would come together on a Sunday and instead of getting out glasses, cards, or dice would take up a book and read from it for the edification of all or would review something from sermons that were heard!"[16]

Spener went on to say preachers cannot instruct people from the pulpit without the assistance of other persons in the congregation to work with them to correct and reform their neighbors. The "little churches in the Church" brought life to a dead orthodoxy.

August Herman Franke (1663-1727) came under the influence of Spener and helped develop Halle as a center of Pietism. Schools were founded, an orphanage begun, and a missionary movement inaugurated that left a lasting impact.

Interestingly, schools for the poor proved so effective that the well-to-do desired them for their children. Teacher training was inaugurated and so highly regarded that Frederick the Great required all who taught on his estate to train under the Pietists! Count Zinzendorf, while a student in the school of Franke, lived in Frederick's home. He later became a leader among the Moravian Brethren, who were to influence the Wesleys and the world. Henry Melchior Muhlenberg, also a follower of Franke, organized parish schools among Lutherans in Pennsylvania.[17] From the Pietists came fresh activity in schools, church life, music, missions, and social concern. Their influence upon life in the churches, community, literature, learning, and leadership was substantial.

In the British Isles Anglicanism borrowed from both the Catholic and Protestant traditions. Dissenters, among them the Puritans, Quakers, and Methodists made significant contributions to Christianity through training of leadership, lay involvement, organization, and dedication in reaching and teaching people.

Because of a growing commitment to an educated and ministering laity,

Christianity pressed for universal education.

Colonists in America established schools to advance learning and train clergy. Harvard College had its beginning in 1636 with the vote of the General Court of the Massachusetts Bay Colony to devote public funds for a school or college.[18] In 1647 the Colony of Massachusetts Bay ordered towns to supply teachers for children. The Old Deluder Satan Law, as it came to be called, began:

> It being one chief project of the old deluder, Satan, to keep men from the knowledge of the Scriptures, as in former times by keeping them in an unknown tongue, so in these latter times persuading them from the use of tongues that so at least the true sense and meaning of the original might be clouded by false glosses by saint-seeming deceivers, that learning may not be buried in the grave of our fathers in the church and commonwealth, the Lord assisting our endeavors,
> It is therefore ordered. . . .[19]

MODERN DEVELOPMENTS IN CHRISTIAN EDUCATION

Robert Raikes (1735-1811) is regarded as the founder of the Sunday school. Begun in Gloucester, England, in 1780, his school was ignored for some time and was even opposed by the clergy. That school on Sunday sought to provide life-related instruction based upon the Bible for poor children of the city on the one day when they were free from their employment.

Conditions were ripe for wide adoption of the school, and it grew rapidly. In America it followed the westward advance of the settlers and often provided the impetus for the organization of churches, libraries, and public schools.[20] Organizations were established for the growth of the Sunday school. The American Sunday School Union was organized in 1824. Regional associations and local and general conventions attracted great interests. Denominations increasingly accepted the Sunday school, and it became a leading means of church growth.

The early public schools were "Protestant" in nature. Pressure to remove sectarianism from the schools led to an increasingly secular education. Private schools emerged to do what the church and parents desired. The potent Roman Catholic parochial school movement began in Philadelphia in 1782 and grew rapidly during peak times of Catholic immigration.[21] Lutheran and other denominational and interdenominational schools made up a growing movement working with children of elementary and secondary school age.

The history of American education shows the gradual acceptance of the idea that the community should support schools for the young and that education should be compulsory. Religious awakenings in the eighteenth and nineteenth centuries led to the formation of voluntary societies to evangelize and educate.[22]

In reaction to a theology that tended to ignore children until they had drifted into sin, Horace Bushnell proposed that "the child is to grow up a Christian, and never know himself as being otherwise."[23] Somewhat reminiscent of Jewish education, he argued that the home, church, school, and community should surround the child with positive influence rather than neglect them until they experienced sin and became ripe for a revivalistic conversion experience.

In 1872 a uniform lesson curriculum for Sunday school appeared. Previous to that time, catechisms, Bible memory, many lesson helps, and sermonizing filled class time. Classes for adults developed rapidly in the 1890s. Graded lessons appeared after the turn of the century. The increased insights into children's learning were forwarded by the growing disciplines of psychology and education. Teacher training was also a major advance in the 1870s.

The YMCA was founded in England in 1844 and came to the United States in 1851. This organization proved to be an effective tool for urban youth and adult evangelism. D. L. Moody received training as an evangelist and administrator in this movement. Christian Endeavor began in 1881. Denominational societies soon followed. Church-related camping began in 1880, although "camp meetings" on the frontier had been a feature of American life for a century.[24] Moody developed one of the first Christian Assemblies in Northfield, Massachusetts, which in 1886 hosted a YMCA college conference that marked the beginning of the Student Volunteer Movement, a major force in world missions. John R. Mott, later to become YMCA international evangelist to university students and one of the originators of the World Council of Churches, found his life redirected to Christian service as a result of the conference.

In 1882 A. B. Simpson founded in New York City a Bible institute that later moved to Nyack, New York. Chicago's Moody Bible Institute began in 1886. Church-related colleges and seminaries are current expressions of Christian commitment to learning and make up a considerable part of the higher education movement.

Vacation Bible school, weekday Christian education, and club programs for children and youth developed in the twentieth century. A variety of parachurch organizations, such as Inter-Varsity, Young Life, Youth for Christ, and Campus Crusade, developed for evangelism and discipleship efforts.

Early in this century leadership in Christian education slowly passed from the laity to the professional. In 1903 the Religious Education Association was founded. A Sunday School Council of Evangelical Denominations formed in 1910 merged with the International Council of Religious Education, which in 1950 became the Division of Christian Education of the National Council of the Churches of Christ in the USA. Protesting liberal theological trends in the council were a group of evangelical publishers and church leaders. Their 1939 meeting preceded a 1942 gathering of evangelicals that launched the National Association of Evangelicals in 1943. In 1945 the National Sunday School Association was formed, which stimulated Christian education work in the post World War II years.[25] The Sunday school convention became popular again, and the National Association of Directors of Christian Education and Professors of Christian Education was developed.

A return toward orthodoxy in the broad field of Christian education occurred at mid-century. H. Shelton Smith and James Smart sought to combat the drift toward liberal theology that John Dewey, George A. Coe, William C. Bower, and Harrison Elliott represented in the first half of the century. In recent years evangelical scholars, publishers, and schools have made solid contributions to the growing field of Christian education.

Christian education is an increasingly recognized field of study in undergraduate and graduate theological education. The growth and nurture of the church requires the tools and concepts of education as the message of the Bible is communicated through church, home, and school.

FOR FURTHER STUDY

1. What role does education have in the life of the church? Provide examples from history.
2. Compare Jewish education with that of the early church.
3. What recurring educational themes have appeared throughout history?
4. Prepare a chart showing who was taught, what was taught, and how people were taught in Judaism, the early church, the ancient church, the medieval period, the Reformation, Pietism, the colonial period, and the present day. What generalizations can be made?
5. Why is Christian literature so important in the life of the church?
6. Learning frequently occurs through socialization. How was this reflected in the Bible and the history of the church?
7. How does music and celebration help to educate?
8. Compare national life in Old Testament days and in the United States or Canada. What religious values are communicated then and now?

NOTES

1. Lewis Joseph Sherrill, *The Rise of Christian Education* (New York: Macmillan, 1953), p. 71.
2. Kenneth Scott Latourette, *A History of Christianity* (New York: Harper, 1953), p. 107.

3. Henry Bettenson, ed. and trans., *The Early Church Fathers* (London: Oxford U., 1956), p. 343.
4. Cited in Kendig B. Cully, ed., *Basic Writings in Christian Education* (Philadelphia: Westminster, 1930), p. 35.
5. William H. C. Frend, "The Church of the Roman Empire, 313-600," in *The Layman in Christian History*, ed. Stephen C. Neill and Hans-Ruedi Weber (Philadelphia: Westminster, 1963), p. 71.
6. Sherrill, p. 302.
7. Thomas M. Lindsay, *Luther and the German Reformation* (Edinburgh: T. & T. Clark, 1900), pp. 13-14.
8. Martin Luther, *Three Treatises*, trans. Charles M. Jacobs, et. al. (Philadelphia: Fortress, 1960), contains the three primary works of the reformer at the height of his struggle with Rome. These translations are from earlier compilations of Luther's literary works.
9. Latourette, p. 715.
10. In addition to other sources cited, see also Frederick Eby, *The Development of Modern Education*, 2d ed. (Englewood Cliffs, N.J.: Prentice-Hall, 1952), pp. 67-79.
11. The reader is invited to review the contributions of individuals to Christian education in Kendig B. Cully, ed., *Basic Writings in Christian Education*, and Elmer L. Towns, ed., *A History of Religious Educators* (Grand Rapids: Baker, 1975).
12. Latourette, p. 847.
13. H. Clay Trumbull, *The Sunday School: Its Origin, Mission, Methods, and Auxiliaries* (Philadelphia: John D. Wattles, 1893), p. 71.
14. Robert H. Glover, *The Progress of World Wide Missions*, rev. J. Herbert Kane (New York: Harper, 1960), p. 43.
15. Latourette, p. 889.
16. Philip Jacob Spener, *Pia Desideria*, trans. Theodore G. Tappert (Philadelphia: Fortress, 1964), p. 13. (Originally published in 1675.)
17. Eby, pp. 256, 258.
18. R. Freemen Butts and Lawrence A. Cremin, *A History of Education in American Culture* (New York: Holt, Rinehart, and Winston, 1953), p. 81.
19. Edward A. Krug, *Salient Dates in American Education 1635-1964* (New York: Harper & Row, 1966), pp. 9-10.
20. Robert W. Lynn and Elliott Wright, *The Big Little School: Sunday Child of American Protestantism* (New York: Harper & Row, 1971), provides a brief, appreciative, and highly instructive sweep of historical highlights of the American version of the Sunday school.
21. Sam Duker, *The Public Schools and Religion* (New York: Harper & Row, 1966), p. 16.
22. Among the resources of religious history that illuminate the American experience are Sydney E. Ahlstrom, *A Religious History of the American People* (New Haven, Conn.: Yale U., 1972); Winthrop S. Hudson, *Religion in America* (New York: Scribner's, 1965); and a shorter collection of materials by Robert T. Handy, ed., *Religion in the American Experience* (New York: Harper & Row, 1972).
23. Horace Bushnell, *Christian Nurture* (New York: Scribner's, 1890), p. 10. His first book appeared in 1847 and was published in final form in 1861. Some consider Bushnell the father of modern religious education.
24. See the author's chapter on the history of camping in Werner C. Graendorf and Lloyd Mattson, eds., *An Introduction to Christian Camping* (Chicago: Moody, 1979).
25. Clarence H. Benson, *A Popular History of Christian Education* (Chicago: Moody, 1943); James D. Murch, *Christian Education and the Local Church* (Cincinnati: Standard, 1943); and C. B. Eavey, *History of Christian Education* (Chicago: Moody, 1964) provide evangelical interpretations of events surrounding the decline of the Sunday school and the assumption of leadership by professionals.

SUGGESTED READING

SPECIFIC REFERENCES

Anderson, Clifford V. "History of Christian Camping." In *Introduction to Chris-*

tian Camping, edited by Werner C. Graendorf and Lloyd Mattson. Chicago: Moody, 1979.

Kennedy, William Bean. "Christian Education Through History." In *An Introduction to Christian Education,* edited by Marvin J. Taylor, pp. 21-31. Nashville: Abingdon, 1966.

Lynn, Robert W. "A Historical Perspective on the Features of American Religious Education." In *Foundations for Christian Education in an Era of Change,* edited by Marvin J. Taylor, pp. 7-19. Nashville: Abingdon, 1976.

Mason, Harold. "History of Christian Education." In *An Introduction to Evangelical Christian Education,* edited by J. Edward Hakes. Chicago: Moody, 1964.

Miller, Randolph Crump. *Education for Christian Living.* 2d ed. Englewood Cliffs, N.J.: Prentice-Hall, 1963.

Pope Pius XI. "Christian Education of Youth." *Seven Great Encyclicals.* Glen Rock, N.J.: Paulist, 1963.

Sherrill, Lewis J. "A Historical Study of the Religious Education Movement." In *Orientation in Religious Education,* edited by Philip Henry Lotz, pp. 13-25. New York: Abingdon, 1950.

Stewart, Donald G. "History of Christian Education." In *The Westminster Dictionary of Christian Education,* edited by Kendig Brubaker Cully, pp. 314-20. Philadelphia: Westminster, 1963.

Taylor, Marvin J. "A Historical Introduction to Religious Education." In *Religious Education: A Comprehensive Survey,* edited by Marvin J. Taylor, pp. 11-23. New York: Abingdon, 1960.

Vieth, Paul H., ed. *The Church and Christian Education,* pp. 19-51. St. Louis: Bethany, 1947.

GENERAL REFERENCES

Bainton, Roland H. *The Reformation of the Sixteenth Century.* Boston: Beacon, 1952.

Barclay, William. *Train Up a Child.* Philadelphia: Westminster, 1959.

Benson, Clarence H. *A Popular History of Christian Education.* Chicago: Moody, 1943.

Bettenson, Henry, ed. and trans. *The Early Church Fathers.* London: Oxford U., 1956.

Bushnell, Horace. *Christian Nurture.* New York: Scribner's, 1890.

Butler, J. Donald. *Religious Education: The Foundations and Practice of Nurture,* pp. 23-121. New York: Harper & Row, 1962.

Butts, R. Freeman and Lawrence A. Cremin. *A History of Education in American Culture.* New York: Holt, Rinehart, and Winston, 1953.

Cully, Kendig Brubaker, ed. *Basic Writings in Christian Education.* Philadelphia: Westminster, 1960.

Eavey, C. B. *History of Christian Education.* Chicago: Moody, 1964.

Eby, Frederick. *The Development of Modern Education.* 2d ed. Englewood Cliffs, N.J.: Prentice-Hall, 1952.

Furnish, Dorothy Jean. *DRE/DCE—The History of a Profession*, pp. 15-47, 97-112. Nashville: Christian Educators Fellowship, The United Methodist Church, 1976.

Glover, Robert Hall. *The Progress of World Wide Missions*. Revised by Herbert Kane. New York: Harper, 1960.

Latourette, Kenneth Scott. *A History of Christianity*. New York: Harper & Row, 1953.

Lindsay, Thomas M. *Luther and the German Reformation*. Edinburgh: T. & T. Clark, 1900.

Lynn, Robert W. and Elliott Wright. *The Big Little School: Sunday Child of American Protestantism*. New York: Harper & Row, 1971.

Murch, James DeForest. *Christian Education and the Local Church*, pp. 13-117. Cincinnati: Standard, 1943.

Neill, Stephen Charles and Hans-Ruedi Weber, eds. *The Layman in Christian History*. Philadelphia: Westminster, 1963.

Sherrill, Lewis Joseph. *The Rise of Christian Education*. New York: Macmillan, 1953.

Sizemore, John T., ed. *The History of Religious Education*. Nashville: Broadman, 1978.

Spener, Philip Jacob. *Pia Desideria*. (Edited and translated by Theodore G. Tappert. Philadelphia: Fortress, 1964.

Towns, Elmer L., ed. *A History of Religious Educators*. Grand Rapids: Baker, 1975.

Trumbull, H. Clay. *The Sunday School: Its Origin, Mission, Methods, and Auxiliaries*. Philadelphia: John D. Wattles, 1893.

Part II

CHRISTIAN EDUCATION AS A DYNAMIC PROCESS

GOD's PROGRAM of education must not only be examined biblically to be understood. It must be viewed in terms of its dynamics to be appreciated. The dynamics—distinctive forces—in Christian education make it a special kind of educational process.

Appropriately, this second unit begins with a chapter on *Jesus Christ—* the Christian educator's supreme teaching example. As gospel writer Luke comments about the master teacher's ministry, ". . . they were continually amazed at His teaching" (Luke 4:32). To study Christ as a dynamic teacher is a richly rewarding experience, an imperative for appreciating the heart, as well as the method, of effective Christian communication.

Also in this unit, theologian Fred Dickason examines the work of the *Holy Spirit* as "our director and resource in teaching and learning God's truth." Here is another major facet of God's educational process—the dynamic of the Holy Spirit, affecting every area in that process.

A third unit chapter considers Christian education's unique ministry of a Book, the powerful, infallible *Word of God.* This is a chapter especially designed to provide guidance for the teacher in studying the Bible for teaching. It presents a series of practical suggestions for personal Bible study.

Another chapter in the unit considers the human dynamic in teaching, as educator Gilbert Peterson analyzes the ministry of the *Christian teacher.*

Finally, the unit includes a study on the use of basic principles for dynamic teaching. The chapter was written by a husband-wife educational team and includes their own illustrative sketches.

4

Christ the Master Teacher

VALERIE A. WILSON

JESUS THE SAVIOR. Jesus the crucified. Jesus the Lord. With those designations we are familiar. But Jesus the teacher? We study His teachings, but the *teacher* Himself? Yet Jesus as teacher is a subject thoroughly worthy of serious consideration, providing unparalleled example for Christian teachers today.

"When Nicodemus came to Jesus by night, he opened the conversation with the words, 'We know that Thou art a teacher come from God' (John 3:2); and history has echoed his verdict. The teaching of Jesus, even though great multitudes throughout the world are still outside its sphere, even though many of his followers have not dared to put it fully into action, has had a power and an effect with which the influence of no other teacher can even for a moment be compared. He stands alone—the 'Teacher.' "[1]

The teacher was an important figure in Israel. Perhaps no other nation so highly magnified the art of teaching or gave to the teacher such an exalted position. "The honor shown to a teacher bordered on that given to God. . . . The Jew gave preference to his teacher over his father; the one gave him temporal life, the other eternal life."[2]

Three things help establish the fact that Jesus was a teacher. In the first place, the people recognized Him as a teacher. Although Jesus never instructed the people to address Him with a specific title, "teacher," or "rabbi," was the most common title given to Jesus.

Not only did the people recognize Jesus as a teacher, the gospel writers described His ministry as a teaching one. References to "teaching" and "taught" abound in each gospel record. Consider these few from Mark's gospel: 4:1-2; 6:2, 6; 8:31; 9:31; 12:35. "Teaching occupied so large a

VALERIE A. WILSON, M.R.E., is a curriculum writer and editor for Regular Baptist Press, Schaumburg, Illinois.

place alongside preaching in His ministry that the impression of the 'Great Teacher' was created and still remains."³

The people recognized Jesus as a teacher, the gospel writers described His ministry as teaching, and His followers were recognized as pupils. "Disciple," meaning "pupil," or "learner," is used over two hundred times in referring to Jesus' followers.

Without a doubt we are on biblical ground in considering Jesus the teacher. Let us remember, however, that "in approaching Jesus as a religious teacher, we are considering more than a dynamic personality and more than a religious genius. We are examining the teaching methods of One who claimed to be the Son of God."⁴

His Qualifications

It is fair to ask about any teacher, "What are his qualifications for teaching?" Depending on the subject to be taught, the answer will vary. We tend to think of diplomas and degrees as qualifications. But sometimes the experiences of life qualify one to teach a given subject. When we approach the qualifications of Jesus the Teacher, experiences rather than degrees are prominent.

It is probable that Jesus received traditional Jewish education as a boy in Nazareth. The town had a synagogue, and Jesus was accustomed to attending it (Luke 4:16). The synagogue was both a religious and an educational institution in Jewish life. Formal education in the synagogue school began when Jewish boys were six years old. During the elementary years, pupils learned to read the Scriptures, to write, and to do simple mathematics. In the secondary years, the emphasis was on learning the law. The Scriptures, especially the Pentateuch, were studied intensely. Jesus' experience in the Temple when He was twelve (Luke 2:46-47) seems to indicate that He had been attending the secondary school of His day.⁵

Benson enumerates five ways in which Jesus demonstrated His educational preparation for teaching: (1) He was a master of the art of reading, as demonstrated in the synagogue in Nazareth (Luke 4:16-20); (2) He was familiar with the less common art of writing, as demonstrated when He wrote on the ground (John 8:6); (3) He knew Hebrew as well as the Aramaic dialect of His day, as shown when He spoke from the cross (Matt. 27:46); (4) He was profoundly versed in the Scriptures; (5) He was familiar with the traditions, the oral law, as demonstrated by His words, "Ye have heard that it was said" (Matt. 5:21, 27, 31, 38, 43).⁶

In addition to His educational preparation, Jesus was qualified in other ways. Perhaps the following six things (taken in part from J. L. Marsh⁷) summarize Jesus' qualifications for His teaching ministry:

1. Jesus was the living embodiment of truth (John 14:6). "He was 100 percent what he taught."[8] Thus He could inspire confidence in His statements.

2. Jesus had authority (Matt. 7:28-29). The authority of the scribes was secondhand. Jesus' authority was "intrinsic, fresh and free."[9]

3. Jesus knew the Scriptures. He quoted from at least twenty Old Testament books; He alluded to others.[10]

4. Jesus understood human nature; He knew His pupils (Matt. 9:4; John 1:47; 2:25; 4:17-18; 6:61, 64).

5. Jesus mastered the art of teaching. "There never was a teacher who was more fully led by the Holy Spirit than was our Lord Jesus Christ, and yet none ever observed the laws of teaching more consistently."[11]

6. He believed in teaching: "You call Me Teacher and Lord; and you are right, for so I am" (John 13:13).

His Pupils

It is easy to think that the master teacher must have worked with perfect pupils. But such was not the case. Remember the disciples? Rough, impetuous Peter; proud John; scheming Matthew; doubting Thomas; dense Philip; greedy Judas.

"To take this small group of undeveloped, unlikely individuals and grow them into a band of developed, well-rounded persons who have been an inspiration to the world is a marvel of the teaching and training art. It has never been surpassed by any other teacher throughout the ages, and has been an inspiration and encouragement to Christian teachers ever since."[12]

Jesus' pupils were mainly adults, but they were not limited to that. Children were in the audience, as is evidenced by a child's ready availability in Matthew 18:2 and the "lad" in John 6:9. Matthew 19:13-15 indicates that Jesus sustained a special relationship to the children, but no direct teaching situations are recorded.

A pattern is discernible in Jesus' ministry. In the beginning He instructed individuals. During the middle period He addressed the crowds. In the end He again worked with individuals, specifically giving intensive training to the twelve.

He encountered pupils everywhere He went. He did not gather them into a classroom or other formal setting. "How remarkably the Master Teacher capitalized on every natural opportunity; whenever He found spontaneous interest and attention, He made of it a vital teaching situation."[13] "Every social occasion, every temporal event, every need, spoken or unspoken, every reference of life, presented Him with an opportunity to convey to men the truths of the Christian life."[14]

HIS PURPOSES

The importance of objectives in Christian teaching cannot be overstated. Someone has said, "Blessed is he who aims at nothing, for he shall not be disappointed." No Christian teacher should ever desire that kind of blessedness! As we look at Jesus the teacher—our perfect example—we see clear purposes in His ministry and an unswerving devotion to fulfill those purposes.

While to know and to feel were part of Jesus' objectives, His aim was to change lives, not merely to affect the intellect or emotions. "His instruction looked to a practical end. He expected progress. To this end, He always appealed to the will of His pupils."[15]

Jesus' purposes could be listed or classified in several ways:

1. Jesus sought to convert His pupils to God (e.g., Luke 13:3; John 3:3). No teaching is complete without this all-important objective.

2. Jesus sought to bring people into harmony with one another (e.g., Mark 12:31).

3. Jesus sought to have His pupils form right ideals (e.g., Matt. 5:48).

4. Jesus sought to deepen His pupils' convictions (e.g., John 21:15-17).

5. Jesus sought to train His disciples to carry His teachings around the world (e.g., Matt. 28:19-20).[16]

Perhaps the best commentary on Jesus' success in achieving His purposes is the book of Acts. The founding of the Christian church, the spread of Christianity in the then-known world, and the presence of Christianity in the world today all attest to the fact that Jesus accomplished in His pupils—particularly the eleven—that which He purposed.

HIS METHODS

SECURING ATTENTION

Securing the pupil's attention must be a top priority with the teacher. "Until the teacher has secured the attention of the class there is no need to try to go any further."[17] Securing attention was not a problem for the master teacher. "He simply and naturally did those attention-winning things which poorer teachers must do with set purpose."[18]

What were those "attention-winning things"? In other words, how did Jesus make contact with His pupils?

1. He used His eyes. "He saw two brothers, Simon . . . and Andrew" (Matt. 4:18); "Jesus turned, and beheld them following" (John 1:38).

2. He initiated conversation. To the woman at the well He said, "Give me a drink," and she immediately answered (John 4:7-9).

3. He asked questions. "When Jesus came into the district of Caesarea Philippi, He began asking His disciples, saying, 'Who do people say that the Son of man is?'" (Matt. 16:13)

4. He invited companionship. After seeing Simon and Andrew, He said to them, "Follow me . . ." (Mark 1:17).

5. He called people by name. "Jesus looked at him, and said, 'You are Simon the son of John' " (John 1:42).

6. He called for attention with words such as "listen," "truly," "behold" (Mark 4:3; Luke 18:17, 31; 22:10; John 3:3, 5[19]).

In every phase of the teaching process, Jesus was the master of the art. His ability to secure attention was no exception.

STYLE

"He was simple yet profound, and used symbolism that effectively conveyed His readily-discernible meaning. By His delightful choice of language He revealed God to men in words they could understand. As He taught profound truths about difficult subjects, He did so in such a way that they became clear and straightforward. . . . 'The people wondered at the gracious words that proceeded out of His mouth,' and 'the common people heard Him gladly.' "[20]

In addition to simplicity and straightforwardness, two other characteristics of Jesus' teaching style should be noted: He taught from the known to the unknown, and He explained the abstract in terms of the concrete.

Teaching from the known to the unknown included the principle of taking people as they were and leading them to the place He wanted them to be. It also included using language that was familiar to the pupil. In dealing with a lawyer (the theologian of His day), Jesus started with a familiar subject—the law (Luke 10:25-37). In dealing with the woman of Samaria, He started with water—the water in the well at hand—and led her to think of *living* water (John 4:6-25). One of His longest recorded lectures, the Olivet Discourse (Matt. 24—25), began with a reference to the Temple, just after departing from it.

The subject matter of Jesus' teaching was largely abstract; it was spiritual. Therefore it was necessary to relate it to His pupils in terms of the concrete. Perhaps one of the clearest examples of this is given in Matthew 13. Jesus was teaching the people about the abstract "kingdom of heaven." He used these concrete illustrations: the sower and seed, the wheat and tares, the grain of mustard seed, the leaven, the hidden treasure, the pearl, the net. It is a recognized educational principle that the abstract should be taught in relation to the concrete. The master teacher did just that!

USE OF QUESTIONS

As we carefully study Jesus' teaching, we see that He used to some degree almost every method we know today. We want to consider several of those, starting with His use of questions. "Questions lay at the very heart of the teaching methods of Jesus; the four Gospels record more than one hundred questions asked by Him."[21]

Jesus' questions were not merely to obtain information. They served a variety of purposes:

1. Some questions *stimulated interest* and formed a point of contact. He asked the disciples, "Who do people say that the Son of man is?" (Matt. 16:13)

2. Some questions helped His pupils *clarify their thinking;* for example, "What did Moses command you?" (Mark 10:3)

3. Some questions *expressed an emotion,* such as disgust or amazement. He responded to the Pharisees, "How can you, being evil, speak what is good?" (Matt. 12:34)

4. Some questions *introduced an illustration.* "Suppose one of you shall have a friend. . . ." (Luke 11:5-6)

5. Some questions were used to *emphasize a truth.* "For what will a man be profited, if he gains the whole world, and forfeits his soul?" (Matt. 16:26)

6. Some questions helped pupils *apply the truth;* for instance, "Which of these three do you think proved to be a neighbor to the man who fell into the robbers' hands?" (Luke 10:36)

7. Some questions were to *provide information* for Himself. "How many loaves do you have?" (Matt. 15:34)

8. Some questions helped *establish a relationship* between the teacher and pupil, as in, "Who touched me?" (Luke 8:45)

9. Some questions were asked to *rebuke or silence* His opposers: "The baptism of John was from what source? . . . And answering Jesus, they said, We do not know." (Matt. 21:25-27)

10. Some questions were *rhetorical;* they needed no answer. "Is not life more than food, and the body than clothing?" (Matt. 6:25)

11. Some questions were asked to *bring conviction;* for example, "Have you never read . . . ?" (Mark 2:25)

12. Some questions were *examinations.* "Simon, son of John, do you love me?" (John 21:15-17)

He was, indeed, the master teacher in His use of questions, "stimulating thought, guiding learning, and challenging pupils to accept the new teaching because they saw its rightness for themselves."[22]

USE OF STORIES

"Jesus presented the most sublime truths in the form of stories [parables]. The story was His favorite method of teaching; no other teacher of whom we have record used parables so freely and so effectively."[23]

"As the master educator, He chose the simplest medium to drive home ideas which have provided food for thought for the most profound minds."[24] "He was unquestionably the world's greatest storyteller."[25] "It is the use of the parable in His teaching by which our Lord is most widely known."[26] About one-fourth of the words of Jesus recorded by Mark and one-half of those recorded by Luke are parables. The word *parable* occurs fifty times in the gospels.

Strictly speaking, a parable is a special literary form. It compares familiar facts with less familiar truths. It may be short and pithy, such as Matthew 15:14, or it may be in extended form. Some of the stories Jesus told were illustrations rather than parables; they were accounts of actual situations, such as, "*A certain man* was going down from Jerusalem to Jericho . . ." (Luke 10:30).

The value of stories in teaching cannot be overstated. "Teaching without illustration is like a house without windows: it may contain many treasures, but they may never be seen."[27] Stories help make abstract truths concrete. They appeal to the imagination. Stories are a free and easy style of teaching. They tend to be informal rather than formal. Stories are an aid to the memory. They are interesting and effective.

Clifford Wilson suggests that the stories Jesus told had these primary characteristics: (1) they were within His pupils' comprehension; (2) they were concise; (3) they quickly aroused interest; (4) the parts followed logically; (5) they led to a satisfying climax.[28]

Although stories can be entertaining, entertainment was never Jesus' sole purpose. At least four purposes are discernible as we look at the stories Jesus told:

1. Some stories were told to secure attention. An example is the parable of the sower as recorded in Luke 8:4-8. After Jesus told the story, the disciples wanted to know more.

2. Some stories illustrated an already-stated abstract principle or truth. The best-known story Jesus told—the Good Samaritan (Luke 10:30-35)—illustrates this purpose. The lawyer who questioned Jesus wanted a definition of "neighbor." In response, Jesus told that immortal story.

3. Some stories were the entire lesson. The trilogy of stories in Luke 15 is an example of this purpose.

4. Some stories summarized the application of a truth. Consider Luke 6:47-49 in this regard.

It is little wonder that people who know almost nothing about the Bible are familiar with some of Jesus' stories. The master teacher demonstrated most vividly the excellence of this teaching method.

USE OF THE DISCOURSE

The discourse, or lecture, method is a systematic presentation of truth. The teacher does most, if not all, of the talking. Jesus often used the discourse when the group was large, but He also used it with a few pupils. He frequently used it in combination with other methods. His discourses "were delivered in the Temple and synagogues, in cities and the country, in the mountains and by the lakes. The subjects range all the way from wealth and divorce to the sabbath and missions."[29] Horne lists over sixty discourses, and classifies them according to audience and subject.[30]

Three of Jesus' lengthier discourses are well known. In the discourse on the Mount (Matt. 5–7), Jesus set forth the superiority of His teachings over those of the law. The disciples were the immediate pupils, but the multitude was evidently within hearing distance (Matt. 5:1; 7:28-29). Perhaps more clearly than on any other occasion Jesus showed His knowledge of the oral law, the Jewish traditions that had taken on authority during the centuries. The surrounding countryside provided objects for His illustrations (the birds of the air, the lilies and grass of the field, Matt. 6:26-30). The discourse included rhetorical questions and illustrations. When Jesus finished, "the multitudes were amazed at His teaching" (Matt. 7:28).

A second well-known and lengthy discourse is that which is recorded in Matthew 24 and 25, the Olivet discourse. The audience seems to have been the twelve. The discourse was given in response to the questions they asked: "Tell us, when will these things [the destruction of the Temple] be, and what will be the sign of Your coming, and of the end of the age?" (Matt. 24:3) Jesus' answer is His major prophetic statement and His admonition to the disciples to be faithful servants while awaiting the Lord's return. Jesus included parables and Old Testament illustrations in this discourse. No reaction on the part of His pupils is given in the gospel record.

A third major discourse is recorded in John 14-16, often referred to as the upper room discourse, although part of it, at least, was given en route to the Garden of Gethsemane. In this instance Jesus was instructing His eleven disciples (Judas was gone). He sought to prepare them for His departure and to instruct them about their mission in the world, describing for them the ministry of the Holy Spirit who would empower and enable them. At the close of the discourse, Jesus prayed for His disciples (John 17). The disciples, seemingly sensing the urgency of the hour, did interrupt the discourse at times with questions and comments. Other than the metaphor of the vine and branches, this discourse does not contain major illustrative material.

"When the Master lectured, the people listened and learned, were informed and stirred, and their lives were enriched. His lectures covered the three-cycle movement of intellect, emotion, and will. The method with him stands out alongside that of the story."[31]

USE OF PROJECTS

Right knowing does not necessarily result in right doing. The teacher must make provision for the carry-over of truth learned to truth applied. Furthermore, actual involvement in the learning process makes learning more permanent. Thus Jesus assigned projects to His pupils. He used the "activity method." Consider these examples from Luke's gospel:

1. In order to demonstrate to Peter His ability to control nature, Jesus commanded, "Put out into the deep water and let down your nets for a catch" (5:4). The result was ships full of fish and a humbled Peter.

2. To enlist Matthew as a pupil, Christ gave the command, "Follow Me" (5:27), and Matthew did just that.

3. To teach that He was Lord of the Sabbath, He used the incident of the disciples' picking corn on the Sabbath (6:1).

4. John the Baptist wanted to know if Jesus was truly the Messiah. Jesus dispatched John's disciples with the instructions, "Go and report to John" (7:22).

5. To put into practice the things they had learned, the twelve were sent forth "to proclaim the kingdom of God" (9:2-5).

6. On another occasion He sent out seventy disciples to witness to the people (10:1-16).

7. To the rich young ruler Jesus assigned the activity of distributing his goods to the poor (18:22). Because the young man chose not to get involved, "He went away grieved" (Matt. 19:22).

8. Before Jesus could instruct him, Zacchaeus had to obey the command, "Hurry, and come down" (19:5). He did, and his life was never again the same.

9. Before Jesus answered the chief priests and scribes concerning the tribute money, they had to get involved. "Show me a denarius" (20:24) was Jesus' instruction. They did, and Jesus answered. As a result, the people were "marvelling at His answer" (20:26).

10. One of Jesus' final instructions to His disciples was, "You are to stay in the city [Jerusalem] until you are clothed with power from on high" (24:49). The book of Acts records the results of their obedience.

Jesus was vitally concerned with His pupils' actions: "Therefore everyone who hears these words of Mine, and acts upon them, may be compared to a wise man" (Matt. 7:24); "You are my friends, if you do what I command you" (John 15:14). As in every other area of His teaching, Jesus was a master in using the activity method, getting His pupils involved.

USE OF OBJECTS

We remember less of what we hear in comparison to what we hear *and see*. Jesus knew the value of having His pupils see. He used visual aids. Here are a few examples of Jesus' use of objects in teaching:

1. He used birds, flowers, and grass to illustrate the heavenly Father's care (Matt. 6:25-31)

2. He used a little child to teach humility (Matt. 18:1-6)

3. He used a barren fruit tree to illustrate the need for faith (Matt. 21:18-22)

4. He used a coin to teach responsibility to government (Mark 12:13-17)

5. He used the example of the widow to teach about right motives in giving (Mark 12:41-44)

6. He used the ripe harvest fields to teach the urgency of doing the Father's work (John 4:35-39)

7. He used the vine and branches to explain the relationship between the Father, Himself, and the disciples (John 15:1-8)

8. His miracles were object lessons, illustrating His deity (John 5:36)

We must remember that the gospels are not textbooks on teaching. The writers did not necessarily record every use Jesus made of an object in His teaching. Enough is recorded, however, for us to know with certainty that Jesus used visual aids, and He used them effectively.

USE OF MODELING

Modeling in the educational use of the term is simply demonstrating the truth. It is "living out" before one's pupils the principles that one teaches. To a degree that no other teacher can approach, Jesus modeled what He taught. Clifford A. Wilson describes Him as "the living embodiment of His own great lessons."[32] "This was one of the greatest elements in the teaching of Jesus: He taught by the example of His own life, for it was a model that others could copy. . . . He was the great Example, able to say with confidence to His pupils, "Learn of Me" (Matt. 11:29).[33]

Only two examples will be given, although in a sense the gospels are one continuous record of Jesus' use of modeling. Jesus modeled for His disciples His teaching about prayer. He instructed them concerning prayer early in His ministry (Matt. 6:5-15). He repeated some of the same material and amplified it in answer to the disciple's request, "Lord, teach us to pray" (Luke 11:1-13). He prayed aloud in the presence of the disciples (Matt. 26:26; John 6:11; 17). But of greater import than His public prayers were His private ones. "But He . . . would often slip away to the wilderness and pray" (Luke 5:16); "He went off to the mountain to pray, and He spent the whole night in prayer to God" (Luke 6:12).

"He was alone praying" (Luke 9:18); with Peter, James, and John, He "went up into a mountain to pray" (Luke 9:28); "He was praying" (Luke 11:1); His testimony to Peter was, "I have prayed for you" (Luke 22:32); again with Peter, James, and John nearby, He spent a night in prayer (22:39-46). What an impression that must have made on the men who were closest to him. They learned to pray from the example Christ set for them.

A second illustration of modeling is recorded in John 13:1-20, the account of Jesus' washing the disciples' feet. Some have called this an object lesson, and it was that. But it was more. It was the Son of God's modeling humility in service, an attitude He often tried to teach His disciples. That demonstration probably did more to convey the truth than all the previous teachings had done.

No wonder Christ is described as "the embodiment of the truth." He was the great example for His pupils of that day. He remains the great example to those of us today who desire to do our part in fulfilling His final command, "Go ye therefore, and teach [make disciples of] all nations . . ." (Matt. 28:19-20). "Christ Jesus was the Master Teacher par excellence because He Himself perfectly embodied the truth, He perfectly understood His pupils, and He used perfect methods in order to change people."[34]

In any endeavor of life, much value is to be gained from studying the example of those who have mastered the same skill, technique, or procedure you are using. Fledgling athletes study the professionals and seek to pattern their lives after them. Budding musicians study the style and techniques of the masters and try to incorporate those into their performances. In the same manner, the Christian educator must be diligent in studying those who have excelled in his field. Such a study well begins with the master teacher.

FOR FURTHER STUDY

1. Read through one or more of the gospels, noting each reference to "teaching" or "taught" or an obvious teaching situation. Make a chart similar to the one shown below on which to record your findings.

Reference	Setting	Pupils	Main Purpose	Methods Used	Results
John 3:1-21	Jesus & Nicodemus alone at night	Nicodemus	To explain the new birth	Discourse, object illustration, questions	Nicodemus was converted (John 7:50; 19:39)

2. List the qualities you feel should be found in the ideal teacher. Note with Scripture references those that are demonstrated in the master teacher.

3. Twelve types of questions are suggested under "Use of Questions." As you read through the gospels, classify the questions of Jesus according to those types. Add other types to the list as you discover them.

4. Using the four purposes of stories as given in this chapter, classify the parables in Luke's gospel. What other purposes would you add to these four?

5. Go through Matthew or Mark and study the activities that Jesus assigned to His pupils. Record the activity, the purpose of it, and the result.

6. Add to the list of objects given under "Use of Objects." From what source did Jesus draw most of His objects? Why? How do you think He would use audiovisual aids if He were on earth today?

7. Study the miracles in John's gospel. In addition to His deity, what did Jesus teach by each one?

8. After studying the chapter, list *specific* lessons you have learned from your study of Christ, the master teacher. How will you apply those lessons in your teaching ministry?

NOTES

1. James S. Stewart, *The Life and Teaching of Jesus Christ* (Nashville: Abingdon, n.d.), p. 71.
2. Clarence H. Benson, *A Popular History of Christian Education* (Chicago: Moody, 1943), p. 25.
3. James D. Smart, *The Teaching Ministry of the Church* (Philadelphia: Westminster, 1954), p. 18.
4. Elmer Towns, ed., *A History of Religious Educators* (Grand Rapids: Baker, 1975), p. 16.
5. Clifford A. Wilson, *Jesus the Master Teacher* (Grand Rapids: Baker, 1974), p. 23.
6. Clarence H. Benson, *The Christian Teacher* (Chicago: Moody, 1950), pp. 258-59.
7. J. L. Marsh, "Principles and Philosophy of Education in the Bible," (Syllabus, Southwestern Baptist Theological Seminary, 1964), pp. 85-90.
8. J. M. Price, *Jesus the Teacher* (Nashville: Convention, 1946), p. 2.
9. Findley B. Edge, *Teaching for Results* (Nashville: Broadman, 1956), p. 3.
10. For a complete statement of this aspect of Jesus' ministry, see Herman H. Horne, *Teaching Techniques of Jesus* (Grand Rapids: Kregel, 1974), pp. 93-106.
11. C. B. Eavey, *Principles of Teaching for Christian Teachers* (Grand Rapids: Zondervan, 1940), p. 19.
12. Price, p. 17.
13. Lois E. LeBar, *Education That Is Christian* (Westwood, N.J.: Revell, 1958), p. 67.
14. Eavey, pp. 73-74.
15. Benson, p. 268.
16. Price, pp. 32-44.
17. Ibid., p. 78.
18. Horne, p. 14.
19. Ibid., pp. 20-21.
20. Wilson, pp. 102-3.
21. Eavey, p. 252.
22. Wilson, pp. 129-30.

23. Eavey, p. 245.
24. Towns, p. 24.
25. Price, p. 99.
26. Benson, p. 272.
27. Towns, p. 22.
28. Wilson, pp. 91-94.
29. Price, p. 107.
30. Horne, pp. 66-69.
31. Price, p. 108.
32. Wilson, p. 116.
33. Ibid., p. 113.
34. LeBar, p. 51.

SUGGESTED READING

*Benson, Clarence H. "The Master Teacher." In *The Christian Teacher*, pp. 257-85. Chicago: Moody, 1950. An excellent study in this perceptive volume on the teacher and teaching.

————. *A Popular History of Christian Education*, pp. 13-29. Chicago: Moody, 1943. A brief overview of Jewish education, including Jesus the teacher.

Eavey, C. B. *History of Christian Education*, pp. 77-81. Chicago: Moody, 1964. Brief overview of Jesus the teacher given in the context of the history of Christian education.

*————. *Principles of Teaching for Christian Teachers*. Grand Rapids: Zondervan, 1940. Several references to Jesus the teacher are used to illustrate the principles of teaching that are presented.

Edge, Findley B. "Jesus Came Teaching." In *Teaching for Results*, pp. 1-13. Nashville: Broadman, 1956. A discussion of the "positive principles followed by Jesus," as well as a presentation of His break with traditional Jewish education.

Gangel, Kenneth O. *Understanding Teaching*, pp. 11-13. Wheaton, Ill.: Evangelical Teacher Training Assoc., 1968. Brief presentation of Jesus the teacher to help answer the question, "What is Christian Teaching?"

*Guthrie, Donald. "Jesus." In *A History of Religious Educators*, edited by Elmer Towns, pp. 15-38. Grand Rapids: Baker, 1975. An excellent overview of the subject.

*Horne, Herman Harrell. *Teaching Techniques of Jesus*. Grand Rapids: Kregel, 1974. A classic work on this subject. Particularly helpful because of its lists and classifications.

*LeBar, Lois E. "The Teacher Come from God." In *Education That Is Christian*, pp. 49-86. Westwood, N.J.: Revell, 1958. A study of principles and examples from the life of Christ in this work on the philosophy of Christian education.

Marsh, J. L. "Principles and Philosophy of Education in the Bible," pp. 82-130. Unpublished syllabus. Southwestern Baptist Theological Seminary, 1964. A study guide for understanding education in the Bible, with a detailed study of Jesus the teacher.

*Price, J. M. *Jesus the Teacher*. Nashville: Convention, 1946. A basic work on this subject.

Smart, James D. *The Teaching Ministry of the Church,* pp. 17-23. Philadelphia: Westminster, 1954. Emphasis on Jesus the teacher in establishing the biblical basis for the teaching ministry of the church.

*Wilson, Clifford A. *Jesus the Master Teacher.* Grand Rapids: Baker, 1974. A basic work on this subject.

*Especially recommended.

5

Principles of Biblical Teaching and Learning

Edward and Frances Simpson

TEN COMMANDMENTS FOR DYNAMIC TEACHING

I

POWER OF THE SPIRIT

Thou shalt depend upon the Spirit to accomplish spiritual goals.

II

EXAMPLE OF THE TEACHER

Thou shalt be what you expect your pupils to become.

III

RELATIONSHIP OF LOVE

Thou shalt demonstrate Christian love for your pupils.

IV

METHODS THAT INVOLVE

Thou shalt select appropriate methods to get attention and hold interest.

V

COMMUNICATION WITH CLARITY

Thou shalt use words and concepts that are clearly understood.

VI

PATTERN OF APPERCEPTION

Thou shalt move from the known to the unknown by easy, simple, natural steps.

VII

JOY OF DISCOVERY

Thou shalt stimulate discovery, not mere listening.

VIII

APPEAL TO THE HEART

Thou shalt elicit emotional response by the pupil.

IX

RESPONSE OF THE WILL

Thou shalt give ample opportunity for volitional response.

X

LIVING DEMONSTRATORS

Thou shalt help the pupil to embody the lesson in everyday living.

EDWARD SIMPSON, Th.D., is professor of Bible, Southwestern College, Phoenix, Arizona.

FRANCES SIMPSON, D.R.E., is professor of Christian education, Southwestern College, Phoenix, Arizona.

THE DEVELOPMENT of productive Christian teaching is guided by the application of basic principles, or guidelines, for teaching.

The teaching situation itself may vary. The location, for example, may be at home, at school, or in the church. It may be formal or informal. The "teacher" may be a parent, a respected adult friend, or a member of the peer group.

But the teaching principles considered here are an integral part of any effective process of guiding students. The list of ten "commandments" is not exhaustive, but suggestive. The first three relate to the teacher, the next three relate to the teaching process, and the final four focus on the learner's response.

I. POWER OF THE SPIRIT

THOU SHALT DEPEND UPON THE HOLY SPIRIT TO ACCOMPLISH SPIRITUAL GOALS (1 COR. 2:10-15).

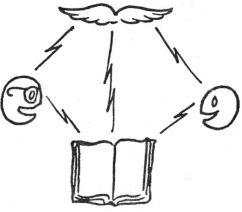

In the last analysis, in biblical education the Holy Spirit is the one who teaches, although He uses human instruments in the process. Christian teachers and students are to be indwelt, enlightened, and empowered by the Holy Spirit, so that He is not only the teacher's assistant, He is the teacher (John 14:26). He is not merely the student's guide into truth (John 16:13), He *is* the Spirit of Truth (John 14:17). It is He who convicts of sin, of righteousness, and of judgment (John 16:8). Persons may structure situations so that there is study of the Scriptures, but the Spirit alone effects the learning. Through the Spirit, learners reassess and change their understandings, attitudes, values, and motives.

Counting on the ministry of the Holy Spirit is not an excuse for sterile efforts at application to life. Rather, the teacher's goal of guiding the student in a continuity of steps toward spiritual maturity can be accomplished only by the *inside inspiration* of the Holy Spirit. As our diagram indicates, the Spirit operates inside the teacher and inside the pupil, communicating the message of the living Word. That is dynamic teaching! The teacher need not despair who knows his Indweller is omnipotent.

Appropriating the Holy's Spirit's power in the teaching situation necessitates (1) prayerful preparation—for understanding of the Bible and for a sensitivity to pupils' needs, (2) prayerful presentation—for effective use of methods, and (3) prayerful follow-up—for achieving lasting results in pupils' lives.

II. EXAMPLE OF THE TEACHER

THOU SHALT BE WHAT YOU EXPECT YOUR PUPILS TO BECOME (1 TIM. 4:12).

As he is assigned the supernatural task of communicating spiritual truth, the effective teacher counts on two indispensible factors: the power of the Holy Spirit (discussed above), and the proof of a holy life. He will know and embody the truth.

Know the truth. Dedicated incompetence is still incompetence. A Christian teacher should know the truth in its biblical framework, seeing God as the source of all truth (Deut. 32:4, KJV*). His goal will be to have experiential knowledge of Christ as the one "in whom are hidden all the treasures of wisdom and knowledge" (Col. 2:3), the one in whom all things consist (Col. 1:17), and the one who is truth (John 14:6). He will appreciate the limitless scope of subject matter, for all truth is God's truth, whether in the spiritual, historical, scientific, artistic, or psychological realms (cf. Col. 1:16). Finally, he will be inspired by the magnitude of his task— that of unveiling the glory of God in every phase of the curriculum.

Embody the truth. Experiencing the truth requires that the process of education be more than lecturing listeners or parroting paradigms. Personal embodiment of truth is the most compelling method. Precepts may fail to impress; Christlike personality never fails. The quality of teaching is determined by the quality of the teacher, for teaching involves the impartation of *life* as well as dogma. We teach more by our walk than by our talk. The above visual suggests the embarrassment of the teacher who fails to practice what he teaches. It may well be said that the master teacher is one who has not only mastered his lesson, but also has been mastered by his lesson. Years ago Marion Lawrence described the ideal Sunday school teacher as one who put his

> Whole mind into his preparation,
> Whole soul into his presentation,
> Whole life into his illustration.

Howard Mayes neatly prods the teacher to humility in this task, remind-

*King James Version.

ing him that he should not be clubbing people with the Word, nor dazzling them with scholarship, but should be modeling truth as a teachable teacher.[1] By God's indwelling power such a teacher dares to say with Paul, "Be ye followers of me as I am of Christ" (1 Cor. 11:1).

III. Relationship of Love

THOU SHALT DEMONSTRATE CHRISTIAN LOVE FOR YOUR PUPILS (1 JOHN 3:23).

It is the Spirit who enables the teacher to embody the truth. Likewise, it is the Spirit who engenders Christian love (Gal. 5:22). Our diagram indicates that by a bridge of love, the teacher can lay hold on Christ and human need and bring them together. Howard Mayes reminds us that establishing such relationships is time-consuming. "It takes time to perk up personal relationships, but it's well worth the effort."[2]

The master teacher is ever our example as we study this principle. "Christ never gave anyone money. He rarely gave them food. He gave them love and service—the greatest gift of all—Himself."[3] In John 4 we read, "He had to pass through Samaria" (John 4:4). There he ministered to one woman with a needy heart. Our teaching may be dead dogma without the life sparkle of the teacher who cares.

Ross Campbell underscores the need for a relationship of acceptance, openness, caring. His conviction is that focused attention is the most demanding need of a child. He needs warm, pleasant eye-contact and unconditional love. Such attention makes the child feel he is the most important person in the adult's eyes.[4]

Campbell's book relates to work with children. But all of us need to communicate Christian love to those we teach, regardless of age. We can use personal notes, phone calls, visits, or invitations to snack times at home or a nearby meeting place. If teachers adopt an earlier check-in time on Sunday, pre-session can also be a productive time for personal communication. We read, "By this all men will know that you are My disciples, if you have love for one another" (John 13:35).

Having looked at the *teacher* in the first three principles let us next examine the *process*.

IV. Methods That Involve

THOU SHALT SELECT APPROPRIATE METHODS TO GET ATTENTION (JOHN 4:7)
AND HOLD INTEREST (JOHN 4).

It has been said that one may observe the difference between the novice and the mature teacher in the first two minutes of the class session. The novice looks at his notes. The proficient teacher looks at his class. Observe the expertise of the master teacher in John 4:7, "Give Me a drink." That opening line caught the attention of that needy student so that she stayed for the lesson! It was a shocker: a Jew asking a favor of a Samaritan; a man addressing a woman; a gentleman approaching a woman-of-the-street!

A dynamic introduction gains interest and suggests, "This is not going to be a ho-hum session." Lawrence O. Richards labels an effective introduction as "the hook." He effectively describes its use with each age level.[5]

Methods are employed to get attention and to hold interest. Pupils need teachers who know how to use creative activity to guide thinking and produce genuine learning. People learn best by experiencing, doing, participating. The triangle depicts this truth: people learn as they hear, but they learn *more* if visuals are added to clarify the message. Meaningful discussion adds further learning, and total involvement brings the fullest results. Teachers need to develop skill in the use of teaching tools.[6]

V. COMMUNICATION WITH CLARITY

THOU SHALT USE WORDS AND CONCEPTS THAT ARE CLEARLY UNDERSTOOD
(1 COR. 2:4; 14:9).

Good communication begins in the mind of the teacher. Sort out the precise message. Then determine how to project it into the mind stream of others. Some teachers are more concerned that they be considered intellectual than that they be understood.

There are guidelines to expedite communication: (1) Step down the high voltage of a thought so that it can be grasped and appreciated by the pupils. Jesus did. Imagine a small boy still having his unopened lunch after an extended teaching session (John 6)! That is evidence of great communication. (2) Avoid technical words if common ones can carry the message. Why say "teleological" when "order" or "goal" might come through more clearly? (3) Clarify simple words when there is danger of misunderstanding. One excellent example of that in these days is the word "love" (John 21:

15-17). (4) Use a multi-sensory approach if it will expedite learning. Use visuals that aid.

Communicating to be understood by the pupils requires insight into the pupil's level of understanding, mind-set, and responses. Let the diagram suggest the need, but not the procedure, for securing such information!

Questions can be an effective tool if the teacher wishes to sense the depth of understanding. However, questions need to be framed carefully, or the response may be disheartening. Let one example suffice: "What are sins of omission?" The student's unfortunate answer: "The ones we ought to have committed, but haven't!"

The good teacher will use a limited number of purely factual questions (Who was Moses' mother? Who was Moses' father?). Such questions can be mere verbal Ping-Pong. Thought questions, which evaluate ideas and assist the student in applying the lesson to life, strengthen the ties of communication.

Techniques such as good questions can be employed to determine whether the teacher has communicated effectively. The essential idea is to get feedback to determine the nature and extent of intake.

VI. PATTERN OF APPERCEPTION

THOU SHALT MOVE FROM THE KNOWN TO THE UNKNOWN BY EASY, SIMPLE, NATURAL STEPS (JOHN 4:7-29; HEB. 5:12).

Apperception, the principle of connecting new ideas with old, is one of J. F. Herbart's greatest contributions to education. John Milton Gregory, in stating his laws of teaching, emphasized the same point: "The unknown must be explained by means of the known."[8] In truth, it is a biblical principle. John underscores the need to adapt teaching to the pupil's developing maturity (1 John 2:12-14). And no perceptive reader of the Pauline epistles could easily miss the apostle's adaptation of new truth to former concepts, with his frequent use of illustrations and figures of speech. Jesus employed the same principle in His parables, illustrations, and visual aids.

Present the lesson in steps small enough so the student can follow the train of thought. Do not give too much information too fast.

Having considered the *teacher* and the teaching *process,* let us now turn to the learner's *response,* for that is the purpose of teaching. The next three principles focus on the three parts of the human personality: intellect (Principle VII), emotion (Principle VIII), and volition (Principle IX). Each part must be activated in a wholesome learning experience to result in a life-changing application (Principle X). This type of learning is the immediate goal of Christian teaching. Pupil response is the cooperative endeavor accompanying teacher stimulation, which can result in personal growth.

VII. Joy of Discovery

THOU SHALT STIMULATE DISCOVERY, NOT MERE LISTENING (PSALM 34:8).

Too often the message of the Word is rejected because this principle is ignored. Many cliches remind us of this, such as "You sit still while I instill."

Gregory, author of the Laws of Teaching, while president of the University of Illinois, reminded his teachers, "Knowledge cannot be passed from mind to mind as apples are from one basket to another, but must in every case be recognized and rethought by the receiving mind."[9]

Education involves the discovery of truth, first by the teacher, and then by the student under the teacher's guidance. In discovery teaching, the teacher opens the gate of understanding and learning. It is a dynamic situation, as the visual suggests, for the teacher may ask a question that lights a fuse.

But discovery learning is possible only when there has been good preparation. The teacher needs to (1) focus on pupil need, (2) relate Scriptures to that need, and (3) select methods that will involve the pupils in participation, evaluation, and application. The learner needs to (1) identify the relation of the study to his need, (2) study the Scriptures to find solutions, and observe how the Bible applies to his personal interests, problems, and needs. The teacher continues as guide.

This kind of learning experience is sometimes described as "the joy of discovery," because there is a unique exhilaration in finding satisfying answers to basic life needs.

VIII. Appeal to the Heart

THOU SHALT ELICIT EMOTIONAL RESPONSE BY THE PUPIL (ROM. 10:10).

After truth has been recognized and interpreted by the mind, it must receive a deeper response. For the Christian, it is "belief in the heart" (Rom. 10:9-10; Eph. 1:18) that produces experience in depth. "From it flow the springs of life" (Prov. 4:23). It is from one's attitudes that one's philosophy of life is made, and in which the great aims to which one pledges one's self are formed.

Too often we teach as if people will do what they *know* is right to do. Psychologists indicate that, on the contrary, people generally do what they *want* to do. One teacher, working with children, noted the principle, "Until you instill the want-to, you can't get them started. Once you inculcate the want-to, you can't get them stopped."

Our diagram symbolically represents the mind, the heart (emotions), and the will (the way a person determines to walk or behave). If we draw the proportions relative to our manner of teaching, we might have a giant head. If we drew it on the basis of how people respond, we would have an oversized heart. If we drew it on the basis of a purely ideal goal, there would be very large feet.

Often it is the emotions that trigger a response of the will. Therefore, a wise teacher needs to be adept at using the methods that cause pupils to respond positively. Undoubtedly, the story is the most useful tool in accomplishing that purpose. Jesus was a master storyteller. In fact, it says of Him, "Without a parable spake he not unto them" (Matt. 13:34). A study of His use of stories would provide guidelines on the skillful employment of that method to elicit response.

Some teachers avoid any appeal to the emotional nature, assuming that appeal to be unwise. But emotions are the fundamental drive of human beings as God made them. Emotions in themselves are neither good nor bad. It is the use of them that makes the difference. They can provide the power to energize the will, and that is the pathway to meaningful action.

IX. Response of the Will

THOU SHALT GIVE AMPLE OPPORTUNITY FOR VOLITIONAL RESPONSE (JOHN 7:17)

Truth must produce a result to be considered learned. The effect may be intellectual, the simple ability to recall a fact; or emotional, an attitude or feeling; or volitional, a decision to act. But the more complete the response, the more effective the learning. Indeed, until and unless there is such a response, a mere knowledge of facts may be  fruitless, frustrating, or even penalizing if moral truth is involved (James 4:17).

It is the challenge of the Christian teacher to provide the suitable stimuli for the desired responses leading to Christian maturity. Ideally the pupil's response involves his whole personality. A total response requires that intellectually there be understanding, emotionally there be appreciation, and volitionally there be commitment to truth by the student. Therefore it is important that the teacher provide opportunity for a volitional response when there has been an emotional appeal. That may be done in a time of quiet prayer at the close of the lesson, when the student makes his personal response to the prodding of the Holy Spirit.

Our visual aid suggests the importance of allowing time in the class session for a final response. Some of the lesson content may need to be condensed if time runs out, to allow ample opportunity for the personal commitment of the pupils. However, we need to recognize that it is at that point that the teacher hits the mark. Failure there may mean that we have been merely marking time.[10]

X. Living Demonstrators

THOU SHALT HELP THE PUPIL TO EMBODY THE LESSON IN EVERYDAY LIVING
(James 1:22-25)

The teacher's purpose is to get the leather-bound Bible into shoe leather—to relate Bible facts to human acts. Carryover activities and projects can be used to implement this purpose, so that impression will be consummated in expression.

Embodiment is the immediate goal of our teaching. After truth is acquired, appreciated, and accepted for action, the life should express it. The educational process, therefore, is completed only as objective truth becomes the subjective experience of the learner. The difference is as marked as that between a Christmas ball, tied on the tree from without, and a luscious orange produced by the life within.

When the teacher espouses this principle as his goal, he evaluates his success not on the basis of his ability to impart facts, but on his skill in helping students to form character. Personal development is his aim. He desires that his students become true disciples, followers of Jesus Christ, acknowledging His lordship, conformed to His image.

In view of this ambitious goal for teaching, the biblical teacher acknowledges the truth of the words of Jesus Christ, "Apart from Me you can do nothing" (John 15:5). But with the apostle Paul he is confident that he "can do all things through Him [Christ]" (Phil. 4:13).

The biblical teacher recognizes that his task is the greatest job in all the world—discipling men and women for Jesus Christ. When God has called him to be a teacher, he'll not stoop to be a king!

> A builder builded a temple,
> He wrought it with grace and skill;
> Pillars and groins and arches,
> All fashioned to work his will,
> And men said, as they saw its beauty,
> "It shall never know decay.
> Great is thy skill, O builder!
> Thy fame shall endure for aye."
>
> A teacher builded a temple
> With loving and infinite care,
> Planning each arch with patience,
> Laying each stone with prayer.
> And men scarcely noted the teacher,
> None knew of the wondrous plan,
> For the temple the teacher builded
> Was unseen by the eye of man.
>
> Gone is the builder's temple,
> Crumpled into the dust;
> Low lies each stately pillar,
> Food for consuming rust.
> But the temple the teacher builded
> Will last while the ages roll;
> For that beautiful, unseen temple
> Was a man's immortal soul.
>
> AUTHOR UNKNOWN

FOR FURTHER STUDY

1. What evidence could a teacher give that he depends upon the Holy Spirit to accomplish spiritual goals?
2. List five of the most important Christian qualities in a teacher. In each case report the way a teacher could demonstrate that quality.
3. What actions by a teacher would communicate to pupils that he loves them?
4. Report the lesson introduction you have observed that most effectively captured the attention of the class.
5. Suggest means by which a teacher can make sure pupils *understand* his words and concepts. Illustrate.
6. Discuss teaching situations in which a teacher put the principle of apperception to work.
7. List methods of getting pupils actively involved in learning by *discovering* rather than mere listening.
8. Report the situation in which a lesson elicited an emotional response in your life. What factors contributed to it?
9. What methods of obtaining a response could be used in a Sunday school class situation?
10. What can a teacher do in or out of class to help his pupils live the lesson out in their daily lives?

NOTES

1. Howard Mayes and James Long, *Can I Help It If They Don't Learn?* (Wheaton, Ill.: Scripture Press, Victor, 1977), p. 46.
2. Ibid., p. 39.
3. Lloyd Cory, *Quote Unquote* (Wheaton, Ill.: Scripture Press, Victor, 1977), p. 132.
4. Ross Campbell, *How to Really Love Your Child* (Wheaton, Ill.: Scripture Press, Victor, 1977), p. 80.
5. Lawrence O. Richards, *Creative Bible Teaching* (Chicago: Moody, 1970), pp. 147-269.
6. Kenneth O. Gangel, *Twenty-Four Ways to Improve Your Teaching* (Wheaton, Ill.: Scripture Press, Victor, 1974).
7. Lois E. LeBar, *Education That Is Christian* (Westwood, N.J.: Revell, 1958), p. 31.
8. John Milton Gregory, *The Seven Laws of Teaching* (Grand Rapids: Baker, 1957), p. 5.
9. Elmer Towns, *The Successful Sunday School and Teachers Guidebook* (Carol Stream, Ill.: Creation House, 1976), p. 28.
10. Elsiebeth McDaniel, *There's More to Teaching Primaries* (Wheaton, Ill.: Scripture Press, Victor, 1976), p. 23.

SUGGESTED READING

Bergevin, Paul. *A Philosophy for Adult Education.* New York: Seabury, 1967. Focuses on adults in the teaching-learning situation.

Campbell, Ross. *How to Really Love Your Child.* Wheaton, Ill.: Scripture Press, Victor, 1977. Underlines love as essential in the learning process, both at home and church.

Cory, Lloyd. *Quote Unquote*. Wheaton, Ill.: Scripture Press, Victor, 1977. A collection of quotes to amuse and to inform. Useful to the Christian educator.

Gangel, Kenneth. *Twenty-Four Ways to Improve Your Teaching*. Wheaton, Ill.: Scripture Press, Victor, 1974. A useful guide for those who wish to develop skills in various methods of teaching.

Gibson, Joyce and Hance, Eleanor. *The Way Juniors Are*. Wheaton, Ill.: Scripture Press, Victor, 1976. Focuses on juniors in the teaching-learning process.

Gregory, John Milton. *The Seven Laws of Teaching*. Grand Rapids: Baker, 1957. A basic text on the principles of the teaching-learning process.

Jacobs, Norman E. *Toward Effective Teaching—Adults*. Anderson, Ind.: Warner, 1969. A basic text on teaching adults.

LeBar, Lois E. *Education That Is Christian*. Westwood, N.J.: Revell, 1958. A basic text in philosophy of Christian Education based on scriptural presupposition.

Mayes, Howard and Long, James. *Can I Help It If They Don't Learn?* Wheaton, Ill.: Scripture Press, Victor, 1977. A textbook for the Sunday school teacher written in a pithy style with a practical message spiced by bubbling good humor.

Murch, James DeForest. *Christian Education and the Local Church*. Cincinnati: Standard, 1943. Part II of this comprehensive coverage of Christian education deals with philosophy of Christian education.

McDaniel, Elsiebeth. *There's More to Teaching Primaries*. Wheaton, Ill.: Scripture Press, Victor, 1976. Focuses on primaries in the teaching-learning process.

Peterson, Gilbert. *How to Get Results With Adults*. Wheaton, Ill.: Scripture Press, Victor, 1977. Chapter 4 emphasizes the use of discovery-learning in teaching adults.

Richards, Lawrence O. *Creative Bible Teaching*. Chicago: Moody, 1970. This excellent text fulfills the promise of its title. Part III applies the philosophy of the author in each age level.

Towns, Elmer. *The Successful Sunday School and Teachers Guidebook*. Carol Stream, Ill.: Creation House, 1976. An encyclopedic text on Sunday school.

Wright, Norman. *Ways to Help Them Learn*. Glendale, Calif.: Gospel Light, Regal, 1972. Part II on adults, "How They Learn," provides practical insights into the learning process.

Zuck, Roy. *Spiritual Power in Your Teaching*. Rev. ed. Chicago: Moody, 1972. An excellent text in describing the dynamic of the Spirit in the teaching-learning process. Chapters 11, 12, and 13 define teaching and learning and list seven basic laws, principles, of the process.

6

The Christian Teacher

GILBERT A. PETERSON

TEACHERS are not only necessary for the life of the church and the perpetuation of the Christian faith—they are indispensable.

Christianity is a unique, personal experience with the living God. In addition, and thoroughly integrated with the personal experience, is a body of truth that God communicated to man through holy and specially guided men of old. This truth that we possess in the Scriptures must be effectively communicated. Believers need it for the proper development of their Christian lives. Unbelievers need to be confronted with their sin and provided with direction for repentance and regeneration. God has chosen the approaches of preaching and teaching as the means of confronting mankind with the truth.

During His three-year ministry, Jesus was known primarily as a teacher. In most of the occurrences where Jesus is directly addressed with a title of some sort, the title is "teacher" or its equivalent.

Nicodemus, in addressing Jesus, first identified Him as a teacher. "Rabbi, we know that You have come from God as a teacher; for no one can do these signs that You do unless God is with him" (John 3:2).

At the end of His earthly ministry, Christ's instructions to His disciples were: "All authority has been given to Me in heaven and on earth. Go therefore and make disciples of all nations, baptizing them in the name of the Father and the Son and the Holy Spirit, teaching them to observe all that I have commanded you; and lo, I am with you always, even to the end of the age" (Matt. 28:18-20).

The disciples were to be a blend of evangelist-teachers. Their evangelizing ministry was to confront people with the claims and life of Christ

---

GILBERT A. PETERSON, Ed.D., is president of Lancaster Bible College, Lancaster, Pennsylvania.

and to call them to a new and living relationship with God through Christ Jesus. Their teaching ministry was to cause people to become conformed to the teachings of Christ. In both cases, lives were to be affected. Changes in thinking were anticipated. Believers were told, "Do not be conformed to this world, but be transformed by the renewing of your mind, that you may prove what the will of God is, that which is good and acceptable and perfect" (Rom. 12:2).

THE PRIVILEGE OF THE TEACHER

It is into a context and great company of outstanding men and women that today's Christian teacher comes. The opportunity of walking in the footsteps of Jesus Christ and presenting the living and true God enthusiastically is before us. To join the ranks of countless individuals who have given of themselves in the selfless task of teaching timeless truth is indeed an honor that should not be lightly bestowed or received. Teaching is both a thrill and a challenge, but, above all, a privilege.

It is a practical privilege, for as we study the Scriptures in preparation for teaching, we become students. As a result we learn more than even the students in our classes. Many teachers have commented that they truly never understood a concept or truth until they were responsible for communicating it to someone else. This is a side benefit of teaching, but a valuable one.

The Christian teacher also has the privilege of investing his life in the lives of others. To recognize that your words and actions are influencing others brings tremendous responsibility as well as honor. James recognizing this, wrote, "Let not many of you become teachers, my brethren, knowing that as such we shall incur a stricter judgment" (James 3:1). Some are eager to speak before groups and enjoy the prominence it brings without being willing to do the careful background preparation. James's warning should not deter a person from the privilege of a teaching ministry, but it does point out that teachers carry heavy responsibility and are answerable for their influence over others.

Lastly, the Christian teacher is being obedient to the scriptural injunction to share one's faith. As Paul instructed Timothy, "And the things which you have heard from me in the presence of many witnesses, these entrust to faithful men, who will be able to teach others also" (2 Tim. 2:2). Paul was instructed by the Holy Spirit and other believers. He in turn taught Timothy. Timothy was to teach other men so that they also could continue the process and teach others. That obedience to the command of Christ, following the example of the apostles and other early church leaders, is our privilege.

THE PREPARATION OF THE TEACHER

Many factors could be cited as important items to be considered in the preparation of a Christian teacher. The following compose at least a minimal list.

A PERSONAL FAITH

It may be stating the obvious to say that a Christian teacher must have a personal relationship with Jesus Christ and trust in Him only for eternal salvation, but that *is* the vital ingredient in the total preparation process. Murch put it well when he wrote concerning the Sunday school teacher, "There should be no doubt in his mind regarding the deity, authority, and all sufficiency of Christ, and he should be able to give a reasonable argument for that faith. He should be a member of the church in good standing and well-known for his loyalty to the cause under all circumstances."[1]

It has often been said that we communicate more by what we are than by what we say. A person's innermost being will not be hidden very long from the observing, searching eyes and ears of students. A phony faith will not stand the test.

A GROWING CHRISTIAN LIFE

A personal faith is the starting point, not the finishing line. The Christian teacher must experience a deepening relationship with Christ. Daily prayer, Bible reading, and recognition of the presence of God in all aspects of life are fundamental to the growth process.

Paul's demonstration of a Spirit-filled, Christ-centered life was a vivid testimony to the Thessalonian church. He was able to refer to his daily behavior when he wrote: "Brethren beloved by God, [we know] His choice of you; for our gospel did not come to you in word only, but also in power and in the Holy Spirit and with full conviction; just as you know what kind of men we proved to be among you for your sake" (1 Thess. 1:4-5). Paul's life-style and mature behavior became a model for the church. The converts then reproduced that behavior and became models for those they met. Christian teachers today must have the same concern and watch their walk to insure that it matches their talk.

The question of spiritual gifts and the gift of teaching in particular deserves comment at this point. There is a spread of opinion on the subject, and there is much debate among believers as to the existence, number, function, and importance of spiritual gifts in ministry. For the purposes of this discussion, it should be noted that we are engaged in a *spiritual* ministry and God has promised to be with us, meet our needs and enable us to fulfill all He requires (Phil. 2:13; 4:19; Heb. 13:5).

As Kinghorn states, "Spiritual gifts function as incarnations of God's power in human life. Sometimes they flow through and heighten our natural abilities, and sometimes they work independently of personal aptitudes. In any case, spiritual gifts complement and blend harmoniously with our humanity."[2] The Holy Spirit does not violate an individual's personality, but rather enables the believer to exercise his ministry in a spiritually effective manner.

"The gift of teaching is the supernatural ability to explain clearly and apply effectively the truth of the Word of God."[3] The teaching gift is supernatural, communicative, results-oriented, and for the purpose of sharing God's truth. A person does not have to wait until he knows whether or not he possesses the spiritual gift of teaching before he begins to teach. It is our privilege and responsibility to teach one another and to trust the unique partnership we have with the Lord in this ministry (2 Cor. 6:1).

A POSITIVE ATTITUDE

Much has been written recently about positive attitudes on the part of both individuals and groups. Paul put it well when he wrote to the Philippian church. "Finally, brethren, whatever is true . . . honorable . . . right . . . pure . . . lovely . . . of good repute, if there is any excellence and if anything worthy of praise, let your mind dwell on these things" (Phil. 4:8). Man, by virtue of his fallen nature, is bent in the opposite direction of all that God intends and desires. Jealousy competes with love, sadness with joy, fear with peace, criticism with praise, impure with pure, and wrong with right. The old nature is continually at war with the new nature, and only those teachers who maintain a close relationship with God can weather the storm and be enthusiastically positive in their approach.

The very word *enthusiasm* suggests a Christian concept. It is derived from a combination of two Greek words, *en*, meaning within, and *theos*, meaning God. An enthusiastic person, therefore, is to be one in whom God dwells. God's presence within produces an outer behavior that is characterized by zeal and optimism. The Christian teacher should thus be contagiously positive and anticipate growth and development.

A BIBLICAL AND THEOLOGICAL KNOWLEDGE

The Christian teacher is one that should be knowledgeable concerning the Word of God and basic theological concepts. Of course there will be different expectancies depending upon the subject area being taught and the level at which the teaching occurs. Seminary teachers and Sunday school teachers are both teaching the Scriptures, but the intensity, purpose, and requirements for both are different.

The Christian physical education, history, or math teacher should have a basic understanding of God's Word, and should integrate biblical and theological concepts with his individual discipline. The degree of biblical and theological sophistication will differ depending on the subject matter and level of instruction, but if the teaching is to be truly Christian, the divinely provided knowledge of special revelation must be brought to bear upon the divinely permitted discovery of general revelation. This is not a once-for-all task, but a continuous one. It should not be done by someone else for the teacher, but every Christian teacher should constantly study the truth of God as it comes to him from both the inspired Word and the natural world that God has created.

A TEACHING EXPERTISE

The job of the teacher is to teach. Teaching is a skill that must be developed, for it necessitates an understanding of people and how they learn, communication concepts and practices, organizational factors, curriculum development, and similar information.

In public education a system has been developed, however imperfect, to systematize that data and teach it to individuals before they are entrusted as teachers with a class of impressionable young lives.

In church education, the training situation is usually critical. Seldom is any teacher training required before starting. In a survey taken by this author of over one thousand churches across the United States, 15 percent indicated no leadership training programs whatever, and another 33 percent reported only a yearly meeting of some type. Sometimes the annual teacher's appreciation banquet was identified as a training session because an outside speaker was engaged. The situation merits our attention, and major work must be undertaken if the situation is to be changed.

The Christian teacher should desire to be skilled to the best of his ability in the art and science of teaching. In a sweeping statement, Paul stated that all of a Christian's words and activities should be done in a most excellent manner. "And whatever you do in word or deed, do all in the name of the Lord Jesus, giving thanks through Him to God the Father" (Col. 3:17).

A CONTEMPORARY ALERTNESS

People do not learn in a vacuum. We are all engaged in varied activities and immersed in a world that is rapidly changing. We live in a visually oriented society and are confronted daily with current events that span the globe. The Christian teacher must be aware of the busy, bustling world around him.

The Christian faith is not a way of looking at special things in life, but a special way of looking at all of life. Sports, education, business, politics, and religious events will often provide a relevant starting point for the sharing of biblical truth. An alert teacher will utilize the events that form the context of our lives to help students learn how to live, understand life, and share that new life in Christ with others.

If there was ever a time in the history of mankind when teachers and leaders needed to be knowledgeable of and sensitive to the contemporary scene, now is that time. The concept of a Christian isolated from the world is foreign to Scripture. Jesus prayed for his disciples that we all would be kept from the evil one while living fully in this present world (John 17:15). Teachers, in turn, must make their students aware of the dangers of the evil one as well as the provisions of God.

A PHYSICAL AND MENTAL READINESS

Lastly, a Christian teacher must take care of the body God has provided. Arriving at class too tired to properly teach or even think is poor stewardship of both teacher's and students' time. Every one who teaches must grapple with the priorities of schedules and activities. This is true whether the individual is teaching Sunday school or college classes. Many important activities, not to mention less noble ones, compete for the attention of Christian teachers. A teacher must be a disciplined person who can make wise decisions, set priorities, and balance his duties and desires.

Good teachers not only plan their lessons well, but also carefully review what they will cover to insure that the materials to be used are available and that they themselves are thoroughly familiar with their planned process. There is no substitute for a physically and mentally well-prepared teacher.

THE PERSPECTIVE OF THE TEACHER

A teacher's philosophy will determine his classroom approach and the results. Many teachers have carefully thought through their educational philosophy and work at implementing it in their classrooms. Others have not faced the issue and have let their past observations of teachers determine what and how they are going to teach. The perspective of the teacher, whether formally deliberated or informally evolved, is important to identify. Several will be identified here. This is not a complete list, but it does represent a number of typical approaches.

Each of the following teacher "types" also represents certain attitudes toward such things as the role of the teacher and learner, content, and learning expectation. Although they are set forth as separate and distinct positions, the reader will quickly note that seldom is anyone's personality or teaching approach so simply defined. The purpose in setting forth these options is to cause teachers to examine their teaching style and think through why they are doing what they are doing.

THE MOTIVATOR

Some teachers believe that their goal in teaching is to inspire their students. They attempt to create an atmosphere of excitement and enthusiasm. Activities are planned to produce an air of expectancy and challenge for the student. The communication of content is low on the priority list. Group feeling, personal satisfaction, and a casual relationship between teacher and student are valued highly.

Humor is used often by the teacher as the main ingredient in the presentation, followed by involvement activities on the part of the student. Assignments are generally geared to a presentation of the student's experience as opposed to fact-gathering and synthesizing.

There is much to commend the teacher as motivator. Learning should be an enjoyable, involving experience, but not at the expense of basic content.

THE MANIPULATOR

The manipulator believes he knows what is best for everyone and so strategizes the teaching experience. He manages the learning situation so that certain answers are always correct and the alternatives appear to be terribly foolish. The manipulator usually believes that he is the dispenser of truth and enforces conformity upon the group. The approach is very close to a propaganda technique, and even when what is presented this way might be truth, the process is questionable. Jesus, when dealing with the rich young ruler, gave him freedom of choice. The man made the wrong choice, but the Lord did not force him to choose the right way.

THE INCULCATOR

There are teachers who do not manipulate, but who believe that certain facts, concepts, skills, and attitudes should be learned by all students. Those teachers we will call inculcators. The inculcator will repeat facts often, frequently admonish, and praise behavior in the attempt to build habits and concepts. It is a form of conditioning, with emphasis on mechanical learning.

As in the case with the manipulator, the inculcator has a body of truth he believes his students should possess. The inculcator is generally open to an individual's learning more than he could possibly teach, but does require of them acquisition of a basic body of knowledge. Most people, especially parents, are to some degree inculcators.

A form of inculcation can be found even in the drill method or the development of programmed learning texts. The student is rewarded for correct responses and must go back and repeat the process until he gets it "right." In some realms of study, this is not only a positive way of teaching, it is necessary. The sciences are an illustration of a type of subject matter that can lend itself to this approach.

THE COMMENTATOR

In ancient Israel one of the most common teaching styles was that of the commentator. Findley B. Edge describes that situation well when he contrasts the teaching of Jesus with that of the rabbis of His day.

"As the old system of Judaism could not contain the spiritual dynamic of his teaching, so the Jewish educational system could not contain his new approach to teaching. He broke with the type of education that had to appeal to ancient authorities to be accepted or believed. The formula found on almost every page of the Talmud, 'Rabbi A. says that Rabbi B. says or Rabbi C. says in the name of Rabbi D.' is lacking in Jesus' teachings. He dared to say, 'You have heard that is was said by them of old time. . . . but I say unto you . . .' (Matt. 5:21-22)".[4]

The teacher who simply gathers a collection of thoughts from other people and reports, "Professor A. says this, or Dr. B. says this, and my former teacher said this," is a commentator in the manner of the rabbis of old.

THE FACILITATOR

A popular teaching philosophy today is that of the facilitator. Taken from the concept of making difficult things easier, the facilitator seeks to design for his students those learning situations that will best accomplish his and their learning objectives. The teacher who is a facilitator generally has certain things he believes should be learned by his students. He also allows his students to establish for themselves those areas of knowledge and experience they feel are important.

Different methodological approaches can and are taken by this type of teacher. At times there will be lecture, at other times group work. Visuals and audio aids are generally employed to enhance the learning experience, and experimentation is valued.

THE ORCHESTRATOR

A word that might describe a holistic approach to teaching is the term *orchestrator*. There are teachers today who have a clear understanding of what they want to see happen as a result of their teaching. On the other hand, they recognize that it is the students who actually do the learning. The role, therefore, is similar to that of the orchestra conductor. He has a concept of what the end product should sound like but is totally dependent upon the players to perform their varied roles if the end product is to be achieved. Different personalities and abilities are recognized. Not all the input is of the same intensity or duration. The conductor provides direction, but the orchestra does the playing.

Many teachers today find that their teaching philosophy and style is like this form. They have studied the content, established learning goals and objectives, and, while working with the entire group, they recognize that each individual's performance is varied, but important. An abundance of equipment and researched techniques await their use, but they select it all carefully in light of both the content and their student's needs to insure an effective and efficient learning situation.

The Performance of the Teacher

A teacher's performance is best measured by his relationship with students. The evidence is in clearly developed lesson plans and the utilization of valid and varied learning techniques. Of course, the teacher's personality is a determining force in each of those realms.

The teacher exists for the sake of the students. For the Christian teacher there is an even greater dimension, that of being part of the Body of Christ. When these two truths are put side by side, the Christian teacher discovers that he has a unique spiritual relationship with his students. Although he is responsible for them, he is also responsible to them.

The successful Christian teacher has a caring concern for those God entrusts to him. The one characteristic that continually marked our Lord's ministry was His compassion. Whether it was with individuals, small groups, or large audiences, He was a man moved by tender care. Today's Christian teacher should be one whose behavioral performance is not that of a cold, detached, or impersonal dispenser of truth. Rather he should be sympathetic, tender, and responsive to the needs of his students. Performance at the highest level in that realm will cover a multitude of mistakes and shortcomings in the more technical aspects of teaching.

The effective Christian teacher will also frame clear, measurable, and achievable learning goals and involve the students in satisfying growing experiences. Edge, in his helpful work *Teaching for Results*, deals with teaching aims in three categories: knowledge, inspiration, and conduct response. Lawrence O. Richards, in his volume *Creative Bible Teaching*, stresses that the teacher must know what to anticipate in terms of a response if the teaching is to be properly targeted. Benjamin Bloom, in his valuable contribution to education entitled *A Taxonomy of Educational Objectives*, sets forth a series of measurable behavior objectives. A teacher who truly desires results in the lives of his students will carefully think through and write down his targets and will identify the evaluation he will use to determine whether or not he has been successful.

No discussion of teacher performance would be complete without some reference to teaching methodology. Our purpose here is not to define the various options available to teachers but rather to briefly explore the relationship between the Christian teacher and method selection and use.

There are certain mechanical factors a teacher must consider when choosing methods. These include things such as the time available for the session, the equipment and facilities, the size of the group, and the age of the student. A wise teacher will carefully weigh the learning setting and choose those procedures that are workable in that situation.

Also, the teacher must carefully think through the content of the lesson to be taught and what is to be achieved. If the development of special skills is in view, then involvement techniques and "hands on" methods are necessary. For example, where the teacher wants to have the student identify a trend that developed over many years and yet do it in a short amount of time, a brief lecture or film clip might serve the purpose. Selection on the basis of appropriateness to the material and lesson objective is vital.

Variety is also of importance to the teacher as he considers his communicating technique. Although that criterion should not outweigh other factors, it still must be considered. Even the most unique and interesting method becomes tiresome if overused.

We all have a tendency to gravitate toward that which is familiar and comfortable. Teachers tend to use the methods that their teachers used. The ability to use only certain methods rather than others most often stems from that type of experience. In order to be able to use a wider variety of instructional techniques, teachers need to be trained in how to actually use different techniques and be given opportunity to practice their new skills. Teaching performance will be enhanced as newer and different approaches are utilized.

THE PRODUCT OF THE TEACHER

Successful teachers are best seen in the lives of their students. This was most effectively stated by Frank B. Stover.

> My little girl has a wonderful teacher. I know this even though I have never visited her class during the school day, and have met her teacher only several times at P.T.A. meetings. I did see the original Christmas play given by her class, visited the science night and physical education exhibitions, and saw the displays in the classroom which featured "Open House" night. I know her life at school because I have watched my daughter grow and change, and in family conversations at breakfast or dinner the story has unfolded.

I know that she has been exploring, whether it be in books or nature walks, or in fields of knowledge which she has entered for the first time this year. . . .

She has furthered her adventures in reading, not only broadly but deeply and for purposes, and even in third grade foresees the endless pleasures and the different uses to which this accomplishment can be put.

Naturally she has been discussing, exchanging her own ideas with others, putting into words the ideas she has heard, and weighing the notions others may bring forth. . . .

I know that she has been observing much, whether it be a film or map or chart, or the behavior of flora or fauna, or the ways in which our community organizes itself for social purposes.

The organizing of ideas, or classroom procedures, or of information gleaned from a trip or a text, is something which her teacher has not left to chance, and practice in this process has carried over into her own part of our family living. . . .

She has had rich experiences in appreciating, whether it be in music or the arts or the story the teacher reads, or just the special contributions each child, regardless of background or ability, can make to the life of the class. . . .

I have observed her reaching, being challenged by her teacher to do her best and a little more, being unsatisfied with a goal set too low, or being anxious for a class project to attain higher ground than it was able to reach. . . .

I might well go on enumerating, but the list is already long enough to suggest a classroom where teaching is an art and a science, where the process of individual development can flourish, where the roots of critical thinking are made to grow by sympathy, understanding and good common sense. We are lucky, her mother and I, and Sally will be even more fortunate if, in the years ahead, her other teachers in school and college know what their fundamental task is: the development of a unique human personality, able to function productively and happily in the society into which it was born.[5]

For the Christian teacher there is that added dimension of leading children, youth, and adults into a vital relationship with Jesus Chirst that enables the individual to live abundantly in this present world and joyfully in the presence of God throughout all eternity. Let the one who has been given the privilege of bearing the title *teacher* vigorously pursue the challenge, and by precept and practice lead people into an enthusiastic and growing spiritual endeavor. Let the sin of dull teaching never once be named among you!

FOR FURTHER STUDY

1. Do an inductive study of the gospel for every situation where Jesus is

teaching. Identify his manner, the lesson being taught, and the method used.

2. Take the word "teach" and do a word study concerning its usage in the New Testament.

3. Locate someone who is recognized by others as an effective teacher. Visit his or her class several times and write a short essay on why the person is successful.

4. Take the teacher expertise aspect of a teacher's preparation and develop the concept in terms of a local church Sunday school teacher training program.

5. Choose one of the six perspectives of a teacher listed in the chapter that you most agree with and identify the strengths and weaknesses of that concept.

6. Do a study of learning aims. Choose a passage of Scripture such as Luke 5:18-26 and write out three different response aims: one for knowledge, one for attitudes, and one for conduct.

7. Using as an example the excerpt from Stover (p. 89), write your own creative story of the most outstanding teacher you have ever met.

NOTES

1. James D. Murch, *Christian Education and the Local Church* (Cincinnati: Standard, 1943), p. 134.
2. Kenneth C. Kinghorn, *Gifts of the Spirit* (Nashville: Abingdon, 1976), p. 34.
3. Leslie B. Flynn, *Nineteen Gifts of the Spirit* (Wheaton, Ill.: Scripture Press, Victor, 1974), p. 74.
4. Findley B. Edge, *Teaching for Results* (Nashville: Broadman, 1956), p .3.
5. Frank B. Stover, "What Is Good Teaching?" *Department of Education Newsletter* (New Jersey Department of Education), 1957.

SUGGESTED READING

Bloom, Benjamin S., et al. *A Taxonomy of Educational Objectives: The Classification of Educational Goals Handbook 1: The Cognitive Domain.* New York: Longmans, Green, 1956. A classical work on the framing of measurable and behavioral learning objectives.

Byrne, H. W. *Christian Education for the Local Church.* Grand Rapids: Zondervan, 1963. A compilation of Christian education information in list and chart form interspersed with helpful comments. Chapter 7 is on the teacher.

Edge, Findley B. *Teaching for Results.* Nashville: Broadman, 1956. A presentation of basic principles of Christian teaching interlaced with realistic illustrations—challenging!

Gangel, Kenneth O. *Understanding Teaching.* Wheaton, Ill.: Evangelical Teacher Training Assoc., 1968. A helpful study book covering the Sunday school teaching process for laymen.

Horne, Herman H. *Jesus the Master Teacher.* Reprint. Grand Rapids: Kregel, 1964. A classical work on the teaching ministry of Christ.

LeFever, Marlene D. *Turnabout Teaching.* Elgin, Ill.: David C. Cook, 1973. A collection of illustrations and practical suggestions for stimulating and enriching teaching.

Murch, James DeForest. *Christian Education and the Local Church.* Cincinnati: Standard, 1958. An overview of the history, principles, and practices of local church Christian education. Chapter 15 is pertinent.

Peterson, Gilbert A. *How to Get Results with Adults.* Wheaton, Ill.: Scripture Press, Victor, 1977. A brief presentation of understanding adult needs and how to meet them in the teaching setting.

Richards, Lawrence O. *Creative Bible Teaching.* Chicago: Moody, 1974. An exciting presentation of the concept and skills necessary for the creative teaching of the Scriptures.

————. *You, the Teacher.* Chicago: Moody, 1972. A simple, readable work on the ministry of the teacher.

Townsend, Edward Arthur and Burke, Paul J. *Learning for Teachers.* New York: Macmillan, 1962. A standard work on teaching, stressing the behavior underlying teaching and learning.

Zuck, Roy B. *Spiritual Power in Your Teaching.* Rev. ed. Chicago: Moody, 1972. A careful biblical study of the role of the Holy Spirit in the educational process.

7

The Teacher's Personal Bible Study

TERRY HALL

EVERY CHRISTIAN needs the Bible: not just a book on a stand beside his bed or somewhere on a shelf, but the counsel of God impacted on his life and thinking. As nothing else, the Word of God will turn his eyes toward heaven, guide him from day to day, renew his spiritual vision and his strength.

Why is it, then, that so few Christians get everyday help from the inspired Scripture? The simple answer is that passive hearing and reading are not enough. We cannot skim over the Bible like a person on water skis. We need to notice what is there; to translate familiar words and passages into ideas and principles, relating them to daily needs and practice. We need to do *personal* Bible study.

But how? Here are seven suggestions, ranging from very simple, basic methods, to more complex approaches. These are usable ideas to help us become involved in studying the Bible for ourselves.

BIBLE INTAKE

The first and most basic suggestion for the Bible study is to program yourself for regular Scripture intake. This means attending a church where the Word of God is preached and taught. Attend regularly and take your Bible.

But you should also make time for personal Bible study. Though some have begun with as little as one or two study times a week, the ideal is a daily time, perhaps five to thirty minutes. Most people find the best time is at the beginning of their day, but this may not be best for you. The important thing is to get Bible intake regularly, each day if possible. Many

TERRY HALL, Th.M., formerly a faculty member of the Moody Bible Institute, is vice president of Media Ministries, Inc., Wheaton, Ill.

with varied schedules find it helpful to make an "appointment" with God for the next day at what seems to be the opportune time.

Find a quiet place where you can read and think, make notes, and study. Expect God's help. Pray for His guidance, and trust the Holy Spirit to give you understanding.

But don't stop with that. Use some of the following techniques to make your time investment pay.

SIMPLE NOTES

One of the most important ways to get more from your Bible is to form the habit of taking simple notes. When you hear a Bible message, jot down the highlights of what you hear. When you read and study the Bible, make a note of what you find. That is important: using pen or pencil as you read can more than double what you get from Bible study.

Notes may be short and simple—the main points of a message, the two, three, or four things you notice in a given passage. Write down chapter and verse so you have the reference for each point and statement.

True, taking notes means work. But searching out what the Bible really says and putting it in your own words will multiply what you get from listening or reading. What should you do with your notes once you

---

Chart 7.1

CHAPTER GROUPINGS WITHIN LARGER BIBLE BOOKS

In larger Bible books, reading and study may be made by separate sections as indicated below. Books not listed are short enough to easily treat as a complete unit.

Genesis	1-11, 12-25, 26-36, 37-50	Proverbs	1-9, 10-24, 25-31
Exodus	1-10, 11-18, 19-24, 25-40	Isaiah	1-12, 13-27, 28-39, 40-48, 49-57, 58-66
Leviticus	1-10, 11-17, 27-28	Jeremiah	1-10, 11-24, 25-33, 34-45, 46-52
Numbers	1-10, 11-21, 22-36	Ezekiel	1-14, 15-24, 25-32, 33-39, 40-48
Deuteronomy	1-11, 12-16, 17-26, 27-34	Daniel	1-7, 8-12
Joshua	1-12, 13-24	Hosea	1-8, 9-14
Judges	1-9, 10-21	Zechariah	1-8, 9-14
1 Samuel	1-8, 9-15, 16-31	Matthew	1-11, 12-15, 16-28
2 Samuel	1-12, 13-24	Mark	1-8, 9-16
1 Kings	1-11, 12-22	Luke	1-8, 9-18, 19-24
2 Kings	1-8, 9-17, 18-25	John	1-12, 13-21
1 Chronicles	1-9, 10-20, 21-29	Acts	1-7, 8-12, 13-21, 22-28
2 Chronicles	1-9, 10-24, 25-36	Romans	1-8, 9-16
Ezra	1-6, 7-10	1 Corinthians	1-10, 11-16
Nehemiah	1-7, 8-13	2 Corinthians	1-7, 8-13
Job	1-14, 15-21, 22-31, 32-42	Hebrews	1-7, 8-13
Psalms	1-41, 42-72, 73-89, 90-106, 107-150	Revelation	1-5, 6-9, 10-18, 19-22

have made them? Even if you throw them away in a day or two, you will find that they will be worth the trouble. But we recommend that you keep them in a notebook or a simple Bible file, preferably in a separate folder for each book of the Bible.

Panoramic View

Reading for a panoramic view is one approach to what is called synthetic Bible study. In this case "synthetic" does not mean "artificial," but describes putting parts together to form the whole. It is always good to do this kind of study before moving on to examine a book in more detail.

To get a panoramic view, you will need to choose a book of the Bible and read it through quite rapidly, if possible at a single sitting. (This is not difficult. Half the books of the Bible are so short they would take up only two columns in a daily paper.) For bigger Bible books, see chart 7.1.

Reading once is good; reading twice is better. You will find, perhaps to your surprise, that each rereading will enrich your understanding.

Before you begin to read, decide on what to look for. The first time through a book, read to find out what it is all about. Make notes. Try to discover what the book is saying as a whole.

Read eagerly with interest, as you would read a new bestseller. What you have is even better.

In a second reading you might look for what some call "the big ideas." Jot down the major events and key people, noting the passage where each event or person is mentioned. Ask yourself, "What really impresses me? What has left a mark on my mind as I've read the book this time?"

You may want to make a special reading in which you look for repeated items—events, people, or even statements that occur again and again.

For example, in reading Numbers, you may note that Israel keeps complaining to God. One student began to watch for those complaints and jotted down the reference in each case. By the time he came to the end, he had listed ten complaints. Then he noted in Numbers 14:22 that God said, "Those men . . . have tempted me now these ten times. . . ." Such observations can provide a whole new insight on the book.

Keep in mind that you may come back to a book for panoramic readings at a later time since there are many different things you can look for. At some future time you may want to reread a book to learn what you can about the author, his background, his family, the changes in his life that especially affected him, his ministry, and his relationships with others.

Or you may read through a book, noting what is different at the end from at the beginning. Have the characters changed location or leadership? Have they had a change of heart toward God?

Another possibility: a reading in which you look for contrasts within the book. Often the Bible contrasts people, as Abraham with Lot, Isaac with Ishmael, Jacob with Esau. Look also for contrasting events, contrasts in place, contrasts in attitudes.

Still another option would be to read the book, looking for turning points in action. What are they? At what points do they come? Another reading might be made to jot down a list of questions you would like to answer in a more detailed study later. Your list might include people you cannot readily identify, and dates or customs you would like to know more about. Following is a summary check of how you might record your panoramic insights in your notebook.

Developing a Panoramic View of a Bible Book

1. Major message of book:

2. Significant events or ideas:

3. Key people:

4. Repetitions within book:

5. Contrasts within book:

6. Differences between beginning and ending of book:

7. Questions for further study:

CHAPTER HEADINGS

Still another good way to get more from your Bible reading is to write out personal chapter headings. That simply involves reading a given book a chapter at a time and writing a short title, or heading, for each chapter.

GUIDELINES FOR GOOD TITLES

Sometimes we need to read a chapter several times before we can see clearly what it really says. Here are four guidelines for a good chapter title:

1. A title should be *distinctive*. It should fit that chapter and no other. "God's Laws," for example, is not a good chapter title because the heading would fit too many chapters.

2. A title should be *original*. It should be the product of your own thinking if it is to help you realize what you are reading. You might use a good reference Bible with splendid chapter headings, but they would not be yours, and copying them would help you very little.

3. A title should be *brief*, no more than four words. Longer titles are hard to grasp and hard to remember.

Sometimes you'll find so many subjects in a chapter that you will think it cannot be summarized in four words or less. When you do, try jotting down a title for each paragraph or subject. Then combine them to form a chapter title.

James 1, for example, seems difficult, but it has only three paragraphs. Verses 1-11 deal with external trials, verses 12-19 with inner temptations, and verses 19-27 with obedience or doing the Word. Combining these, one student chose: "Trials; Temptations; Doing Word"—a heading that, though telegraphic, reminds one of the chapter's three big ideas.

4. A good title should also be *descriptive*. That is, it should bring to mind the chapter's major themes.

BENEFITS FROM TITLING CHAPTERS

Making your own chapter headings does several things. First, it slows you down and makes you more reflective. You have to read more carefully and usually must reread several times.

Reading for chapter headings also reminds you that you are looking for what the Bible says. You have to think about what you are reading and must notice, too, what the Bible emphasizes and what it covers rather briefly.

Composing original chapter titles also provides a way to remember the content of the Bible and helps relate one part of the Bible to other parts. For example, jot down the chapter headings of the book you are reading. Then think about or memorize the headings. That way you can remember and use a large part of what you have read.

RECOMMENDED READING PLAN

You would find it very profitable to read through the entire Bible, chapter by chapter, writing original chapter headings. If you decide to do that, however, it is suggested that you read them in the order shown on chart 7.2.

In this way you would read first the Old Testament books that summarize history from creation through Israel's captivity and return—Genesis,

Exodus, Numbers, Joshua, Judges, 1 and 2 Samuel, 1 and 2 Kings, Ezra, and Nehemiah. Then read the New Testament books that summarize history from John the Baptist to the apostle John's revelation of things to come.

After that, with the span of all Bible history in mind, you would be prepared to appreciate the books in the next column, reading through them preferably in the order indicated.

Chart 7.2
CHRONOLOGICAL READING SCHEDULE OF BIBLE BOOKS

A. Read these books first to open Bible history	B. Then read these corresponding contemporaneous books to fill in more about each period
Genesis	Job
Exodus	Leviticus
Numbers	Deuteronomy
Joshua	
Judges	Ruth
1 Samuel	
2 Samuel	1 Chronicles, Psalms
1 Kings	2 Chronicles, Song of Solomon, Proverbs, Ecclesiastes
2 Kings	Obadiah, Joel, Jonah, Amos, Hosea, Micah, Isaiah, Nahum, Zephaniah, Jeremiah, Habakkuk
[Babylonian Captivity]	Lamentations, Ezekiel, Daniel
Ezra	Esther, Haggai, Zechariah
Nehemiah	Malachi
	[400 silent years]
Mark	
Matthew	
Luke	
John	
Acts	Galatians, James, 1 and 2 Thessalonians, 1 and 2 Corinthians, Romans, Ephesians, Colossians, Philippians, Philemon, 1 Timothy, Titus, 1 and 2 Peter, 2 Timothy, Hebrews, Jude
Revelation	1 John, 2 John, 3 John

SURVEY CHARTS

Once you know how to write original chapter titles, you are well on the way to being able to picture entire books of the Bible by making original survey charts.

Making such charts teaches one about a book in a way that almost nothing else can do. You will learn by gathering material and making the chart. When it is finished, the chart also pictures what you have learned so that you can refer to it easily and quickly.

A survey chart helps view the book's component parts and how they fit together. It is invaluable if you want to share the book with others in a Bible class or other situation in which time is limited.

Making a Bible survey chart is not difficult. Begin by reading through the book of the Bible you have chosen, noting original chapter titles as already described.

Now, beginning about two inches from the top of the page, list in a column on the left-hand side the chapter numbers with the original titles you have written. Leave three or four spaces between each entry. If the book is long, tape several sheets of paper end to end, so you have a long column of chapter headings. Or, chart a longer book by separate smaller sections as shown on chart 7.1.

Next, draw a series of vertical lines about one-half inch apart at the right of your list of chapter titles. This will give you several columns at the right in which you can trace the treatment of a major subject throughout the book as shown in the illustration.

For example, if you are charting Nehemiah and you discover that there are many prayers throughout the book, label one of the vertical columns "Prayers." You then go down the column indicating the verses in each chapter in which you find one or more such prayers. You can also indicate what kind of prayer appears in each chapter.

Other spaces may be used for charting subjects such as "Leadership," "Motivation of Others," "Confession." Still other columns can be used to indicate contrasts and comparisons you may have noted in your reading.

Nehemiah 1-6, for example, is concerned with physical work; chapters 7-13 deal largely with spiritual work in the lives of the people. One column, or even two, might therefore be used to show the portion of the book that deals with physical work; another will show the chapters stressing work in the hearts of the people.

The subjects you trace through on your chart can be chosen on the basis of your own interest and findings. Ask yourself who is involved throughout the book, what happens to them, when it happened, where it happened, and why it happened. Your answers to such questions will lead you to

Chart 7.3

SAMPLE SURVEY CHART OF NEHEMIAH

Chapter Titles	Major Event	Setting	Time	Prayer	Climax	Major People	Places
1. Report and Response	Rebuilding Wall (Physical Work)	Conditions	4 Months	Confession of Sin		Hananiah, Nehemiah, Samaritans, Jews	Shushan
2. Review and Rousing				Help			
3. Register of Workers		Construction	52 Days		Rebuilding Wall		
4. Rebuke to Samaritans		Conflict					
5. Redemption of Children				For Victory over Enemy			
6. Repeated Opposition Overcome					Wall Done		
7. Register of Returnees	Reforming People (Spiritual Work)	Census	1 Week			Ezra, Nehemiah Priests	Jerusalem
8. Reading of Law		Congregation Together		Praise to God	Revival		
9. Remorse in Prayer				Confession of Sin			
10. Record of Intentions		Census	13 Years				
11. Recruits for City							
12. Rejoicing in Dedication		Consecration to the Lord		Dedication of the Wall	Wall Dedicated		
13. Reformation of Temple				Help	Reforms		

discoveries about the book, which can be shown (as in the accompanying sample survey chart) on your original chart.

When you have finished, you will be surprised at how much you have learned about the book. And when you come back to the same book later, your chart summarizes your earlier findings as a base for deeper digging.

"Whose Responsibility?" Analysis

Many portions of the Bible emphasize God's commands and the blessings that follow obedience. Such passages come alive when studied and analyzed in the light of what God asks us to do and what He in turn promises to do for us. This kind of study can be carried out with great profit by making a "Whose Responsibility?" analysis of a given passage in which you list God's commands on one side of a sheet of paper and His promises on the other.

HOW TO PROCEED

To do the analysis, begin by drawing three vertical lines on a sheet of paper so that the sheet is divided into four columns. The three columns on the right should be about three inches wide, the far left column somewhat less. Head the columns, "Verses," "My Responsibility," "Results and Miscellaneous," and "God's Responsibility." (See sample form.)

The object is to read the passage in the light of what it says to you—personalize it—summarizing your findings point by point in the appropriate columns.

The things God's Word says you are to do should be listed in the "My Responsibility" column; the things God promises to do for you should go in the "God's Responsibility" column. The things the Word says will follow as a result go in the "Results and Miscellaneous" column, along with items that do not belong in either of the other two categories.

EXAMPLE FROM PSALM 119

Use a literal translation, not a paraphrase, for this type of study. The King James and *New American Standard* versions are most highly recommended. Psalm 119:1 in the *New American Standard Bible* reads, "How blessed are those whose way is blameless, who walk in the law of the Lord." This tells you that you have two responsibilities: one is to keep your way blameless, the other to walk in the way of the Lord. Both go in the "My Responsibility" column as entries for verse 1.

The same verse says that the one who does this is blessed. You cannot bless yourself; God has to do it. So write "God will bless" in "God's Responsibility" column. Verse 3 says those who do the things in verses 1 and 2 will "do no unrighteousness" and "walk in his ways," so write those in the "Results and Miscellaneous" column.

Chart 7.4

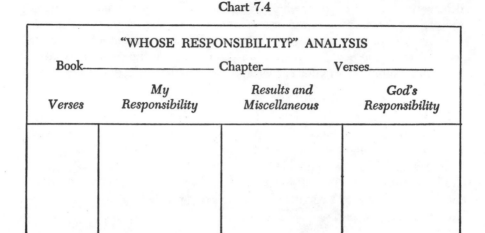

Analyze the entire passage verse by verse and statement by statement in that way, noting your findings in the appropriate column. Verse 5, "Oh that my ways may be established to keep Thy statutes," by implication seems to say that you should pray for that, so write, "V. 5—Pray that my ways will be established to keep God's statutes" in the "My Responsibility" column. There are also "My Responsibility" entries for verses 6, 7, and 8; "Results" entries for verses 6 and 7; and an entry in the "God's Responsibility" column for verse 8.

HOW TO GET DEEPER INSIGHTS

It takes about fifteen minutes to go through eight verses this way. Once you have made entries, look up definitions of key words such as "blessed" in verse 1 or "testimonies" in verse 2 to make sure you really understand what the Bible is talking about. A dictionary will help here or, even better, a *Strong's* or *Young's* concordance, which give biblical definitions of the words involved. (*Strong's* lists every word in the King James Version, what each means, and every place in the Bible it occurs!) It is suggested you write those definitions very briefly right on the analysis page where you can fit them in.

"But this takes careful thinking," someone may say. Exactly. That is why it works. You are listening to God, thinking about what He is really saying, and thinking about how to put His Word into practice.

Also make a note of any implications. For example, in verse 1, your responsibility is to keep your way blameless and walk in the law of the Lord. This implies that you must know what the law of the Lord says; so write that in. And there may be implications to be noted in the "God's Responsibility" column.

Is there some aspect of God's law you need to be especially concerned about today? If so, write that down. (After all, you are searching the Scriptures to let them change your life!)

That leads to a very important step—turning all the entries into personal prayer. Items in the "My Responsibility" column may prompt you to thank God for what you have discovered in Scripture, especially about Himself. Or you may be led to confess a sin or failure, or pray for help. Items in the "God's Responsibility" column lead to thanks for what He promises to do or to prayers of expectation, trusting God to do what He has promised.

Psalm 119 is an excellent passage to study using the "Whose Responsibility" method. Its twenty-two sections of eight verses each give you ideal reading portions for twenty-two days.

If you like the method, you can then go back to Psalm 1 and do the entire book of Psalms in about a year. Or you can use this method to study the New Testament epistles or the Old Testament prayers.

THREE-STEP CHAPTER ANALYSIS

Three-step analysis is a good approach to discovering the nugget truths in any chapter you may wish to study. The steps are: (1) observation, or, What does it say? (2) Interpretation, or, What does it mean? and (3) application, or, What does it mean to me? You may do these a step a day or all three steps at a single sitting. Longer chapters could be done by individual paragraphs at a time.

STEP 1, OBSERVATION

Observation can be taken by writing out original chapter titles as explained. For a more detailed approach, use a literal Bible version that divides the chapter into paragraphs. Write original summary titles for each paragraph. Or, you may simply jot down a list of the important facts or ideas appearing in the chapter.

STEP 2, INTERPRETATION

Interpretation can be done by asking and answering six basic questions: who? what? where? when? how? why? You can apply those questions to the chapter as a whole, to each paragraph in turn, or to each fact or happening. Write out the answers briefly.

Most of the answers to those questions will be clear from the Scripture context, though you may find help from cross-references in your Bible or from a Bible dictionary, Bible handbook, or passages located by means of a good concordance.

The important thing is that you examine every facet of the chapter. Most people are surprised at what the written answers reveal. The reason:

you will have forced yourself to examine, to question, to think of what the Bible says (see sample analysis).

Another way of doing the second step is to write out an original paraphrase; that is, restate the chapter in your own words, using "I" and "me" whenever possible. (Try to work from a very literal version like the King James; then compare what you have done with one of the good modern paraphrases.)

STEP 3, APPLICATION

Don't forget this important final step. What do the facts you have discovered mean to you?

One way of noting application is to write down answers to five basic questions. Does the passage speak of:

1. A sin to be forsaken?
2. A promise to be claimed?
3. An example to be followed?
4. A command to be obeyed?
5. A stumbling block or hindrance to be avoided?

As a final question, ask yourself, "Is there something here that I should do today?"

Note that the first letters of the five key words—sin, promise, example, command, stumbling block—spell SPECS. We therefore call these the *SPECS?* questions, adding a final question mark to remind us of the "Is there something for today?" question.

Another way to close such an analysis is to write out a very specific first-person prayer. You can thank God for the truth or example given, or ask for help in applying what God has said, or make a confession of what you have failed to do. Once you have used the three-step approach you will find it can be used with real profit in relatively little time. And you will find the Bible speaking clearly to the needs of daily life.

These are, of course, but a few of a number of methods available for personal Bible study. Never forget that Bible study methods can degenerate into "mechanics." Let them always just be a tool the Holy Spirit can use to a better end—fellowship with God. The Bible is not designed just to satisfy our mental curiosity, but also to touch our emotions and move our wills to choose God's ways. We do not just study the Bible—we live it!

SAMPLE THREE-STEP CHAPTER ANALYSIS

JONAH 1

1. OBSERVATION (*from the Bible only—what the chapter says*)

CHAPTER TITLE: Jonah's Flight from God

KEY VERSES 1:10, "Then were the men exceedingly afraid, and said unto him, Why hast thou done this? For the men knew that he fled from the presence of the LORD, because he had told them" (KJV).

KEY WORD OR WORDS: flee, fear

2. INTERPRETATION (*from the Bible, Bible dictionary, and concordance*)

WHO:

A. Jonah, prophet in Israel called to carry God's message of judgment to Nineveh. At first fled in opposite direction.
B. Sailors on ship who got converted transporting a prophet being disciplined by God.
C. The Lord (Jehovah, the self-existent, eternal One) who graciously pursues His sinning prophet.
D. Great fish prepared by God to rescue Jonah.

WHEN:

Eighth century B.C.—reign of Jeroboam II of Israel (2 Kings 14:25).

WHERE:

A. Nineveh, capital of Assyria on northern headwaters of Tigris River.
B. Joppa, Israel's seaport 35 miles west of Jerusalem on Mediterranean (From Jonah's home town of Gath-hepher in Israel, Joppa is southwest and Nineveh is northeast!)
C. Tarshish (probably near Gibraltar, in Spain)

WHY:

A. Why did Jonah try to run from God's call?
   1. Afraid God's mercy would win out and Nineveh would be spared (4:2).
   2. Pride—Jonah afraid his message of judgment would not come true.
   3. Fear—knowing Assyria's might and cruelty in war, prophet may have feared God would save Assyria to judge Israel.
B. Why did God send the terrible storm and great fish?
   God will not let us run from His will. In love God pursued Jonah, not to punish so much as to save him from himself and bring him to a place of willing obedience.

3. APPLICATION (*from Bible only, answering question, What does this mean to me?*)

Principles:

    A. I cannot run away from God, even though I may try.

    B. God loves all people and acts to bring them word of salvation.

    C. God is in control of His universe and will use everything in it to bring a believer to a place of willing obedience.

    D. God will let people pay their own way into sin, but He will graciously pay their way out—not always by the means we would choose!

    E. I should obey God the first time He speaks. I will end up doing His will anyway!

SPECS? analysis of Jonah 1

Sins to Forsake: Disobedience in what I believe God wants me to do.
Delayed obedience: obey now.
Following my own reason instead of what God reveals.

Promise to Claim: His continual, inescapable, loving presence (implied).
God in love will work out His good purpose in my life.
He will graciously pursue and discipline me for my good.

Examples to Follow: I should go to any length of sacrifice to spare others (as sailors).
I should make commitments to God after He has dealt with me in a special way to make sure I profit.

Commands to Obey: Great Commission to make disciples of all nations (strongly implied).

Stumbling Blocks to Avoid: I should never let self-will stand in the way of doing God's will.
I should never let what may seem like favorable circumstances be the only test of God's will.

What Do I Do Now? Begin to cultivate a deeper relationship with a neighbor to whom I believe God would have me speak.

FOR FURTHER STUDY

PERSONAL PROJECTS TO IMPLEMENT THE CHAPTER

1. Ask God to make clear to you what He wants *you* to be doing with His Word.
2. Organize a spiritual growth notebook with sections and pages for:
    a) Sermon and lesson notes
    b) Prayer requests and answers
    c) Personal Bible study notes
    d) Illustrations and insights

3. Set up a personal file with separate folders for each book of the Bible. Go through all the notes and clippings you have accumulated in the past and file the ones you really want to keep.

4. Take notes on sermons and Bible lessons you hear for at least the next month. Each time:
   a) For review recopy the notes soon after taking them, filling in further from your own thinking on the Bible text.
   b) Compare your notes with someone else's on the same message.
   c) Write down a specific, personal goal as the outgrowth of that message.

5. Read a small book of the Bible, like Jonah, several times for a "panoramic view." Record your findings in your notebook.

6. Make up your original four-word (or less) chapter titles for each chapter of Jonah. Write them in your notebook and also on a card to carry with you until you know them well.

7. Make a survey chart of Jonah like the sample in chart 7.3. Headings for columns to the right of your chapter titles could be:
   a) People
   b) Places
   c) Prayers
   d) Jonah's attitudes
   e) Miracles
   f) God's sovereignty
   g) Repentance
   h) Others of your choosing

8. Study Psalm 119 by the "Whose Responsibility" method at the rate of eight verses a day for twenty-two days. For each group of eight verses:
   a) Rewrite every word of each verse into the appropriate column(s).
   b) Define key words from a dictionary or Bible concordance like *Strong's* or *Young's*.
   c) Pray each column back to God.

9. Practice the "Three-Step Chapter Analysis" as explained in this chapter on Jonah 2, 3, and 4. For each of these short chapters:
   a) *Observe* by titling each paragraph and listing significant ideas or events in each.
   b) *Interpret* by answering the six questions and rewriting each chapter in your own words.
   c) *Apply* by personal and specific answers to "SPECS?" (see "Three-Step" Chapter Analysis) and write out a first-person prayer from the chapter.

10. Use the study methods on successively larger Bible books.

11. Make a commitment with a close friend to meet together once a week to share with each other what you have done in Bible study in the past week. Covenant to pray regularly for each other, asking not only for a fruitful time in Bible study, but also for Bible fruit in your life.

SUGGESTED READING

BOOKS ON PERSONAL BIBLE STUDY METHODS

Jensen, Irving L. *Enjoy Your Bible*. Chicago: Moody, 1969. Excellent, popular-level explanation of how to approach the Bible by books, chapters, paragraphs, sentences, words, and topics.

————. *Independent Bible Study*. Chicago: Moody, 1972. Advanced Bible analysis. Use as a sequel to same author's *Enjoy Your Bible*.

Search the Scriptures: An Approach to Chapter Analysis Bible Study. Colorado Springs: NavPress, 1974. The title says it! A proved and workable system.

Souter, John C. *Personal Bible Study Notebook*. 2 vols. Wheaton, Ill.: Tyndale, 1973, 1976. Ready-to-use forms to guide Bible study and record your findings.

Sterret, T. Norton. *How to Understand Your Bible*. Downers Grove, Ill.: Inter-Varsity Press, 1974. Best lay-level book on how to get the true meaning of Scripture.

Tenney, Merrill C. *Galatians: The Charter of Christian Liberty*. Rev. ed. Grand Rapids: Eerdmans, 1960. Learn nine different Bible study methods by practicing them on Galatians.

Vos, Howard F. *Effective Bible Study*. Grand Rapids: Zondervan, 1956. Good, though somewhat sketchy, overview of different methods.

Wald, Oletta. *The Joy of Discovery*. Rev. ed. Minneapolis: Augsburg, 1975. Guided practice in observation, interpretation, and application. A classic in the field.

REFERENCE BOOKS FOR BIBLE STUDY

Books are listed in descending order of recommendation, both by categories and within categories.

1. Bible Concordance
   Strong, James H. *Strong's Exhaustive Concordance of the Bible*. Nashville: Royal, 1890.
   Young, Robert. *Young's Analytical Concordance to the Bible*. Grand Rapids: Eerdmans, 1955.
2. Bible Dictionary
   Unger, Merrill F. *Unger's Bible Dictionary*. Chicago: Moody, 1957.
   Tenney, Merrill C., ed. *The Zondervan Pictorial Bible Dictionary*. Grand Rapids: Zondervan, 1970.
3. English Dictionary
   Woolf, H. Bosley, ed. *Webster's New Collegiate Dictionary*. Rev. ed. Springfield, Mass.: Merriam, 1975.

4. Bible Commentary

Harrison, Everett F., and Pfeiffer, Charles F., eds. *Wycliffe Bible Commentary*. Chicago: Moody, 1962.

5. Bible Handbook

Alexander, David, and Alexander, Patricia. *Eerdman's Handbook to the Bible*. Grand Rapids: Eerdmans, 1973.

Halley, Henry H., ed. *Halley's Bible Handbook*. Rev. ed. Grand Rapids: Zondervan, 1975.

6. Bible Atlas

Pfeiffer, Charles F. *Baker's Bible Atlas*. Grand Rapids: Baker, 1961.

7. Bible Customs

Wight, Fred H. *Manners and Customs of Bible Times*. Chicago: Moody, 1953.

8. Bible Introduction

Archer, Gleason L. *A Survey of Old Testament Introduction*. Chicago: Moody, 1973.

Harrison, Everett F. *Introduction to the New Testament*. Grand Rapids: Eerdmans, 1964.

8

The Holy Spirit in Teaching

C. FRED DICKASON

THE OFTEN NEGLECTED PERSON in the teaching-learning process is actually the most important. The Holy Spirit is the sovereign, most wise, and ultimate teacher of spiritual truth. He makes God's truth relevant to the persons involved and enables application that causes life and growth. Our teaching and learning efforts are in vain unless we cooperate with the Spirit.

Since the Holy Spirit was appointed by the Father, and since He is emminently qualified in His own right, we need to know Him and His role in the teaching-learning process that we may cooperate with Him in effective life and service for the Son of God.

HIS REALITY AS A PERSON

What is the Holy Spirit? He is a *person* just as are the Father and the Son. Since we are made in the image of God, much of what we consider ourselves to be as persons applies to the Spirit. With the great amount of evidence and analogy available, we should have no trouble thinking of Him as a genuine person.

As do all persons, divine and human, the Spirit possesses intellect (1 Cor. 2.10-11), emotions (Eph. 4:30), and will (1 Cor. 12:11). His works also affirm His personality. He is the intelligent creator (Gen. 1:2), the giver of personal life (John 3:5). He teaches (1 John 2:20), guides (Gal. 5:16-18), and speaks (Acts 10:19; 13:2). Pronouns that refer to persons are used of Him (John 15:26; 16:7, 13-15). He is the object of our personal trust, whom we may obey (Acts 10:9-21) or disobey (Isa. 63:10). And as a person, He is associated with the other persons of the Trinity (Matt. 28:19; 2 Cor. 13:14). He meets all the definitions of a person.

The Holy Spirit is also *deity*. The Bible equates the Spirit with *JHWH* (Jehovah) of the Old Testament (compare Isa. 6:9-10 with Acts 28:25). Christ includes the Spirit in the name of deity (Matt. 28:19; note the one "name" with three personal titles). Peter says that to lie to the Spirit is to lie to God (Acts 5:3-4). The Spirit has attributes that only God possesses: omniscience (1 Cor. 2:10-11), omnipresence (Psalm 139:7-11), and omnip-

---

C. FRED DICKASON, Th.D., is chairman of the Department of Theology, Moody Bible Institute, Chicago, Illinois.

otence (Job 33:4). He works as God only can work. He creates and sustains life (Gen. 1:2; Psalm 104:30). He raises the dead (Rom. 8:11). He reveals God's truth (1 Cor. 2:10-11), and He creates divine life in the believer in Christ (John 3:5; Titus 3:5). He is fully God, as are the Father and the Son.

Our director and resource in teaching and learning God's truth is a genuine person and genuinely God. Without Him we could do nothing.

His Role as a Teacher

Since the Holy Spirit is a person and a member of the Godhead, He is qualified to teach as is no human. But how does He teach?

FALSE CONCEPTS

Roy B. Zuck identifies four erroneous views regarding the role of the Holy Spirit.[1] First, that He is the *total* (only) teacher. His teaching excludes human teaching, for He illumines each believer directly, and human teachers may obstruct His work. This subjective, mystical view ignores the revealed fact that the Spirit uses human teachers, as evidenced in the Great Commission (Matt. 28:19-20); the involvement of church leaders (Acts 5:42; 15:35; 18:11; 20:20; 28:31); the command to Timothy (2 Tim. 2:2); and the gift of teaching to believers (Rom. 12:6-7; 1 Cor. 12:28; Eph. 4:11). This view further limits education, either because it is not needed, or because it excludes information or stimulation by other teachers. It can also lead to an attitude of superiority and infallibility since one's information comes directly from the Holy Spirit (fallible human understanding minimized).

A second false view sees the Spirit as a *totalitarian* teacher. He takes over the individual's responsibility for personal study or development. Human teachers need little or no training or preparation, for the results in ministry come from the Spirit. This imbalanced view results from a false view of the teacher. The teacher is more than a live book presenting truth. He is personally involved as example, expresser, and encourager for the truth. (1 Tim. 4:12-16). He is personally concerned and contributing to the life and welfare of others (Acts 20:27-37; 1 Tim. 5:1-3, 17-18).

Third, some regard the Spirit as a *tandem* teacher. He adds His part after the human teacher has done his part. We give the facts, and sometime later the Spirit inserts the catalyst that activates the spiritual factor. This view fails to recognize that God works in us and through us to will and to accomplish His good plan for our lives and others (Phil. 2:12-13). As members of Christ's Body, the church, we have spiritual gifts that are to be exercized in the power of the Spirit, including teaching (Rom. 12:4-7). As Zuck points out, "When God is educating, the human teacher and the pupils are involved together in the teaching-learning process, and at the same time the Spirit is working within the teacher, on the Word of God, and within the pupils."[2]

The fourth mistaken view regards the Holy Spirit as if *tethered*. Bound by a humanistic philosophy of teaching, the Spirit is regarded as unnecessary to religious teaching. With the proper materials, equipment, personnel, and program, creative and well-meaning teachers can operate efficiently on natural grounds without the aid of the Spirit. This view fails to comprehend the biblical estimate of man's finiteness and fallenness, and has its only resource in sinful "flesh" (1 Cor. 2:14; 3:1-3). It elevates man's creativity and methods over God's and fails to realize that only the Spirit can accomplish the spiritual goals of Christian education.[3]

The common failure of the above erroneous views is that they fail to consider the balanced biblical revelation concerning the Spirit's role.

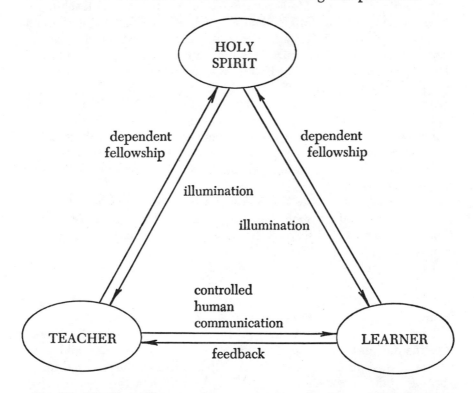

Fig. 8.1. This diagram pictures the communication aspects among the persons involved in the teaching-learning process. The Spirit may teach the learner directly, or indirectly through the teacher. At any time, there may be transmission and feedback along the channels indicated. A biblically informed approach to teaching-learning will take into account the dynamics suggested by the relationships involved. The Spirit illumines and enables both teacher and learner. Each, as a believer-priest, has direct communication with the Spirit. They may communicate on a human level with the Spirit controlling both of them. Teaching-learning tends to be maximized as these factors, among other pedagogical principles, are remembered and facilitated.

PROPER CONCEPT

It seems clear from Scripture that there are certain principles by which the Spirit operates in the teaching role.

First, there is the principle of *personal cooperation*. Though salvation is totally the saving work of God by grace apart from human effort (Eph. 2:8-9), sanctification in any of its phases requires the God-assigned cooperative effort of the believer. Every command addressed to the human will is evidence of this. We are told to grow in grace (2 Pet. 3:18), to diligently add virtues (2 Pet. 1:5-8), to teach others (2 Tim. 2:2), to take pains to do the job well, not neglecting our spiritual gifts (1 Tim. 4:14-16).

"The Holy Spirit seeks to teach through human channels or instruments. Human teachers should seek to be under the full employment of the Spirit, as clean and capable instruments. . . . in the final sense, it is not they who teach, but the Holy Spirit. As instruments of the divine Teacher, they teach what the Spirit of God has revealed in His Word."[4]

This should not be understood as "letting go and letting God" in the quietistic, passive sense. The fruit of the Spirit is self-control (Gal. 5:22-23). As Ryrie puts it: ". . . The Scripture does say very plainly that *I* am to do certain things that are a vital part of the process of sanctification. . . . But even in verses where the Spirit is mentioned as being involved in carrying out the exhortation, the individual is also included as a necessary part of the process."[5]

This type of cooperation is required of the teacher (1 Tim. 4:13; 2 Tim. 2:2; Titus 1:9) and of the learner (Matt. 7:24; Heb. 5:12; James 1:25). The Holy Spirit is a person who enables the person of the teacher and the person of the learner to communicate and interact with God's truth for personal and corporate growth.

Second, there is the principle of *personal cultivation*. The Holy Spirit revealed that we are persons made in the image of God. That means we are persons with intellect, sensibility, and will (Gen. 1:26; James 3:9). Though mankind fell and lost holiness, the image of God is retained, but terribly marred by sin. For believers in Christ, the Holy Spirit has renewed our righteousness and holiness according to the image of Christ (Eph. 4:24). This was accomplished by His regenerating us (John 3:3, 5-6; Titus 3:5-6). He is now cultivating that new life He created within us to grow into more Christlikeness.

The teacher and learner should both recognize the great worth of the individual person made in the image of God. The Lord Jesus did. A person is of greater value than many sparrows (Matt. 6:26), than all the riches of the whole world (Matt. 16:26). In fact, the worth of man is best seen in the tremendous price of eternal death that Christ paid for each of us. Though unworthy of the least consideration because of our eternal debt and guilt, yet our worth, as made in the image of God, is indelibly written in the blood of the God-man. He did not invest His life in worthless creatures, but in unworthy sinners. That makes the job of teaching a matter of cooperating with the Holy Spirit in the cultivating of persons of extreme worth.

Cultivating is an individual responsibility. The teacher and learner have many of the same imperatives addressed to them both. Each will be evaluated for his works when Christ rewards His servants (1 Cor. 3:13; 2 Cor. 5:10; Gal. 6:4-6). The Holy Spirit cultivates both teacher and learner in a very personal way, and we must do the same.

The goal toward which we strive is personal maturity. That is one reason the Spirit gave the Word (2 Tim. 3:16-17). That is why He changes us from one stage of glory to another (2 Cor. 3:17-18). That concern must be shared by us as cooperative servants of God the Spirit.

Third, there is the principle of *interpersonal communication.* The Spirit operates in the individual's life; but He also operates in the corporate life, the body life of the church. The church is the Body of Christ, her risen, exalted Head (Eph. 1:20-23). Through the Spirit, Christ has supplied His Body with spiritual gifts, capacities to serve others in various functions within the assembly (1 Cor. 12:4-7; Eph. 4:7-11). In the body no members are without gifts. Further, no member is independent, but all members are interdependent (1 Cor. 12:14-26). In this complex of personal relationships, there is not just one teacher and not just one learner. We all in some ways are teachers and learners. All should contribute in balanced fashion, under the Spirit's control and with His gifts, to the welfare of the whole body (1 Cor. 12:7; Eph. 4:12-16).

We must note here that the popular concept of discipling persons one by one through a particular leader is valuable to some degree, but no one person is sufficient for the complete task. Disciplers themselves must also be discipled. The whole body must be involved in the total process.

It is also evident from Scripture that not all body life relationships occur in the formal teaching situation or even in the meetings of the assembly. Teaching-learning may be sponsored by the Spirit in any real life experience, in any personal encounter with truth, and in any interpersonal communication. The Holy Spirit can work on a personal basis before, during, and after any formal teaching-learning contact to cultivate spiritual life and maturity. However, the assembly provides the best context for total operation of spiritual gifts and overall teaching-learning (Eph. 4:11-16).[6]

"Let it be said again, the work of Christian leadership is always shown within the context of the universal church. There is no organization or institution which has any authority in Christian service apart from its connection with the church as represented by some local assembly. Everything that was done by God's people in the New Testament was church-related."[6]

To honor Christ with eternal effects and spiritual efficiency, any teaching-learning situation must apply the foregoing principles revealed by the Holy Spirit as those by which He operates.

HIS RESPONSIBILITY IN TEACHING

In the administrative council of the Trinity, the Holy Spirit has been assigned by the Father and the Son the responsibility of application of the truth of God. What does He contribute to teaching?

RELATED NAMES

Certain names of the Spirit help us to grasp His contribution to teaching. The title *Spirit of Truth* indicates that He as deity is the revealer and applier of God's truth to human hearts (John 14:17; 15:26; 16:13). He makes God's objective, revealed Word of truth (John 17:17), centered in Christ who is the truth (John 14:6), to be subjectively applied truth (Eph. 1:17).

The title *Helper* (sometimes "Comforter," "Advocate") from the Greek *paracletos,* refers to one called alongside to help according to the need. This title is connected to the revealing and teaching ministry of the Spirit (John 14:26; 15:26). He is our helper in teaching, apart from whom we could teach nothing (Gal. 5:16-17, 25).

The title *Spirit of Wisdom and Revelation* speaks of the Spirit's work as "wising us up" by revelation. Again this points to His deity. The work involved here might have once included fresh revelation, as to the Ephesians in a day when Scripture was not yet complete and the gift of prophecy was still needed for the beginning stages of the church age. But with the completion of the whole New Testament canon, the Spirit's job is to give us wisdom concerning what has been already revealed as the complete and adequate guide for truth and practice (2 Tim. 3:16-17; Jude 3). His primary responsibility in teaching centers in the revealed truth of Scripture.

RELATED WORKS

With mention of objective truth and subjective application, we should consider the Spirit's ministries that relate to those and so to teaching.

The work of *revelation* is a disclosing of truth about God's person or will. Though God has revealed His truth in various ways,[7] His primary means were through His Son, the incarnate Word, and His Scriptures, the inscribed Word. The revelation in the Old and New Testament Scriptures was the work of the Spirit (1 Cor. 2:9-13; 2 Pet. 1:20-21). The Spirit is not now revealing new truth, hitherto undisclosed, to believers; but He is directly, or through the gift of teachers who explain the truth, applying the truth already revealed in Scrpiture.

The work of *inspiration* refers to that process of the Spirit when He superintended human authors so that, using their own personal powers, vocabulary, and style, they composed their contribution to the written Word of God without error in the original manuscripts.[8] Inspiration, then, gave us the inerrant record of God's choice, including revelation in propositional statements and historic events. This is the objective subject matter we are to teach (Matt. 28:19-20; 1 Tim. 4:13; 2 Tim. 4:1-4). It involves all of Scripture (2 Tim. 3:16-17) and all its teachings (Acts 20:20, 27).

Inspiration differs from *teaching* by the Spirit. Only biblical writers were involved in inspiration, whereas all believers may share in His teaching. The special superintendence upon the writers that guaranteed inerrancy in the Bible cannot be claimed under the Spirit's teaching. There is no such claim in Scripture, and teaching involves the understanding of finite and fallen minds, even though they be renewed by the Spirit. Appropriation of truth is always considered in Scripture to be subject to error.

As Zuck aptly puts it, ". . . the Spirit's purpose in teaching is to make clear to the minds and hearts of God's children the truth which He has inspired."[9]

The work of *illumination* involves the Spirit's making clear and applying the truth of Scripture. This seems to be His work with Christians that Paul mentioned in Ephesians 1:17-18. The psalmist cried for it (Psalm 119:18). Christians need illumination to discern the truth and to grow by it (1 Cor. 2:15; 2 Cor. 3:18). No new truth is revealed in the Spirit's illuminating; He is teaching on the individual level the truth that has already been revealed.

The unsaved man is unable on his own to receive the truth (1 Cor. 2:14). He must first be convicted by the Spirit of the truth of the gospel and then respond to it in faith to receive the light of the gospel in the person of Christ (John 16:7-11; 2 Cor. 4:3-6). Then, having received life and light in Christ, a person may benefit from the Spirit's illuminating the Scripture. That teaching causes growth as we receive biblical truth (1 Pet. 2:1-2). Again Zuck helpfully contributes:

> In teaching, the Holy Spirit operates on (or activates) both the written Word and pupils: one He animates and the other He illuminates. It is in this way that He communicates, or teaches, God's truth. . . . illumination is the communication of the *meaning* of the truth. . . . He guides into truth already revealed. Of course, to the believer being illumined, the truths may be new, for he has never before known them.[10]

Neo-orthodox or existential theologians hold that revelation takes place today when men respond to the witness and record of God's revelation in the Bible. To them the Bible is not the Word of God objectively. It merely *contains* the Word, which comes to us by revelation when we respond to it in some crisis situation of life. If we do not respond, it is not God's Word. By such doctrine they not only confuse revelation with illumination, but more disastrously they also reject any objective revealed truth. Liberal theologians confuse inspiration with illumination. A man is inspired when he sees God's truth and responds to it with a life change. They, too, forfeit objective truth in recorded, inerrant form.

We must distinguish revelation, inspiration, and illumination used in the biblical sense. *Revelation* refers to God's objective act of disclosure in words or events. It speaks of truth's source: God. *Inspiration* refers to God's superintending men to write. It speaks of truth's inerrant record: Scripture. *Illumination* refers to God's clarifying the Scripture to believers. It speaks of truth's application: understanding.

At this point we should consider several major works of the Spirit performed for the individual. They in a large degree precede and are a prerequisite for any effective teaching ministry of the Spirit.

First, *conviction* brings the unbeliever to the place of acknowledging that the gospel is truth and that it applies to him. This work is absolutely necessary to overcome the deadness of man's sin nature and the delusion cast by Satan (John 16:7-11; 1 Cor. 2:14; 2 Cor. 4:3-6). By this the Spirit causes personal agreement with the gospel so that men may intelligently trust in Christ.

Second, *regeneration* creates a new capacity to think, feel, and perform with God. It renews the moral base of personality and allows both learning and teaching to be carried on through the Spirit (John 3:5-6; Eph. 4:24; 1 Pet. 1:23—2:3).

Indwelling brings the person of the Spirit within the person of the believer. That results in a permanent personal relationship that allows the resident Spirit to work in and through the new nature implanted by regeneration (John 14:16-17). The Spirit's indwelling presence is God's gift to every Christian the moment he receives Christ (Rom. 8:9; Gal. 3:2). That is the basis of His teaching ministry in believers. However, full enjoyment of His teaching is reserved for those who are filled with the Spirit.

Fourth, *baptism* by the Spirit places the believer into Christ and into His Body, the church, upon receiving Christ (Rom. 6:1-4; 1 Cor. 12:12-13; Gal. 3:26-28). Not only does this far-reaching work place the believer into the sphere of right standing "in Christ," but it also dethrones the old sin nature through co-crucifixion with Christ (Rom. 6:6-14). This legal and moral union with Christ grants the possibility of saying no to sin and yes to God. In uniting us to Christ, the head of the church, the Spirit also places us into our own peculiar positions as members of Christ's Body. With the Spirit's gifts to us, we now may function to honor Christ and serve fellow Body members (1 Cor. 12:7, 11-13). Baptism occurs once for all at receiving Christ (Gal. 3:26-27). All Christians have it (1 Cor. 12:13). It is not to be sought; since all have it, and we are never exhorted to seek it. Not all Christians, however, have the same gift; nor do all Christians have any one particular gift (1 Cor. 12:7-11; 28-30).

Fifth, the *filling* of the Spirit means the control of the person of the Spirit over the person of the believer (Eph. 5:18). Filling is the basis of all genuine and effective Christian living and service (Eph. 5:18—6:18). The Spirit keeps the old nature dethroned and under control (Rom. 6:12-14; 8:2-4; Gal. 5:16-17). This occurs only when we are given over to His will and are allowing Him to cultivate our lives and empower our service (Rom. 6:12-13; 12:1-6). His control does not eliminate our control, making us passive tools; but He operates in us and through us, in our individual personalities and abilities, to cultivate us and others through us (Gal. 5:13, 22-23; Phil. 2:12-13). Filling and baptism must not be confused. Baptism grants us position, our standing in righteousness in Christ; filling controls our practice, our expression of righteousness in the Lord. Baptism occurs once at faith, but filling occurs and continues only when we walk in obedience to God's Word (Gal. 5:16-17; Col. 3:16-17).

The teaching ministry of the Spirit is free to operate in the life of the Spirit-filled believer.

REALITY OF TEACHING

We have mentioned His names and His works, and we come now to the reality of His teaching. We have already introduced many aspects of His ministry, but there are other factors we must consider.

Transmitting the truth. The Bible presents Christianity as objective truth from God centered in the historic God-man (John 14:6; 17:17; Col. 2:3), not merely an ethic, life-style, or service. The title "Spirit of Truth" refers not to truth centered in man's person or social relations, but to truth centered in God, from whom the Spirit receives the content of His message and for whom He discloses it to men (John 16:13-14; 1 Cor. 2:10-13).

So then the Spirit is concerned with a "given" body of objective truth concerning God, Christ, God's plan, man, salvation, and Christian life and witness. To be sure, "all truth is God's truth"[11] even in the arts and sciences, and it should be treated in the context of Scripture and under the control of the Spirit. However, the Spirit's teaching operates *primarily* in the realm of *revealed truth.*[12] This seems clear from statements of Christ

(John 14:26; 16:13; 17:17) and of Paul (1 Cor. 2:9-13; Eph. 1:17-18). This is the truth centered in Christ that makes us free (John 8:32).

It is that truth objectively revealed in which the Spirit would make us subjectively walk. It is called moral "light" as opposed to "darkness" of sin (John 1:5-8; 2:4-8; 2 John 1-4; 3 John 3). And it is that biblical truth that we are required to transmit under the Spirit's teaching.

We might profitably consider at this point the contribution of John 14:26; 16:13; and 1 Corinthians 2:13 to the subject. John 14:26 contains Christ's promise to the disciples of supernatural recall of His teachings. It obviously refers to teaching and remembering concerning all the things He spoke while He accompanied them on earth. The promise was to those in the upper room who had previously heard His teachings. That was necessary so that they might transmit His truth accurately in oral form. It would also enable those who would contribute to the written form of His truth in the Scriptures yet to be produced. So then it is not a promise to believers today that the Spirit will recall accurately to mind whatever we have studied in Scripture. We may extend, though, the Spirit's purpose to the preservation of the Word in manuscripts and to His participation in teaching the inspired, preserved Word. The Spirit who inspired the Word is vitally interested in teaching the Word.

John 16:13 promises, "But when He, the Spirit of truth, comes, He will guide you into all the truth. . . ." Again the "you" refers to the apostles to whom Christ had been telling many new truths connected with Himself and with the age in which He would be absent from earth and present with the Father. (Note the mystery truths, freshly revealed and not found in previous revelation, as in Matt. 13:11, 17; Eph. 3:5-6.)

He had many more things to tell them, but conditions were not then ready. But after He sent the Spirit, He would continue revealing God's new truth for this age, completing God's disclosure centered in Christ so that the final product could be labeled "all the truth" (John 16:13). This is "the faith which was once for all delivered to the saints" (Jude 3), and was completed with the final "revelation of Jesus Christ" (Rev. 1:1) in the last writing of John. Again, John 16:13 does not speak primarily of the Spirit's teaching, but of His revealing objective, normative truth for the church.* We may extend the principle of His purpose again, as in John 14:26. His

---

*Zuck, pp. 36-38, holds John 14:26 and 16:13 to be valid references to the Spirit's teaching ministry today. But we must note (1) the immediate hearers were the apostles, who needed supernatural recall and revelation, (2) the context of many new truths being revealed (John 13-16, particularly 16:12), (3) the terms "teach" and "speak" may refer to revelation (John 6:63; 7:17; 12:49-50; Acts 2:16, 31; 28:25; 1 Cor. 2:13; Heb. 1:1-2), (4) references to the Spirit's receiving truth from the Father and disclosing or announcing it to the apostles (John 16:13-15), and (5) the problem with how all believers would be taught the whole truth even of Scripture.

interest in revealing new truth about Christ from God to the apostles would suggest that He would certainly be involved in the teaching of that truth.

Some consider 1 Corinthians 2:13 to refer to the Spirit's teaching ministry to all Christians. However, there are factors in the context that seem to limit that teaching to revelation and/or inspiration. The teaching falls into the sequence of communicating new truth, humanly unattainable to men such as the Corinthians and us. The order of communication is (1) truth in God's mind, (2) the Spirit's discerning God's mind, (3) revelation by the Spirit, (4) to apostles, "we" of verses 12-13, (5) in Spirit-selected words, as in Scripture, (6) to all men, who are either natural, carnal, or spiritual, as in 2:14—3:4.

Again we may say that the Spirit is interested and involved in the teaching of objective truth in His chosen words. That is evident from allusions to His lack of work in the natural man (v. 14; see also Jude 19) and from His obvious work in the spiritual man (v. 15). The "we" of 1 Cor. 2:13 cannot be a reference to the Corinthians, who were so obviously carnal (3:1-3); for they would not be fit channels for the Spirit, nor would they qualify for infallible teaching of the Word that judges all men. Further, the "we" must be distinguished from those who are judged as spiritual through the reception of their words.

The most pointed references to the Spirit's work of teaching the believer are found in 1 John 2:20, 27. The Spirit is here named "the anointing from the Holy One," and "the anointing which you received from Him [the Son]," and "His anointing." This one "abides in you," "teaches you about all things, and is true." Those are obviously references to the Holy Spirit with terms John has used before John 14-16. He is teaching all believers to apply the truth He has previously revealed and is alerting them to false doctrine. He is distinguished from the Father and the Son in the context (vv. 23, 27). The Greek *didaskei* (teaches) refers to an authoritative, doctrinal teaching, and the content of the teaching is connected to and based on what they had "heard from the beginning" from the apostles (v. 24). This is the central passage on the Spirit's teaching all believers the truth of the Word of God. He transmits an authoritative body of truth in His teaching ministry. He has revealed it; now He applies it.

Guarding the truth. In 1 John 2, the truth is opposed by the lie. False teachers with false teaching pervade the world, all purporting to have the truth. The Spirit raises the danger flag. He makes believers who know the basics about Christ and the gospel to be sensitive to false teaching. Consequently we can know all we need to know of true doctrine and discern error. This parallels the Spirit's specific teaching and warning about false doctrine of which Paul speaks (1 Tim. 4:1-6). He expects us to test all teachings and to bring them into comparison with the truth in Christ (1 John 4:1-6). He is greater than the false spirits behind the false teachers. All proposed systems and speculations must be brought captive to the obedience that Christ demands, according to His truth (2 Cor. 10: 3-5). The Christian must not belong to the "cult of the open mind." He must prove all things on the basis of the Scriptures (1 Thess. 5:21-22). The Spirit will never teach or lead a believer contrary to what He has painstakingly inspired in the Bible.

Cultivating persons in the truth. We have mentioned the worth of the individual created in the image of God, and the investment of Christ's redemption of the individual. Now we need to be reminded of the personal interest the Spirit has in the individual. He jealously desires to have us fully enjoying and walking with Christ. James says, "The Spirit which He has made to dwell in us jealously desires us" (James 4:5, NASB margin). That means He is dedicated to the good of the individual and directs His activities to that end. He is doing more than producing good instruments for God; He is cultivating our persons so we may know God and love and enjoy Him forever as a person (John 17:3). Both teachers and learners are more than tools in a process. As Wayne E. Oates points out, "A *person,* however, is more than, other than, and different from the roles he perceives and enacts."[13]

We are cultivated directly by His teaching through illumination of the Word. He teaches us indirectly through godly men who have received gifts of teaching from the Spirit (1 Cor. 12:8-11, 28; Eph. 4:11). He builds us up corporately in the Body of Christ (Eph. 2:21-22; 4:12-16). He may teach in any combination: one on one, one on many, many on one, many on many. Teachers and pastor-teachers seem plural in the local assembly (1 Tim. 5:17; James 5:14), and both sexes may be involved, each teaching in his proper sphere under proper authority (Acts 18:26; 1 Tim. 2:11-15; 3:2-3; 5:17; 2 Tim. 2:2; 4:1-2; Titus 2:3-4).

We must never sacrifice the person in the process of teaching. We need lovingly to consider the person whom the Spirit highly regards, regardless of gifts, abilities, traits, position, sex, race, or station in life (1 Cor. 12:13, 22-25; Gal. 3:28; James 2:1-9).

His Results in Learners

The Spirit's teaching is designed to produce certain basic effects in the life of the believer. First, He produces *spirituality,* which is the immediate result of the Spirit's control. Carnality characterizes those controlled by the flesh (Rom. 8:1-13; 1 Cor. 3:1-4; Gal. 5:19-21); but spirituality characterizes those controlled by the Spirit (Rom. 8:4, 12; 1 Cor. 2:15-16; Gal.

5:16-18, 22-23). Spirituality is that dynamic relation to the Spirit that enables growth and service (Gal. 5:25—6:10). The Spirit teaches us the Word that we may obey it (Eph. 5:18; Col. 3:16). That results in spirituality.

Second, He produces *growth*. When the believer walks according to the Word he has been taught, he may at any stage of life experience growth in grace and knowledge of Christ (2 Cor. 3:18; Eph. 1:17-19; 1 Pet. 2:1-2; 2 Pet. 3:18). Growth, in turn, leads to greater comprehension, which expands ability to learn from the Spirit.

Third, He produces *maturity*. Growth with resultant maturity is a process made up of various phases, each in its own time and under the proper conditions set by the Spirit. Maturity is a condition of life in which we are grown-up to some extent, properly adjusted to life's relationships, duties, and demands, with proper attitudes and development of character. Spirituality may be instant, but maturity takes time. It is the Spirit's purpose for us, and we need to plan and encourage teaching to that end.

Fourth, He produces effective *ministry*. As the Spirit has given gifts, so He encourages development of them to become more effective in various services (1 Cor. 12:7; Eph. 4:12; 1 Tim. 4:14; 2 Tim. 1:6). That involves diligent self-preparation and faithful cultivation on our part. The Spirit prompts works of edification (1 Cor. 14:12; Eph. 2:10; 4:12) and witness to the unsaved (Acts 1:8; 4:29-31). He uses His inspired Word (2 Tim. 3:16-17) and cultivates our personalities and skills. Our teaching should involve training the whole person and the proper preparation in Scripture and practical matters to evangelize and edify.

Both Zuck and Lawrence O. Richards make a pointed contribution to this subject.[14] Zuck emphasizes that Spirit-motivated learning is the highest form of intrinsic motivation.[15] The Spirit creates awareness of need, promotes desire to learn truth, and directs into relevant learning.

His Requirements of Teachers and Learners

There must be spiritual alignment with the supreme teacher, the Spirit of God, if any truly effective and eternal results are to be achieved. Any success must be measured by the Spirit's standards in His inspired Word (Gal. 6:7-10; 2 Tim. 3:16-17). Other standards and measurements must be checked by this (Isa. 8:20; Col. 3:16). To cooperate for successful teaching, certain conditions are mandatory, according to His Word.

There must be *a right relationship to Christ*. Without receiving Christ there is no spiritual life (John 1:12-13; 3:36). Only teachers and learners who know Christ through regeneration by the Spirit qualify for spiritual growth and service.

There must also be *a right relationship to the Holy Spirit.* For effective service, teacher and learner should be filled with the Spirit (Eph. 5:18). Only under His control may we operate to honor Christ (John 15:1-5; Gal. 5:16-17; 5:25—6:10).

The one general condition, simply stated, for the filling of the Spirit is *obedience,* which involves heeding three basic commands. First, "Do not "quench the Spirit," or do not resist Him (1 Thess. 5:19). That requires submission of the whole life and of each step of our lives to Him (Rom. 12:1-2). Our lives must be dedicated and directed by Him for effective teaching and learning (Rom. 12:4-8). Second, "Do not grieve the Spirit," or have no unconfessed sin (Eph. 4:30). The dedicated life can yet run into occasional sin, and it must be confessed for restored fellowship (1 John 1:9). Moment by moment cooperation with the Spirit results in enjoyment of Christ and enablement to perform His will. Third, we must "walk by the Spirit," that is, depend upon His power and His direction for the cultivation of effective life and service for Christ (Rom. 8:4; Gal. 5:16-17). We must not "be conformed to [the customs of] this world" (Rom. 12:2). Our goals, motives, and expressions should not be shaped by the world's creature-centered pleasure philosopy, but we must be transformed by the Spirit to know and do the good, acceptable, and perfect will of God.

Effective Christian teaching is enhanced by *proper gifts of the Spirit.* Not all can be as effective as some in teaching. Though all teach to some degree, the Spirit's gift of teaching gives to some the capacity to excel. Teaching is the ability from the Spirit to explain and apply the truths of God's Word, showing harmony and detail and making it personal. The Spirit teaches each Christian in the reception of the truth; however, He uses teachers to communicate that truth in digestible form. All believers should be taught by the Spirit, but not all believers communicate effectively to others what they have been taught. The gift of teaching rates first in importance after the gifts of apostles and prophets (1 Cor. 12:28; 13:8-10; Eph. 2:20; 3:5-6). We need to recognize that gift and provide opportunity and encouragement for its use.

The gift of teaching, as any other gift and perhaps more so, may be improved in quality by training and exercise. We must stir it up to full flame and keep it going and growing (1 Tim. 4:14; 2 Tim. 1:6). We must study the Word given by the Spirit with all diligence, privately and perhaps formally (2 Tim. 2:1-2, 15). We must also cooperate with the principles of God's pedagogy, learning to communicate effectively by all proper means, adjusting the teaching to the learners. So shall the Spirit's teaching become more effective by us to produce genuine learning.

FOR FURTHER STUDY

1. Write two short paragraphs on your concept of the person of the Holy Spirit and your relationship to Him. Share this for comparison and encouragement with others who might be studying with you.
2. On a biblical basis, define and distinguish the following ministries of the Spirit: revelation, inspiration, illumination, teaching. How do they relate to each other and to us?
3. How may a person cooperate with the Spirit (*a*) as He teaches us, and (*b*) as we teach others?
4. Do an in-depth study on the gift of teaching, noting its nature, place of importance, purpose of ministry, need of development, and places of use. What should a church provide to enhance the benefits of this gift?
5. Make a list of truths the Spirit would have a new Christian know and appropriate. Suggest how those might be communicated effectively to the Christian.
6. Distinguish and relate the Spirit's baptism and filling. What function does each perform? How are they related to teaching-learning?
7. Relate how diligent self-preparation is consistent with the Spirit's control and will enhance any teaching-learning situation.

NOTES

1. Roy B. Zuck, *Spiritual Power in Your Teaching*, rev. ed. (Chicago: Moody, 1972), pp. 59-65.
2. Ibid., p. 63.
3. Ibid., p. 64.
4. Ibid., pp. 81-82.
5. Charles C. Ryrie, *Balancing the Christian Life* (Chicago: Moody, 1969), pp. 64-65.
6. Kenneth O. Gangel, *Leadership for Church Education* (Chicago: Moody, 1970), p. 185.
7. Charles C. Ryrie, *The Holy Spirit* (Chicago: Moody, 1965), pp. 34-35.
8. John F. Walvoord, *The Holy Spirit* (Grand Rapids: Zondervan, 1954), pp. 56-58.
9. Zuck, p. 44.
10. Ibid., p. 56.
11. Frank E. Gaebelein, *The Pattern of God's Truth* (Chicago: Moody, 1968), p. 20.
12. Zuck, pp. 34-35.
13. Wayne E. Oates, *The Holy Spirit and Contemporary Man* (Grand Rapids: Baker, 1974), p. 42.
14. Zuck, pp. 119-23; Lawrence O. Richards, *Creative Bible Teaching* (Chicago: Moody, 1970), pp. 90-99.
15. Zuck, pp. 124-28.

SUGGESTED READING

Gaebelein, Frank E. *The Pattern of God's Truth*. Chicago: Moody, 1968. Treats problems of integration in Christian education.

Gangel, Kenneth O. *Leadership for Church Education*. Chicago: Moody, 1970. Suggests educational programming and leadership principles; puts teaching in perspective.

Oates, Wayne E. *The Holy Spirit and Contemporary Man.* Grand Rapids: Baker, 1974. An interesting and sometimes helpful insight into communication from a leading psychologist, existentially inclined and not given totally to biblical authority and inerrancy.

Richards, Lawrence O. *Creative Bible Teaching.* Chicago: Moody, 1970. Good insights into the theory and practice of teaching the Bible.

Ryrie, Charles C. *Balancing the Christian Life.* Chicago: Moody, 1969. Excellent presentation of the essence and expression of the spiritual life.

————. *The Holy Spirit.* Chicago: Moody, 1965. Brief, helpful, balanced treatment of the doctrine of the Holy Spirit.

Walvoord, John F. *The Holy Spirit.* Grand Rapids: Zondervan, 1954. Extended theology of the Holy Spirit.

Zuck, Roy B. *Spiritual Power in Your Teaching.* Rev. ed. Chicago: Moody, 1972. Excellent and only in-depth treatment of the Holy Spirit's work in the teaching-learning process; thoroughly biblical.

Part III

THE PERSON IN CHRISTIAN EDUCATION

It is natural, says Lois LeBar, to describe the local church in terms of its activities, its work as an institution; *but everything the church does,* she emphasizes, *is for the sake of people.*

People—big people, little people, people in all shapes and colors—that is what a family is, and that is what a Sunday school class is. As parents and as teachers we share our lives with those God-created beings, each with such magnificent potential for providing joy or frustration.

This unit looks at the person in education. Chapter 9 is a practical study of *children* by a person who has himself raised a family. It is designed to give both parent and teacher useful insights into working with learners from birth through eleven years.

A chapter on youth follows the approach begun in the children's chapter. The critical years of early and middle adolescence are reviewed in terms of key characteristics. As the young person is followed through the junior high and senior high years, basic suggestions are given for working with this transition person.

In keeping with the growing contemporary concern on adult education, chapter 11 provides a solid overview of teaching for adults. Although emphasizing established basics, it touches such new areas as "caring groups."

If our focus in teaching is to indeed be on the person, it becomes necessary to plan for that focus. An important chapter in this unit, therefore, concerns lesson planning, and chapter 12 takes us through some steps for effectively communicating the Word of God to the learner.

Finally, people respond differently to teaching approaches. Some enjoy a discussion method; others prefer well-planned lecture. The final chapter of this unit introduces the subject of teaching methods and their use in working with people.

9

The Learner: Children

Robert E. Clark

The Children We Teach

The learner is a most significant part of the teaching-learning process. In Christian teaching, even though the Word of God is central as our final authority and foundational textbook, the learner must be kept in focus. The Word of God is taught to enable him to become more Christlike.

Learners must be understood as developing people. God has ordained that individuals grow through various stages in life. Each stage contributes to and lays a foundation for the stages that follow. As the individual develops, different kinds of needs are met. Each stage has its growth, developmental patterns, and characteristics that are generally typical of that stage. However, each individual may display differences in the developmental patterns that make him uniquely an individual.

One of the purposes for understanding the individual learner is to meet his needs as a total person. Many divergent activities and experiences will enable parents and teachers to do that. Individuals grow at their own rate of development as needs are met and new needs emerge. Growth in the lives of the pupils is one of the greatest rewards in teaching and learning.

This chapter is designed to help parents and teachers have a better understanding of their children and to provide practical suggestions for meeting the needs of the child.

The childhood years are foundational, during which the basic structure of personality, habits of life, and character are fairly well developed. Those patterns of life become increasingly complex and more difficult to change as a person enters adolescence and adulthood. The significance of the earlier years cannot be overemphasized in teaching and learning. A basic

---

Robert E. Clark, Ed.D., is professor of Christian education, Moody Bible Institute, Chicago, Illinois.

understanding of the characteristics and needs of children is essential to help them most effectively in their development.

Children come in all sizes, shapes, and behaviors! In many respects children are alike and yet different because they are individuals in their own right. Children are not miniature adults, and we should not expect adult behavior from them.

Childhood is as distinct a period in life as the youth or adult years. Childhood extends from birth through eleven years of age. Child development authorities are especially emphasizing the importance of prenatal development from conception until birth. Research studies have shown that a child is affected through his environment as he develops during his mother's pregnancy. "Nutrition, drugs, radiation, illness and even the expectant mother's emotions may influence child development."[1]

CHARACTERISTICS AND NEEDS OF CHILDREN

Children have several general characteristics. Physically, they are very active and energetic. They are growing rapidly in every part of their personality. They have periods of uneven growth and sometimes reach plateaus in their physical development.

Mentally, children are discovering the world about them, and their mental development expands tremendously during those first eleven years of life. Though they are sharp intellectually, they have some limitations. They are literal in their thinking and have difficulty understanding abstractions, symbols, and generalizations. Children think specifically and do not readily relate ideas together. Jean Piaget suggests four stages of development in the thinking processes of children: (1) The sensorimotor period is approximately from birth to two years of age. The infant differentiates himself from objects. He relies heavily on sensory experiences as his chief source of learning. (2) Preoperational thought includes the years from two through seven. He can classify or categorize, but uses only one attribute at a time. He makes judgment on how things appear rather than on the basis of a mental operation. (3) Concrete operations range from about seven to ten or eleven years. The child is able to define, compare, and contrast in logical thought patterns. However, he is still concrete in his thinking. (4) Formal operations begin at eleven or twelve years of age. The individual can think and reason abstractly. Religious symbolism begins to have meaning.[2]

Emotionally, children are learning self-control. Twos and threes have great difficulty controlling their emotions, but children develop emotional control as they learn to relate to people. Usually, by the time a child is eleven he has learned to control his emotions and may often repress them to conform to adult or peer pressure and behavior standards.

Socially, most children tend to be friendly. As they grow, children learn to relate to other people in the social context. They realize they can be happier and more secure by complying to standards of behavior imposed on them by adults. As they gain self-control, they discover they can work in groups and enjoy interacting with others, particularly those in their own peer group. A primary child feels more secure when he pleases and is accepted by adults. By the time a child is a junior, he is definitely more influenced by his peers and is seeking peer approval. He is also beginning to show signs of seeking independence from adults and even his parents. Children today are likely to be more expressive and outgoing due to the permissiveness of our society, the desire to be involved actively and vocally, and the stress placed on personal development, self-discovery, and self-expression.

Spiritually, children can grasp biblical concepts and apply scriptural principles to their lives if the concepts are taught on their intellectual level and related to their everyday experiences. *How* children are taught those concepts is almost as important as *what* they are taught. Children are very capable of learning new concepts, but they are often influenced more by attitudes and actions than by the concepts they learn. The foundation for spiritual development is laid early in life. The positive Christian example of parents probably influences the child more than any other source.

The majority of children do not receive Christ as Savior until the primary or junior years. However, if children are reared in a Christian home, they may be ready for salvation much earlier. During the preschool years, basic concepts and attitudes are taught, but children must understand what they are doing. Intellectual development precedes spiritual readiness and comprehension. As a child understands spiritual concepts mentally, he can respond intelligently. It is imperative that the plan of salvation be presented simply and literally so the child can understand how he can put his personal faith in Christ as Savior.

THE INFANT AND TODDLER

Life begins at the moment of conception. Research studies indicate that a child is affected by his mother's actions, the food she eats, and her personal habits.

> Even before the mother is aware that conception has taken place, the growth of the new individual is proceeding at a remarkable rate. During the weeks that pass before the first evidence of pregnancy (usually the cessation of menstruation), development has already progressed from the first to the second stage of the prenatal period—from a zygote, smaller than the dot over this i, to an embryo ten thousand times larger, com-

plete with rudimentary eyes, ears, mouth, and brain, simple kidneys, a liver, a digestive tract, a blood stream, and a tubelike heart that begins to beat on about the twenty-fifth day. All this in a body about one quarter inch long.[3]

After the miraculous development of a new life has run its course, and the birth process has taken place, it is time for Christian education to begin. The very young child passes through two major periods of growth. *Infancy* is usually considered birth through twelve months, and *toddler* describes the child from thirteen to twenty-four months. The major development of the child is in physical growth. Each child grows at his own rate; some children learn to walk by eight months, and some take longer, even up to twenty months. "No period in one's life is as important as the first two years. . . . Psychologists and educators agree that never again during his entire life will a person learn as fast or as much as he does in the first two years."[4]

Physically. During his first year an infant learns to turn over, sit up, crawl, scoot, toddle, walk, and communicate his needs. Parents must exercise patience and wisdom to allow the child to develop at his normal pace. The time table varies greatly with each child. It is unwise to compare brothers and sisters in their development since each one is a unique individual. Intellectual development becomes more evident as the child nears his first birthday, though signs of his progress are evident even before that time. A baby responds by crying, smiling, or cooing. He reacts through facial expressions, gestures, and emotional outlets. The very young child depends on those responses since he cannot communicate with word symbols to let his needs be known.

As the child continues through his first year, he is growing very rapidly. In fact, he has tripled his birth weight, as a rule, and has grown ten to fifteen inches. His coordination is increasing, and he is constantly on the move whether he is awake or asleep.

Many remarkable changes are seen in the child from one to two years of age. He still continues to grow rapidly but is able to move about more freely because of improved coordination. He begins to investigate his surroundings and becomes a discoverer to see what his world is all about. He still prefers the familiar surroundings but is discovering everything within his reach. He relies heavily on his five senses. He tastes, touches, feels, hits, bangs, and smells to become acquainted with his limited world. It is absolutely amazing what a very young child can learn about himself and his world in the first two years of life. Is it any wonder that early childhood education has made such an impact in the past decade when we realize how much a young child *can* learn in such a short period of his total life span?

Mentally. The intellectual and language development of the toddler can be stimulated by adults who talk properly to the child. Baby talk should be avoided since it can build improper speech habits. The child can be read aloud to; an adult can sing and talk with the child in simple, concrete language. The attention span of a toddler is very short and must be considered in communication. Most children at this age have an attention span of one minute or less. Repetition plays a very important role in the learning process.

Ruth Beechick suggests that instead of thinking in terms of minutes, it is more helpful to think in terms of tasks. Is a task an appropriate level of difficulty for the child, and does he stick with a task until it is finished? All who work with children know that at times, in certain tasks, children's attention spans can be surprisingly long.[5]

Emotionally. The underlying need of the infant, and he has many, is that of love and security. Parents are undoubtedly in the best position to meet his needs, though workers in the church and day care center are also able to contribute to the child's well-being and development. Love is communicated more effectively through attitude and action than through verbalization for the young child. He feels deeply and responds to a quiet, calm, and unhurried atmosphere in which he feels secure and comfortable. Those who work with young children should be calm, collected, and secure themselves in order to transmit those same feelings to the children.

Socially. The infant lacks control emotionally and expresses himself as he feels. He relates best to his parents, siblings, and other familiar household visitors. He is an individualist and can be very demanding on those who care for him.

Spiritually. Spiritual teaching must be done on an individual basis. A loosely structured curriculum is essential. The use of sensory experiences and much repetition are the best ways to communicate with the infant and toddler. The program should be individualized, with the learning geared to the needs of the child. Especially in spiritual development, children assimilate more in attitudes and actions than from understanding concepts. For example, a child may be taught to bow his head, close his eyes, and fold his hands when he prays, though he does not understand all the theological implications of prayer. The child has a simple faith and trust and imitates what he sees his parents and others do.

Research will continue to provide guidelines for teaching very young learners. We certainly need to regard these children as persons who have needs to be met. Though the teaching is informal, much learning can take place by teaching literal, concrete, and simple concepts provided by a model-example of parents and teachers.

Nursery children are delightful people (most of the time), who range from two to three years of age. Sometimes they are referred to as the "Negative Nursery"! It is really amazing what they can learn, even as young as they are. In fact, the twos and threes are in one of the most formative periods of life, particularly in laying foundations for the remainder of life. What are they like? Here is a brief description of the nursery child as a total personality.

Physically. He is about three feet tall and has varied development as an individual. He is concentrating on larger muscular development. His smaller, or finer, muscles are not developed, and he can do very few things that require skillful coordination. He is continually active, but he tires easily and needs to have alternating periods of activity and rest. His five senses are very hungry, and he reaches out for sensory experiences. He is very sensitive to atmosphere, color, and beauty. He needs space to move about freely. He needs activities that require minimal skill and provide opportunities to use his five senses.

Mentally. The two-and-three-year-old lives in a limited world, which is confined largely to his immediate family. He has a limited vocabulary of three hundred to nine hundred words. Some of the more common words in his vocabulary are *me, my, mine,* and *no*! He does not understand concepts that deal with time, space, and numbers. He has a very undependable memory and needs much repetition. His attention span may vary from one to five minutes, depending on the individual and the activity in which the child is engaged. He needs teachers who can communicate with him on his level and use vocabulary he can understand.

Emotionally. He tends to be unstable and intense emotionally. He craves security, love, and attention. He has little control over his emotions and may throw temper tantrums. Sometimes he cannot express *how* he feels, but his feelings are usually evident through his actions. He has many intense fears, which result from the insecurities of the unfamiliar or unknown. He has already begun to develop trust in people or a lack of it through his home environment, especially his mother. He needs a stable, calm, and quiet atmosphere in which he feels secure.

Socially. The two-or-three-year-old is an individualistic, self-centered person who lives in a small, narrow world. He is most familiar with and dependent on members of his family. He does not know how to relate to people generally, or even to those his own age. He likes to play alone but does not object to parallel play. He finds sharing very difficult. He often expresses himself negatively and responds with "NO"—sometimes because he does not know what else to say, or because he may not understand. He needs teachers and parents who cultivate much patience and can provide individual attention.

Spiritually. The nursery child learns spiritually through example, attitudes, and actions. His spiritual concepts are very limited, and what he learns must be taught simply and in view of his mental development. "Jesus loves me, the Bible is God's special book to me, and the church is where I can learn about Jesus and His love for me" are basic concepts the nursery child can learn. He believes what he is told, and therefore, needs the truth taught literally, simply, and clearly.

THE KINDERGARTEN CHILD—AGES FOUR AND FIVE

How is a four-and-five-year-old best described? There is a vast difference between the early four-year-old and the late five-year-old. Each child is an individual and will develop at his own rate. How can we view the child as a total personality?

Physically. He is growing rapidly—faster at four, somewhat slower at five. He is growing taller, and his larger muscles are still growing. He likes to hop, skip, and jump to stretch the larger muscles. He lacks in smaller muscular coordination. His eye-hand coordination is not good, but is improving. He needs a program in which he has freedom of movement, alternated with periods of activity and rest.

Mentally. Sometimes he is called the "Keen Kindergartner" because he has a very keen imagination that has reached its peak. He likes to pretend and sometimes tells exaggerated stories. He often mixes truth with error or fact with fantasy. He needs help in telling the difference, even when he is five. He is a literalist and thinks concretely. He uses many words he does not understand, mainly because he likes the sounds of BIG words! His functional vocabulary may range from five hundred to fifteen hundred words. His concepts of time, space, and number are limited, and he lives in the here and now. His attention span can stretch from five to seven minutes, with the maximum time usually being about ten minutes. If the activities are too long, he gets restless and wants to move physically. Parents and teachers will have fewer discipline problems if they provide change in activity and are personally involved.

Emotionally. The four-and-five-year-old has better control emotionally than his younger friends, although he may still have emotional outbursts. He has learned many fears. Some fears are due to insecurities in a growing, expanding world. He needs a stable and secure environment with adults he feels he can trust.

Socially. The kindergarten child's awareness of people and how to relate to them has increased greatly, and now he is becoming more interested in some group activities. He is conscious of "the group," but may be shy to join with others readily. He makes friends (some children more quickly than others), but changes friends frequently. Since he has a larger vocabulary, he talks more freely and is able to express himself more clearly. His emotions may be vented negatively through actions such as biting, scratching, shoving, or hitting, toward a younger brother, sister, or playmate.

Spiritually. The child's concepts are growing if he has been instructed properly in Bible knowledge. Parents play a major role in the spiritual development of the child. Spiritual teaching must be done in concrete and literal terms and related to everyday living. Jesus and God (he does not distinguish between the two) are very real to him, and he loves them very much. That love is best communicated through the example of his parents and teachers. He is credulous, and therefore, needs to be taught the truth. He likes to go to Sunday school and learn about Jesus. He likes to pray and tell Jesus he loves Him. His prayers are simple, self-centered, short, and usually sincere. A few children are ready to receive Christ as Savior, but need sufficient background in spiritual teaching to respond intelligently on an individual basis. Foundations in readiness in spiritual development are extremely important.

THE PRIMARY CHILD—AGES SIX THROUGH EIGHT

What is unique about the primary child? How is he different from the four- or five-year-old, or the energetic junior? Why is the primary child referred to as the "Pleasing Primary"? What is he like as a total person?

Physically. The primary child is growing rapidly and unevenly, and is uncoordinated in his finer muscles. He does not like long, intricate projects because of a lack of coordination. He has much energy and wants to be actively involved doing things with his entire being. It is possible for him to overdo because of his excessive energy and uneven growth. Individual development is erratic, and children should not be compared solely on the basis of their sizes.

Mentally. The primary child is a careful observer. He likes to see how things work and shows greater interest in the process than the product. He enjoys tearing things apart but usually gives up in putting them back together again. He is beginning to reason more verbally and express himself fluently. His vocabulary is increasing rapidly, with a vast difference evident between the early first grader and the later third grader.

He is beginning to learn the skills of reading and writing. Usually, the formal process begins in first grade, though the kindergarten has done much to prepare the child for the more formal steps. By the third grade the child has made great strides in reading and writing skills and in making the transition from printing to cursive writing.

The primary child is literal and concrete in his thinking and still does not make the transition from literal to symbolic or abstract thinking. Parents and teachers need to communicate on his level without talking down to him as though he were a little child. Primary children are developing a world view and are beginning to relate to the past and future. Most of their thinking and reasoning, however, are related to the immediate present. They do not think logically or chronologically.

He likes to please adults and attain to their standards, and as a result works toward perfection. He may become frustrated if too much is required of him and may get discouraged and give up if standards are set too high. The primary years are very important in developing a positive self-image. Parents and teachers need to do all they can to encourage and build wholesome self-concepts.

Emotionally. The primary child is very sympathetic to those his own age. He may be so moved by a story or illustration that he becomes tearful as he identifies with a child who has been injured, ill, or mistreated. He has a tender compassion and wants to express his love and concern in practical ways. What an ideal time to lay a foundation in missions!

He is still unstable in his emotional control. He has learned to gain more self-control through adult or peer pressure but expresses how he feels without thinking at times, especially when he is fatigued. Most of the time he is happy, noisy, and giggly, and one would think he does not have a care in the world. But he may be troubled about something at home or school and have difficulty in expressing his feelings. He needs to learn to express himself in acceptable ways so he does not become withdrawn or repressed.

Socially. The primary child is usually a friendly person who makes friends quickly, even with strangers. His friends tend to change often. Girls and boys have short-lived girl-and-boy-friend relationships. In the early primary years girls and boys play together frequently, but as they approach the third grade level, a gradual change takes place. Different interests develop. Play activities definitely become more selective. Most boys and girls choose members of the same sex for their playmates.

Group work is very appropriate for the primary child. He enjoys group activities and has begun to learn how to relate and socialize with other members of the group. He can take simple leadership roles and participate actively. A cooperative rather than a competitive spirit, with an emphasis on teamwork, is possible with adult supervision and guidance. Primaries can be taught to respect authority, be aware of others and their needs, and build positive interpersonal relationships through group work.

Spiritually. The Lord Jesus Christ can be real to primary children. If the children have been taught about Him, He is their very best and wonderful friend who can do anything! The primary child can understand literal biblical concepts that are taught on his intellectual and spiritual level. Parents and teachers can be models through their life example in such matters as consistent attendance and participation in church activities.

A primary knows right from wrong and can tell the difference between fact and fantasy. Scripture needs to be applied to familiar, everyday experiences. Salvation can be made understandable. The child may be ready to receive Christ as Savior. Home background will make a difference in ability to understand and comprehend the plan of salvation. The analogy of the human family and God's family may be one of the most effective ways to present the gospel. Terminology needs to be defined simply and clearly with literal and concrete explanations. The primary child may need assurance of salvation and what to do if he sins after becoming a child of God. With adult guidance, primary children can grow in Christ and witness for the Lord as they live for Him day by day.

> How should you teach primaries? In the ways they learn best—stories, questions, projects, role playing, reading, singing and drawing. Some learning activities demand seeing and hearing; other activities demand bodily movement, creative thinking and small muscle control. Spending an hour in one activity is never justifiable. Be ready to change activities to meet the children's needs and to accomplish your teaching goals.[6]

THE JUNIOR CHILD—AGES NINE THROUGH ELEVEN

What makes juniors different from other people? Why are they sometimes called "Jumping Juniors"? What are they like as total personalities? Juniors are in grades four, five, and six in school and are in the prime of life in many ways. The word "doer" can be written across their total personalities because they are *doers* in every way! What are they like more specifically?

Physically. They are abounding with energy! Juniors are very active and never seem to tire. They have excellent health and love the out-of-doors. Their lives are filled with many adventurous activities. They have slower and steady growth and are well coordinated in larger *and* finer muscles. Sometimes they are untidy in their personal appearance and care for personal property because they are too busy to be bothered.

Mentally. Juniors are exciting people to teach. They are alert, keen, and critical The questions they ask are thought-provoking and indicate they can think and reason logically. They may even question authority. Their concepts of time, space, and number have grown greatly. They now have a world view and can study maps, geography, and history. They are in the "golden age" of memory and therefore can memorize quickly and easily if challenged. They are beginning to understand symbolism and abstractions but have limitations in their thinking processes and still think literally.

Emotionally. The nine-through-eleven-year-olds have fewer fears than younger children. They like to impress people with their bravery and dislike being called "cowards" or "sissies." Sometimes they cover up their feelings because of peer pressure. Juniors enjoy telling jokes and have a strong sense of humor. Many times they are quick-tempered and react hastily in situations where they are put on the spot. Juniors can be loud, boisterous, and obnoxious, but can control their emotions if they are taught properly. They need teachers who are stable emotionally and do not get sentimental or upset easily.

Socially. Juniors have more awareness of their peers and are eager to be with them. It is more evident that they are seeking independence from adults. They are entering the "gang stage" with fellows or girls of the same sex. They thrive on competition because they are better coordinated, have slower and steadier growth, and are capable of practicing their skills. They are becoming more capable and need to assume greater responsibilities for their actions and behavior.

Spiritually. What age group is so ready for salvation? Juniors are very responsive to salvation and Christian growth if careful foundations have been laid in the earlier years. They are very capable investigators and can discover truth from the Bible for themselves with proper guidance. They can distinguish between right and wrong, and have a tender conscience toward God. They may try to cover up their spiritual needs by showing off or saying they really do not care. Hero worship is typical of juniors, and they are ready to be pointed to Jesus Christ as the perfect example whom they should follow. Those who have accepted Christ as Savior are able to have personal devotions and dedicate themselves for service to the Lord. Many juniors have given their lives to Christ for service because of their willingness and eagerness to be used.

> Building clubhouses, playing football, experimenting with chemistry sets, wrestling with their friends—juniors enjoy them all. Juniors are active and noisy and full of life. And they do not leave their interests and liveliness at home when they come to the church for Sunday school, worship, or club meetings. Juniors bring all of themselves along, sometimes to the dismay of the adult leaders. But to know junior-age children is to love them. They have a keen sense of loyalty, and if they know an adult appreciates them, they identify with that adult, are loyal to him, and learn much from him.[7]

Juniors are great people and have much in-depth potential if they are challenged. What a privilege and opportunity it is to get involved with them.

How to Teach to Meet Needs

Children are total personalities, and we must be aware of them as whole persons as we teach them. If a child is not feeling well physically, his mental capacities will be affected; he may be antisocial and display unacceptable behavior. He may not respond spiritually. Since he functions as a total person, we must acknowledge his needs for well-being in every area of personality. Sometimes a child does not know how to respond because he does not understand himself and why he feels the way he does. As we teach children we recognize several factors that must be considered.

TREAT AS INDIVIDUALS

Even though he may be similar in many ways to others his own age, each child is a unique person. We must respect and develop that uniqueness. A child may develop a low self-image if he is not accepted or is discouraged in his development during early childhood. Parents may tend to compare brothers and sisters and be negative in their comments and attitudes; that is not a wholesome practice. Naturally many children will be more outgoing, whereas others will be slower in their development, and some will be more attractive physically than others. All will probably be immature emotionally because they are children. Even with all the differences in maturation, we must treat each child as a special creation of God and work with the Lord in bringing out the best in each child. That is a great challenge to every parent and teacher, but will pay great dividends as the child develops as an individual.

BEGIN EARLIER IN LIFE

We cannot begin too soon to mold and guide children. Childhood specialists emphasize the importance of the prenatal period and the effects that a child's mother has on him during pregnancy. When a child is born, he knows little about his immediate environment and the expansive world that lies beyond. It is absolutely amazing what the child learns in those first few months of life! We cannot tell how much he is growing as a total person except in physical development. Researchers are discovering more about early childhood development in the intellectual, social, and emotional areas. We do not want to miss the opportunity to give children the best learning environments possible during the foundational years of development.

BEGIN WHERE CHILDREN ARE INTELLECTUALLY

We must begin where children are intellectually and challenge them to their maximum potential. The learning environments from which they come, their own intellectual capacities, the age levels represented, the vocabulary they use and understand, and the abilities they have in expressing themselves are all parts of their intellectual development. Children are eager learners, are curious creatures, and want to discover many things for themselves. Sometimes adults thwart children's learning because they "tell" them everything rather than let children discover for themselves. Why is it that many children lose the desire to learn or have their curiosity dulled by the time they have completed the elementary school years? Have teachers and parents capitalized on children's desire to discover and eagerness to be creative? If we are going to teach children effectively, we must know them as individuals, be aware of what capacities they have intellectually, recognize their strengths and limitations, and be alert to special areas of need.

BE AWARE OF HOW CHILDREN THINK AND LEARN

We must be aware of how children think and learn. Children think in literal, concrete, and specific terms. They cannot think symbolically, generally, or abstractly. In fact, Piaget in his studies found that children are not able to think abstractly until they reach the ages of eleven or twelve through fourteen. Many teachers and parents approach children on the adult level and teach them as though they were adults intellectually and spiritually. In the process, children learn to parrot and give answers they think adults want to hear without comprehending what has been taught. Children must learn with understanding in literal, concrete, and simple vocabulary that is on their level intellectually and spiritually. They need teaching that utilizes the sensory experiences, provides familiar, everyday, life-related experiences with which they can identify. They need to be involved in the self-discovery process during which they can discover truth for themselves. We cannot assume children understand and comprehend concepts without explanation. Naturally, children want to please; they will seek to gain recognition and acceptance by responding whether their answers make sense to them or not.

PROVIDE A MODEL-EXAMPLE

Parents and teachers need to provide a model for children to follow. There is probably nothing we can do that will have any greater affect on children than the example we live before them. What we *are* is far more significant than what we *say* or *do*. In Deuteronomy 6 we are reminded of the importance of parent-modeling in everyday life. Children are careful observers and see more than we realize. They sense the inconsistencies in adult lives, even though they may have difficulty in putting it all together. If we really love God, then we must *show* that love in reality with our actions as well as our words. If we say it is important to attend church, we must be consistent in attendance ourselves. If we say we ought to be loving, kind, and forgiving, then we must exemplify those qualities in our own lives. For children, the spiritual dimension is often caught more than taught. As adults, we have a tremendous responsibility to pliable and easily molded children.

TEACH WITH VARIETY IN PROCEDURE AND METHODOLOGY

Because of their short attention spans and need for activity, children must have variety. Adults can sit for longer periods of time, but children need to get up and move about to release energy stored in growing muscles. In fact, the younger the children, the more movement and space they need. If parents and teachers do not consider the need for variety and change, they automatically will have more behavior problems. Teachers need to be sensitive to the need for change of activity; when children become restless and begin to squirm, that is usually the signal for a change of pace.

Variety in methodology is important as we work with children. The variety may require physical as well as intellectual change. Children need methods that encourage self-discovery, interaction, and participation. The two-and-three-year old child needs ten to twelve changes of activity per hour, while the junior does not require as much physical change in activity. He can sit for longer periods of time if he is intellectually stimulated and has changes of mental activity. Younger children thrive on repetition of the same activities used in the same way. Older children at primary and junior levels need repetition but in a variety of ways to decrease boredom and stimulate their intellectual curiosities.

With the wide variety of modern technological equipment and current methodology, teachers need to broaden their use of creative methods to meet the needs of children. Of course, methods and resources should be chosen in view of the objective for the teaching session, but the teacher must be concerned about variety and involvement of the learner in the process.

MAKE TEACHING MORE LEARNER-CENTERED

The teacher has traditionally been central in the teaching-learning process. He plans the sessions, presents the content, and may do most of the talking. If we are concerned about meeting the needs of the student, we must shift the learning activities from the teacher to the learner. The role of the teacher changes from one who presents material to a guide or resource person. John Dewey said that the teacher is an advanced learner in the group. He certainly should know more than the pupils, but he serves as a guide and facilitator in the learning process. The child's interests and needs are met meaningfully through the process of self-discovery, interaction, and involvement. He becomes personally involved in the process. The session is planned to meet his needs and help him grow as a person.

Actually, the teacher will probably learn as much or more than the pupils. At least he will begin to be aware of individual needs and how he can meet those needs, stimulate individual pupils to learn and to grow, and observe significant changes in their behavior over a period of time. The teacher's responsibility is not to teach content, but to teach *pupils* the content that will produce changes in attitudes and behavior. What a challenge for the teacher who wants to meet individual needs and build interest in learning!

DEVELOP CREATIVITY THROUGH TEACHING

Children have much creative potential, but that potential must be developed. One of the reasons that children may not develop creativity is that they are stifled by adults. A parent or teacher may say, "Oh, you can't do that," or, "That is much too hard for you. You'll have to wait until you are more grown up to do that." Of course, the basic step in developing creativity is for the parent or teacher to set a good example of being creative himself. Rather than limit or discourage the child, the teacher can build positive attitudes toward being creative. He can encourage the child to try. An inquisitive spirit, a different way of doing, or an eagerness to learn a new task may develop the creative potential waiting for release.

Opportunities for creative thinking and doing must be integrated into teaching-learning situations. Opportunities for choice based on interest will encourage the child to venture out and try new ways of doing.

How to Discover Needs of Learners

Learners have many different kinds of needs. Some are basic to all, such as affection, security, belonging, and success. Other needs are unique to the age group. Young children need space to move about, thus providing opportunity for growth of muscles and to release excess energy. Some needs are individualized. Bill needs to know Christ as his personal Savior. Maria has a great need to learn patience with her younger brothers and sisters. How can we discover those needs?

Casual observation will reveal needs of learners. Be alert as you observe the group and individual. Comments, facial expressions, gestures, or questions asked may reveal a need. Seek to observe the individual in different types of situations to discover more about him as a total person. Personal discussion will also reveal needs.

Individual and small group counseling may help discover needs. Individuals may express themselves in small group sharing or in a one-to-one setting. The teacher can arrange to get together informally with an individual or plan a formal counseling session.

Become familiar with characteristics and needs of age groups. What is expected of children at a particular learning level? What are their needs as related to those expectations?

Social activities of various types will be helpful in determining needs as children display "the other side" of themselves, which may not be evident in a classroom setting.

THE RELATIONSHIP BETWEEN THE PERSON, HIS NEEDS AND TEACHING

In Christian teaching-learning we are concerned about what is happening to people. We teach people, not merely content or lessons from a manual or book. Each person must be taught as a total individual. Therefore, we must have a good understanding of the individual—his characteristics, patterns of growth and development, and his needs.

When we teach people we teach to meet needs. In Christian teaching the most important needs are spiritual. However, in order to meet spiritual needs, we must consider other areas as well. For example, a person must be comfortable physically if we hope to meet his intellectual and spiritual needs.

Needs in a teaching-learning situation may be as different as the number of individuals present. Some may be lacking in basic psychological areas such as love, acceptance, or recognition. Other learners may have problems with self-esteem or needs relating to their relationships with other people. Some individuals may need Christ as Savior, while others are in the process of growing in Christ and need help in specific areas of Christian growth. The teacher is confronted with the task of meeting various kinds of individual and group needs. In his preparation time, the teacher may find it helpful to list key pupil needs that he can consciously plan to meet through the content he is teaching. Whatever his approach, the teacher must be cognizant of needs and seek to meet those needs as he teaches. One of the great satisfactions in teaching-learning is when needs are being met and individuals are growing as persons.

FOR FURTHER STUDY

1. Select a child whom you know that you can observe in a variety of situations: home, play, church, and other settings. How does that child fit the characteristics described for his particular age group? What are some of his needs as a result of his characteristics?

2. Observe children at each department level in your church. Write a summary for each department. Describe the children physically, mentally, emotionally, socially, and spiritually. How does one group differ from another? How do your ideas compare with what is given in the text for each group?

3. Choose one department level from childhood with which you are most familiar. Imagine you are asked to speak to a group of teachers at that department level. What are several specific and practical suggestions that you could make to the teachers as they teach those children?

4. Select a particular age group in childhood. What basic theological concepts would you teach the child? Since the child is literal in his thinking, and cannot understand symbolism and abstractions, how would you teach him those concepts?

5. Make a list of the headings under the "How to Teach to Meet Needs" section. Observe a teaching-learning situation in which children are being taught. Evaluate the teaching being done in view of each of the factors listed.

NOTES

1. John Bergan and Ronald Henderson, *Child Development* (Columbus, Ohio: Merrill, 1979), p. 70.
2. Elsiebeth McDaniel and Lawrence O. Richards, *You and Children* (Chicago: Moody, 1973), pp. 19-21. See also Jack Smolensky, *A Guide to Child Growth and Development*, 2d ed. (Dubuque, Iowa: Kendall/Hunt, 1977), pp. 92-94.
3. Gladys Jenkins and Helen Shacter, *These Are Your Children*, 4th ed. (Glenview, Ill.: Scott, Foresman, 1975), p. 35.
4. Roy B. Zuck and Robert E. Clark, *Childhood Education in the Church* (Chicago: Moody, 1975), p. 58.
5. Ruth Beechick, *Teaching Preschoolers* (Denver: Accent, 1980), pp. 17-18.
6. Elsiebeth McDaniel, *There's More to Teaching Primaries* (Wheaton, Ill.: Scripture Press, Victor, 1976), p. 15.
7. Zuck and Clark, p. 107.

SUGGESTED READING

Bergan, John, and Henderson, Ronald. *Child Development.* Columbus, Ohio: Merrill, 1979. An excellent introductory child development text, which integrates developmental principles and processes with ages and stages in childhood.

Bolton, Barbara J., and Smith, Charles T. *Bible Learning Activties, Grades 1 to 6.* Glendale, Calif.: Gospel Light, Regal, 1973. Projects, games, discussion, and research designed to involve children in making personal discovery from God's Word.

Brubaker, Omar, and Clark, Robert. *Understanding People.* Wheaton, Ill.: Evangelical Teacher Training Assoc., 1972. An overview of the developmental stages in life with practical suggestions on how to meet needs.

Elkind, David. *The Child and Society.* New York: Oxford U., 1979. A book of essays that deal with issues in applied child development with the hopes of protecting and conserving children, our all important human resources.

Haystead, Wesley. *You Can't Begin Too Soon.* Glendale, Calif.: Gospel Light, Regal, 1974. A combination of biblical principles and educational insights on how to teach children theological concepts.

Jacobsen, Margaret. *What Happens When Children Grow.* Wheaton, Ill.: Scripture Press, Victor, 1977. Traces each age level through childhood by years with practical illustrations and suggestions particularly helpful to parents as teachers.

Jenkins, Gladys, and Shacter, Helen. *These Are Your Children.* 4th ed. Glenview, Ill.: Scott, Foresman, 1975. An excellent study of children by age levels based on clinical evidence and scientifically controlled research findings in child development and child experiences.

Jersild, Arthur; Telford, Charles; and Sawrey, James. *Child Psychology*. 7th ed. Englewood Cliffs, N.J.: Prentice-Hall, 1979. A classic work on child psychology.

Kagan, Jerome. *Understanding Children*. New York: Harcourt, Brace, Jovanovich, 1971. An integration of current psychological knowledge about children into practical suggestions for adults interested in understanding and educating children.

Larson, Jim, ed. *Make Learning a Joy*. Glendale, Calif.: Gospel Light, Regal, 1976. Practical helps for teachers and leaders of children, Grades 1 to 6.

McDaniel, Elsiebeth. *There's More to Teaching Primaries*. Wheaton, Ill.: Scripture Press, Victor, 1976. Practical how-to book for teachers of primary children, with suggested ways to improve teaching.

McDaniel, Elsiebeth, and Richards, Lawrence O. *You and Children*. Chicago: Moody, 1973. A book that gives practical helps in ministering to children. It includes the basic issues and suggests ways to grow in skill in communicating Bible truth to children.

Piaget, Jean. *The Child and Reality*. New York: Penguin, 1976. A highly refined and easily understood exposition of Piaget's nine essays, which provide a valuable resource in a study of human nature, development, and behavior.

Smolensky, Jack. *A Guide to Child Growth and Development*. 2d ed. Dubuque, Iowa: Kendall/Hunt, 1977. An informative and interesting book on child understanding based on new concepts, practices and research from sociological, psychological, anthropological, and medical areas with practical application integrated throughout the text.

Zuck, Roy B., and Clark, Robert E. *Childhood Education in the Church*. Chicago: Moody, 1975. A comprehensive volume treating all aspects of teaching children in the church.

10

The Learner: Youth

CHARLES H. NICHOLS

THE TEENAGER, with his wide-ranging and often colorful characteristics, is a major force in American culture. In the simplest identification he is a person who lives in a transition period between childhood and adulthood, in the age span from twelve to eighteen.

Broadly labeled as *youth*, he has a culture and characteristics all his own. Those who would work with him in a Christian context will do well to carefully consider both.

YOUTH CULTURE

Culture is defined as the habits, beliefs, value systems, and thought forms of a given people at a given time. Culture is at the very heart of our life-style. Larry Richards highlights this concept when he writes: "When we think of youth culture in Christian Education we need to break away from visions of long hair and loud music. What is important to us is not merely the symbols of youth difference, but the substance. And this substance consists of the set of values—the 'what's important to me'—that lies at the root of their understandings and experiences of life, and at the root of their decisions and choices."[1] To help us understand that culture, let us examine four areas involved.

Thrill seeking and living for the now are the *habits* of this age group. Thrill seeking has been a pastime of youth for generations, although existential humanism has heightened the impact. Thrills can come from many areas including taking risks, becoming involved in adventures, and seeking pleasures. Closely associated with seeking thrills is the emphasis on the immediate. The past is distant, the future remote, so all that is left is to

---

CHARLES H. NICHOLS, M.A., is chairman, department of Christian education, Grace College of the Bible, Omaha, Nebraska.

"live for the now." A resultant problem, of course, is the failure to recognize consequences, thereby opening the door to failure, frustration, and misspent living.

Beliefs of this age group are idealistic and superficial. With the jump from dependent childhood and the flight to "independent" adulthood comes the desire to champion a cause and to be free. Since youth feel they have broken what they sometimes consider adult oppression, they desire to do the same for others. But they have not lived long enough in the real world, thus life is often seen in a romantic "Don Quixote" perspective.

The "Belong Bunch" best describes their *value system.* Peer pressure governs much of what youth do. Although peer pressure has always been strong, there is a stronger thrust on the small group today. The mass pressure of the latter sixties and early seventies has waned. It is replaced by tight-knit subcultures. With the stronger emphasis on love (love based on what seems right), those peer groups challenge parental authority and personal convictions. Lawrence O. Richards summarizes by noting that there "seems to be a tendency for decisions to be made nonrationally, on impulse within a situational framework, and without conscious testing or extension of values."[2]

Paradoxical is the key word to describe youth *thought patterns.* Youth are seeking fun, but often find no happiness; freedom, but no liberty; moving, but nowhere to go. Since their habits, beliefs, and value systems are in a state of flux and are bombarded by the existential humanism of today, it is no wonder teens are confused in their thinking. Gone are the absolutes, only to be replaced by the pressures of conformity. They are told to grow up, then told that they are not old enough to do so.

What is our response to their culture? Several suggestions can be projected. First, develop a solid, biblical philosophy of youth ministry that emphasizes the constructive side of youth culture. Second, allow for their culture. Encourage the positive aspects. It is also vital that we do not try to be part of their culture. Youth do not need twenty-, thirty-, or forty-year-old teenagers. Third, know the specific youth culture of your area. Culture differs from place to place, and we cannot lump all youth into one mold.

YOUTH CHARACTERISTICS

The youth period is normally divided into two major stages. Early adolescence, ages twelve to fourteen, is normally identified as junior high. Middle adolescence, ages fifteen to seventeen, is titled senior high. To provide a comparative developmental study the two stages are viewed for each of the major areas: physical, mental, social, emotional, and spiritual. This will provide not only a basic understanding of each age group but will also emphasize the developmental pattern.

PHYSICAL

A. *Early Adolescence*
   1. Body development is rapid and irregular, causing awkwardness and self-consciousness.
   2. Body contour starts to show signs of adulthood, causing difficulties if body over- or underdevelops.
      a. Girls tend to develop narrow shoulders, larger bust, broad hips, and curved legs.
      b. Boys tend to develop broad shoulders, narrow hips, muscular build, and deeper voices.
   3. Internal organs also develop rapidly, which results in energetic people who tire easily. There are rapid lung development, large heart capacity, and active glandular changes.
   4. General health is good, but posture is a problem.
   5. Physical capabilities of reproduction (puberty) heighten sex drives.

B. *Middle Adolescence*
   1. Body development has taken on adult features with boys usually gaining the height advantage.
   2. Body contours are even more pronounced, which can cause greater trauma for those who develop irregularly. (A physically over-developed individual can have as many problems, if not more, than a physically underdeveloped person.)
   3. Internal organ growth starts to level out, although acne is still a major glandular problem.
   4. General health is good, although sleeping and eating habits are generally poor.
   5. Sexual feelings and drives are more active and intense in boys than in girls, although once aroused the sex drive of girls tends to last longer.

C. *Principles for parents and teachers*
   1. Create an acceptance of the physical makeup. You accept them the way they are. Share Psalm 139:13-16.
   2. Develop a spiritual attitude toward the body (Rom. 12:1-3; 1 Cor. 6:19).
   3. Develop a concept that the body is a vehicle for worshiping God.

MENTAL

A. *Early Adolescence*
   1. There is a problem with distinguishing between the real and the imaginary because of the imaginative process carried over from childhood.

2. There is a tendency to be critical and make snap judgments because of developing abstract thought, independence, and lack of experience.
3. Junior high youth tend to be inquisitive and curious because new reasoning powers are developing.
4. They are often hesitant in expressing themselves or answering questions, but that is due more to a fear of failure than lack of knowledge.
5. This is the time to link Bible truths in chronological order, since their ability to group the meaning of the historical past is improved.

B. *Middle Adolescence*
   1. They are "why," "what," and "how" oriented, because their minds are maturing.
   2. Because of broader experience, they are developing interest in various career fields.
   3. Because they have a sharpening ability in abstract thought, senior high students like to debate and discuss.
   4. They are thinking independently, and they challenge ideas and concepts previously accepted.

C. *Principles for parents and teachers*
   1. Work with their interests, not yours.
   2. Teach the difference between improper criticism and honest evaluation.
   3. Use their ability to think and ask questions as positive teaching tools.
   4. Be honest about your own knowledge.

SOCIAL

A. *Early Adolescence*
   1. This is a period of expanding social experience and contacts, thus it is a socially demanding time.
   2. This period is marked by immature behavior and teasing because they want social recognition but do not know how to get it.
   3. Junior high youth are marked by a craving for status and acceptance.
   4. Discipline becomes a real problem because social acceptance is more valued than authority structure.
   5. Parental problems start to arise because of the natural drive from dependence to independence.

B. *Middle Adolescence*
   1. Parental problems become more acute. They especially abhor "overprotection" and "apron strings."

2. Deeper friendships develop, especially in the dating or "going steady" process.
3. Conformity to the group gets stronger, especially in dress, language, and fads.
4. High school youth desire to be popular and want leadership positions, especially among their peers.
5. They do show social concern, especially to those who are going through struggles.

C. *Principles for parents and teachers*
   1. Provide information, interpretation, and example to help develop scriptural social attitudes.
   2. Give them qualified approval and acceptance. (Accept the person, not necessarily the action.)
   3. Present Jesus Christ as the ideal social man.

EMOTIONAL

A. *Early Adolescence*
   1. Self-concept is very important, especially in evaluating the actions of others toward them.
   2. Emotional instability is extremely high because of the changing glandular conditions. Emotional responses will be greatly varied, will hit extremes, and will change rapidly.
   3. This is a period of crushes, especially on older youth and adults. Those crushes will pass quickly if not encouraged.
   4. Emotions are generally expressed through outbursts that tend to be more physical than verbal (withdrawal, hitting, and similar actions).
   5. Discouragement and feelings of guilt and frustration are felt strongly because of the lack of emotional control. This usually results in temporary withdrawal from activities and people.

B. *Middle Adolescence*
   1. High school youth tend to become self-centered, often thinking more highly of themselves than they ought to.
   2. Emotional control is improving but moodiness is still a major problem. (Their moods last longer than when in early adolescence.)
   3. Fear, anger, and love are usually the strongest emotions displayed, and they are interlaced in an intricate network.
   4. Greatest emotional needs are acceptance and security, without which they develop either an inferiority complex or an aggressive attitude.
   5. Their feelings run deep, which often causes misunderstandings, confusion, and frustration.

C. *Principles for parents and teachers*
1. Judge emotional responses at the proper age level.
2. Show emotional consistency and maturity yourself.
3. Share scriptural values of sex, love, and other emotional responses.
4. Take time to be with youth so you know their emotional needs.

SPIRITUAL

A. *Early Adolescence*
1. Because of the natural individual differences in young teens, they will differ in spiritual readiness and understanding.
2. Junior high students' lack of maturity and discernment gives them a mixed sense of right and wrong.
3. Because they have a desire for acceptance, they are sensitive in conscience.
4. Major moral problems for young teens seem to be profanity and stealing.
5. They are able to make and understand total commitment.

B. *Middle Adolescence*
1. Because of their questioning minds, fifteen to seventeen-year-olds start to doubt spiritual things and want to question why and how.
2. Because of their idealism, they want reality and genuineness in their Christianity.
3. They desire clear, biblical, spiritual leadership that demonstrates practical Christianity.
4. They are asking three basic questions: Who am I? Where do I fit in? Is it worth it?
5. Youth at this age want and need to be challenged spiritually.

C. *Principles for parents and teachers*
1. Get *them* into the Word of God. (Do not spoon-feed.)
2. Channel their efforts into outreach ministries.
3. Help them develop biblical principles and godly habits.
4. Be there to help them and be an example.

What is our response toward teenagers? Again, three positive steps can be taken. First, see each youth as a total person. How he feels about his appearance affects his social life. His mental concepts affect his emotions. All of his characteristics need to be brought under the discipline of the Holy Spirit so he can become conformed to the image of Christ. Second, use those characteristics. Work with them, using the guiding principles noted at the end of each characteristic area. Third, develop yourself as a total person. Youth ministry is people-to-people oriented. If our example is to be vital, then we, too, must conform to the image of Christ.

YOUTH WORK

There is no one pattern for successful youth work. Variations in the local youth culture, the particular talents and abilities of the youth workers, and a variety of similar factors all relate to the effectiveness of a given youth ministry.

However, there are some basic factors to keep in mind. The first of these is the foundation of a *life-related theology*. "A Christian youth ministry should be an extension of one's theology. The accent should not be on problem-solving (overcoming fears, gaining confidence, improving one's self-concept), but on helping youth to become aware of possibilities found in a relationship with Jesus Christ."[3]

Close behind its biblical orientation, youth work demands *exemplary leadership*. Those who teach and minister with youth are obliged to demonstrate what they share. This was the pattern with Jesus Christ.

Merton P. Strommen summarizes as he comments on the responses of successful youth leaders: "Virtually all, in some part of their free responses, used a desire to influence youth in directions consonant with the Christian way of life as their predominant motive. And this motive clearly arose out of love, concern, and profound respect for youth."[4]

Finally, there is *goal-oriented programming*. Although programs are secondary to relationships in ministry, they are necessary. A good teaching situation, an active youth meeting, or a good social all need content and direction, and that is programming. Youth programming must be based on clear objectives, such as confronting youth with the biblical message in a meaningful relationship to their environment; developing principles for effective, independent study of God's Word; or developing godly patterns of living.

Goal-oriented programming is planned with the needs of the youth group in mind. It is also planned in terms of balance. That balance must not only relate to elements of programming (worship, fellowship, instruction, service), but also to levels of commitment. Lawrence O. Richards points out in *Youth Ministry: Its Renewal in the Local Church* that a major problem in youth programming is that it is often directed toward the fringe and unreached (see figure 10:1). He suggests that more attention be given to the attenders and especially to the core group. That means that the deeper the young person's commitment, the greater his need for personal involvement with adults and other youth believers in programming related to discipleship development, service opportunities, and in-depth Bible study. "Big events" and interaction sessions are needed for the fringe and unreached groups.

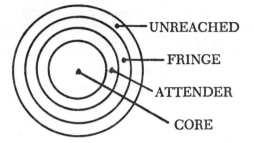

1. *Core Youth* = I am personally committed to Christ and this fellowship.
2. *Attender* = I enjoy coming regularly to this group.
3. *Fringe Youth* = I attend when it is something that interests me or when I don't have something else to do.
4. *Unreached Youth* = I could care less.

Fig. 10.1

FOR FURTHER STUDY

1. To better understand today's youth, interview three teenagers and relate the interview to the contents of the chapter.
2. Do a comparison chart of various approaches to youth ministry.
3. Discuss the concept that "youth are the church today." Is that true? What are the implications to the youth? To the church?
4. Write your own philosophy of youth ministry. State what you believe the Bible teaches about youth ministry and what you consider especially important.

NOTES

1. Lawrence O. Richards, *Youth Ministry: Its Renewal in the Local Church* (Grand Rapids: Zondervan, 1972), p. 22.
2. Ibid., p. 21.
3. Merton P. Strommen, *Five Cries of Youth* (New York: Harper & Row, 1974), p. 30.
4. Ibid., p. 118.

SUGGESTED READING

Felske, Norma. *Teaching That Grabs Young Teens.* Wheaton, Ill.: Scripture Press, Victor, 1976.

Frans, Mike. *Are Junior Highs Missing Persons from Your Youth Ministry?* Wheaton, Ill.: Scripture Press, Victor, 1979.

Hooton, Ardith, and Heidebrecht, Paul. *Teaching Today's Teens.* Wheaton, Ill.: Scripture Press, Victor, 1976.

Ignatius, Keith, and Carroll, John. *Youth Ministry: Sunday, Monday and Every Day.* Valley Forge, Pa.: Judson, 1972.

Kessler, Jay. *Let's Succeed with Our Teenagers.* Elgin, Ill.: David C. Cook, 1973.

Komarnick, Dan. *Teenagers Are People.* New York: Exposition, 1968.
Reed, Bobbie, and Reed, Ed. *Creative Bible Learning for Youth.* Glendale, Calif.: Gospel Light, Regal, 1977.
Richards, Lawrence O. *Youth Ministry: Its Renewal in the Local Church.* Grand Rapids: Zondervan, 1972.
————. *You and Youth.* Chicago: Moody, 1973.
Zuck, Roy, and Benson, Warren. *Childhood Education in the Church,* Chicago: Moody, 1978.

11

The Learner: Adults

Rodney G. Toews

THE CHRISTIAN EDUCATION of adults in the North American church has experienced a wide diversity of expression in recent history. At one extreme churches are offering a highly organized system of Bible study classes, home prayer-and-share groups, weeknight Bible seminars, and men's and women's study groups, to complement a strongly didactic emphasis from the pastor in the pulpit. At the other end of the continuum, Christian education for adults is no more than a Sunday morning sermon or Bible class lecture led by the pastor or one of the elder statesmen of the church.

Unfortunately, the latter end of the spectrum appears to be the prevailing one. Churches tend to relegate the Bible teaching ministry to the pastor or to someone else in the congregation who can "tell them what they need to know." The systematic approach to Bible study with adults, emphasizing personal and small group interaction with the Scriptures under the guidance of a capable teacher (not just an accomplished theologian), is definitely a minority situation.

Furthermore, observation has shown that Christian education for adults in most churches is subservient to Christian education for the other age groups. Christian education funds, teacher training efforts, facilities, equipment, and curriculum resources may be funneled generously into the Bible instruction of children and youth. Often, though, it is only whatever money, room, equipment, or other teaching material is left over from teaching the younger learners that is available for the adult classes. That is why many adult Bible classes meet in church kitchens, pastors' studies, or similar secondary classrooms.

RODNEY G. TOEWS, B.D., is vice president of ministries, Gospel Light Publications, Ventura, California.

But some provocative information is surfacing on adult population trends that has much to say to the struggling, straggling adult Christian education program. Whereas the sixties and early seventies were the years of the booming youth culture, the last quarter of the twentieth century is seeing a marked growth in the adult population. The post-World War II baby boom swelled the midcentury American population with young people. But the postwar babies and midcentury young people have grown up. They are now the young and middle adults of the last two decades of the twentieth century.

The United States Department of Commerce reported that in 1970 people under age 21 accounted for 40 percent of the population, whereas young adults (aged 21-39) made up 24 percent. But the commerce department also projects that children and youth will constitute only 32 percent of the population by 1990, whereas young adults will account for 30 percent (an increase of 6 percent). During the same time span, middle-aged adults (40-64 years) will remain 26 percent of the population, but the elderly (65 and over) will increase from 10 percent to 12 percent of the population.[1]

Secular adult education has been reflecting the groundswell of that population shift for some time in the rising popularity of continuing education programs for adults. But the shift also has far-reaching implications for the Christian education program in the local church. No longer can the adult department be expected to meet the needs of its growing constituency with the "leftovers" from the other departments. Those churches that will successfully meet the challenge of the new influx of adults must make Christian education to adults a priority in their planning.

CHARACTERISTICS AND NEEDS OF ADULTS

At some time after graduating from high school, reaching age eighteen, enlisting in military service, securing a full time job, and/or marrying, a young person in our culture is labeled "adult," a label that stays with him until death. Because adulthood covers such a wide time span in a person's life, and a general description of characteristics and needs of adults cannot accommodate specific traits of each stage of adult development, adulthood will be discussed in three categories—young adult, middle adult, and older adult.

YOUNG ADULT

One word that accurately summarizes and characterizes the young adult age group (18-35) is *decision*. During those early years of adulthood the young adult is called upon to make several decisions that will affect his life-style for the remaining years of life. Even though early decisions can be reversed, those choices make a lifelong impact on the individual and others whose lives the decisions intersect.

Deciding about faith. The most critical decision to be made as a young person launches into adulthood regards his Christian commitment. It is to be hoped that the individual who has grown up in a Christian environment has, in his childhood or youth, made the leap from his parents' faith to his own personal faith in God. But many persons rely on the religious expression of their parents or Christian environment as long as they are in that environment. With the dawn of adult independence, which may take shape in leaving home for school, work, marriage, or military service, each individual must affirm a personal decision to walk with God. That decision will affect every other decision made throughout adulthood.

Deciding about marriage. Generally during young adulthood, each person must decide whether to travel alone or in tandem through the journey of adult life. Those who opt for marriage acrue an entire package of decisions that will dominate much of their young adulthood and beyond: Whom and when shall I marry? How do I compatibly assimilate another person into my life-style? Shall we bear children? If so, how many and how soon?

Those who choose to marry, but do not find a suitable marriage partner, must decide how to adapt to a life-style that, in their minds, is a secondary preference. Those who choose to remain single face decisions regarding their relationship to a predominantly family-oriented culture.

Deciding about education and occupation. Once the requirements of mandatory education are met, the young adult must decide between continuing education, in college or trade school, and seeking immediate full-time employment upon which to base a career. Those who opt for education must decide where to attend and what course of study to follow. Those who look toward an immediate career must choose a trade or line of work in which they want to invest their lives.

Deciding about social relationships. Whether single or married, the young adult needs to select a peer group with whom he will interrelate and find his needs for social interaction met. Those needs will often motivate a young single or couple in their search for a church group, a social club, a neighborhood, or even a community or geographic location that appeals to them.

Young adults feel a need to achieve a desired level of status through occupation, financial security, and social acceptance. The church can be of ultimate service to young adults by affirming and assisting them as they find their way through the valley of decision which is young adulthood.

MIDDLE ADULTS

The years of middle adulthood (36-59) could be called the *earning* years. By this stage of adulthood most people have established and are in the process of maintaining or improving a pattern for present and future economic stability.

Paradoxically, middle-aged adults often find themselves uncomfortable living out the choices made in young adulthood and in the evaluation judge them to be no longer valid. It is not uncommon to find men and women in middle age jettisoning well-established careers and families in search of fulfillment for their midlife values and interests. Although the Christian subculture in America traditionally reports much more stable and lasting family relationships than the norm, midlife career change seems to be as evident among believers as in the general population. In the midst of re-evaluating some of the decisions of young adulthood, middle-aged adults have a unique set of responsibilities all their own.

Civic and social responsibility. Middle-aged adults tend to bring an aura of stability to civic, social, and church activities. During early adulthood, participation and membership in community, church, and business groups is low but peaks in middle age. Many middle adults have a greater appreciation for their social relationships and have more freedom to devote to those activities.[2] Their financial stability is a major factor in the success of many of those programs.

Guiding teenagers to adulthood. Those couples who produced children as young adults now experience, in middle adulthood, the responsibilities, pressures, and rewards of leading their offspring across the bridge between childhood and adulthood. Those years often place great strain on the family as teens exercise their wings of independence. Middle-aged parents must find the delicate balance between maintaining family unity while gradually untying the apron strings.

Facing the empty nest. Parents who have centered their young- and middle-adult years on their children often face a critical dilemma when the last of the offspring leave home: What do we live for now that the kids are gone? Parents need to prepare for living as a couple alone even while the children remain at home. Then when their children leave home they will be well prepared for their life-style changes.

Accepting and adjusting to physical change. A major concern among middle adults is the physical effect of aging. Though the diminishing of physical strength and vitality is often overstated, middle age is normally the beginning of physical deterioration of many bodily functions. Middle adults must adapt a continuingly positive attitude about their limitations (energy, vision, hearing, for example) and make adjustments in their life-styles accordingly.

OLDER ADULTS

With the advancement of medical technology and emphasis on healthful diet and life-style, the years of older adulthood (60 and over) hold bright promise for the senior citizens of our culture. The idea that the usefulness of senior adults is minimal is an improper generalization.

Physical adjustments. Certainly there are increased physical limitations for those above sixty, but they should in no way be considered useless or inferior. Senior adults have a great reservoir of wisdom and experience upon which younger generations may draw with profit. But there are certain characteristics of older adults that must be kept in mind. Older adults do not possess the strength, agility, or endurance of younger adults. Often their liabilities mask their keen minds and other abilities.

Economic adjustment and retirement. With the major share of his earning days behind him, the older adult must rely upon the nest egg of his pension, investments, social security, or other preplanned provisions for his livelihood. Furthermore, a retiree must adjust to accommodate a new role—if not as a productive worker in a post-retirement career or avocation, at least as a creative occupant of increased leisure time. Many adults at retirement tend to "unplug" themselves from society and activity, and thus find themselves with little to occupy their quiet days. Such a posture of "giving up" can lead to early deterioration of physical and mental faculties. Older adults need to find creative ways of occupying their time within the framework of possible budget limitations due to reduced retirement income.

Adjusting to the loss of loved ones. Many couples anticipate a long and productive retirement together. Then suddenly one partner is gone, and the surviving mate faces the prospect of a lonely end. Women experience losing their spouses at a much higher rate than men, and most of the women left alone by the death of a spouse do not remarry.

When death occurs in the senior years, the partner is cast again into the valley of decision: Shall I continue to live alone? Where shall I move? What about living with the children? What about a retirement home? Who will care for me? A widow or widower in the senior years must be helped to find activities and friends to help fill the void left by a partner's death and to combat the gripping loneliness that can result.

THE DISTINCTIVES OF ADULT CHRISTIAN EDUCATION

Many of the principles discussed in this chapter broadly apply to Christian education at all age levels. But the Christian education of adults has some unique qualities that must be honored in the program of the local church. Teaching adults is *not* the same as teaching children. Several factors that are not present in the Christian education of younger learners come to bear on the adult learning experience.

When children and youth attend Sunday school and other educational experiences, they come with a backdrop of a week-long, formal learning atmosphere. They spend many hours in the secular classroom, so the Bible classroom blends with other learning experiences.

But the adult comes into the Christian education arena from the world of business, politics, and social experiences. Therefore it may take longer for adults to adjust to the formal learning atmosphere than it does for younger learners. The teacher of adults must carefully foster the learning atmosphere that is often absent in the adult's business/family-oriented life.

Second, adults come into the Bible classroom with a wealth of personal experiences from the years they have spent as adults. That experience provides a valuable resource for the Christian educator to draw upon in the application of Bible truth to life situations.

Similarly, adults attend Bible study with more concrete, established ideas than younger Bible students have. As such, adults may find it more difficult to accept new ideas into their already solidified thought patterns and opinions. Care must be taken to introduce new ideas carefully and gradually in order for adult learners to integrate them through the existing grid of time-honored notions, traditions, and patterns of thought.

Third, adults are more capable of self-directed learning than are children and youth. A group of adults may accept a Bible study assignment and carry it to successful conclusion and application with little direction from the teacher. But younger learners must be supervised more closely in order to keep them on track and guide them to the desired conclusions.

The Objectives of Christian Education for Adults

In one sense, to reach adulthood is to arrive at a plateau of achievement and growth not equaled in scope throughout the remainder of an adult's life. Formal schooling is basically completed, independence is achieved, autonomy is realized. But growth and development do not end for an individual simply because he or she has married, enrolled in college or graduate school, or taken a first job on the stairway to a promising career. Adults continue to grow, change, and develop emotionally, mentally, socially, and spiritually. They will enlarge their capacities and establish and reach goals throughout their lifetimes. Indeed, when the process of growth and development ceases in adults, stagnation begins a downward spiral that can eventuate in early death.

Curiously, the church has sometimes lost sight of the onward growth needs of adults. Many local churches have fostered the attitude that adults have finished their Christian education when they graduate from the high school or college department of the Sunday school. "We know all the books of the Bible, the key Bible stories, and we have memorized several years worth of Bible verses," comment many adults. "My Christian education is complete."

But continuing growth and development in the area of Christian education is as much or more of a need for adults as other adult developmental needs. The need for Bible study and its application to all of the ever-changing facets of adult life never ends. Christian education is a lifelong endeavor.

Four objectives must be kept in focus when considering a program of Christian education for adults. Each is distinct in its purpose, but the four dovetail to form a unified emphasis for adult ministries.

WARMTH AND ACCEPTANCE

Every person alive has a basic need to be accepted and loved by others. But our fast-paced, impersonal, computerized life-style tends to isolate individuals and groups and often prevents this basic need from being met. Furthermore, approximately 27 percent of the population of the United States moves its residence every year, leaving friends and associates behind again and again. Sociologists state that that mobility contributes to people's being set adrift on a sea of anonymity. Loneliness and a feeling of isolation have become characteristics of modern existence, and people are finding their need for friendship, love, and acceptance unmet.

What better place is there for a person to find warmth and acceptance than in the local church setting? But building an atmosphere of warmth and acceptance among adults means more than potluck suppers, baby showers, and men's fellowship breakfasts. True fellowship is the discipline by which individuals begin to accept and care for each other through specific, selfless words and actions. Deep, caring relationships result from consistent, disciplined interaction between persons who are willing to commit themselves to each other for the edification and growth of one another.

Obviously an individual cannot commit himself to care for an entire church on a personal basis. A person can only care effectively for a limited number of persons; there are not enough hours in the day to care for one's entire church or community. Even Jesus, though he ministered to multitudes, was involved in a relationship of caring and fellowship with only twelve men. The greater the numbers, the greater the difficulty in maintaining a level of commitment to individuals, which requires time, effort, and sometimes even money.

The most effective and naturally available vehicle for the ministry of caring among adults is the adult Sunday school. In most cases, the adult department of the Sunday school is already divided into departments of managable size (young adults, singles, college-career, couples). A person who could not realistically care for his entire church could care for a small group made up of class members. Theoretically, if every individual in the church belongs to a class (if not in person, at least on the records), and each class is diligently committed to meeting the needs for warmth and acceptance in each of its members, then all the adults will be cared for. It may never work out quite as idealistically as it sounds, but at least it illustrates the practicality of using the adult Sunday school as the basis for creating an atmosphere of warmth and acceptance among the adults in the church.

Many churches are finding that the formation of caring groups in the adult Sunday school class or among the adult members of the congregation is a practical way to express warmth and acceptance. Caring groups are people voluntarily meeting together in organized small groups for the purpose of Christian edification.[3] Often an adult Sunday school class is broken into small groups (six to twelve persons each), which meet regularly at a time other than Sunday morning to get better acquainted, pray and share, study the Bible, and reach out to others in their church and community.

The caring group becomes for each adult the focus of caring and a resource for warmth and acceptance for a set period of time (six months to one year). Each person will get to know his caring group better than any other group of people in the church, and in turn they will get to know him, his needs, his victories, and his hurts. Within the framework of deepening relationships, caring groups are able to "rejoice with those who rejoice, and weep with those who weep" (Romans 12:15) in more specific and meaningful ways than is possible with a large congregation.

BIBLE STUDY

A second objective for adult Christian education is consistent Bible study. The depth and riches of God's Word are immeasurable. No one can exhaust its treasures in a lifetime. Nor does any one person ever reach a point where he can say, "I know the Bible completely," or, "There is nothing new for me to gain from studying God's Word." Adults have the constant and continuing need to explore and discover what God's Word says and means in their lives.

Bible study implies firsthand interaction with God's Word. Bible *preaching* is the ministry of one individual, which enlightens the listeners to the point where they are inspired and challenged to commitment. Bible *teaching*, however, is the process of one individual's guiding another (or group of others) in the firsthand discovery of what God's Word says. In preaching, the preacher *tells* the listener what he believes God wants him to know. In teaching, the teacher creates a learning environment in which the learners are brought into contact with the Word through personal reading, discussion, interaction, and creative activity to the point where they are discovering for themselves, under the teacher's careful guidance, what God is saying to them through His Word.

Most churches generously provide ample preaching for their constituents—a sermon on Sunday morning, Sunday evening, and possibly in a midweek service. Churches need inspiring Bible preaching, but they also need in-depth teaching that involves adults in reading, outlining, discussing, and explaining the Word of God together.

Why is it so important to involve adult learners in Bible study? Is a good Bible lecture not sufficient to instill the principles of God's Word into the lives of adults? Several independent studies have verified that people learn best when they are involved in the teaching-learning process. That is why it is much easier to teach a person how to swim by making him experiment with simple strokes and kicks in the shallow end of a pool than to have him study a chapter on swimming fundamentals in a textbook. The Bible is not a series of principles merely to be memorized and meditated upon, but contains guidelines outlining how people should live. Thus the exercise of studying God's Word and applying its principles to life as adults is a skill to be learned and practiced. The skill of godly living, just like the skill of swimming, driving a car, balancing a checkbook, or hitting a tennis ball, is learned best through the give-and-take involvement of learning with other adults. Therefore Bible study, in order to produce the consistent Christian life-style in adults, must be learner-involving in its nature.

There are at least two approaches to basic Bible study for adults. One approach is to study the Bible in a book-by-book, verse-by-verse fashion. Studying the Bible in that manner allows the learner to discover and appropriate life principles as they appear in the flow of each complete Bible book. A second approach is to focus on common themes of Scripture in topical studies of the Bible. In the former approach, a class may study prayer when it arises in the course of studying a Bible book. In the latter, the theme of prayer may be selected first, and learners directed to many sections of the Bible where instructions on prayer may be found.

Both approaches have their merits, but both are most effective when the teaching techniques employed are those involving the learners in discovering God's truth for themselves.

As in the warmth and acceptance objective, the most available vehicle for adult Bible study in the local church is the adult department of the Sunday school. Sunday morning Bible classes are traditionally the most accepted period in the church week for in-depth Bible instruction. As such, many churches find success in making the Sunday school hour the main Bible study hour for the week, whereas weeknight caring groups hold the focus of bringing groups together to foster fellowship, group building, and mutual acceptance.

APPLICATION TO LIFE

There are three basic questions in Bible study that each teacher of adults must lead the learners to answer for themselves: (1) What did the Bible passage mean to the original readers? (2) How does that meaning apply to the lives of Christians in the twentieth century? (3) What personal response shall I make to what God is saying in the passage?

The first question helps the learner discover what the passage *says,* whereas the latter two questions lead the learner to apply to his life-style the message of the passage. The first emphasis relates to Bible *information,* the second relates to Bible *application.* Both are indispensable to meaningful Bible study.

Bible information without Bible application can become sterile religious history and philosophy. Many people have memorized large sections of the Bible, but their lives remain largely unchanged because their contact with Scripture was solely at the informational level. Bible information must lead to Bible application.

Similarly, Bible application without the firm foundation of Bible information can be dangerous. Trying to establish principles for living and relating to God and others without researching the information of the Bible is like trying to build a house without a blueprint. There is no guarantee that the finished product will be reliable protection from the elements. Likewise, an authentic Christian life-style must be based on the authority of the *Word* of God or it is no better than the code of ethics created by any godless heathen.

The focal point of the application of Scripture in the life of the adult learner is his personal response to what God has said. In other words, each individual learner must assume personal responsibility to respond by the application of Scripture to his life. The alert adult teacher will include in his instruction opportunities for learners to help each other make those life-changing responses.

OUTREACH

As the first three objectives of adult Christian education are being reached, the fourth will happen almost automatically. When people find themselves in an atmosphere where they are accepted, appreciated, and cared for, and when they discover the Bible to be the living, life-changing, need-meeting Word of God as it is applied to their lives, they will want to share their blessings with others who may be aimlessly enduring an unfulfilling life.

Even though much outreach may be a spontaneous by-product of a successful Christian education program for adults, the church should provide some structure for the systematic outreach of those outside its boundaries. Again, the adult Sunday school class offers a viable framework for adult outreach. The adult class stands as a half-step into the fellowship of the church due to its less threatening size and generally winsome informality. An individual who steadfastly refuses an invitation to a worship service may be kindly disposed to attend a class social event or home group activity with his believing neighbors. Once the invitee experiences the warmth and acceptance of the small group and becomes introduced to the life of the church through the medium of the adult class, his attitude toward the church and God may be healed.

Other aspects of adult outreach that come into play in the local church might include visitation of class absentees, visitors, and prospects; evangelistic Bible studies or campaigns; neighborhood canvass and census; and intensive training for personal evangelism.

The goal of outreach must be seen as enlisting adults to begin the cycle of the previously noted objectives.

NOTES

1. "America's Adults: In Search of What?" *U. S. News and World Report,* 21 August 1978, p. 56.
2. Monroe Marlowe and Bobbie Reed, *Creative Bible Learning for Adults,* (Glendale, Calif.: Gospel Light, 1977), p. 32.
3. Neal McBride, *The Adult Class: Caring for Each Other* (Glendale, Calif.: Gospel Light, 1977), p. 5.

SUGGESTED READING

Carrier, Wallace H. *Teaching Adults in Sunday School.* Nashville: Convention, 1976.

Cole, W. Douglas. *Working with Senior Adults in Sunday School.* Nashville: Convention, 1977.

Gould, Roger L. "The Phases of Adult Life: A Study in Developmental Psychology." *The American Journal of Psychiatry,* November 1972, pp. 33-34.

Gross, Ronald. "Toward a Learning Society: Adult Educators Engage a World of Challenge." *Lifelong Learning—The Adult Years,* January 1978, pp. 18-24.

Hollaway, Ernest, and Fitch, James. *Working with Adults in Sunday School.* Nashville: Convention, 1974.

Knowles, Malcolm. *The Adult Learner: A Neglected Species.* Houston: Gulf, 1973.

Lawson, Linda. *Working with Single Adults in Sunday School.* Nashville: Convention, 1978.

Leypoldt, Martha M. *40 Ways to Teach in Groups.* Valley Forge, Pa.: Judson, 1971.

————. *Learning Is Change.* Valley Forge, Pa.: Judson, 1971.

Marlowe, Monroe, and Reed, Bobbie. *Creative Bible Learning for Adults.* Glendale, Calif.: Gospel Light, Regal, 1977.

O'Neill, Nena, and O'Neill, George. *Shifting Gears.* New York: Avon Books,, 1974.

Schaller, Lyle E. *Hey, That's Our Church!* Nashville: Abingdon, 1975.

Sheehy, Gail. *Passages: Predictable Crises of Adult Life.* New York: E. P. Dutton, 1974.

Zuck, Roy B., and Getz, Gene A. *Adult Education in the Church.* Chicago: Moody, 1970.

12

Planning for Teaching

Lois E. LeBar

WHEN WE BEGIN to prepare a Bible lesson at home, we must begin with the Lord; when we begin to teach pupils in a class, we should begin with those pupils. Since the Lord is the teacher's Teacher, we must first wait before Him for His directions. Acknowledging that the wisdom and power are His, we offer ourselves to be used as the human instruments. When we are aware of the intimate integration of the human and divine in the Christian learning-teaching process, we say with Paul, "I labor, striving according to His power, which mightily works within me" (Col. 1:29).

After we know what Scripture passage we will be teaching, we ought to immerse ourselves in it and ask God to speak to us personally through it. We must study it intensively no matter which age group we shall be teaching, so that we may understand it, feel it, live it. We then ask the Lord to speak personally through it to our class in terms of their daily lives here and now.

God has given the Holy Spirit to illumine the Word to us, to take the things of Christ and show them to us. He supervised the writing of His written revelation so that it may be authoritative for us. But because evangelicals have such a high view of Scripture, we sometimes use it as an end in itself, without getting through the written Word to the living Word. Christ said to the Jews in John 5:39-40, "You search the Scriptures because you think that in them you have eternal life; and it is these that bear witness of Me; and you are unwilling to come to Me, that you may have life." The symbols Scripture uses to describe itself speak of means to the end of fullness of life—lamp to illumine, seed to produce, rain and snow to water the earth, milk and meat and honey to nourish, fire to burn, hammer to

---

Lois E. LeBar, Ph.D., has taught Christian education at the Moody Bible Institute, at Wheaton College, in Africa, and in Asia.

break the hardest heart, sword to pierce, mirror to reflect, critic to discern. The purpose of the written Word is to lead us to the living Word, who Himself is *life*.

The Lord also uses teachers, teaching aids, and programs to bring people into relationship with Himself. People sometimes learn to love their teachers before they love their teachers' God, and they sometimes see Jesus in teachers before they believe that He is real. Students may answer correctly all the questions in their Sunday school workbooks without being related to Christ. It is easy to feel successful when we have put on a smooth program, but the crucial question is, What is happening to people? The test of our teaching is the changed life of the person who has had dealings with the Lord of glory.

In our lives as teachers, we have to watch out that the Lord's blessings and the Lord's service do not overshadow or compete with His person. As we get involved with the complexities of using His good gifts or ministering in His name, He may no longer be the center of our activities. Even though there are many things to think about in preparing to teach, the focus of everything must be the personal relationships between the teacher and the Lord and between our pupils and the Lord.

Wording Aims

If a lesson is to effect changes, it must move toward a goal. When we teachers have discovered the richness of God's Word, it is often a temptation to wander off on interesting bypaths that fail to further the progress of the lesson. Unless we have a clear aim, we have no basis for selecting and rejecting ideas that come to us and to our students. Many teachers are frustrated because they try to cover all the material that is suggested in a manual. Since printed material is written for general use, we have to adapt it to fit our own classes.

The Lord deals with us as whole persons and is concerned about every aspect of our lives. Bible teaching can overemphasize *knowing* at the expense of *feeling* and *doing*. Teachers can mistakenly assume that knowing will automatically lead to the corresponding feeling and doing. But that is contrary to Scripture. "To one who knows the right thing to do, and does not do it, to him it is sin" (James 4:17). Knowledge alone is seldom potent enough to lead to action. Feelings are the energizers, the natural mainsprings of action. Feelings are fickle; we cannot rely on them, but we cannot deny them. They can force the mind to supply rationalizations for what they want to do. Usually we cannot think right if we do not feel right. Moreover, we all have good intentions that never get carried over into action. Aims must be expressed in terms of feeling and doing as well as knowing.

Primarily the mind is involved in knowing truth. But the body is not going to make difficult changes unless the will makes a definite decision and commands it to disrupt its established routines. The will has to focus the whole person. It has to be strong enough to integrate the pulling and hauling of the whole being. Feelings prefer to do whatever is easy and pleasant. If the mind says that the plan of God is logical and sensible, the will must be strong enough to tell the body to move in that direction even though the feelings may be protesting.

When we appreciate all that is involved in changing conduct, we will not count on knowledge alone. Behavioral changes cannot be expected unless we aim at motivation and practice as well as knowledge.

For younger people each lesson should include knowing, feeling, and doing. For older students a curriculum unit will include all three; for instance, the first lesson might be primarily at the feeling level of motivation, the middle lessons would be on discovering God's answers to a problem, and the final lesson or lessons would involve carrying out the word of truth.

An aim should be worded concisely, specifically, and personally. It should be expressed as briefly as possible so that it can be kept at the center of attention during the whole lesson. It should be specific enough—in a doing aim, for example—for the pupils to visualize clearly what they can do during the week to obey the Lord. It should be personal enough for the individuals to apply it to their own living conditions.

DISCERNING NEEDS

If we seek to work with God to effect changes in people, we will start our class where a change is needed. Every pupil comes to class with many kinds of needs.

One of the first that he is aware of is the way he feels about himself. Is he comfortable in the group? Does he feel good about himself in relation to the teacher and to his peers? Or does he feel inferior, afraid that he will not be accepted or make his contribution, or that the whole thing will be boring to him? Does he see himself as made in the image of God, special, one of a kind, just as God wanted him to be for His particular purpose? If we feel good about ourselves, we can forget ourselves and concentrate on the problem at hand, can be free to improve ourselves, and minister to others. The way we feel about ourselves provides our frame of reference, the grid through which we screen everything that happens. It usually pays to spend the first hour in a new group getting acquainted with each other so that everyone feels at ease.

A good teacher has a genuine appreciation for the general needs of people. We bring our whole beings to Bible class, and God is concerned about physical and psychological needs as well as spiritual: health, safety, love, security, self-esteem, belonging, recognition, freedom, new experiences, and self-fufillment. It is from the ancient Greeks, not from Scripture, that we get the mistaken idea that the mind overshadows all other aspects in importance.

Some teachers act as if the first and great commandment were expressed as knowing all the facts of Scripture rather than in terms of loving. Loving is the essential link between knowing and doing; loving is based on knowing and leads to doing. We are not wasting time when we cultivate attitudes and work on emotional problems. The answers to those as well as mental questions are found in Scripture.

In addition to appreciating general needs, teachers can keep a file of their pupils' spiritual needs. Those include needs for salvation, dedication, daily commitment, vital prayer, fullness of the Spirit, natural witnessing, genuine worship, depth of knowledge and insight, Christian fellowship, self-discipline, sacrifice, fruit of the Spirit, and development of Spiritual gifts.

Christianity works inside out; not by natural outward means, but by infiltration of the Spirit. It is natural to emphasize the outer factors in teaching the Bible, for most of our means are outer—the Bible, teacher, pupils, environment, teaching aids. The challenge is to work with the Holy Spirit to motivate the deep *inner* springs of action that will result in changes that endure.

The age group we teach is the one with which we can best identify. The secret of the apostle Paul's personal work is expressed in 1 Corinthians 9:19-23; he freely became the servant of all kinds of people, to find common ground with all kinds, that by all possible means he might bring them to God. It takes patience to teach, especially in working with those whom we do not understand, for we need to learn why they behave as they do and to know how to deal with that kind of behavior.

PLANNING APPROACHES

What happens when a speaker or teacher begins by a monotonous reading of Scripture? Even when we try to follow the reading, our thoughts are often diverted to other Scriptures, or to some personal experience, or to some problem, or to something about the reader himself. He has suggested no direction for our thoughts, nothing within ourselves with which to connect it. In His teaching Jesus seldom simply started with eternal truth; He taught at the level of life. We cannot expect full attention unless we plug into the listeners' lives. So many voices surround us these days that we have formed the habit of turning off those not personally related to us; they hold little interest and often no meaning. What a waste of time and energy for teachers to present irrelevant Scripture when pupils come with so many needs to be met. We need to become skilled in making connections between our pupils' current needs and the Scripture that best answers them. When preparing to teach, list your pupils' needs, focus on one need, then select Scripture references that apply.

We must keep alert to the group's current needs, and ask the Lord which need it will be most ready to consider at classtime. He knows, even if we do not. He will guide in selecting the group's most common need. Then we take time to focus on and discuss the subject until it is in the forefront of attention. If the pupils are genuinely concerned about it, they will put forth effort to find God's solution. We can then direct them to the Scripture that provides the clearest answer and is closest to their experience.

If our Scripture has already been provided, as when we are following a manual, we use the same procedure from the other direction. We ask the Lord: Where does this truth meet the students' current needs? How will it make a difference in what they want to do here and now? We begin with a personal question that is expressed from their point of view in their language.

When we are planning and teaching in the Spirit, the Lord can guide specifically ahead of time. But we cannot know before the session an urgent need that some person may bring up in class. When that happens, we send up a quick little SOS for guidance. Shall we continue the lesson as planned? Can we answer the need with the scheduled Scripture without distorting the passage, or shall we discard the planning in favor of the new need? Of course, revising the lesson plan in class requires extensive knowledge of Scripture as well as the pupils. But what is the use of teaching the Bible if we do not teach it to people? We have a great advantage when we catch the teachable moment.

If there is little time for the build-up of motivation, at least we can word a personal question that is answered by the Scripture. If they come to class with a relevant question, we can go immediately to the content.

If the Word is taught faithfully in relation to human needs, Bible class will often provide effective group counseling. But the attitude with which a person comes to a personal counseling session is often very different from his attitude toward a Sunday school lesson. When a person comes to a counselor he is ready to voice a personal need; when he comes to Sunday school, too often it is only because "it's Sunday." Many people have not learned to find the answers to their daily needs in the application of Scripture.

DISCOVERING GOD'S ANSWERS

WITH PEOPLE WHO CANNOT READ

If children and others are not able to use their own Bibles, God can reveal Himself to them through the medium of a story. They should be prepared to look for something, to listen for what God says about a problem that they have discussed. Every teacher should be a good storyteller, for all ages appreciate illustrations. Children who have pleasant associations with Bible stories feel that no stories are as good as Bible stories. They are full of action, color, conflict, strong personalities, and the power of God. They should be carefully constructed in the light of the attention span, experience, and vocabulary of the age group.

Stories need to be carefully prepared for telling. The important beginnings and endings may be memorized, but the action should be lived dramatically by the teller. He should portray the events so graphically that the listeners feel as if they just happened. He does not fumble for words, because he visualizes each scene vividly. Visuals aid understanding of the setting and culture. To fill out the Bible scene, details may be added if they are most probably true to the background.

WITH PEOPLE WHO READ

Many children can begin to use their own Bibles. After the teacher poses the problem and describes the setting of an active incident, juniors enjoy finding definite answers in specific verses.

Youth and adults need a teaching session as well as a preaching session on Sunday morning, not two sermons. The genius of teaching is the small intimate group in which overt interaction is possible. "When He, the Spirit of truth, comes, He will *guide* you into all the truth; for He will not speak on His own initiative, but whatever He hears, He will speak; and He will disclose to you what is to come" (John 16:13, italics added). A teacher is essentially a guide in discovering God's revelation. He is also ready to declare, but his chief method is guiding. He seeks to make his students independent in securing their own spiritual nourishment (to study the Bible as scholars do), to achieve depth in Bible study by training their powers of observation.

When students are trained to ask questions of the text, they see exciting things that they had no idea were there when they read superficially. Good teachers seek to become skilled in the art of asking good questions. Not only do we need to see how the Bible relates to students' needs, but we need to help them think up good questions to discover the truths for themselves.

Even when drawing out facts, questions may be worded to make the students think. In the light of the lesson aim we ask in the direction we want each question to take us. If questions are carefully worded in advance, they can be clear, clearly grasped, and kept in mind. If a friendly conversational atmosphere is maintained, students will feel free to think aloud and learn together. (See chapter 7 for detailed suggestions for personal Bible study.)

Concluding with Action

People come to Bible class, hear the Word of God, and go out to do nothing about it. When that continues, teachers do not expect anything to happen, pupils do not expect anything to happen, nothing *does* happen.

Learning involves change—change that affects the whole being, not just the mind. Christianity is revolutionary, for we all start self-centered as children. God seeks to break up selfish patterns in order to establish a new set around Himself. It is natural to resist that inner change. We try all kinds of outward improvements rather than take apart our inner beings. Change is threatening because it undermines our security, our self-esteem. We feel we will lose something. It takes extra time and effort. In order to change, we have to see clearly why it is necessary and exactly how to bring it about.

If we as teachers are going to work with the Spirit of God to make personal inner changes, our teaching will have to be personal. Some people apologize for being personal, but not the Bible. How many personal references there are in Paul's letters that have become part of canonical Scripture! God could have given His written revelation in the form of systematic theology; how much controversy that would have saved His people. But He did not. Scripture contains many personal elements in history, narrative, biography, poetry, and very personal letters.

In our day, home Bible classes are springing up all over the world. One reason is that they are informal and personal and people feel free to seek help for their daily problems.

If pupils are going to practice the truth during the week, they must clearly visualize what they can do realistically at home, school, work, and play. That does not mean that teachers will point their fingers at individuals and tell them what to do. But they will save time at the end of a lesson to ask: What is God saying to *you* in relation to your home, your office, your school, your friends? What will be hard as you make this change? How can we help each other?

Most of our difficulties are not with what we do not understand but with what we do understand. Wisdom is the ability to apply biblical knowledge to practical situations. We must not substitute the art of communication for the art of living.

The following lesson outlines are examples of the above principles, using the same Scripture for primary through adult departments. Note how concisely the whole lesson can be outlined, and how a sharp aim gives direction and movement.

DEPARTMENTAL LESSON OUTLINES USING EXODUS 3:1–4:17

Primary

Aim: To feel God's nearness instead of being afraid.

Approach: What can I do when I'm afraid?

Content: Emphasis on "Certainly I will be with you."

Action: Dramatize doing hard things with God (facing lightning, meeting big dog); plan to do one hard thing this week.

Junior

Aim: To experience the various ways in which God speaks to us.

Approach: How does God speak to us? Only through the Bible?

Content: God speaking by means of the burning bush, His voice, His power (snake).

Action: Keep a list of all the ways God communicates with us, as in nature, storm, sickness.

Junior High

Aim: To work with God to strengthen one weakness.

Approach: Who am I that God could use me for anything?

Content: God's personal communication and great promises.

Action: List our weaknesses and work with God to strengthen one.

Senior High

Aim: To use one created potential that has been dormant.

Approach: "What is in your hand?" Your created potential?

Content: Moses' spiritual home, palace training, rod in his hand, brother Aaron.

Action: Use one potential in a new way this week.

Adult

Aim: To allow God to mature and use one undeveloped aspect of my life.

Approach: How does God recruit and train leaders?

Content: Freedom from self, no excuses, God's empowering.

Action: Take one new step toward leadership.

USING PRESESSION MOMENTS

When teachers come late to class and busy themselves with preparations, what does that communicate to the class? The fifteen to twenty minutes when individuals are arriving before group activities begin may be an integral part of the session serving three valuable purposes: (1) to help us get to know individuals as the unique persons they are, (2) to allow us to check on the carry-over of last week's lesson, and (3) to give us leads into the new lesson.

The first thing a new pupil learns about his teacher is how much he cares about him as an individual. Does the teacher care enough to find out who he is, what his family is like, what he enjoys doing, what is hard for him? Many a child comes to Sunday school early because he has found that his teacher will spend a few minutes with him alone. That develops a special rapport; he is no longer just one of a group. None of us bares his real self to strangers, but after we have talked superficially, we dare go deeper to see how far we can trust the other person with the things that really matter to us. Some people have no one at home in whom they can confide.

Second, as individuals arrive we find out how they carried out last week's lesson. Nothing is so encouraging as seeing the Lord work. We are ready to go on with Him when we see results in our own lives. If nothing happened in someone's life during the week, we analyze why and figure out how the teacher or the class can help in the future. That enables teacher and class to pray definitely for individual needs.

Presession can also give us opportunity for up-to-the-minute leads into the new lesson. If our aim is to develop self-discipline or self-control, early arrivals may post on the bulletin board pictures or clippings showing positive or negative control. Personal questions on the chalkboard may prompt a spontaneous discussion. The students may see if they want to add anything to a list of main problems in relation to discipline. The teacher may select one of the shared experiences for role playing to start group activities. A resource person may be brought in to raise real problems. Puzzles or games may motivate new ideas for children. Youth and adults may be given a checklist to indicate their needs, interests, and experience with the subject at hand.

Evaluating Our Teaching

Although the Lord rewards faithfulness, He has said, "I chose you . . . that you should go and bear fruit, and that your fruit should remain" (John 15:16). If we have worded concise aims in terms of changed lives, it is easy to keep checking for results. Of course people must know the truth and have right attitudes before they will obey the Word, but the ultimate test is action. It is God who gives the tests, and He gives them in daily life situations. We are delighted when in class someone gains new insight, shows love to another, or shares a spiritual experience. But we may not know the small changes that add up to the big changes that take place out of class unless we are acquainted with the daily lives of our pupils. The teacher's reward is seeing them make steady progress toward maturity in Christ.

The way to keep improving our teaching is to keep evaluating. After each session, ask yourself: When was the presence and power of God most evident? What did I do to facilitate His working? What was weak in this hour? How could that weakness have been avoided? What difference will this experience make in my praying for the next session? What have I learned about the individuals in my class that I should record in my file?

"Therefore, my beloved brethren, be steadfast, immovable, always abounding in the work of the Lord, knowing that your toil is not in vain in the Lord" (1 Cor. 15:58).

FOR FURTHER STUDY

1. How has the Lord recently spoken to you through Scripture during a preaching service? During a teaching session? During your private devotions?
2. Find a Bible verse that expresses God's aim for this universe, and another for God's aim for every believer in Christ.
   Write your own personal aims for this year, this quarter, and this week; be as concise and specific as possible.
   Write one personal aim for each pupil in your class, or, if you are not teaching, for several of your friends.
3. Freely paraphrase the ideas in 1 Corinthians 9:19-23 in terms of a teacher with a class of children, youth, or adults.
4. Examine suggested lesson approaches in teaching materials that you are now using. Which ones would get your class excited? How could you revise the others to meet the particular needs of your group?
5. Make a line graph of the spiritual experiences of your life, indicating when you made upward progress toward God, when you went downward away from Him, and when you remained on a plateau. What were the chief causes for each movement?

SUGGESTED READING

Comenius, John Amos. *The Great Didactic.* 1657. London: Adam and Charles Black, 1896. A classic, one of the first to emphasize growth from within, wholeness of the learner, knowledge that is useful, learning by doing, importance of early years, value of visuals, truth derived from Scripture, and nature.

Fritz, Dorothy B. *Ways of Teaching.* Philadelphia: Westminster, 1965. The *why* and with *whom* of teaching, including the person in a setting, the meaning of method, discovery, and taking responsibility as learning.

Hyde, Douglas. *Dedication and Leadership.* South Bend, Ind.: U. of Notre Dame, 1966. What we can learn from the Communists about working with people.

Jaarsma, Cornelius. *Human Development, Learning and Teaching*. Grand Rapids: Eerdmans, 1961. Christian educational psychology, notably the development of personality.

*Joy, Donald M. *Meaningful Learning in the Church*. Winona Lake, Ind.: Light and Life, 1969. Strategies that help lay teachers communicate the distinctives of the Christian faith.

*LeBar, Lois E. *Education That Is Christian*. Old Tappan, N.J.: Revell, 1958. Principles of the learning-teaching process derived from Scripture.

————. *Focus on People in Church Education*. Old Tappan, N.J.: Revell, 1968. The educational cycle in its context in the church, with emphasis on people rather than programs.

Lederach, Paul M. *Reshaping the Teaching Ministry*. Scottdale, Pa.: Herald, 1968. Reevaluating the context, objectives, settings, and strategy for the present day.

*Leypoldt, Martha M. *Learning Is Change: Adult Education in the Church*. Valley Forge, Pa.: Judson, 1971. An experience as well as a description of zestful learning with practical suggestions for reflection and personal activity.

Mager, Robert F. *Developing Attitude Toward Learning*. Palo Alto, Calif.: Fearon, 1968. A creative, practical study of influencing students' attitudes.

————. *Preparing Instructional Objectives*. Palo Alto, Calif.: Fearon, 1962. Demonstration as well as description of preparing behavioral objectives.

Mayes, Howard, and Long, James. *Can I Help It If They Don't Learn?* Wheaton, Ill.: Scripture Press, 1977. A humorous treatment of five important principles of teaching.

Merjanian, Pepronia. *The Joy of Teaching*. Chicago: U. of Chicago, 1966. Teaching as an invitation to love, requiring meeting needs and planning creatively.

Richards, Lawrence O. *Creative Bible Study*. Grand Rapids: Zondervan, 1971. Overcoming the problems of perspective, isolation and understanding in Bible study.

————. *Creative Bible Teaching*. Chicago: Moody, 1970. Bridging the gaps between truth and implication.

*————. *A Theology of Christian Education*. Grand Rapids: Zondervan, 1975. Life as the focus of Christian teaching, goal of discipling, communication by modeling, dynamic of interpersonal relations.

Rood, Wayne. *The Art of Teaching Christianity*. Nashville: Abingdon, 1968. The vision for preparing, teaching, follow-up.

Russell, Letty M. *Christian Education in Mission*. Philadelphia: Westminster, 1967. The context of Christian education in a witnessing community, the structure of dialogue, method of participation, life-style.

Swain, Dorothy G. *Teach Me to Teach*. Valley Forge, Pa.: Judson, 1964. A group of learning teachers discussing the teacher's purpose, pupils, communication, lesson planning, evaluation.

*Wald, Oletta. *The Joy of Discovery*. Minneapolis: Bible Banner, 1956. A brief, practical explanation of how teachers can guide students in making their own discoveries in Scripture.

*Especially recommended.

13

Methods in Teaching

William B. Haburn

Methods are an essential part of teaching. As a teacher, the methods you use express your attitude and convictions. What you believe about people and how they learn is also shown by the methods you choose.

Roy Zuck in *Spiritual Power in Your Teaching* states that the Holy Spirit "works through methods to bring about spiritual nurture. The creative use of a variety of methods facilitates learning, and thus fosters spiritual change and maturation."[1]

Content is communicated by the method chosen. The way you approach something determines, to a degree, what is learned. "Method does teach, in itself. And the method used has a great deal to do with the atmosphere of a group, with group interrelationships, and therefore is directly related to some of the intangible but basic learning and change that take place in persons."[2]

As Christian teachers we are interested in maximum learning. If we hope to move beyond the minimum learning level we must approach our class with a well-thought-out plan utilizing a variety of teaching methods. Five fellows do not get together and win basketball games without planning their strategy. They fulfill their purpose by following specific plays (methods).

Definition of Method

Different terms are used to describe methods. Some emphasize the communication of content.

> Method is simply an instrument used by the teacher to communicate to the learner the knowledge, ideal or truth under consideration.[3]

William B. Haburn, Ed.D., is academic dean and professor of Christian education for Western Baptist Bible College, Salem, Oregon.

> The word method is simply descriptive of processes used by a teacher to communicate information to the students.[4]

Others emphasize the experience itself.

> Methods are tools or ways of teaching; they are links for uniting content and experience. Methods are vehicles for bringing learners in vital contact with Christ and the Word.[5]

> A method is simply an activity designed to hook students, to communicate information and meaning, to lead to insight, or to encourage response.[6]

The use of words such as "tools" or "instruments" allows audiovisual equipment to be included as teaching methods, although technically the method would be how the equipment is used.

Our definition of method must point toward something that can be used in such areas as securing the interest of the student, assisting the student in understanding the biblical content, relating the biblical content to life, and securing personal commitment. Thus methods are instruments (tools, vehicles, activities, processes) that a teacher utilizes in leading a student through a learning experience that causes the learner to change and grow.

Methods do not replace knowledge of the subject, spiritual concern for the students, or the need for prayerful dependence upon God. "[Methods] will not run on their own educational power alone, or on your skill alone. . . . You still will need to seek the ever-willing aid of the Holy Spirit if any teaching idea or procedure whatever is to achieve the outcome you desire."[7]

GUIDELINES IN USING METHODS

The use of teaching methods, if they are to be other than gimmicks for teachers to use, should follow some basic guidelines.

The first guideline: *The teacher should prepare the content of the lesson before determining the teaching method to be used* (this, of course, relates to the first law of teaching).[8] Choosing your methods will be less difficult when you know what you are going to present. "If you understand what you are trying to accomplish, you can select or invent an activity to accomplish it. Master the parts of the lesson process, and method skill will follow."[9]

The second guideline: *The teacher shall select methods that are appropriate.* Factors that should influence your decision include the age of your students, biblical content, and the time available. Some methods bridge all age levels when they are used in the appropriate manner, but others are best used with specific groupings.

The third guideline: *The teacher shall utilize a variety of methods.* That does not mean only variety within the time span of a single lesson, but particularly variety over a time span of two or three months. It is wise to keep a record of methods used and the effectiveness of each method. Review your record to see if one method is being used excessively. "A teacher who uses only one method is in danger of developing only one group of skills in his pupils and only part of his own powers as an educator."[10] There is always some risk in using one not used before, but risk is often necessary for growth. To fulfill this principle, you will need to study new methods.

The fourth guideline: *The teacher shall use methods to open channels of communication.* Communication is to take place between individuals within the class and between the teacher and the student. The Bible must be lived to be learned. If a student is to receive maximum benefit from a Bible study, methods must result in each student's becoming actively involved in expressing his personal insights and inner feelings. "[Communication] involves more than simply giving Bible information. For you, and for every teacher of God's Word, communication means sharing. Sharing your understanding of the Word you teach. Sharing your feelings as you experience God's dealing with you in your life. Sharing your values and your choices as you attempt to harmonize these with the Word. Sharing honestly and openly whatever is real to you."[11]

The fifth principle: *The teacher shall arrange the room to facilitate the method to be used.* Some methods require a specific arrangement. For example, a group may find it difficult to secure open communication if the students are sitting in rows, whereas a circle allows each person to see the others and speak directly to them. The use of a small picture requires that you be able to move to a position close to each student. Teachers may be limited in their choice of a method by the arrangement or size of their rooms, but that is also a challenge for developing and using methods that do fit into the available facilities.

TYPES OF METHODS

Teaching methods are classified in various ways. Leavitt in *Teach with Success* identifies methods of impression and methods of expression.[12] Another author classified them according to types of learning or learning purpose. Learning types would include methods to develop knowledge, understanding, skills, attitudes, interests, or values.[13]

Gangel uses the approach of emphasis on people to identify four basic categories. Those are *group work* (buzz groups), *teacher and students* (question and answer), *student to teacher* (creative writing, memorization), and *teacher to student* (lecture).[14]

To those four categories Gangel adds the designation of *instructive play* for methods with smaller children (puzzles). Finally, there is a category that can be identified as *nonclassroom activity* (field trips).

To illustrate the use of methods in the various categories, examples will be considered for each category, with guidelines for their use.

GROUP WORK: BUZZ GROUPS

The class is divided into smaller groups of three to six people who will meet together to discuss a specific topic related to the lesson for a limited period of time. Guidelines:

1. Prepare a specific topic for the groups to consider (same for all or different for each group).
2. Prepare an instruction sheet for each group. Provide sufficient space on the sheet for summary of the group discussion. Include time limits.
3. Divide class as equally as possible.
4. Assign a leader/reporter for each group, or explain how groups are to choose leaders.
5. Circulate to encourage and assist the groups.
6. Reassemble as a class.
7. Have each group share discussion conclusions. Teacher summarizes the findings.

Buzz groups encourage the quiet student to interact in a small group setting, generate new ideas or insights, allow for the application of Bible truth, and provide for student participation and interest. Group reports can be retained for future use.

TEACHER AND STUDENTS: QUESTION AND ANSWER

This method provides for interchange between students and teacher. The use of questions is the first step toward meaningful interaction in the classroom.

Questions can be used in securing and holding attention, actively involving the student in the learning process, provoking thought, clarifying ideas, and determining what a student knows or is remembering. Further, they provide opportunity for leading into a Scripture passage, relating one concept to another, and assisting the student in applying scriptural truths to his own life.

There are various types of questions. *Factual* questions are used to secure information or to open a discussion. For example, Paul uses the term "fitly joined together" in Ephesians 2:19-22. A carpenter in the class might be asked to explain how he joins the parts of a building together. That requires factual knowledge. We might also use an *interpretive* question like "What does Paul mean by using the figure of a building fitly joined together, and how can that relate to church membership?" This question asks how the information applies to what we are studying.

Thought questions may or may not require an immediate answer. We could ask, "How can we today be joined together in the manner suggested by Paul?" This question challenges the student to think. *Rhetorical* questions generally have the answer implied in the question. Christ asks a rhetorical question in Luke 12:25. *Alternative* questions offer the student a choice. They require one to determine which alternative is correct.

Justification questions provide an opportunity for a student to clarify a decision or an act. These kinds of questions can expose fallacious reasoning or cause a student to examine his motives. When you ask a student to answer a question asked by another student it is called a *relay* question. Such questions encourage interaction between class members.

Guidelines for questioning:

1. Direct questions to the class as a whole before asking a specific person to answer.
2. Ask easier questions to set the tone and then proceed to more difficult ones.
3. Ask factual questions prior to interpretive questions.
4. State questions in a clear, concise way, restricting them to one idea per question.
5. Plan your lessons in such a way that questions are a natural part of the class session. Plan questions.
6. Ask questions according to the students' level of knowledge.
7. Use questions that allow the student to interpret or apply the truth to his own life.
8. Ask questions that encourage an honest, exploring, open-mind approach to the lesson.
9. Avoid the use of questions that can be answered with yes or no.
10. Consider "feeling" questions that involve the student emotionally.
11. Ask questions that point toward actions that can take place immediately following the lesson or even during the lesson.
12. Use questions of a general nature before becoming specific when drawing the application to the lesson.*

STUDENT TO TEACHER: CREATIVE WRITING

Creative writing refers to specific projects given to your students in which they write in their own words what they are studying in the Bible or in a related subject. Students will retain more when they write their thoughts, beliefs, feelings, and ideas. There are various forms of creative writing.

Scripture paraphrasing requires more than just facts from the Word. When you ask your students to paraphrase, they must comprehend the key

*For more information on questions, read chapter 4, "Christ the Master Teacher" and note His use of questions.

idea of the passage and then restate it in current terminology. It is helpful if you allow your students to read their paraphrases to each other and rewrite them.

Letter writing helps your students to identify with biblical characters and events in letter form. There are many variations of this method. The younger student, for example, could identify with the boy giving up his lunch for feeding the five thousand (John 6) by writing a letter about it to his grandfather. Young people might want to put themselves in the place of Jacob and write to Rebekah about his experiences at Uncle Laban's house (Genesis 29). A person of any age could be one of the natives seeing Paul bitten by the snake, or a prisoner in jail when Peter was released (Acts 12), and write to someone about those experiences.

An understanding of day-by-day events is accomplished when students write entries into an imaginary *diary*. A very rewarding diary project for young people is to place themselves into Scripture as a Bible character and write a diary of his or her teen years.

Students could be asked to write a *newspaper article* or editorial based on an assigned text. If they write an article, it would be written as a factual news item. If they write an editorial, they are allowed to insert their own convictions, since an editorial is written to convince someone of a particular position.

Creative writing could also include writing poetry, new words to a familiar hymn, radio scripts, short plays, open ended stories or situations, tracts, bumper stickers, or slogans. Keep the content of Scripture as the focus when creative writing is utilized. The purpose of creative writing is to make Scripture more meaningful and understandable.

TEACHER TO STUDENT: LECTURE

Teacher focus methods are usually represented by the lecture, where the major activity centers on the speaking of the teacher. This is a traditional but useful method when augmented by other methods such as discussion, question and answer, and the use of audiovisual aids.

As in effective lecturing, a method may represent a number of major types. One such example is *role playing*, which has elements of student focus, teacher-student participation, and group setting. It is a contemporary method, effectively used with youth and adults. The term "role" refers to how a person behaves in a given situation. Role playing itself is "a brief, spontaneous, unrehearsed presentation of a problem in which certain members of the class act out certain roles. There is no script prepared, no memorizing of parts. . . . The problems which are enacted may deal with human relations or social situation[s]. Or the problems may deal with personal-emotional feelings."[15]

The use of role play as a teaching method can be illustrated by this example. An adult Sunday school class was studying the topic of Christian service. Since many people agree that the Bible teaches the need for the Christian to participate in serving Christ while being unwilling themselves to participate, a role play situation was used to bridge between study and application.

Two women were chosen for the role play. One assumed the role of the daughter of a man who had died of cancer within the last six months. The other assumed the role of a recruiter seeking volunteers to participate in the cancer fund drive by canvassing one block near her home. In the play, the recruiter knocked on the door and discussed with the daughter the need for funds for cancer research. The daughter agreed with everything until she was asked to contact people for the fund drive. Her attitude changed, she began giving numerous excuses, and would not do it even though she believed it was necessary and valuable. A discussion of the feelings expressed and parallels to the class lesson then followed the role play. This led naturally to the basis for Christian service and its place in the sincere Christian's life, as well as specific areas of service in the church.

Gangel emphasizes that "role playing is based on the philosophy that meanings are in people, not in words or symbols," and thus it requires that "we must first of all share the meanings, then clarify our understandings of each other's meanings, and finally, if necessary, change our meanings."[16] Since meanings are in people rather than words, the change takes place through involvement in actions that are realistic and life related. Role playing provides just such an opportunity.

Guidelines for role playing:

1. Devise the situation to be acted out. Keep the situation simple. Make the situation relative to your class.
2. Establish an appropriate classroom climate. Place yourself in the position of a guide. Help students to anticipate the situation. Maintain an attitude of respect.
3. Select the characters to play the roles. Explain that they are representing roles and not necessarily their own attitudes. Choose students with self-confidence for the first role plays. Encourage participants to express their feelings in a spontaneous manner.
4. Prepare the class to observe the role play. Provide key questions that will help the audience to identify feelings or ideas displayed during the role play. Suggest that each observer choose one character and determine how he would respond if he were playing the role.
5. Play the incident. Maintain discipline during the role play and do not let it get out of hand. You may want to stop the role play for discussion and then continue it.

6. Discuss the role play. Discuss the details of what happened. Identify the feelings that were expressed. Discuss how the role play could apply to our lives. Determine the personal application.

CONCLUSION

Your expertise as a teacher will be enhanced by developing a working knowledge of methods and creatively using them. Teaching presents a new challenge each time you enter the classroom as an active participant in the teaching-learning process. Under the guidance of the Holy Spirit you serve both as a teacher and as a learner. The effective use of methods will enhance both experiences.

FOR FURTHER STUDY

1. Research the concept that the teaching methods we choose reveal what we believe about people.
2. Prepare a paper that may be used in a class presentation on audio-visuals as a teaching method.
3. Lead a discussion on the topic "Risks in Using Methods that are Unfamiliar to You."
4. Research the meaning of communication and how an adequate understanding of communication will improve your teaching ability.
5. Write a paper on the topic "How Theology Should Influence Our Methodology."
6. Select a teaching method not presented in this chapter and write a short paper explaining what it is and how to effectively use it.
7. Prepare a short teaching session demonstrating one method of teaching.
8. Prepare an outline for a teacher training session that explains the various categories of teaching methods.

NOTES

1. Roy B. Zuck, *Spiritual Power in Your Teaching* (Wheaton, Ill.: Scripture Press, 1963), p. 139.
2. Sara Little, *Learning Together in the Christian Fellowship* (Richmond, Va.: John Knox, 1956), p. 33.
3. Findley B. Edge, *Helping the Teacher* (Nashville: Broadman, 1959), p. 75.
4. Kenneth O. Gangel, *Twenty-Four Ways to Improve Your Teaching* (Wheaton, Ill.: Scripture Press, Victor, 1974), p. 7.
5. Zuck, p. 137.
6. Lawrence O. Richards, *Creative Bible Teaching* (Chicago: Moody, 1970), p. 112.
7. Rice A. Pierce, *Leading Dynamic Bible Study* (Nashville: Broadman, 1969), p. 25.
8. John Milton Gregory, *The Seven Laws of Teaching* (Grand Rapids: Baker, 1957), p. 112.
9. Richards, p. 112.
10. Gilbert Highet, *The Art of Teaching* (New York: Random, 1950), p. 112.
11. Lawrence O. Richards, *You the Teacher* (Chicago: Moody, 1972), p. 69.
12. Guy P. Leavitt, *Teach with Success* (Cincinnati: Standard, 1956), p. 86.

13. H. Norman Wright, *Ways to Help Them Learn—Adult* (Glendale, Calif.: Gospel Light, 1972), p. 86.
14. Gangel, p. 9.
15. Edge, p. 128.
16. Gangel, p. 24.

SUGGESTED READING

Bolton, Barbara J. *Ways to Help Them Learn—Children Grades 1-6*. Glendale, Calif.: Gospel Light, 1972. Well-written and practical book that presents characteristics and organizational plans in addition to selected methods.

Brown, James W.; Lewis, Richard B.; and Harcleroad, Fred F. *AV Instruction: Methods and Materials*. New York: McGraw-Hill, 1959. A standard college AV text. It is written in a clear style and well illustrated. Chapter 20, "Using Still Pictures," is recommended reading.

Edge, Findley B. *Helping the Teacher*. Nashville: Broadman, 1959. A standard text that is useful to the Sunday school teacher.

Ford, LeRoy. *Design for Teaching and Training*. Nashville: Broadman, 1978. A programmed text. Based on the Bloom's taxonomy, it leads the student through the teaching process. Well done and useful book.

————. *Using the Case Study in Teaching and Training*. Nashville: Broadman, 1969.

————. *Using the Lecture in Teaching and Training*. Nashville: Broadman, 1968.

————. *Using the Panel in Teaching and Training*. Nashville: Broadman, 1970.

————. *Using Problem Solving in Teaching and Training*. Nashville: Broadman, 1971.

The above four books are all excellent. Each one has visual illustrations and well-written explanations. Purchasing is recommended.

Gangel, Kenneth O. *Twenty-four Ways to Improve Your Teaching*. Wheaton, Ill.: Scripture Press, Victor, 1971. A brief presentation of twenty-four teaching methods. Very profitable for teacher training. A teacher's guide is available.

Highet, Gilbert. *The Art of Teaching*. New York: Random, 1950. A classic work that should be read.

Leavitt, Guy P. *Teach with Success*. Cincinnati: Standard, 1956. Practical book. Brief presentations. Good check charts.

LeBar, Lois E. *Education That Is Christian*. Westwood, N.J.: Revell, 1958. A well-written, meaningful book. Excellent correlation of biblical examples with effective teaching.

Lee, Mark W. *So You Want to Speak*. Grand Rapids: Zondervan, 1951. Brief, meaningful ideas to improve your speaking ability.

LeFever, Marlene D. *Turnabout Teaching*. Elgin, Ill.: David C. Cook, 1973. A concise but thorough explanation of seven methods. Excellent illustrations are included.

Little, Sara. *Learning Together in the Christian Fellowship*. Richmond, Va.: John Knox, 1956. One of the earlier books that provided for active involvement by the student. Recommended reading.

Mayes, Howard, and Long, James. *Can I Help It If They Don't Learn?* Wheaton, Ill.: Scripture Press, Victor, 1977. A fun book to read. Concepts are presented with different terminology.

Morrison, Eleanor S., and Foster, Virgil E. *Creative Teaching in the Church*. Englewood Cliffs, N.J.: Prentice-Hall, 1963. Excellent ideas as to methodology, but the book must be used with direction among evangelicals. The authors have a low view of inspiration.

Pierce, Rice A. *Leading Dynamic Bible Study*. Nashville: Broadman, 1969. Based on group process and gives good information on how to involve people as they learn.

The Psychology of Teaching Methods. Chicago: National Society for the Study of Education, 1976. A technical, research-oriented book with a good historical overview of teaching methods.

Richards, Lawrence O. *Creative Bible Teaching*. Chicago: Moody, 1970. Practical help in scriptural philosophy of teaching, learning, and lesson planning.
————. *You the Teacher*. Chicago: Moody, 1972. Will change you. An account of a teacher's experiences.

Sanders, Norris M. *Classroom Questions*. New York: Harper & Row, 1966. Based on Bloom's taxonomy of educational objectives—questions are categorized according to the various levels. One of the very few books available on this subject.

Stoop, David A. *Ways to Help Them Learn—Youth Grades 7-12*. Glendale, Calif.: Gospel Light, 1973. Well-written and practical book that presents characteristics of youth and organizational plans in addition to selected methods.

Wright, H. Norman. *Ways to Help Them Learn—Adult*. Glendale, Calif.: Gospel Light, 1972. Another practical, well-written book that presents characteristics and organizational plans in addition to selected methods.

Zirbes, Laura. *Spurs to Creative Teaching*. New York: Putnam's, 1966. Written for teaching standard subjects. This book has some excellent ideas and illustrations. Sometimes it is too wordy with educational jargon, but the first three chapters are beneficial to any teacher.

Zuck, Roy B. *Spiritual Power in Your Teaching*. Wheaton, Ill.: Scripture Press, 1972.

Zuck, Roy B., and Benson, Warren E. *Youth Education in the Church*. Chicago: Moody, 1978.

Zuck, Roy B., and Clark, Robert E. *Childhood Education in the Church*. Chicago: Moody, 1975.

Zuck, Roy B., and Getz, Gene. *Adult Education in the Church*. Chicago: Moody, 1970. The *Education in the Church* series has various chapters in each book on methodology. Helpful ideas are given for the total span of life. Ideas can be adapted from one level to another.

Part IV

THE FAMILY IN CHRISTIAN EDUCATION

BIBLICAL EDUCATION begins in the home, and the Christian education implications of Deuteronomy 6 and Ephesians 6 have a continuing validity.

It is essential, therefore, for the evangelical church as well as individual believers to have a basic understanding of the family as an educational ministry. For that purpose two special chapters are included in the text.

The first chapter, by a husband and wife team, provides a biblical perspective on the family in contemporary culture.

The second chapter follows that perspective into the implications of spiritual training in the home.

Although brief, the unit supplies a critical introduction to educational thinking for a day of troubled homes and marriages.

14

Biblical Perspective for the Family

ALFRED and DOROTHY MARTIN

CONTEMPORARY VIEW OF MARRIAGE AND FAMILY

The decadence of today's society is evident in the frequency with which the family is declared to be obsolete. The traditional picture of a family—father and mother united in marriage, with children legitimized by the sacred marriage bond—is a caricature in the eyes of many. Changes in the family structure in recent years seem to support this view.

More and more frequently men and women live together in temporary alliances. A marriage license is considered unnecessary as long as the couple has a "meaningful relationship."

Pregnancy of unmarried women carries little or no stigma in the view of contemporary society. Abortion is to many people the accepted answer to an unwanted baby, whether conceived outside of or within marriage.

The divorce rate continues to soar and is high even among Christians, who often dissolve their marriages on other than biblical grounds.

The sexual revolution ranges from the approval of infidelity and immorality in snickering jokes on television situation comedies to the push for homosexual rights. The demand is increasing that homosexuality be recognized and legalized as a legitimate life-style with the option of "marriage."

One excuse given for this slide in society's values is that nothing is wrong because there are no absolute moral standards. "If it feels good, it must be right," is the prevailing wind of the day. That is not a new idea. Long ago a society existed in which "everyone did what was right in his own eyes" (Judg. 21:25). The current emphasis on personal fulfillment, regardless of who might be hurt in the process, tears apart the family fabric.

ALFRED E. MARTIN, Th.D., was dean of education at the Moody Bible Institute until 1981.

DOROTHY MARTIN, M.R.E., is an author-educator.

But throughout history even thinking pagans have recognized the need for a stable family life if civilization was to endure. One cause of the collapse of Greece and then Rome was the disintegration of marriage and the family. So today, thoughtful people *outside* the church are warning of the yawning chasm that will swallow civilization if society continues its plunge toward moral chaos.

Some psychologists and sociologists are shifting their permissive views and speaking out in alarm at the undermining of family life. Others are daring to swing the pendulum back and say that a woman can proudly be a mother, that marriage should endure, and that the family unit is important.

But those voices in the moral wilderness, while welcome, speak from a sociological, not a biblical, viewpoint. Their well-intentioned advice is tenuous, for its basis is faulty. The advice is given from a human perspective that ignores God. The only foundation on which to build a lasting marriage is the standard God has established.

BIBLICAL VIEW OF MARRIAGE AND ITS RELATIONSHIPS

In the face of the denials of and uncertainties regarding the validity and sanctity of marriage and the family, Christians must constantly reaffirm the teaching of Scripture. The Bible clearly states that that human institution is of divine origin. God intended it to be an indissoluble union, valid for a man and a woman as long as each lives.

God created man in His own image (Gen. 1:26-27), male and female. He made wise and loving provision for the procreation of the human race *before* man's sin and fall. The family was in the world before sin entered. God's instruction to Adam and Eve, "Be fruitful, and multiply, and fill the earth, and subdue it" (Gen. 1:28), is the basis of the family.

In that respect humanity is utterly different from the angels, each of whom was individually created by God. God did not choose to create human beings as separate individuals. When God created Adam, He made him a racial being, the progenitor of all other human beings. Eve, the first woman, was taken from the first man (Gen. 2:21-23), thus assuring the absolute unity of mankind.

In both the Old and New Testaments the relationships of husband and wife and of parents and children are prominently featured. The marriage bond is pictured as the closest and most intmate of any human experience. The physical union is important not only for its own sake, but also because it symbolizes the complete oneness of husband and wife. That takes from marriage any concept of its being for either partner's selfish fulfillment and invests it with a dimension found only in Scripture. The Bible says, "A man shall leave his father and his mother, and shall cleave to his wife; and they shall become one flesh" (Gen. 2:24).

God designed marriage as a teaching tool, although its purpose was not apparent in the Garden of Eden and was not made clear until centuries later. Throughout the Old Testament are intimations that this wonderful relationship was to typify another, higher relationship. The figure of a husband is used repeatedly to describe God's relationship to His people (Isa. 54:5). The Old Testament gives beautiful pictures of bridegrooms and brides: Adam and Eve, Isaac and Rebekah, Jacob and Rachel (Gen. 2; 24; 29). The picture becomes more delicately explicit in the experience and expressions of the bridegroom and bride in the Song of Solomon, in which the married lovers show their complete and holy delight in each other's person.

The New Testament gives the full disclosure of God's purpose in establishing marriage in the Garden of Eden. The apostle Paul, directed by the Holy Spirit, explained that God intended marriage to illustrate the relationship between Christ and the church, His redeemed ones. In Ephesians 5, which deals with the mutual responsibilities of the husband and wife to each other, the apostle concludes, "This mystery is great: but I am speaking with reference to Christ and the church" (verse 32).

The word *mystery* when used in the New Testament means literally "a secret." It is used in a technical sense to refer to something that is not revealed, or at best is only vaguely intimated, in the Old Testament, but which is clearly and fully revealed in the New. Therefore it is an open secret to the people of God. Those who will not believe God's Word find it still to be a mystery and a source of controversy.

ROLES IN MARRIAGE

God makes clear in His Word that He established an order in the marriage relationship, putting the husband at the head of the home. This order has often been ridiculed. Recently it has come under particularly vehement attack with repercussions even among Christians. Some attempt to make Scripture imply that because the husband is the leader, he is inherently better than the wife and that men are superior to women. Scripture does not say that. An analogous picture may be seen in the choosing of the nation Israel as God's special people (Deut. 7:6-8). God the sovereign Creator invested family leadership in the husband. That is God's pattern for an orderly, smoothly working family unit. That families do not follow the pattern does not change its original establishment.

Some attempt to explain away the scriptural order by insisting that references to marriage and the family are culturally conditioned, and that what applied to roles within the family in Old Testament times or in Paul's day are not valid in today's culture.

That view, held even by many Christians, affects more than simply the question of husband and wife roles. It raises the question of the authority of God's Word for other areas of life. Paul's words in Ephesians 5, in 1 Corinthians 14, and in 1 Timothy 2 *were* culturally oriented since he wrote to specific churches at a particular time in history. But, since he wrote under the inspiration of the Holy Spirit, the words apply to any age, to the present age as well as to first-century Christians. Ephesians 5:22-24 is as much a part of the Scripture that was "given by inspiration of God" as is John 3:16.

Often Galatians 3:28, "There is neither . . . slave nor free . . . male nor female . . . you are all one in Christ Jesus," is used to assert the total equality of men and women, wiping out any distinction of headship.

Such an assertion comes from a confusion of two entirely different categories. The verse refers to equality of status before God as redeemed sinners; it does not erase the different and distinctive roles of men and women that God began in creation. Every human being who has been saved by grace through faith in the Lord Jesus Christ has the same relationship to the heavenly Father as every other saved human being. In the light of eternity, distinctions based on racial, cultural, or sexual status are unimportant. In that respect there is no distinction between male and female.

But we *are* still either male or female. No amount of human argument can erase that distinction; no ignoring of the distinction will remove it. The unisex movement, which tries to explain away the basic differences in men and women, will not change what God did in creation. It is clear that He did not create two males or two females. Scripture explicitly condemns any type of sexual relationship other than that between a man and a woman united in marriage (Genesis 19; Leviticus 18; 1 Corinthians 5-6).

The Christian must not be guided in these matters by his own opinion or by the views of others, but by the question, What does Scripture say? God says there is equality in status before Him, but differences in roles. Christians err when they adopt the attitude of the world and imitate its flouting of God's command to husbands and wives. The marriage relationship is cheapened by unseemly jesting about the true place of husband and wife. Often given is a one-sided emphasis, which distorts the perfect picture God has painted in His Word.

Men too often emphasize just the wife's responsibility of submission to the husband. This *is God's* command not to be lightly dismissed: "Wives, be subject [submit] to your own husbands, as to the Lord" (Eph. 5:22). But the command is set in a context in which the husband's responsibility is also clearly delineated: "Husbands, love your wives, just as Christ also loved the church and gave Himself up for her" (Eph. 5:25).

Such love clearly is a quality above and beyond the ordinary. The reference is not to the normal sexual love, which would not need to be commanded, but to a love even more desirable and needful for both partners.

It is right for husbands and wives to want sexual fulfillment, for God established and sanctified sex within marriage. But that is only a part of the relationship, which will be enhanced and glorified if it is accompanied by a continual spirit of self-sacrifice that causes each one to put the other's welfare completely ahead of his own. Sex is an earthly and temporary condition anyway, even though it was created by God and blessed by Him from the beginning. One day the sexual need will be eliminated (Matt. 22:30). God intended the spiritual, mental, emotional, and sexual aspects of marriage to blend into a joyous oneness in love.

What God commands in the Ephesians passage is a volitional love, a love that can be *willed*. It is not a passing sexual urge or a romantic feeling, nor does it depend on external appearance or even on a response from the one loved. The individual chooses to love regardless of any circumstance. Often husband and wife must make that choice consciously over and over again in the wearing of life.

The verses that precede the instructions regarding husband/wife roles are often ignored in the contemporary controversy. When God tells husbands to love their wives as Christ loved the church, He sets a standard that is impossible to obey. When He tells the wife to submit to her husband as unto the Lord, He gives her an impossible standard. Yet He expects each to live by the standard. The solution to that dilemma lies in the fact that God Himself gives the power to obey as He does for every other command He gives His children.

The instructions in Ephesians 5:22–6:9 that govern the relationships normal to everyday living grow out of one of the deepest doctrines to be found in all of Scripture. It is the command to believers to be filled with the Holy Spirit (Eph. 5:18). One of the evidences that a Christian is filled with the Spirit is his obedience of submission—husbands and wives, parents and children, employers and employees. No one is exempt.

Marriage requires that both partners lay aside a fundamental human need for self-acceptance and self-esteem and make fulfillment of the other's welfare and pleasures more important than one's own. That is possible only through the ability given by the Holy Spirit.

This is the background against which God commands the wife to be in subjection to her husband. It is true that husbands may abuse the responsibility of leadership. But that does not negate the order God set in the family. Nor does the fact that many wives are superior to their husbands in intellect, ability, or spiritual discernment alter their position of submission. A wife who is not a Christian may indeed find this a "hard saying." But a Christian wife can rest in the assurance that an all-wise, all-loving God has so ordered the marriage relationship for the highest good of herself and her husband. When her submission, given voluntarily, is secure, the blessings God has ordained in marriage follow naturally.

Complications arise, of course, when one of the partners is an unbeliever, yet the principle remains unchanged. The Scripture tells the believing wife that her quiet submission to and prayer for her unbelieving husband may win him to Christ (1 Pet. 3:1-2). The specific command of Scripture is that a believer must not marry an unbeliever (2 Cor. 6:14). If a Christian has disobeyed God in this matter, he may confess his sin and be forgiven. But that does not alter the fact that the two are still married and should remain so, difficult as it may be. The believer cannot use that verse as biblical ground to divorce the unbelieving partner.

Another complication arises when two unbelievers marry and one subsequently becomes a Christian. The biblical principle already referred to is true in such a case also. If one is already married to an unbeliever, one cannot change the fact. Instead, he goes on in obedience to God from the point where God finds him (1 Cor. 7:12-14). In such cases the context in Ephesians 5 becomes even more urgent; all headship and all submission in such relationships is possible only as it is done "as unto the Lord."

The scriptural view of divorce, which many Christians dare to challenge, reaffirms the sanctity of God's ordinance of marriage (Mark 10:1-9). There must be a continual reminder that marriage is the illustration to the world of the relationship between Christ and those who belong to Him. That bond, forged at Calvary, can never be broken.

PARENT-CHILD RELATIONSHIPS

God considered the family to be so fundamental that He incorporated the duty of children toward their parents in the Ten Commandments: "Honor your father and your mother, that your days may be prolonged in the land which the LORD your God gives you" (Exod. 20:12). In His instructions through Moses, God shows repeatedly that a child learns respect for and obedience to other authority, including ultimately the authority of God, by learning to obey his parents. That is the emphasis in Leviticus 19, for example, where God connects obedience to parents with the repeated statement of His very being: "I am the LORD." The creator and ruler of the universe is the source of all authority.

The New Testament repeats and enlarges the theme. The passage in Ephesians 5-6, which discusses the mutual duties of husbands and wives, also states those of parents and children. Children are to obey; parents are to raise children "in the discipline and instruction of the Lord." Both are possible only through the power of the Holy Spirit.

BIBLICAL VIEW OF THE FAMILY

Scripture reveals God as creator, sovereign ruler, sustainer of the universe, judge. The Bible speaks of His majesty, eternality, omnipotence, omniscience, holiness. Those attributes, so far beyond human comprehension, could arouse only fear and awe.

But the Bible also reveals God as a loving Father (Psalm 68:5). "Just as a father has compassion on his children, so the LORD has compassion on those who fear Him" (Psalm 103:13). Other references show God's Father relationship to His people. Our family relationship as His dear children enables us to "draw near with confidence to the throne of grace" (Heb. 4:16) for His comfort and help.

God's dealings with the human race through the centuries were expressed in family terms. The value God places on family life is evident in His Word. Children are called the "gift of the LORD" (Psalm 127). God chose to have His Son come into the world through a human mother (Gal. 4:4-5) and grow up in a family, thus stressing the spiritual significance of marriage and the home. Even the supreme truth of salvation is explained in terms of birth into the family of God. The Lord Jesus spoke of children in the tenderest of terms.

The earthly home is the teaching tool to illustrate the relationship of God the Father to those who are His children through faith in His Son. It is that faith that will enable them one day to be secure in the heavenly home. To know God's high concept of the family will guard against being swept away by the false views so prevalent in this age.

CHRISTIAN EDUCATION IN THE HOME

Child education authorities have long agreed that the home is the most vital factor in childhood growth and adjustment to life. The home atmosphere in the early critical years shapes and molds attitudes that carry throughout life.

The pattern of Christian education in the home is foreshadowed in the Old Testament. Deuteronomy 6 indicates a constant, day-by-day instruction in the ordinary circumstances of life. Such training is not to be a once-a-week instruction or teaching only at special times. It is a total commitment of thought and action that covers all of life and should take precedence in the parents' thinking. Everything in ordinary living is to be a vehicle to convey in childhood the spiritual truth that is essential to coping with life beyond the home.

The emphasis in the Deuteronomy passage is on a naturalness in talking about God and our response to Him. Children are to learn early that life is not dissected into entirely separate categories of sacred and secular, but that a personal relationship to God must permeate the whole of one's experience and affect the way one lives. God says, "Even a child is known by his doings, whether his work be pure, and whether it be right" (Prov. 20:11). He makes it clear that training in holy living begins very early.

The most important part of Christian education in the home is acquaintance with and continual use of the Word of God, lived out in daily life. Paul reminded Timothy that he had been instructed from childhood in the "sacred writings, which are able to give you the wisdom that leads to salvation through faith which is in Christ Jesus" (2 Tim. 3:15).

CHRISTIAN EDUCATION THE RESPONSIBILITY OF PARENTS

God told *parents* to teach their children (Psalm 78:4-8; Prov. 1:8). Such teaching does not automatically insure that children will grow up to follow God. The disintegration of many Christian families is heartbreaking evidence that the family that prays together does not always stay together. Faith in God cannot be inherited, for each human being must make an individual response to Christ. But the spiritual attitudes of one generation can affect the next, as Psalm 78 indicates. Timothy's faith "first dwelt in [his] grandmother Lois, and [his] mother Eunice" (2 Tim. 1:5). God holds Christian parents responsible for providing a home atmosphere that will point their children to Him.

Basic to that is a fact that parents dare not overlook. Deuteronomy 6 makes clear that God's Word must first be in your heart before it can be taught to children.

Both mother and father are involved in the teaching, but the father carries the greater burden because of his position of leadership in the home (Eph. 6:4; Col. 3:21; 1 Tim. 3:4, 12). That position cannot be taken lightly, for it carries the responsibility of overseeing the spiritual nurture of the family. The position of leadership should neither be lightly treated by a husband nor coveted by a wife.

EXAMPLES IN SCRIPTURE

Noah showed his wife and sons what it meant to follow God in spite of the ridicule of neighbors and friends (Gen. 6).

Abraham gave his son Isaac a never-to-be-forgotten lesson in obedience when he walked with him up Mount Moriah to offer him as a sacrifice in response to God's command (Gen. 22).

Joshua took responsibility for his family when he declared to fellow Israelites as they faced the choice of serving God in a new land, "As for me and my house, we will serve the LORD" (Josh. 24:15).

Job 1:4-5 gives a picture of a father who prayed daily on behalf of his children, even though they had established their own homes and he was no longer directly responsible for them.

Hebrews 11:23 makes clear the trust Moses' parents had in God's ability to keep their son safe in His will.

But Scripture also gives the somber account of fathers who did not provide a home atmosphere that turned their children naturally to God. Eli, though himself a godly man, was judged "because his sons brought a curse on themselves and he did not rebuke them" (1 Sam. 3:13). And Samuel, the great man of God, had sons who "did not walk in his ways, but turned aside" (1 Sam. 8:3).

Parents must use line-upon-line verbal instruction coupled with godly example in nurturing children for the Lord. The home is the place where God's Word is taught in living.

DISTINCTIVES OF THE CHRISTIAN FAMILY

Should a Christian family be different from a non-Christian family? God's Word rings a positive yes! A home inhabited by those who have been redeemed by the precious blood of Christ is to have "all bitterness and wrath and anger and clamor and slander . . . along with all malice" put away from it, and they are to be kind to one another (Eph. 4:31-32).

That is hard, for every human being is born a sinner and demands his own way. The home is the place to learn how to adjust, how to handle frustrations, how to love—again through the power of the Holy Spirit.

Scripture is permeated with the emphasis that Christians are different and are to live in a manner different from the world because of what God has done for them. The call to commitment in Romans 12:1-2 is preceded by a "therefore," which refers to the recital of God's mercies in earlier chapters. The practical, godly living that is exhorted in Ephesians 4-6 is based on and made possible by the spiritual blessings God has already given in Christ and that are outlined in the first three chapters.

Christian parents cannot hope to keep out of the home every bit of the moral rot that pervades society. It creeps into every home, Christian and non-Christian alike, in both blatant and subtle ways through newspapers, magazines, television, and different values and life-styles of friends, neighbors, and relatives. Since the home is the first influence a child knows, it must be the first line of defense against evil. Christian parents must take the offensive against anything, no matter how innocent it may seem on the surface, that leads children's hearts and minds from God.

The Christian home where people live who have experienced Christ's redeeming love should be characterized by many qualities. Among them:

1. *Love.* The wonder to the pagan world of the first century was this quality in Christians, so evident that those observing it exclaimed, "Behold how they love one another!" Love within a Christian family is not to be put on and taken off at will. In fact, God's Word warns that one's claim

to love God is evidenced by how he loves his brother (1 John 4:20). It is the "love of God . . . poured out within our hearts" (Rom. 5:5) that makes possible harmonious family living. The circle of a loving family gives emotional security and is a safeguard against the power of the evil one.

2. *Knowledge of God's Word.* God gave the Bible for doctrine and reproof and correction to help us know how to live (2 Tim. 3:16). Each family must search out its own method of developing a hunger for God's Word like that which characterized Jeremiah. He found it a "burning fire" in his bones (Jer. 20:9).

3. *Reverence for God.* Christian homes must balance the teaching of God's loving forgiveness of sin with the reminder from Habakkuk that His eyes are "too pure to approve evil." If true reverence for God is the center of the family, its members will have a reaction like that of Isaiah, who, seeing God's holy glory, was conscious of his own unworthiness (Isa. 6).

4. *Personal holiness.* The process of becoming "holy and blameless" (Eph. 5:27) begins with the small child in the home and goes on in little ways day after day. Children have a right to expect their parents to be an example of what it means to live "sensibly, righteously, and godly in the present age," as Titus 2:12 requires.

5. *Disciplined members.* This includes both parents and children together controlled by an inner compulsion of love rather than an outward sense of compelled duty. Discipline is everything that takes place in a home to bring each member to be mature sons in God's family, to the "measure of the stature which belongs to the fulness of Christ" (Eph. 4: 13-14).

6. *Joy.* Those who have experienced the depth of the peace of God through Christ can know also the depth of joy that God's presence gives (Psalm 16:11).

7. *Hospitality.* Throughout the Old Testament, God instructed His people to be mindful of strangers and to care for their needs, because, He said, "You were aliens [strangers] in the land of Egypt" (Lev. 19:34). The Christian family adds a deeper dimension to this concern for others as it reaches out beyond the home to share the riches of God's grace.

BIBLICAL VIEW OF SINGLENESS

It is impossible in a few paragraphs in one chapter on marriage and family to adequately present God's view of singleness. The best that can be done is to remind of the overall theme in Scripture, the personal accountability of every human being. God always speaks first to the individual and says that each one is to "give account of himself to God" (Rom. 14:12). One day marriage will no longer exist; as individuals we will go on eternally loving and serving God.

Scripture does indicate that God's general plan for mankind was marriage. He intended it to be the means of ultimate happiness here on earth. Had sin not entered God's perfect world, marriage would have remained the perfect state God designed it to be. Instead, human nature is warped, so that marriage does not guarantee happiness.

Remaining single is an alternative option to marriage, an option some choose voluntarily, and one others are forced by circumstances to assume (Matt. 19:12). To be single does not mean to be unfulfilled, unwanted, or unloved. All of that can be equally true of married people.

No one should have marriage as a sole goal in life. Whether married or single, the goal of every believer should be commitment to Christ. When we ask for God's will, we do not know if it will include marriage or, if it does, how long a marriage partner will live. It is only by *first* accepting God's will that we find it is "good, and acceptable, and perfect" (Rom. 12:2).

The truth of 1 Corinthians 7:7, 32-34 is hard to understand completely, and is one of the areas of truth we can only see "through a glass darkly" now (KJV). But the verses underscore a singleness of purpose, the purpose of being fully dedicated to God. We are not our own, but are bought with a price (1 Cor. 6:19-20) and our chief end is to "glorify God and enjoy Him forever."[4]

God's will, whatever it is, whatever it brings, *is* perfect, and every one of His dear children, married or single, can rest in that confidence.

Conclusion

The purpose with which God began marriage on earth culminates in heaven with a glorious marriage supper (Rev. 19:7-9). All the marvelous truths about the family come to a climax as the redeemed from every tribe and kindred and nation are united forever with their Redeemer, their Bridegroom, Jesus Christ.

The Christian family, God's exhibit to the world of His gracious provision of salvation for "whosoever will come," must never allow itself to be torn apart by inner dissension or by the scorn of the world. The high calling of the family is to be an example of the Lord Jesus Christ, who "loved the church and gave Himself up for her; that He might sanctify her, having cleansed her by the washing of water with the word, that He might present to Himself the church in all her glory, having no spot or wrinkle or any such thing; but that she should be holy and blameless" (Eph. 5:25-27).

FOR FURTHER STUDY

1. Observe newspapers for one week noting articles (including advice columns) on men/women and parent/child relationships. Contrast with the biblical view outlined in this chapter. Note areas of agreement; areas of disagreement.
2. Analyze the goals of the women's liberation movement in biblical perspective.
3. Contrast love as defined in Scripture with the contemporary expressions found in rock music.
4. Use a concordance to find passages that give the Old Testament emphasis on the family.
5. Study Deuteronomy 6:7-8. List specific ways a family can use the time periods given there to give spiritual training.
6. How can personal holiness be taught objectively to primary age children? junior age? adolescents? List methods to use, and compare for differences in each age level.

SUGGESTED READING

Adams, Jay E. *Christian Living in the Home.* Grand Rapids: Baker, 1972.

Anders, Sarah Frances. *Woman Alone: Confident and Creative.* Nashville: Broadman, 1976.

Andrews, Gini. *Sons of Freedom: God and the Single Man.* Grand Rapids: Zondervan, 1975.

Augsburger, David. *Cherishable: Love and Marriage.* Scottdale, Pa.: Herald, 1971.

Christenson, Larry, and Christenson, Nordis. *The Christian Couple.* Minneapolis: Bethany Fellowship, 1977.

Engelsma, David. *Marriage: The Mystery of Christ and the Church.* Grand Rapids: Reformed Free Pub. Assoc., 1975.

Epp, Theodore H. *Guidelines for Christian Parents.* Lincoln, Neb.: Back to the Bible, 1967.

Getz, Gene. *The Christian Home in a Changing World.* Chicago: Moody, 1972.

Guder, Eileen. *To Live in Love.* Grand Rapids: Zondervan, 1967.

Hancock, Maxine. *Love, Honor and Be Free.* Chicago: Moody, 1975.

Lum, Ada. *Single and Human.* Downers Grove, Ill.: Inter-Varsity, 1976.

Martin, Dorothy. *Creative Family Worship.* Chicago: Moody, 1976.

Martin, Norma, and Levitt, Zola. *Divorce: A Christian Dilemma.* Scottdale, Pa.: Herald, 1977.

McGinnis, Marilyn. *Single: The Woman's View.* Old Tappan, N.J.: Revell, 1974.

Schaeffer, Edith. *What Is a Family?* Old Tappan, N.J.: Revell, 1975.

15

Spiritual Home Training

V. Gilbert Beers

The Meaning of Spiritual Training

Traditionally the child spends the first eighteen years in the home. Eighteen years is 6,574 days, 157,776 hours, and sixty times that many minutes. Theoretically that is the time available to parents for spiritual training. In a very real sense, it is much less, for by the time a child reaches the teen years, a parent's influence has peaked, and the child begins to test ideas with other persons in other places. Thus, it is likely that the parent has less, not more, time for spiritual training than the traditional eighteen years.

What would the average Christian parent of a young child say if asked, "What specific goals do you have for your child by the time age eighteen comes around? Exactly what spiritual ideals would you project for your child at that age?"

Many parents have probably never defined such goals for their children. Thus the desired result of spiritual training remains a blur, which produces a similar uncertainty concerning the manner and methods that should be used to provide spiritual training for the child.

Some parents do have goals, but are content that such goals are limited. Later they may discover that half a loaf is not necessarily better than no loaf at all. For example, the goal for a child to accept Christ as Savior is basic for every Christian home. But to set that as the ultimate goal of all family spiritual training, neglecting goals of growth in Christ, can prevent the spiritual growth necessary to mature Christian living. To provide a thorough training in God's Word is another basic goal for every Christian

---

V. Gilbert Beers, Ph.D., Th.D., is a former professor of Christian education and is now president of Books for Living, Inc. and the author of a number of books for family and children.

home. But if that training focuses on facts and information to the point that it overshadows application of the Word to daily living, the child may grow to believe that an informed Christian is a mature Christian and the proficiency with which information is recited is a gauge of spirituality.

Christian maturity should never be measured by the degree to which a child has become an extension of his parents.[1] This kind of conditional growth, in which we as parents measure maturity by our own yardstick, refuses to allow the child to grow beyond parental ambitions or attainments. It is possible, although difficult for most parents to accept, that a child has the capacity to grow far beyond his parents' level of spiritual maturity.

Spiritual training is on a road with many crossroads, a way marked by many alternatives. That road is life. The most basic choice is the decision to continue as is, committed to self, or to commit life to Christ as Savior and Lord and follow Him. That choice may also relate to other alternatives—religion versus personal Christian commitment, surrender versus rebellion, obedience versus disobedience, Christian community versus the world, Christian values versus a value-vacuum kind of society.

The parent who comes to grips with the responsibility of spiritual training for the child may be uncertain about the role expected of him. Because of that uncertainty or unwillingness to commit himself to the task at hand, he may simply abdicate his responsibility. He is willing to let the church or Sunday school do it, let someone else do it, or let the spouse do it. Happy is the parent who is not overcome by the sense of responsibility, but joyfully assumes the opportunity to influence his own flesh and blood for eternal benefits!

SPIRITUAL TRAINING FOR THE TOTAL PERSON

In an effort to focus on certain functions in life, a child is often compartmentalized into the physical, or biological, being, the social being, the intellectual, or mental being, and the spiritual being. Although there is value in concentrating on one of those areas at a given time, there is also danger in moving from a recognition of the total person as a living symphony. The spiritual part of our being does not reside in a separate corner of our lives, hidden from and refusing to participate with the other "parts" of our being. The parent must keep that in mind in spiritual training, recognizing that what may at the moment seem to be physical, social, or intellectual training may indeed have profound spiritual impact on the child. For example, a father who is physically harsh in his discipline may be conditioning his child against the concept of a loving Father in heaven. The child may find it difficult to accept a basic spiritual concept because of his father's physical behavior.

Piaget held that "biological acts are acts of adaptation to the physical environment and organizations of the environment."[2] Perhaps that thought can be transferred to the spiritual world. If so, we would say that spiritual decisions and activities are those that acclimate us to the spiritual world and to the organizations and institutions that are established to promote the welfare of that world. Or, to put it another way, spiritual decisions and activities put us in harmony with God and His kingdom.

Since the kingdom of our God extends to the here and now, and is not merely that segment of eternity that we spend with Him in heaven, it becomes important to consider spiritual training as training for this world as well as training for the world to come. That means that the reconciliation of our physical, mental, and social beings with our spiritual beings is an essential act of harmony. It means also that our spiritual decisions, attitudes, and actions should rule and overrule in all other matters of life. We cannot be in tune with God in our souls and out of harmony with Him in our conduct. To believe one thing and live another promotes a disharmony of our mental and social well-being and often causes physical sickness and suffering.

Parents are urged to remember this essential ingredient in spiritual training. First, they themselves must be at peace with God in their hearts and hands, as well as in mind and social relationships. To train their children effectively in spiritual growth they as parents must first bring spiritual harmony to their physical, mental, and social lives. More will be said later about the parent as a model.

SPIRITUAL TRAINING—CLIMACTIC EXPERIENCES OR PROCESS OF GROWTH?

Paul's experience on the Damascus road has led many to look more favorably on climactic relationships with Christ as opposed to slow and steady growth in Him. Too often the validity of conversion is measured by the drama associated with the moment of conversion or by the contrast of life before conversion. To be sure, such a conversion commands more attention, especially if the new Christian was once a criminal or was well-known for his evil ways.

But conversion that is less dramatic, brought about through the patient, steady foundation laid by Christian parents in the home, is not only as valid but often gives the Christian a stronger, more secure base upon which to build his new life. The validity of conversion is not based upon its drama or climactic qualities, nor is the reinforcement of the Christian life based upon a repetition of climactic experiences. Spiritual training in the home is a slow, steady process of growth.

Does spiritual training take place before a child makes a definite decision to be a Christian? Of course, for there must be foundational training to prepare the child for such a decision and to provide much that will be needed once that decision is made. It is true that spiritual training becomes much more productive after the child makes a decision for Christ, for there is more purpose now in all that is learned.

SPIRITUAL TRAINING—DUTY OR OPPORTUNITY?

Enforced spiritual training may not only fail to be productive, but may even be counterproductive. When learning the Word of God becomes a duty rather than an opportunity, that duty may become a chore, and chores lose their luster (if they ever had any!) when they can no longer be enforced.[3]

Christian conduct by guilt is never a worthy substitute for Christian conduct by desire. Parents can never produce enough guilt in a child to make him love the Lord with all his heart, soul, mind and strength. But they can produce enough to cause him to fear, which does not make for a good, growing love relationship with either God or the parents. Happy are parent and child who build a warm, loving, exciting atmosphere of joy and desire so that the child's greatest motivation in life is to please God, read and share His Word, and to be sure to perpetuate the atmosphere of Christian love that has surrounded him in his home.[4] This is the fabric from which commitment is woven, and commitment is the basic requirement for a lasting relationship in marriage and Christian living.

SPIRITUAL TRAINING AS A SYSTEM OF PRIORITIES ON A SCALE OF VALUES

Christian living is often a choice of priorities on a scale of values. Spiritual training in the home should focus on the wise choice of those priorities.[5] Parents who refuse to give up an extra margin of income to provide proper time to be good Christian parents have made a poor choice. Their priorities are weighted toward greater materialism rather than a more vital spiritual destiny of their children. Families that become so preoccupied with television that the Word of God and wholesome Christian family activities are neglected have made poor choices.

Life is not a sharp division between plus and minus. Children need to learn early that some people are more honest than others, even after conversion. They need to discover early that some Christians are more loving, more giving, more forgiving, more temperate, or more joyful than other Christians.

Spiritual growth for the Christian is becoming more of those things that honor God and build His people. It is also a recognition that becoming a Christian does not exclude one from suffering, heartache, sin, trouble, and a host of other problems. Becoming a Christian puts us "in Christ" and Christ in us, the Christ who alone can give us wisdom and strength to overcome those things.

As a child grows he enters more and more into a world in which others compete for his mind and heart. In any given day the child is overwhelmed by a multitude of such competitive overtures. Television commercials compete for his money and affections, peers compete for his loyalties or friendship, and even teachers compete for his discipleship.[6] A parent must help the child sort out the various challenges to his system of priorities. Spiritual training is part of that "sorting out" process, providing the child with God's perspectives on the things that matter most in life. Spiritual training is a growing awareness of God's priorities, helping the child not only to put first things first, but to recognize what those first things are.

THE PARENT'S ROLE IN SPIRITUAL TRAINING

Parents are often bewildered when they view the responsibility of preparing their child spiritually for this life and the next. They are frequently uncertain concerning their role as spiritual leaders. Many feel they are inadequately trained to do the job.

Of course, Abraham, Isaac, and Jacob were inadequately trained also if one thinks of formal training. So the lack of formal training in child development or theology should not frighten parents. As adults we learn doctrine or theology primarily through verbal communications of other adults. But as children we learn those things mostly through adult models.

The most important work a parent can do in providing spiritual training to the child is through his role as model. Consistency between our role as model and our role as verbal communicator is essential. Confusion will result in the child's mind if we verbally communicate one doctrine or perspective and he perceives something quite different in our behavior.

The basic spiritual training for "God is love" is first found in the parent not only verbalizing "I love you," but in that love being evidenced in all of life's daily contacts with the child. It is confusing for a child to learn of a loving heavenly Father when he has seen little or no love in his own father's relationships to him.

A delightful, rewarding prayer life may be learned best from an always-accessible parent. If the child grows up with the abiding realization that he can go to the parent at any time for any purpose and will be received with love and understanding, he will learn a most important lesson about prayer. But if the parent is quick to say, "I'm busy, don't bother me," or, "Why did you bother me with *that*?" the child may fail to learn that God is ever present and ever willing to help.

To a small child the parent is the model of omniscience, omnipotence, and omnipresence, for to him the parent has all wisdom, all power, and is always present to solve his small problems. Somehow growth brings a creeping realization that a parent is *not* all-powerful or all-wise, and a parent does well to help the child adjust to that growing realization, shifting the child's confidence in the parent's "superhuman" strength and wisdom to the Person who truly deserves it. Thus spiritual growth is often a gradual shifting of "bigger-than-life" images from parent to God, as it should be.

The attributes of God are ideally seen first in the parent, not as God but as a reflected image of God. The qualities of a rewarding prayer life are first seen in the verbal and nonverbal communications between parent and child. The idea of Christ as rock, shelter, savior, and deliverer is first seen in the secure relationship between the child and the parent who not only cares, but is always a refuge, a "very present help" from the troubles of the outside world. The child must be assured that the parent is "with him" no matter what. Like God, the parent must never communicate "I'll love you only if you do things *my* way." Thus home and parents become a source of strength when all else fails.

As the child grows and shifts the godly attributes from parent to the God who deserves them, it becomes increasingly important that the parent maintain an honest verbal communications role.[7] Too often parents hold some false kind of modesty or seek to preserve an endangered ego in communicating their true feelings or an expression of their weaknesses or failures. Later, when the child reaches the teen years, the parent is surprised and hurt that his child "clams up" and does not communicate his inner feelings.

Of course parents must be judicious in sharing their private weaknesses or most personal failures. Children are not able to bear some burdens, for they may be too heavy. But a warm, loving exchange of experiences and "bearable" feelings and thoughts will help the child realize that parents are honest and open and are pilgrims on the same road as their children.

One of the warmest, most rewarding times in parenthood is when the path of the parent as the communicator of his inner feelings and the path of the child as the communicator of his inner feelings begin to merge. The two recognize at last that they are headed in the same direction, and that they can be of mutual help, strengthening one another. Happy is the parent who recognizes that some day his child, probably in the teen years, merges onto that communications road and does indeed become a strengthening force in the parent's own spiritual growth. That is a switch that many parents are too proud to accept—that there comes a time when the "child shall lead them." But when a parent's desire throughout the training of the child has been for the child some day to exceed his own maturity, it becomes easier for the parent to recognize it when it does happen and to rejoice instead of being hurt.

Thus the communications role between parent and child is a critically important role in life. We communicate nonverbally with the parent as model for doctrine and conduct, but also verbally, when feelings and experiences are shared with love and mutual concern.[8]

An important part of the parent's communication role is that of listener, just as it is an important part of God's communication role with us. As parents expect God to give undivided attention when they pray, so should parents give undivided attention when the child has a need to express. It is most important for the child to realize that when he has something to say, the parent has focused his attention solely on the child and his need and has not divided that attention with "something more important" at the moment. *Nothing* is more important at that time!

THE PLACE OF DISCIPLINE IN SPIRITUAL TRAINING

The traditional view of discipline is that of a child doing something wrong and the parent spanking him for it. After enough spankings, the child turns from the wrong.

Punishment is certainly an important part of discipline. God punishes for sin, and we can do no less as parents. The child must learn that sin, or wrongdoing, brings punishment and therefore discourages the child from doing the things that are wrong.

However, discipline is much more than punishment. Discipline suggests making disciples, and Jesus did not spend the three years of His earthly ministry spanking or punishing His disciples daily. There is a positive side to discipline that is even more important than punishment. The parent becomes a friend, helper, and guide, working with the child to recognize and eliminate those things in life that will cripple or destroy.

Discipline is helping a child know what is wrong, why it is wrong, and why he will be punished if he does it. But it is also helping a child know what is right, why it is right, and why he will enjoy certain rewards if he does that.[9]

Discipline is protection against foolish decisions, a refusal to let a child walk into the "lions jaws," or go beyond the bounds of what is best for him and his family and his God. Discipline is drawing a circle of love around the child and offering security and love within that circle, with freedom of movement in harmony with the child's level of maturity to make certain decisions. It is warning against the unhappiness and frustration that lie beyond the boundaries of that circle, and the parental help and strength and wisdom to motivate the child to stay within the circle.

Discipline is also a recognition that punishment or reward does not increase or diminish parental love. Indeed, it is love that brings discipline, so the love level should remain high, or perhaps peak, throughout the time of discipline, and mutual forgiveness from a child and parent should be swift afterward.

SEX EDUCATION AND SPIRITUAL TRAINING

Does sex education fit at all into a program of spiritual education? Or should it fit more properly into a program of biological education?

To be sure, sex education has a biological base. But it has deeply spiritual implications.[10] The highest goal of sex education for the child is to teach the child the sanctity of sex; that the process so badly maligned in the locker rooms and on television is a spiritual process by which two people give themselves to each other. It is also an act of creation by which a woman, a man, and God unite to create new life. Thus, sex education and spiritual training go hand in hand.[11]

PROCESSES AT WORK IN SPIRITUAL TRAINING

What, then, are the processes through which we accomplish spiritual education in the home? Traditionally we think of a certain time that may be called family altar, devotional time, Bible study time, or any one of many names. Often families feel guilty if they cannot make this specific time work as a time of spiritual training.

There is value in having such a specific time and in following a specific plan of action. By doing this, it is easier to set goals and fulfill them. But the great men and women of the Bible probably never trained their children at a limited time. They were admonished to teach their children throughout the day in all exercises of living. Spiritual training was a continuous process in which the parent looked for opportunities throughout the day and in all circumstances to tell the child about God and how God expected him to live.[12]

During formal, or structured, family worship, a parent must seek to apply creativity of approach to maintain a high level of interest. Such a time can become deadly dull if the same approach is used day after day.[13] It is far more important to build a lifelong appetite for God's Word and family worship than to impart certain facts and doctrines.

Much spiritual home training can be accomplished through outreach or Christian service. The best way to learn how to please God is to enter into some service for Him and learn while serving. Families can serve in remarkable ways, such as visiting nursing homes, children's homes, or homes for retarded adults and sharing love through music, testimony, and personal interest. Families can help other families in need and share Christ along with tangible gifts gathered for the needy. These are but a few of many kinds of outreach from the home, and of course through the church and Sunday school there would be numerous other kinds, too.

Spiritual training recognizes certain levels of learning and what a child can accomplish at each level. To move too fast or too slow, or to expect too much or too little can be frustrating to a child.[14]

The end result of spiritual home training is for a child to come to know Jesus Christ as Savior and Lord and to discover ways to live to the fullest for Him. It is to help the child grow into a mature adult Christian who can assume the role of Christian mother, father, or other adult spiritual leader who can help to train others in living the Christian life. Learning is dynamic change in the learner's life, so something should happen throughout the learning process. The wise parent will seek to make learning not only dynamic, but enjoyable, for to desire to study the Word of God and practice the Word in daily living is far more important than merely to know what one should do.

FOR FURTHER STUDY

1. Conduct a survey of college-age young people to determine the type of spiritual training given to them as children, how they reacted to it then, and how they react to it in retrospect. This might include also a study of how many would use the same techniques and approaches if they become parents.
2. Through a Sunday school class or other group of elementary-age children, survey reactions to the spiritual training they currently receive at home and how the children would like to see that training change to be more interesting and effective.
3. Using a textbook on doctrine, develop a related chart showing how the parent as model would teach each doctrine nonverbally to his children.
4. Do a study of discipline as a positive force in spiritual training as opposed to a punitive force.
5. Develop a comprehensive presentation of the various methods or processes by which spiritual training of children in the home can be accomplished.
6. Present a plan for sex education for children, showing the relationships to spiritual training. Show specifically how certain facets of sex education may relate to specific doctrines or attitudes about spiritual life.

NOTES

1. For additional reading from a psychological point of view, see Suzanne Strait Fremon, *Children and Their Parents* (New York: Harper & Row, 1968), pp. 35-36.
2. Barry J. Wadsworth, *Piaget's Theory of Cognitive Development* (New York: McKay, 1971), p. 9.
3. Gladys Hunt, *Honey for a Child's Heart* (Grand Rapids: Zondervan, 1969), captures this sense of opportunity in joy through reading with children in the home.
4. See Arline Cate Thrash, *Little Things That Keep Families Together* (Nashville: Broadman, 1976).

5. David Wilkerson, *Parents on Trial* (New York: Hawthorn, 1967), focuses on the wise and unwise choice of priorities by parents and children, showing how much juvenile delinquency is actually a result of poor parental choices of priorities in giving spiritual training to their children.
6. Chapter 2 in Gordon MacDonald, *The Effective Father* (Wheaton, Ill.: Tyndale, 1977) has some excellent thoughts concerning these competitive forces.
7. Fred Roach, *Let's Talk* (Old Tappan, N.J.: Revell, 1977) presents some good ideas to help get family conversation going.
8. Virginia Satir, in *Peoplemaking* (Palo Alto, Calif.: Science and Behavior, 1972), has some excellent discussion on the place of communications in the family.
9. See James Dobson, *Dare to Discipline* (Wheaton, Ill.: Tyndale, 1976) for a good discussion of discipline for children.
10. See Clyde M. Narramore, *How to Tell Your Children About Sex* (Grand Rapids: Zondervan, 1958).
11. Mary E. LeBar, *Children Can Worship* (Wheaton, Ill.: Scripture Press, Victor, 1976) presents some good ideas on spiritual training, especially chapter 4 on family worship.
12. Helpful here are resources such as the Victor Family Concern Series, a set of books, leader guides, and workbooks covering major family concerns (Scripture Press Publications).
13. Dorothy Martin, *Creative Family Worship* (Chicago: Moody, 1976) gives excellent help on putting variety and interest into family worship time.
14. See Roy B. Zuck and Robert E. Clark, *Childhood Education in the Church* (Chicago: Moody, 1975), chapter 10, for a table of doctrinal learning levels.

SUGGESTED READING

Anderson, Doris. *How to Raise a Christian Family*. Grand Rapids: Zondervan, 1960. A mother tells how to make family living a happy experience, including family worship and spiritual training in the home.

Brandt, Henry, and Landrum, Phil. *I Want to Enjoy My Children*. Grand Rapids: Zondervan, 1975. Principles of parenthood with a section about discipline.

Christenson, Larry. *The Christian Family*. Minneapolis: Bethany Fellowship, 1970. A guide to family relationships, especially "God's order" for mates, wives, children, parents, husbands.

Collins, Gary R., ed. *Living and Growing Together*. Waco, Tex.: Word, 1976. Twelve authors write about important areas of family relationships, including chapters on evangelism in the home.

*Dobson, James. *Dare to Discipline*. Wheaton, Ill.: Tyndale, 1976. A psychologist's view of discipline, both from a positive and punitive perspective.

Drescher, John M. *Seven Things Children Need*. Scottdale, Pa.: Herald, 1976. Seven things include significance, security, acceptance, love, praise, discipline, and God.

Edens, David, and Edens, Virginia. *Why God Gave Children Parents*. Nashville: Broadman, 1966. About parental responsibility in various areas, specifically in Christian nurture and growth.

Fairchild, Roy W., and Wynn, John Charles. *Families in the Church: A Protestant Survey*. New York: Association, 1961. A research study of family life, based on group discussions, questionnaires, and data from previous research.

*Fremon, Suzanne Strait. *Children and Their Parents*. New York: Harper & Row, 1968. A psychological work on parent-child relationships. Has many good principles that can be applied to spiritual training.

*Especially recommended.

Galloway, Dale E. *We're Making Our Home a Happy Place*. Wheaton, Ill.: Tyndale, 1976. Suggestions for new approaches to family living, with a section on communications and another on fun in the family.

Gangel, Kenneth O., and Gangel, Elizabeth. *Between Christian Parent and Child*. Grand Rapids: Baker, 1974. Some chapters on family worship and fun as a family.

Getz, Gene. *The Christian Home in a Changing World*. Chicago: Moody, 1972. A small guidebook relating biblical principles to Christian home relationships.

Goldman, Ronald. *Religious Thinking from Childhood to Adolescence*. New York: Seabury, 1964. A descriptive account of how school pupils think about religion and the way they are taught religion.

Haystead, Wesley. *You Can't Begin Too Soon*. Glendale, Calif.: Gospel Light, Regal, 1974. Child's various relationships to people and the principles that will develop him spiritually.

*Hendricks, Howard G. *Say It with Love*. Wheaton, Ill.: Scripture Press, Victor, 1972. Emphasizes communicating the gospel with love. Chapter 9 talks about living the gospel with the children in the home.

Hubbard, David A. *Is the Family Here to Stay?* Waco, Tex.: Word, 1972. Examines the biblical origin of the family and guidelines for the problems a modern family faces.

*Hunt, Gladys. *Honey for a Child's Heart*. Grand Rapids: Zondervan, 1969. An excellent book about the imaginative use of books in family life and how spiritual growth can come through reading.

Jacobsen, Margaret Bailey. *What Happens When Children Grow*. Wheaton, Ill.: Scripture Press, Victor, 1959. Last chapter talks about the spiritual training in the Christian home.

Jones, Jessie Orton. *The Spiritual Education of Our Children*. New York: Viking, 1960. A discussion of ways to build religious values in home and school.

*MacDonald, Gordon. *The Effective Father*. Wheaton, Ill.: Tyndale, 1977. The role of the father as seen through the eyes of a pastor and father.

Martin, Dorothy. *Creative Family Worship*. Chicago: Moody, 1976. Ways to improve family worship.

Meier, Paul D. *Christian Child-Rearing and Personality Development*. Grand Rapids: Baker, 1977. Role of parent as viewed by a Christian psychiatrist.

Merrill, Dean. *The Husband Book*. Grand Rapids: Zondervan, 1977. The husband's role as seen from the masculine perspective.

Miller, Randolph Crump. *Your Child's Religion*. New York: Hawthorn, 1962. Discusses child in relationship to religion through church, home, and community.

Narramore, Bruce. *An Ounce of Prevention*. Grand Rapids: Zondervan, 1973. A guide for parents in directing the moral and spiritual growth of their children.

————. *Help! I'm a Parent!* Grand Rapids: Zondervan, 1972. Brings biblical and psychological truth together to answer questions about the role of modern parents, including a good section on discipline.

*Especially recommended.

Narramore, Clyde M. *How to Tell Your Children About Sex.* Grand Rapids: Zondervan, 1958. Small but good book with psychologist's views.

Olson, Nathanael. *How to Win Your Family to Christ.* Westchester, Ill.: Good News, 1977. Talks about ways to win various family members to Christ.

Rice, Shirley. *The Christian Home: A Woman's View.* Norfolk, Va.: Norfolk Christian Schools, 1965. Husband-wife relationships and spiritual training of the child in the home.

Roach, Fred. *Let's Talk.* Old Tappan, N.J.: Revell, 1977. Ideas to start family conversations.

Royal, Claudia. *Teaching Your Child About God.* Westwood, N.J.: Revell, 1940. Emphasizes importance of parental understanding and guidance in the religious development of the child.

Ruddock, Eugenia Ramsey. "The Discipline of Children in the Christian Home." Master's thesis, Wheaton College, Wheaton, Ill.: 1959. Seeks to clarify the place of discipline in the Christian home.

Rafferty, Max. *What They Are Doing to Your Children.* New York: New American Library, 1963. A criticism of education of children in the public schools by the Superintendent of Public Instruction of California.

*Richards, Lawrence O. *A Theology of Christian Education.* Grand Rapids: Zondervan, 1975. Chapter 17 is about the home as a nurture center, and chapter 18 offers suggestions for an alternative to the traditional Bible teaching approach.

*Satir, Virginia. *Peoplemaking.* Palo Alto, Calif.: Science and Behavior Books, 1972. About family relationships. Based on the premise that "all of the ingredients in a family that count are changeable and correctable." Some excellent challenges to our thoughts about spiritual training.

Strauss, Richard L. *Confident Children and How They Grow.* Wheaton, Ill.: Tyndale, 1975. Seeks to apply biblical principles to the task of raising children in a Christian home.

Taylor, Florence M. *As for Me and My Family.* Waco: Word, 1976. Advice to parents from a biblical perspective.

Thrash, Arline Cate. *Little Things That Keep Families Together.* Nashville: Broadman, 1976. Homey family experiences that have helped bring the author's family into a closer relationship.

Wadsworth, Barry J. *Piaget's Theory of Cognitive Development.* New York: McKay, 1971. A presentation of Piaget's ideas concerning intellectual organization and adaptation to the environment. Some good principles that can apply to spiritual training.

Westley, William A., and Epstein, Nathan B. *The Silent Majority.* San Francisco: Jossey-Bass, 1969. Two psychological studies of emotional health of students as they relate to families. Although students are college age, the root of their problems is in spiritual training in earlier childhood.

*Wilkerson, David. *Parents on Trial.* New York: Hawthorn, 1967. From personal experience with young people who have fallen into drugs and street

*Especially recommended.

life, Wilkerson tells how parental influence and neglect in their earlier childhood have contributed to delinquency.

Wilt, Joy. *An Uncomplicated Guide to Becoming a Superparent.* Waco, Tex.:
Word, 1977. A mother's view of parental roles with the framework for spiritual climate in the home.

*Zuck, Roy B., and Clark, Robert E., eds. *Childhood Education in the Church.*
Chicago: Moody, 1975. A basic textbook in Christian education for children.
A number of chapters relate to spiritual training of children, including chap-
ters 9, 10, 11, 19, and 28.

Part V

ORGANIZING THE CHURCH FOR CHRISTIAN EDUCATION

PEOPLE, RESOURCES, and programs must be properly organized and coordinated for the church to effectively carry out its educational mission of guiding persons to maturity in Jesus Christ (Eph. 4:13). Although the degree of simplicity or complexity in the organizational plan is largely determined by the size of the church, planning is essential.

Nehemiah organized family groups for adequate division of labor. The early church found it necessary in Acts 6 to assign ministries to qualified persons. Paul emphasized the training of faithful men who could in turn teach others.

This unit begins with an overview in chapter 16 of the total church program. The pastor is then considered in his key role as "equipper" (Eph. 4), where he not only preaches and teaches the Word but ultimately supervises that total church program. Chapter 18 discusses the multiple staff-team concept in the church, which may add such professional leadership as director of Christian education, youth pastor, children's director and/or family ministries director.

Chapter 19 defines organization and describes its outworking through the board of Christian education. The structure, or framework, of organization calls for placement of people in areas of ministry and the improvement of the quality of their ministry. Chapter 20 discusses administration and supervision and the relationship of organization to leadership. Developing, enlisting and training that leadership are considered in chapter 21.

The last two chapters of the unit relate educational curriculum and facilities and equipment to the organizational aspect of Christian education. Gaines S. Dobbins's chapter 23, for example, provides a rationale for a building philosophy as well as a practical guide to form and function.

16

The Church's Educational Ministry

Doris A. Freese

Today's CHURCH seeks to meet the biblical imperatives of evangelism and edification (Matt. 28:19-20) through its total program. Although both evangelism and edification occur in all aspects of that program, edification frequently takes form in a more systematic way through the agencies or programs that constitute the church's educational ministry. An accurate assessment of the extent of edification and the effectiveness of educational programs or ministries may be made when certain questions are asked. What biblical principles underlie the church's educational ministry? How does the total church program seek to carry out such principles? What process can be used as a guide in determining and implementing ministries or programs? What educational ministries currently exist in our churches as a means of evangelizing and edifying?

BIBLICAL PRINCIPLES

General agreement exists in today's Christian society about the role and importance of the home in teaching (see chapter 14). Old Testament passages command and identify the educational primacy of the family in the transmission of faith from one generation to another. Likewise the New Testament describes the place of nurture and training in the home. Gene Getz cautions in his book *The Measure of a Family* that although functions are clearly identified in the New Testament, little is said regarding what actual form or pattern the home teaching should take.[1]

The Scriptures also describe the function of teaching as it relates to a body larger than the family, gathered specifically for instruction. In the Old Testament, Israel gathered together to hear the reading of the law. The Deuteronomy 6:6-9 passage, which outlines the teaching responsibility

Doris A. Freese, Ph.D., is an associate professor of Christian education at the Moody Bible Institute, Chicago, Illinois.

of the family, occurs within a body of instruction given to Israel by Moses. In other words, the gathered body was taught how to teach and live in their families. The great history of Israel was frequently rehearsed verbally by the leaders to the entire congregation (Josh. 24). Duties of Old Testament priests included teaching the law along with the sacramental duties of Tabernacle and Temple worship (Lev. 10:11; Deut. 31:10-13; Mal. 2:7). Ezra, identified as priest and scribe (Ezra 7:11; Neh. 8:1-4), assumed a key role in teaching the law to the exiles who returned to Israel from Babylon.

New Testament pictures of teaching begin with Jesus Christ Himself as the master teacher, who taught gatherings varying in size from one (Nicodemus; the Samaritan woman) to several persons (small groups of disciples) to huge crowds (five thousand sitting on a hillside). With the inception of the church as recorded in the book of Acts, teaching emerged as an essential means of instruction in doctrine and Christian life-style as the infant church grew under the teaching of the apostles (Acts 2:42). Paul's ministry included not only evangelizing the unsaved but also teaching new converts and strengthening them in the faith (Acts 14:21-22). Among the gifted persons in the church were those who served as pastor-teachers (Eph. 4:11) and those who taught (Rom. 12:7; 1 Cor. 12:28). Paul encouraged Timothy to observe the principle of multiplication in his ministry—to commit God's truth to men who would be able to teach others also (2 Tim. 2:2).

Getz's caution regarding function versus form also applies to the educational ministry of the church. Although the *function* of teaching is clearly indicated, the form, pattern, or design it should take is indistinct. The local church, therefore, is free under the guidance of the Holy Spirit to design ways to teach within certain guidelines.

THE TOTAL CHURCH PROGRAM

Both function and form are reflected in what a local church does. Whatever program a church plans and implements, it must carry out the ultimate purpose for which the church, the Body of Christ, exists. That purpose is to make disciples as summed up in the Great Commission, "Go [or more accurately, "Going," or, "As you go"] therefore and make disciples of all the nations, baptizing them in the name of the Father and the Son and the Holy Spirit, teaching them to observe all that I commanded you . . ." (Matt. 28:19-20). The responsibility includes both *evangelizing,* to bring persons to Jesus Christ, and *teaching* them in His commandments and in the doctrines of the Word. Implied in the Great Commission is the aspect of training and equipping. How can one "go" unless he has been equipped in some way to do so? (Compare with Eph. 4:12-13.)

The church, in its efforts to carry out the Great Commission, must marshal its entire program in the direction of that purpose. The total church program, therefore, can be defined as the entire, complete program that a local church carries on to bring persons to Christ as Savior and Lord, to guide them in growth toward Christlikeness, and to equip them for effective service in the will of God. All ministries of a local church, such as pastoral, teaching, music, evangelism, extension, and preaching, will focus on the three major areas of evangelizing, edifying, and equipping.

Every age level will receive a proper and balanced emphasis in salvation, Christian growth, and service. Children, youth, and adults will be confronted with the claims of Christ for salvation. Christian children, youth, and adults will be taught biblical truths at their level of comprehension and will be encouraged to walk and grow in Jesus Christ. Christians of all ages will be trained, simply or more complexly, to share their faith in Christ and to participate in the growth process of one another through service and expression.

In the development of its program, the church will seek to allow for involvement of and ministry to the total person. Each person possesses intellect, attitudes, feelings, will, and capacity to relate to God and to others. In order to meet the needs of the whole person, the program should include four major elements: instruction, worship, fellowship, and expression-service.

Those four elements are reflected in the early church as described in Acts 2:42-47. Note that the new believers devoted themselves "to the apostles' teaching" (instruction); devoted "themselves . . . to fellowship, to the breaking of bread and to prayer" (fellowship); continued "in the temple . . . praising God," (worship); and shared possessions with those in need (expression-service). Furthermore, they had favor with all people throughout the city and God added "to their number day by day those who were being saved" (evangelism).

Instruction, through preaching and teaching, relates primarily to the intellect and involves the transmission of biblical information, doctrines, and truths. It also includes training, such as the development of teaching or leadership skills. Since teaching and preaching seek to go far beyond mere intellectual exercise and expansion, instruction lays the foundation for movement toward maturity in Christ as persons grow in the knowledge of Him and His word.

Worship serves as a means of expressing our thoughts about God to God. From the old English word "worthship," it denotes the worthiness of the individual receiving reverence and honor. A right attitude that acknowledges who God is and His right to receive our praise and adoration is essential in worship. Although worship or heart expression involves the person primarily at the feeling level, it should be a result of what he knows about God. Lois E. LeBar states, "worship is adoring God for Himself, thanking Him for all His goodness to us, and in His presence adjusting our will to His will. While instruction informs the mind, worship challenges the will and emotions. On the basis of Scriptural truth, our attitudes are shaped and conformed to His likeness."[2]

A third element that should be an essential part of the total church program is *fellowship*. Not only does the believer seek fellowship with his Savior and Lord, but he seeks mutual edification within the church, the Body of Christ (Eph. 4:15-16; 1 John 1:3). True fellowship goes beyond mere social or recreational activities, which may be used as a means of gathering people together and helping them feel comfortable within a group, to the building up of one another through expressions of concern, prayer and share time, utilization of gifts and abilities, and development of warm Christian friendship. Such fellowship can take place at any age level. Even children can develop a sense of community through activities that promote cooperation rather than competition.

The fourth element, *expression-service*, focuses on the need for each individual believer to act upon his knowledge and faith. It can take a variety of forms—believers can speak of their faith, teach, visit, serve as deacons or deaconesses, assist in the administration of the local church, train others, demonstrate hospitality, care for the sick in the congregation, pray, or lead a Bible study. Not only are possibilities for service numerous within any local body of believers, but also all ages—children, youth and adults—can be involved.

Evangelism, the presentation of the gospel, is a major aim of Christian education as well as a biblical imperative. It is not considered one of the major elements, but it permeates all four. Instruction, worship, fellowship, and expression-service can all be used in the evangelization efforts of the church to win others to Jesus Christ. For example, at camp, which includes all four elements, a senior high student may find Christ as Savior through one of several activities. He may hear and respond in a Bible hour (instruction); he may make a decision at an evening campfire (worship); or he may be led to Christ by some fellow campers in his cabin (fellowship, expression-service). The local church should ask, Do the persons involved in our various programs and ministries clearly present the claims of Christ for salvation so that the unsaved can and will respond? Is there an emphasis on salvation as well as on Christian growth and service?

A careful examination of programs for a particular age level may reveal either an overemphasis or lack among the four elements. Each department does well to chart all the programs planned for any given year (Sunday school, Sunday evening programs, camp, vacation Bible school, weekday club), and indicate the elements that receive primary emphasis in each specific program. Once a department has developed its chart, the following questions may be asked: On which elements is the most emphasis currently being placed? What elements are either missing or have an inadequate emphasis?

THE EDUCATIONAL PROCESS

One must view the church program of Christian education as composed of various parts or ministries that are educational in nature, that seek to meet the needs of the whole person, and that carry out biblical imperatives. All too frequently a program or ministry is launched on the basis of its attractive curriculum materials, its success in some other church, or its emphasis on a current issue or problem. Likewise, a program in existence may be continued for a variety of reasons ranging from tradition and entrenchment to fear of trying something new. Rather than developing or continuing programs on such bases, the local church can plan and implement ministries following a sequential order or process—the educational process.

THE EDUCATIONAL PROCESS*

Biblical Imperatives and Objectives

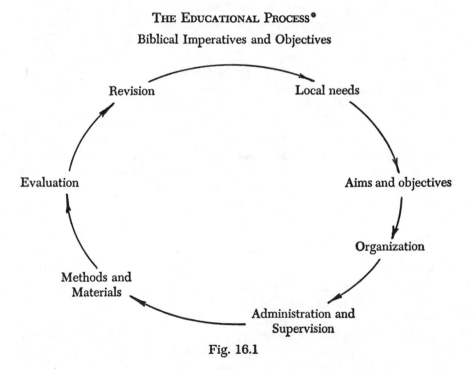

Fig. 16.1

*Diagram adapted from materials suggested by LeBar, Gangel, and Getz.

The educational process begins with the biblical imperatives of evangelism and edification as seen in Matthew 28:19-20 and the related objectives determined by the local church as it views its mission in carrying out those imperatives. The following illustrates the first step in the educational process:

Biblical imperative: Edification—"teaching them to observe whatsoever I have commanded you" (Matt. 28:20).

Biblical objective: The local church will provide the means for effective edification whereby believers of all ages can develop into spiritually mature and effective Christians.[3]

NEEDS

When clear objectives have been written, the next step is to determine the more specific needs of the local church as they relate to the objectives. It may be well to look at particular age groups, as well as at the larger fellowship of believers.

A representative body composed of teachers, leaders, and parents might meet to discuss and identify the needs, for example, of youth. Both general and specific needs should be identified. Some needs will be common to all ages; others will apply specifically to one age group. Needs relate to various aspects of the whole person (physical, mental, emotional, social, and spiritual) as well as to organizational, administrative, and supervisory areas. For example, the following represent several kinds of needs:

Need	*Area*
A need for a plan that provides fellowship for senior citizens	Organizational
A need for the juniors (grades 4, 5, 6) to learn to do simple Bible study	Departmental
A need for a quality library for our teachers' use	Organizational
A need for trained teachers for our Sunday school	Supervisory
A need for Steve and Diane to receive Christ as Savior	Personal

AIMS

The next step in the process is to write aims or objectives that arise out of the identification of needs. An aim or objective is simply a statement of what the group or individual plans to accomplish. It gives direction to planning and implementation and serves as a checkpoint as progress of the plan is assessed. Aims will be both immediate and long-range. For example, leaders of an educational agency like the Sunday school can ask questions such as: By the end of the year, what enrollment increase can we achieve? How will teachers receive training for improvement? What visitation programs will be included in the Sunday school? A teacher, who is also determining aims, will ask questions such as: By the end of the year in this class what will my pupils know about God, Jesus Christ, the Bible, the Christian life? How will their attitudes grow and change? What new or additional steps will they take in their Christian walk?

Aims may be general or specific. General aims tend to express in broad terms what is to happen within a group or individual, whereas specific aims can be linked with very particular needs. However, aims of any kind—immediate or long-range, general or specific—should be written with the following characteristics, and these characteristics should be evident whether the aim is for a person, program, administration, supervision, or lesson:

> Clear enough to be written down
> Concise enough to be kept in focus
> Specific enough to be accomplished
> Accomplishable within a designated time period

Educators refer to four kinds of aims or objectives: cognitive (having to do with the mind), affective (having to do with feelings and attitudes), skill (having to do with motor development), and behavioral (having to do with conduct). A similar way of looking at aims is to identify them as *know, feel, skill,* and *do* or *conduct* aims. The Christian worker senses the importance of communicating knowledge, but he is aware that the purpose of teaching goes far beyond the accumulation of information and facts. He therefore writes aims that not only will help persons to study and discover God's truth but will also guide them in finding ways to apply the truth to their lives. The leader, concerned with his students' overall Christian growth, writes aims to guide in that direction. He may write a single *feel* or *do* aim, or he may write a series of aims, *know→feel→do,* but he is ever concerned with immediate and long-range changes in the lives of persons.

ORGANIZATION

The church exists as an organism or a living body that transcends time and space. Only God Himself can see the Body of Christ in its entirety at one time, and the church will continue to grow until the return of Christ. The local church body is but a small part of a much larger whole. It exists as an organization or a local gathering of believers with some structure or form that is both visible and definable. Even local fellowships that hold to a minimum of organization have some identifiable form.

When needs of the local body have been identified and aims have been written, the next step is to organize the educational ministries program to carry out the aims, which in turn meet the needs. Organization, or the framework underlying the plan, has to do with the grouping and arranging of the persons and programs.

Organization is *person-related*, with job descriptions used to explain relationships and responsibilities.

It is also *program-related*. It defines the relationships of each agency or ministry to the total church program. Statements of policy and procedure help identify the task and operating plan of each agency.

Organization should evidence several characteristics. First, it should be *unified*. Whatever is done in the name of program should contribute to and be an integral part of the total ministry. It helps to carry out the overarching biblical objectives of the church.

Second, organization of the program should be *simple*. It should allow the persons involved to minister freely within a minimum of necessary boundary lines. It helps facilitate rather than impede ministry.

Organization should also be *flexible* in order to change when change is required—If when a plan or program must be altered, supplemented, strengthened, or even discarded.

Fourth, organization should be *cooperative* with a sense of God's authority.* All persons involved in a local church ministry should be willing to follow the simple lines of authority set forth in God's Word: God, Christ, man, woman.

Fifth, organization should be *correlated* in that persons within a particular agency in the church education program understand its relation to other agencies. Such relationship will be evidenced in curriculum, programming, and departmentalization. Correlation of each agency within the church education program avoids overlapping and gapping.

Finally, organization should be *participative* so that members within various agencies are involved in setting goals, determining programs, and evaluating progress. The Christian worker acknowledges the picture presented by Paul in Ephesians 4:16 of the body with its many members, which in proper working order "causes the growth of the body for the building up of itself in love."

Kenneth O. Gangel reminds those involved in leadership, "In the process of departmentalization, unification, correlation, construction of organizational charts and all the rest, we dare not lose sight of the fact that in the final analysis we are dealing with an *organism* and therefore must allow the church's spiritual aspects to constantly permeate the organizational process."[4]

*LeBar in *Focus on People in Church Education*, p. 72, uses the expression "democratic under God's authority." True unity and cooperation among believers takes place only as those believers follow and function within the authority structure laid down by God in His Word.

ADMINISTRATION AND SUPERVISION

Organization of the program leads to administration and supervision. *Administration* has to do with guiding and directing the persons toward desired goals within the structure, or framework, of organization. It is the organization fleshed out in people who by common agreement now move forward to accomplish their task.

A thorough treatment of administration is given in chapter 20 by Dr. Ronald Chadwick. He suggests that the function of administration includes planning, organizing, staffing, initiating, delegating, directing, overseeing, coordinating, evaluating, and motivating. Perhaps, for this discussion, those functions can be summarized under two major headings: delegation and coordination.

Delegation seeks to distribute responsibility among those involved in ministry. It involves selecting the right person for the task and holding him accountable as he fulfills his responsibility.

Coordination provides the thread that weaves its warp through all that takes place in the educational ministry of the church. The administrator leads his workers in understanding and implementing the purposes and goals of the total church program.

Supervision relates to improving the quality of both leadership and program. It involves overseeing, motivating, maintaining proper relationships, and evaluating performance and product.

A good supervisor will guide his workers in setting and maintaining standards. He will be aware of his workers' strengths and areas that need improvement. He will seek to train them to be more effective in their ministry.

The following chart (fig. 16.2) illustrates organization, administration, and supervision as they relate to one another.

METHODS AND MATERIALS

The educational process to this point has concentrated on the persons involved and the programs or tasks to be implemented. Persons, of course, will utilize methods and materials to carry out the tasks. Byrne defines method as an "orderly, systematic procedure employed to carry out some purpose or to gain some preconceived goal."[5] Method is simply a way of doing the task, whereas materials are the tools or aids used in any given method. Byrne places methods into two categories; administrative and instructional.

The "how" or method of the educational ministry of the church builds on an understanding of both content (curriculum) and educational process (teaching-learning). Those aspects are discussed in detail in chapters 5 and 22. LeBar stresses the importance of scriptural method by which the

Organization	Administration	Supervision
Board of Christian Education — Library Committee [chart] Set up a library committee as a part of the Board of Christian Education.	Appoint a librarian and three assistants to catalog and circulate books and other library resources.	Evaluate effectiveness of the committee and make three monthly reports to the Board of Christian Education.
Sunday school — teacher training — visitation [chart] Develop a plan for systematic visitation.	Enlist and train leadership for visitation.	Maintain high quality of visitation program through refresher training every six months.

Fig. 16.2

teacher serves as a guide to help pupils "discern their own real needs, discover the answer in Scripture, and practice the truth."[6] A variation on her diagram of boy-Book-boy shows the relationship of pupils' needs, the Word of God, the teacher, and the Holy Spirit.

When emphasis is placed on guiding pupils to discover answers and to respond, the teaching methods take a specific approach. Rather than concentrating on delivery of a large amount of content, the teacher carefully selects methods that involve pupils in active Bible study and discovery. Interaction methods, such as question and answer, discussion, Bible search, buzz groups, and role play, will be used along with teacher focus methods such as lecture and story-telling. Curriculum materials will be selected not only for the quality of content, that is, how clearly and accurately the Word of God is taught, but also for the process or method that is used to guide pupils in learning.

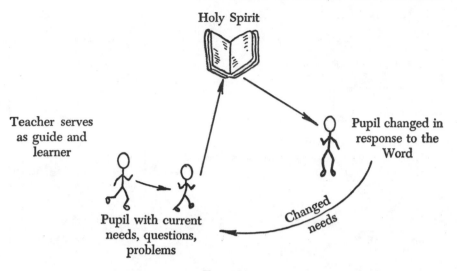

Fig. 16.3

EVALUATION

The final step in the educational process, evaluation, is in no sense a termination point. Continual evaluation occurs as key aspects of the total educational ministry are examined. Evaluation looks at program, pupil, process, progress, and product. Each aspect is examined and evaluated by asking questions such as:

> To what extent are persons' needs being met?
> To what extent are aims being accomplished?
> What spiritual results are evident?
> How can results be conserved?

More specific questions can be asked that relate to a particular program or curriculum or to individual pupils within a class. In each instance evaluation seeks to measure progress and to determine what has been accomplished. The evaluative process then results in a reassessment of needs, which may be different as a result of the accomplishment of earlier goals. New aims are written and the educational process continues.

MEETING NEEDS OF PEOPLE THROUGH VARIED MINISTRIES

What are some forms that might be utilized to carry out the church's Christian education program? As stated before, although function is described in the Scriptures, very little is said about exact form, pattern, or design. Since a church cannot have function without form, examination of a particular form or ministry should include an assessment of its function. Does it emphasize teaching (instruction) or worship? Does the ministry allow for edification of believers through fellowship? To what extent does the program encourage expression and service?

Three major time frames serve as a backdrop for examination of Christian education ministries: Sunday, weekday, and seasonal. Some teaching ministries, such as Sunday school, occur every Sunday during the year, whereas some may coincide with the public school year, such as children's church or training hour.

Weekdays provide opportunity for a variety of ministries not only in form but in duration. Such ministries may take the form of weekday clubs, fellowship organizations, Bible classes, prayer and share meetings, and training sessions. Time frames vary from short-term, such as several weeks for a training series in a particular department, to long-term, such as clubs that keep pace with the school year.

A third time frame recognizes the growing interest in and use of summer months and vacation periods such as Christmas and spring breaks. Vacation Bible school, camp, and retreat programs take advantage of such blocks of time that allow for in-depth ministry to a particular age level or group of people in the church.

SUNDAY SCHOOL

Although in some cases Sundays or weekends tend to see an evacuation of people from the home area, Sunday still remains the day on which most people choose to worship the Lord and seek instruction in His Word. For two hundred years the Sunday school has served the purpose of instruction—originally to teach lower class children to read and write and later to teach the Word of God to both the unchurched and the churched. Today the Sunday school has been identified as the church at study, involving people in the Word of God and training them to study it together.

What characterizes the Sunday school of today? First, it is a school that meets on *Sunday*. Sunday is still freer than other days of the week for many people and offers opportunity for the church to gather together for the purpose of instruction in the Word as well as for worship. Even churches with innovative approaches to worship and program structure provide some Sunday educational experience for children, and often for youth and adults, prior to or following the morning worship time.

Second, the Sunday school is a *school*. Its main purpose has been instruction, and it has committed itself to a systematic teaching of the Bible. In no other educational ministry of the church do so many age levels receive such a systematic approach to the Scriptures. The Sunday school can teach not only biblical truths and general doctrines but can also stress the distinctive doctrines of each church. It is committed to the Great Commission, both in evangelizing and in edifying or "teaching them to observe whatsoever I have commanded you" (Matt. 28:19-20).

As a school, the Sunday school can departmentalize in order to teach persons on their individual levels. Although some Sunday schools use an intergenerational pattern (grouping persons across a variety of age levels), the advantage of teaching persons at their comprehension level remains strong. Children who think literally and concretely need to be taught Bible truths in that way, whereas youth and adults, who can deal with more abstract concepts, can study the same Bible truths at a more mature level.

Third, the Sunday school has been and is essentially a *lay movement.* Both in England and in the United States the Sunday school began as a movement launched and taught by lay persons rather than by clergy. In fact, it was not until the early 1800s that the church began to recognize the Sunday school as a viable and legitimate teaching agency of the church.

The spirit of 2 Timothy 2:2 is exemplified in the lay emphasis of the Sunday school. Leaders teach persons who in turn teach others. The pastor of a local body of believers can capitalize on the lay aspect of the Sunday school as he seeks to put into operation the pattern of Ephesians 4:11-12—"He gave . . . some as pastors and teachers, for the equipping of the saints for the work of service, to the building up of the body of Christ." The pastor serves as the equipper or facilitator, teaching and training believers to do the work of the ministry—specifically, teaching in the Sunday school. The Sunday school has further served as a training ground for church leadership. Because teachers of all ages are needed to teach all ages, the Sunday school has proved to be both a recruitment and training center for current and future leadership.

Fourth, the Sunday school is *evangelistic* in its ministry. Boys and girls, youth and adults throughout the history of the Sunday school have found Jesus Christ as Savior through the ministry of faithful teachers. Though the Sunday school seeks to reach entire families for Christ and to teach all members of the family, it also provides opportunity for evangelism and teaching of children whose parents do not attend church or Sunday school. Busing of children to Sunday school is often predicated on the fact that parents are not opposed to letting their children attend. Every effort should be made, however, to reach the entire family at the same time the children are being taught.

CHILDREN'S CHURCH

Whereas Sunday school serves a teaching function, the children's church provides opportunity for children to worship at their level of understanding and ability and to participate actively in worship. Churchtime for children is not intended to be either a second Sunday school or a substitute for Sunday school (that is, a place to leave children while parents attend only the morning worship service). Rather, children's church builds on the Sunday school experience and capitalizes on the additional time for Christian education. It provides opportunity both to train children in worship and reverence and to train them in leadership and service. Most curriculum materials for children's church provide for age-level groupings and for child participation. For best results, the children's church leadership will be selected with the same care taken in selecting Sunday school teachers. Continuity of leadership is desirable for the sake of the children and their continued growth in biblical truth and spiritual walk.

TRAINING HOUR

A third educational ministry that utilizes Sundays is the training hour, often geared for all ages. Its major purpose has been primarily instruction and expression with a view toward developing leadership qualities in children, youth, and adults.

In some churches the time slot on Sunday evening is used for youth meetings with an emphasis on Bible study, singing, and fellowship. Where adults are involved, the training hour may take the form of instruction in elective studies such as Bible books, doctrine, teacher training, current issues, missions, family life, and leadership training.

WEEKDAY CLUBS AND BIBLE STUDIES

Weekdays also provide time for various kinds of ministry. Groups of children may meet in the afternoon or in the evening in clubs such as Awana, Pioneer Girls, and Christian Service Brigade, where there is a strong emphasis on fellowship, expression, activity, and achievement.

Home Bible classes for children, such as Child Evangelism Fellowship clubs, Bible Club Movement clubs, and Joy Clubs, tend to an evangelistic approach.

Young people may meet in the early morning before school, in the evening, or on Saturdays for Bible study or a variety of social and recreational activities. Adults utilize a variety of times in a wide range of ministries: early morning Bible study and prayer for working men, morning Bible studies for mothers, and evening Bible study and/or fellowship times. Often the club or home Bible class may serve as a means of evangelism.

SEASONAL MINISTRIES

Summer months and vacation periods as well as weekends have the advantage of offering blocks of time when groups can engage in in-depth experiences such as camps, retreats, vacation Bible schools, and seminars.

Such experiences usually include all four program elements: instruction, worship, fellowship, and expression-service. With the exception of seminars, which often focus on a particular topic such as teacher training and therefore reach a special group, seasonal ministries may be intergenerational as well as age-graded. Family camp, family retreat, and family vacation Bible school allow all ages to learn from and fellowship with one another. The relaxed, informal atmosphere of the less structured, longer time frame allows for a kind of learning to take place that more closely resembles that which occurs in the home. Even intensified study, such as that at a family life retreat or seminar, appears informal because of the relaxed setting and atmosphere of fellowship.

Church educational ministries may and do take a variety of forms as history and current practice indicate. The basic function of teaching, however, must continue to be evident. The church must continue to serve both as reinforcer of the educational ministry of the home and as educator, equipping saints and causing the growth of the church body for the building up of itself in love (Eph. 4:12, 16).

FOR FURTHER STUDY

1. Using Acts 2:42-47 as an illustration of the elements in the total church program (instruction, worship, fellowship, expression-service), trace the elements throughout the book of Acts.
2. Locate five statements of biblical imperatives that emphasize evangelism and five that emphasize edification.
3. Write objectives for the ten imperatives above. Reflect your own local church mission in your statements.
4. Guide the leadership of a particular church educational ministry, e.g., the Sunday school or a weekday club program, in using the educational process as a basis for planning and implementing a year's plan.
   a) Identify key needs in the particular agency or ministry. Select a few priority needs that can be met in one year.
   b) Write aims to meet the selected needs.
   c) Determine the organization, administration, and supervision aspects necessary to carry out the aims.
   d) Plan methods and materials to be used in implementation.
5. Write, or adapt from other sources, an evaluative instrument for an educational ministry that will measure progress during the year as well as at the end of the year.
6. Make charts for children, youth, and adults, that list the ministries to each age level, the time frames, and the emphasis of each on instruction, worship, fellowship, and expression-service. Determine over-

lapping and gapping areas and what should be done to strengthen the ministries to a particular age level.
7. Use the boy-Book-boy diagram by LeBar (fig. 16.3) as a guideline for laying out a Bible lesson.
8. Identify the educational ministries in your church that are specifically designed to train prospective and future leadership. How can the training aspect be built into each existing program?

NOTES

1. Gene A. Getz, *The Measure of a Family* (Glendale, Calif.: Gospel Light, Regal, 1976), p. 7.
2. Lois E. LeBar, *Focus on People in Church Education* (Westwood, N.J.: Revell, 1968), p. 39.
3. From Gene A. Getz, *Sharpening the Focus of the Church* (Chicago: Moody, 1974), p. 265.
4. Kenneth O. Gangel, *Leadership for Christian Education* (Chicago: Moody, 1970), p. 60.
5. H. W. Byrne, *A Christian Approach to Education,* 2d ed. (Milford, Minn.: Mott Media, 1977), p. 185.
6. LeBar, p. 50.

SUGGESTED READING

Brown, Lowell E. *Your Sunday School Can Grow.* Glendale, Calif.: Gospel Light, Regal, 1971. A sourcebook of practical ways to plan for and improve the Sunday school.

Byrne, H. W. *A Christian Approach to Education.* 2d ed. Milford, Minn.: Mott Media, 1977. A Christian approach to education for Christian schools and colleges, setting forth the basic differences between secular and Christian education.

Calhoun, Mary. *Vacation Time, Leisure Time, Any Time You Choose.* New York: Abingdon, 1974. A sourcebook on developing models for planning and implementing leisure time ministries.

Freese, Doris A. *Vacation Bible School.* Wheaton, Ill.: Evangelical Teacher Training Assoc., 1977. A helpful sourcebook on planning and implementing a vacation Bible school.

Gangel, Kenneth O. *The Effective Sunday School Superintendent.* Wheaton, Ill.: Scripture Press, Victor, 1975. An excellent work on the qualifications and responsibilities of the Sunday school superintendent.

————. *Leadership for Church Education.* Chicago: Moody, 1970. An examination of general principles of administration and management and their relationship to the task of the local church, particularly the educational program.

————. *Twenty-four Ways to Improve Your Teaching.* Wheaton, Ill.: Scripture Press, Victor, 1974. A helpful survey of specific methods for teaching children, youth, and adults.

Getz, Gene A. *Sharpening the Focus of the Church.* Chicago: Moody, 1974. A study of the church through the lenses of church history, New Testament principles, and contemporary needs. A discussion of why the church exists, how to build the church through proper edification, New Testament principles of administration and organization, and communication of the principles of New Testament evangelism.

Larson, Jim. *Churchtime for Children.* Glendale, Calif.: Gospel Light, Regal, 1978. A guidebook of practical ideas, resources, and instructions for implementing a churchtime program for children in grades one through six.

LeBar, Lois E. *Focus on People in Church Education.* Westwood, N.J.: Revell, 1968. A blueprint from which teachers, Christian education workers, and ministers can build their programs and by which they can survey and evaluate their particular local situations.

Self, Margaret, ed. *How to Plan and Organize Year Round Bible Ministries.* Glendale, Calif.: Gospel Light, Regal, 1976. A valuable sourcebook for planning and implementing Bible ministries for children, utilizing summer and other vacation times.

Westing, Harold J. *Make Your Sunday School Grow Through Evaluation.* Wheaton, Ill.: Scripture Press, Victor, 1976. An excellent work describing standards and suggesting tools for the evaluation and improvement of the Christian education program.

17

The Pastor and Christian Education

Sherman Williams

Gaines Dobbins states it well in his book *Building Better Churches* when he says: "By virtue of his calling the minister is committed to the Word of God as sufficient, authoritative and final. From it he preaches and teaches; without it he would have neither a ministry nor a church. He finds himself preaching and teaching essentially the same truths as those preached and taught by those through whom the Scriptures came . . . [He has a deep] conviction that he needs no other Christ, no new Gospel, no improvement upon the Christian system of truth."[1]

The Pastor's Role as Preacher and Teacher

God has chosen certain men as pastors to preach and teach, to lead and guide, to guard and train all those who believe on Jesus Christ through hearing the gospel. Having enriched those chosen men by His Spirit, God has given them to the church to teach and train believers and prepare them for the work of the ministry unto the edification of the entire Body.

The church was designed by God to meet needs. Among the major means for meeting those needs is the ministry of preaching. Nothing can take the place of Spirit-filled preaching; it has a central place in the ministry of the church. The task of preaching, however, as far-reaching and vital as it is, is only a part of the work of the pastorate.

The apostle Paul in writing to his young friend Timothy, for example, admonished him to entrust the gospel to faithful men who were apt to teach. Three main duties of the pastor as outlined in 1 Timothy 4:13 (NASB) are "reading, exhortation, teaching." In other words, the pastor is to read and proclaim the Word publicly, to appeal to the hearts of the people through exhortation, and to teach or provide instruction.

Sherman Williams is pastor of Redwood Chapel Community Church in Castro Valley, California.

The pastor is the key person in the Christian education program of the local church. In the vast majority of our churches he is the only professionally trained staff person. Even in a church that has Christian education staff, the nature of Christian education is such that the pastor must be vitally related to it. Since the aim of the church is to bring people to a knowledge of Christ and to lead them to a place of spiritual maturity, thoroughly furnished unto every good work, the church becomes fundamentally an educational institution, and the minister is in essence a teacher. The method and the program of the church is essentially educational; the church should indeed be a school in Christian living. That is why the pastor must function not only as a preacher and teacher but also as an educational leader in the local church.

Jesus was most often referred to as teacher. He spoke of Himself as teacher and called His followers His disciples. He gave the greatest block of His time to teaching the twelve. In His Great Commission He sent His followers out to make disciples of all men everywhere, to teach them to observe all things that Christ commanded. Among the gifts Christ gave to the church are pastor-teachers. Through preaching and teaching the lost are to be won, then built up in faith and character.

In 2 Timothy 2:24 and Titus 1:9 Paul expands the idea of the pastor's teaching ministry, "both to instruct them who desire instruction and to convince those who speak against the truth to overturn it." In his preaching and teaching the pastor must be sure to provide a balance between evangelism and edification. It is important to "preach the Word" with great patience and instruction, as well as to be faithful to "do the work of an evangelist" (2 Tim. 4:2, 5).

The Pastor's Role in Helping the Church Develop a Philosophy of Christian Education

By his attitude and his action, the pastor must clearly indicate his high regard for the total ministry of Christian education in his church. He must emphasize through the pulpit and in public and private statement that the work of the church is done by the combined efforts of its people using their gifts in the development of the ministry.

The pastor, realizing that its workers comprise the greatest evangelistic team that could ever come to the church, must take an active interest in the Christian education program. That team adds the advantage of remaining in the church with a teaching and training program throughout the entire year.

It is strategically important that the pastor teach his people that Christian education is not just a department of the church, but that it provides a unifying foundation and framework for the church and its ministry. It is not a substitute for spiritual life; it provides channels through which the life of the spirit can flow.

The areas of Christian education ministry are concentrically related to the major thrust of the church; as spelled out in Ephesians 4:11-16, preparing Christians for their work of the ministry and bringing them to a place of spiritual maturity, "to the measure of the stature which belongs to the fulness of Christ" (Eph. 4:13). The elements used in accomplishing that are listed in Acts 2:42-47 and Acts 5:42. They are: instruction (or doctrine), worship, fellowship, and evangelism. First, people must be brought to Christ and become recipients of a Christian nature, then they are to be built up in Christ, nurtured, and edified. With a certain maturity they are then sent out to reproduce themselves.

Christian education, as a basic part of the church's total ministry, provides essential agencies for carrying out the elements. Those agencies must, of course, be correlated to prevent overlapping and omission, as well as graded to meet particular needs of each group.

An especially critical part of the church's educational ministry is in the area of church-home cooperation. The church is faced with the responsibility of making provision for Christian family education and involvement. There should be a division of emphasis between peer group and family group activities. In developing a sound program of Christian education these characteristics must be considered:

1. *Comprehensiveness.* It should include every member of the church's constituency in its program. There should be a job for every worker and a worker for every job. The leaders should plan a balanced program to meet individual needs.

2. *Unity.* The various programs of Christian education must be organized into a unified plan of action, with coordinated planning and direction.

3. *Grading.* There are some activities in which age togetherness is desirable. This is true of public worship, based upon a pattern that makes possible the maximum participation of old and young. The focus in this case is vertical and not horizontal, so any number of people can be meaningfully involved. Some service projects in which the church is engaged may be shared by persons of all ages. There are many activities, however, that are best carried on in graded groups. These include the areas of instruction in the Sunday school and other Bible study classes, children's worship programs, and most of the social and recreational activities.

4. *Participation.* Where Christian education is properly organized, it distributes widely within the fellowship the responsibility for communication of the Christian message. Thus, the various talents and interests of the different members of the constituency are utilized, avoiding overworking a few faithful participants and providing many people with the

joy as well as the discipline that comes from service to the church. There is perhaps no more important way for vitalizing Christian faith than to become involved in training others to share that faith.

THE PASTOR'S ROLE AS EQUIPPER

The total Christian education ministry of the church must be under the general direction and in the spiritual concern of the pastoral leadership. The pastor's role is to equip the saints for the work of the ministry and to build up the Body of Christ, according to Ephesians 4:12. At the very heart of the pastor's work is his teaching ministry, which is a part of almost all that he does. Although many share in the instructional life of the church, the pastor is the chief teacher. He must teach and train others that they might be able to teach and lead.

Many pastors do not clearly comprehend the importance of their ministry of teaching and training others. Though the pulpit is a point of beginning, it is of course only that. The successful pastor must prepare and train others and assign to them tasks according to their gifts. The major work of training for Christian service and preparing people for their work of ministry must be done in the local church under competent leadership. That training should include knowing Bible content and understanding Bible theology. Every church member must have a basic understanding of the Christian faith in order to fulfill his ministry. And, he must know methodology—how to teach and lead.

The development of leadership in the church must take place at three levels: first, the development of *pastoral leadership* to equip teachers and other leaders for their task; second, the development of *lay teachers and leaders* to equip members for the work of the ministry; third, the development of the *laity* as serving members. Since the ministry of the church was given to the church as a whole, every member is a minister and needs to be trained for his ministry.[2] Talents and gifts for the tasks of the church are to be found and developed in each congregation. The pastor can neither do everything himself nor can he neglect any phase of the work of his church.

There are two basic types of leaders. The leader in articulation sizes up the problem, maps out a workable plan in his own mind, and explains his ideas to the other individuals in the group. The leader in action plunges into the actual work, provides a lead for the others, and gets them to fit into the course of action that he has already taken himself. A good pastor-leader has both qualities. He recognizes the importance of his personal leadership in motivating others. He is a leader in action as well as in articulation. See 1 Peter 5:2-3 and 1 Thessalonians 2:3-10.

Our Lord gave us a pattern of wise leadership. He instructed His disciples; He showed them how to do it! Then He led them forth to do the work. He inspired them with His words; He challenged them with His acts. He involved them in doing the work with Him. They watched Him and then followed Him.

The pastor, if a good leader, provides first the right kind of atmosphere to encourage everyone's participation. He emphasizes the "workers together" concept. He realizes that God in His wisdom has placed in every church a group of believers gifted by the Holy Spirit, capable of contributing to the upbuilding of the entire Body. Recognizing that principle, with humility and confidence he looks for help as the Holy Spirit directs him. Whether they be unpaid lay-workers, or part/full-time salaried workers, he works with them in the role of a supervisor. He stimulates their sense of oneness in the Lord's work and encourages their team spirit, as members of the church together employing their spiritual gifts for the building up of the Body of Christ.

Second, he administers wisely. He starts where he is with what he has and prayerfully determines where he wants to go and what is necessary to get there under God. He considers the elements involved, the agencies needed, the staff required, and the facilities that will be necessary. He leads the people in the establishment of long-range goals as well as intermediate goals—goals that are stretchable but reachable.

Kenneth L. Cober in his book *The Church's Teaching Ministry* shares some excellent insights regarding leadership. He writes:

> Leadership is the performance of a service by a person with a group of people in such a way as to help them further the purpose of their group. . . . The results of one's leadership are not to be determined by what the leader achieves but rather by what he enables the group to achieve. The best leader is the one who could stimulate the group to its maximum performance . . . leadership is effective only as it helps the group to advance the group for the purpose for which it exists. . . . The leader's relationship to the group is that of servant and not of a master. He thinks of leadership as function, and not in terms of status. He masters the skills of leadership, so he can help the group to achieve its purposes effectively.[3]

Time must be spent with people at the various leadership levels, beginning with the governing board of the church and working down through the various levels until every lay member has been reached and trained for a particular area of ministry. As mentioned before, the pastor must be a leader in action as well as in articulation. He must show the way. He must be concerned for individuals, leaving the isolation of the pulpit and the safety of the "church crowd" to make contact with individuals. He must encourage and lead, not drive and harass. God has given him people that he might build them up, not magnify himself at their expense. There comes a time when the pastor must look directly into the eyes of a member, describe the need and the kind of worker needed, and quietly and persuasively state his belief that God has gifted that member for that task. That may be done by pastoral calls, through scheduled conferences in the church office, or over a cup of coffee in the home. In a larger church, the Christian education director or a similar staff person will assist in that kind of personal enlistment.

Equipping the people for their work of ministry is the responsibility of the pastor. The job is well done when the believers in the Body become "ministers" to the Body. Of course, if the church is large enough to have a minister of Christian education, then the pastor will share with him in a spirit of teamwork the responsibilities being considered. Do not hire a staff member to do someone else's work. Hire him to do the work of which he is uniquely capable according to his natural interests and spiritual gifts.

Peter Wagner in his book *Your Church Can Grow* writes,

> Pastors of growing churches who work with a loyal and competent staff are aware of the essential contribution that each staff member makes toward the growth of the church. No pastor should take credit for what a staff colleague is doing. So the pastor will frequently say, "Don't think I am responsible for this; I am just one member of a fantastic team."
>
> A good pastor will want to give credit to his people and will be careful to make sure that the people of the congregation are well aware of his dependence on them, and he will remind them of it as often as possible. So as not to jeopardize the spiritual dynamic already at work among the people he will be very hesitant to accept public credit for the growth of the church. No pastor, regardless of how gifted he is, can make a church grow alone.[4]

THE PASTOR'S ROLE AS SUPERVISOR OF THE TOTAL CHURCH PROGRAM

The majority of churches in America are not large enough to maintain a staff of professionally trained Christian education workers. That means the pastor must either surrender the education ministry to his Sunday school superintendent and other lay leaders, who are often untrained, or he must assume the responsibility of directing the program of Christian education as part of his pastoral ministry. Even the pastor who has other professional leaders on staff cannot afford to retreat from his responsibility to the total church educational program. He must know enough about the program of Christian education to give wise, kind, and sympathetic support to his colleagues. He must support the program wholeheartedly and be informed as to its nature and progress and always show an active interest in each facet of the work. Whether the church is large or small, urban or rural, the pastor is the key person in the program of education. His attitude will either inspire or discourage the people. Enthusiasm is contagious, but so is indifference.[5]

The church program must be integrated by the pastor—his vision, his love for Christ and the people, his enthusiasm, his efficiency—those will determine the course of the church's ministry. The pastor must remember that he is pastor of all the organizations.

The pastor must be a good supervisor. That requires both "super-vision," the ability to see more and farther and act accordingly, and "super-direction"—helping his people set goals so that they know where they are going and why. As supervisor of the total church program, the pastor must guide his leaders into a meeting of minds and mutual respect regarding goals, standards, and principles of operation.

The life of the church is an organism that demands unity, correlation, and coordination. The health of the whole depends upon the health of all the parts. Each part of the Church's program must strengthen and support the ministry of the rest.

The pastor as a church-builder is faced with inescapable administrative responsibilities. He must not be overly absorbed in practical administrative matters, but he must develop skills to make administration a means toward spiritual ends. Church administration is primarily concerned with persons, not methods and systems. Putting the right person in the right place of responsibility is important. Most churches use very little of their membership power. To strengthen our churches we must provide a continuous process of increasing the number of those who are active and involved.

Supervision is therefore a basic function of the pastor. It may be defined as the process of achieving unity and harmony of effort and effectiveness in the accomplishment of organization and spiritual goals. It is concerned with developing a smoothly functioning team effort. On the basis of the example of Christ in such references as Mark 6:1-31 there are some simple suggestions for the pastor in his supervision.

1. *Develop leadership.* The success of a pastor depends largely upon his ability to gather about him a group of potential leaders, officers, and teachers and train them to do what needs to be done in the total ministry of the church (2 Tim. 2:2). Any pastor can multiply himself by teaching others.

2. *Define the job.* Develop a job description for each worker. Jobs must be clarified and skilled people matched with the tasks to be done.

3. *Use delegation.* Delegation, the sharing of responsibility and authority, is a process that cannot be ignored but rather should be recognized and employed intelligently by every church leader.

Henry R. Brandt has stated, "As the church grows the pastor's administrative duties must change. He can no longer do much of the work himself and be solely responsible for every detail. He must turn over some of the work to others; see to it that others assume responsibility."[6]

The pastor gets things done through other people by delegating authority and duties. Jesus followed that principle in sending out the twelve and seventy, and that is what was followed in the early apostolic days when deacons were selected.

4. *Require accountability for responsibility.* After the twelve disciples had gone forth to minister, they returned to Jesus and "reported to Him all that they had done and taught" (Mark 6:30). So it is the pastor who must provide for reports to be given regarding work performance in the ministry of the church. Lay out the plan, set up the goal posts, and then check the score to see what is happening.

5. *Give counsel and direction.* The pastor must assume the place of inspirational leadership. His spirit, his Christian experience and character, his knowledge and zeal, his devotion and loyalty, his willingness and skills, his love and personal concern provide and sustain much of the motivation of the leaders who surround him. He becomes a model for them in the development of other inspired and enthusiastic leadership.

The pastor must care! When he does, he has the indispensable foundation for healthy, satisfying relationships. Unless he really cares about the other person, even his most helpful actions may bring resentment instead of appreciation—if he does not care, every act, every courtesy, every generosity extended to the other individual may only arouse suspicion and block cooperation.

Here are some signs of caring: First, a recognition of every individual's uniqueness. Second, seeing people as ends, not means. (He helps to achieve personal goals as well as do a better job in the whole program for which the leader is responsible. He does not think of people as mere objects—tools to help him achieve his purposes—for that poisons human relationships. Until a pastor is willing to serve the purposes of each individual as well as the common purpose in which he is interested, he cannot be said to really care.) Third, he goes out of his way to help others. Fourth, he takes the responsibility for others. Fifth, his acts toward his people are not simply keyed to the rewards he gets for caring. If he is being considerate only because he wants them to give what he needs to perfect his ministry, then he will lose their loyalty in the end.

Finally, a good pastor is one who has a genuine love for God and for the people that he serves.

The Pastor's Wife and Her Role in Christian Education
in the Church

The wife of a pastor should share with him his call to Christian service and ministry—she should feel called to give herself to a life of service for God and people. It is important that she share his ministry and recognize her need to continually grow spiritually and mentally with him so that their interests remain one and the same. In a sense she has not only married a husband but has married his job. That is not true with most husbands' occupations.

The effective pastor's wife has more satisfaction as a woman than many other wives because the special partnership of man and wife extends to her professional as well as her personal relationship with her husband. Very few occupations impose such teamwork requirements on marriage partners.

Welthy Fisher, in *Handbook for Minister's Wives*, writes, "The role of a pastor's wife is different from that of most women for two reasons. First your husband's profession calls for one of the most inclusive combinations of requirements, skills and obligations required of one human being. Second, as a minister's wife, you cannot escape a special kind of relationship to both the people and the task, local and national, that make up your husband's work."[7]

Of course, the primary duty and privilege of the pastor's wife is to make the home what it ought to be. She and her husband must recognize the importance and value of a Christian home. They must give evidence that they believe that the home is the first concern of the Christian education program. The modeling they do in the home in the husband/wife, parent/child relationships is one of the most effective educational tools to be used.

In his book *The Multiple Staff in the Local Church* Herman J. Sweet writes in the chapter entitled "Distaff": "The role of the pastor's wife is a difficult role to play. She lives in a glass house. Her attitudes, appearance, her management of her family, her social contacts, are all subject to severe scrutiny."[8] He adds that the "hidden" factor in the success or failure of a pastor's ministry is to be found in the attitude and influence of his wife.

The pastor's wife must avoid the twin evils of either withdrawing from responsibility or rushing into jobs and usurping responsibility. She can, however, make a tremendous impact and exert great influence with women. Much can be done without holding office. She can encourage and train other women to employ all their gifts in the service of Christ. She should know how to discreetly steer and give directions to others as an ex officio member of many women's groups and organizations within the church. Quietly and efficiently she can help women organize all their activities and serve as counselor to those who have the responsibility of direct leadership.

She will attend the church services regularly and be active in the church in serving to the degree that her husband would expect any other woman to serve. She might well serve as a hostess in greeting strangers and visitors, and help her husband become acquainted with them as well as minister with friendly graciousness to all. She is also in a good position to search out the talent and gifts of the people of the church and assist the personnel and recruiting department in finding suitable work for the talents and gifts of members. Great responsibilities and trials come to a pastor's wife, but she will have exquisite joy in serving with her husband in a life ministry under God.

When a church is small, it is often necessary for the pastor's wife to serve in a number of ministering areas. She and her husband must determine where her abilities and gifts can best be used. As the church grows in numbers and staff members are added, she can with her husband help develop the kind of team spirit and camaraderie that are so essential.

CHRISTIAN EDUCATION IN PASTORAL TRAINING

A Christian college or seminary should have a strong department of Christian education to provide that essential part of the pastor's training. Since Christian education is vital to the function and ministry of the church, the Sunday Bible school and other educational ministries, together with preaching and public worship, pastoral work and administration should all be considered at the heart of a Bible college or seminary curriculum.

In many schools, though several courses are listed in Christian education, only a couple of semester courses are required for graduation. As a result, those courses become incidental or postscript to the whole thrust of pastoral education.

Peter P. Person writes in his book *The Minister in Christian Education:*

> The seminarian dream focuses on the pulpit. First, because the mass media of pulpit oratory is far more dramatic than teaching a Bible class or visitation. In the second place, he has probably been captivated by the personality of some eloquent preacher. The third reason . . . he has been trained to preach. It is quite natural therefore, for him to dream of himself occupying the pulpit of a large urban church with an assistant to do the calling, a Director of Christian Education to care for the ministry to the children and youth and an efficient office secretary. He is thus free to devote himself to preparation and study for pulpit appearance . . . but he is apt to have a rude awakening from his dream after graduation when he finds himself not in the church of his dreams.[9]

Our schools must emphasize that one of the most important aspects of a pastor's training should be in the development of lay leadership to work in the various areas of Christian education. The pastor must be a creator of leadership vision and capability. He is the chief teacher, the teacher of teachers, and plays an important part in preparation of leaders in all of the church offices. The pastor is God's man who helps the church fulfill its total ministry, in which teaching is a major part.

In a large church, a team ministry must be established, and the pastor must lead that team so that all members have the same goals. It is vital to the success of the pastor's God-given ministry that he be prepared by our schools to effectively administer and clearly communicate.

The great objective in Christian education is the birth, growth, and maturation of believers in the church of Jesus Christ. Whatever is necessary in the accomplishment of that great task is of vital concern to the pastor.

FOR FURTHER STUDY

1. Develop a statement on how the pastor can accept responsibility for the total church program, without getting involved in all the details.
2. Work out a statement of church educational aims from a pastor's viewpoint.
3. Do a biblical study on the relationship of preaching and teaching in the ministry of Christ.
4. Draw up an outline of a church educational program and indicate where each part of the program fits into the pastor's ministry, viewed both as responsibility and as opportunity.

NOTES

1. Gaines S. Dobbins, *Building Better Churches* (Nashville: Broadman, 1947), p. 29.
2. Helpful reading here is Kenneth L. Cober's book *The Church's Teaching Ministry* (Valley Forge, Pa.: Judson, 1964), especially chapters 2, 6, and 7.
3. Ibid., pp. 99-100.
4. C. Peter Wagner, *Your Church Can Grow* (Glendale, Calif.: Gospel Light, 1976), p. 56.
5. A helpful book is J. Clark Hensley, *The Pastor as Educational Director* (Kansas City: Central Seminary, 1946).
6. Henry R. Brandt, *The Pastor and Church Management* (Wheaton, Ill.: Scripture Press, 1966).
7. Welthy Honsinger Fisher, *Handbook for Ministers' Wives* (New York: Women's Press, 1950).
8. Herman J. Sweet, *The Multiple Staff in the Local Church* (Philadelphia: Westminster, 1963), p. 82.
9. Peter P. Person, *The Minister in Christian Education* (Grand Rapids: Baker, 1960), p. 10.

SUGGESTED READING

Blackwood, Carolyn P. *The Pastor's Wife.* Philadelphia: Westminster, 1951.
Brandt, Henry R. *The Pastor and Church Management.* Wheaton, Ill.: Scripture Press, 1966.

Cober, Kenneth L. *The Church's Teaching Ministry.* Valley Forge, Pa.: Judson, 1964.

Dobbins, Gaines S. *A Ministering Church.* Nashville: Broadman, 1960.

————. *Building Better Churches.* Nashville: Broadman, 1947. An exhaustive study and guide on the subject.

Fisher, Welthy Honsinger. *Handbook for Ministers' Wives.* New York: Women's Press, 1950.

Hensley, J. Clark. *The Pastor as Educational Director.* Kansas City: Central Seminary, 1946.

LeBar, Lois E. *Education That Is Christian.* Westwood, N.J.: Revell, 1958.

Olson, Richard A., ed. *The Pastor's Role in the Educational Ministry.* Philadelphia: Fortress, 1974.

Person, Peter P. *The Minister in Christian Education.* Grand Rapids: Baker, 1960.

Sanders, J. Oswald. *Spiritual Leadership.* Rev. ed. Chicago: Moody, 1980.

Sweet, Herman J. *The Multiple Staff in the Local Church.* Philadelphia: Westminster, 1963.

Vieth, Paul H., ed. *The Church and Christian Education.* St. Louis: Bethany, 1947.

Wagner, C. Peter. *Your Church Can Grow.* Glendale, Calif.: Gospel Light, 1976.

Washburn, A. V., and Cook, Melva. *Administering a Bible Teaching Program.* Nashville: Convention, 1969.

18

Professional Church Leadership in Christian Education

RAY SYRSTAD

THE USE OF THE TERM "professional" in local church ministry is a relatively recent development. Even though today some may still hesitate to use the term, it simply refers to those who have trained for specific ministry in the local church and are paid a salary for the service they render.

Until the early part of the twentieth century there was generally only one person in the local church who qualified for the title "professional"— the pastor. He performed the expected duties of preaching and the conduct of worship, visiting the sick and shut-ins, performing wedding ceremonies and funerals, and whatever responsibilities his particular congregation attributed to the role of the pastor.

In recent years, however, professionals in the local church have greatly increased in number and variety of ministry. A number of the largest churches today include well over one hundred salaried professionals, many of which are involved in very specialized ministries.

A 1974 article in *Christianity Today* predicted, "In the next decade the churches that will 'make it' are those that emphasize staff and program more than plant, and associate ministries (or paraministry) will be the main occupational growth area in the church."[1]

It was suggested that a worthy goal for churches is one full-time staff worker for every 100-125 persons who attend. It was also indicated that soon the main work of evangelism, teaching, and Christian nurture in the churches will be performed outside the pulpit.[2]

Recent years have witnessed a dramatic growth in the number of people engaged in "support" ministries in the local church. Those include:

RAY SYRSTAD, B.D., is minister of education, Peninsula Baptist Church, Rancho Palos Verdes, California.

Minister of Christian Education   Minister to Senior Citizens
Administrative Pastor   Minister to the Deaf
Minister to Adults   Church Secretary
Minister to Singles   Activities Director
Youth Director   Camping Director
  (Junior High Director,   Preschool or Christian Day School
  Senior High Director,   Administrator
  College Director)   Director of Children's Ministries
Business Administrator   Educational Associate
Minister of Counseling   Minister to Families

Also included in the category of the professional in church ministry must be the rather recent development of the professional-in-training or what has come to be known as the intern. The intern is most often a student who serves under the supervision of a full-time staff member. It is a mutually beneficial arrangement, particularly if the staff member is willing to share himself and his ministry with the student and not simply assign to the intern the less desirable tasks.

Professionals as Equippers

The professional called to minister in a local church must begin with a clear philosophy of what he believes the Bible teaches about the church. Findley B. Edge says that the central problem in the modern church is that "we don't know who we are or what we are supposed to be as the People of God."[3]

Edge not only poses the problem, but he also arrives at some important conclusions. "When one is called by God to be a part of His people, he is also called into the ministry." Every believer is called to be a minister through whom God can work to build His church. Edge's second conclusion is: "The primary responsibility for God's ministry in the world is the responsibility of the laity and not the clergy."[4]

Contrary to much church thinking, *church members cannot pay a church staff to do their work.* God has called all believers to serve Him with the gifts and abilities He has given them. It therefore becomes the task of the pastor and his staff to *equip the people* to do the work of the ministry (Eph. 4:12).

Foremost in the equipping process is a strong pulpit ministry by the pastor or pastors who share the responsibility of communicating God's truth through preaching. The first contact an individual has with a church is generally through attending a morning worship service. What he hears from the pulpit will often determine whether he returns to eventually become a part of the fellowship. There will rarely be an opportunity to equip the believer through the other ministries of the church unless the pastor has first been a faithful feeder of the flock of God (1 Pet. 5:2).

It is significant to note that many of the rapidly-growing churches of today are those in which the pastor has placed primary emphasis on the teaching of the Word of God from the pulpit. Dan Baumann classifies such a church as "The Classroom Church" in his book *All Originality Makes A Dull Church.*[5] He describes one such church in Southern California: "Sermons are expository; sermons are longer than average (and there is much appreciation for this pattern); sermonic aids are provided; laity expectations have undergone redefinition. The pastor is expected to be the teaching pastor and, as such, spends most of his time in the study."[6]

The effectiveness of a professional staff person in church ministry is closely related to his ability to involve the people of the church in meaningful ministry. In her book *Focus on People in Church Education* Lois LeBar quotes John R. Mott as saying, "He who multiplies the doers is greater than he who does the work."[7] The staff person may find that it is often easier and less time-consuming to do a task himself. But that equips no one and eventually results in an overworked, frustrated staff person.

Those who have served in the local church ministry normally agree with Gaines S. Dobbins that "the quality and adequacy of leadership determines more than any other human factor the success of the church."[8] How eagerly we look in our churches for the "born leaders," but Dobbins points out, "The truth seems to be evident that leaders are made rather than born and that the qualities of leadership are acquired rather than inherited."[9]

Equipping, then, means that the staff professional is continually involved with enlisting and training the people for ministry. Seeing the task as equipping will guard against the tendency to feel that it is a thankless, never-ending chore of trying to convince people that they ought to serve the Lord. We must not succumb to the tendency to use human manipulation to provide only what God can supply. Our Lord reminds us of the primary ingredient that we often neglect: "Therefore beseech the Lord of the harvest, to send out laborers into His harvest" (Luke 10:2*b*).

We may think of equipping only in terms of formal training classes that we conduct for our people. Classes and seminars, both within and outside the local church itself, can be important equipping tools. But there are other ways the professional staff person in the church can contribute to the growth and spiritual effectiveness of the people. Spiritual encouragement is often overlooked. In his reforms, Josiah, king of Judah, gave a good example of how to work with people. He "set his priests at their tasks," but he did not stop with that. He also "encouraged them for the service of the house of the LORD" (2 Chron. 35:2). For Josiah, enlistment was not enough. He followed it with encouragement.

Providing a variety of reading material through a church library or a table where books are available for purchase can be an effective equipping tool. The Christian Booksellers Association reports that a relatively small percentage of Christians ever frequent a Christian bookstore. Therefore one minister of Christian education initiated the concept of bringing the bookstore to the people. Working on a consignment arrangement with a local bookstore, he brought a wide variety of books to the church and made them available for purchase. Now, ten years later, that ministry has grown from a single table to an entire room, and it has contributed significantly to the growth and edification of the people.

Committed to the biblical concept of the priesthood of believers, the pastor, staff, and lay leadership of a local church must continuously evaluate the many tasks in which they engage to see if they are indeed contributing to the equipping of the saints for ministry. As Findley B. Edge urges:

> Also by this principle can we evaluate the effectiveness of the church's program. Is the curriculum designed to give specific training in equipping the saints for the work of the ministry? If not, it ought to be changed. Are the activities of teaching and training in the various organizations of the church actually equipping the saints for the work of the ministry, and are the people actually engaging in this ministry in the world? If not, the work of these organizations needs to be modified to achieve this fundamental objective.[10]

THE MULTIPLE STAFF-TEAM CONCEPT

It is a healthy, encouraging sign to see churches growing to the point where they need more than one full-time staff professional to adequately serve and give guidance to the Body. Staff growth, however, brings corresponding problems, and there is much room for potential confusion unless both the church membership and the professional staff clearly understand the functions and relationships of a multiple staff in the local church.

Marvin T. Judy gives a helpful summary of what he calls "Presuppositions for a Doctrine of the Multiple Ministry in the Protestant Church" in his book *The Multiple Staff Ministry*.[11] He categorizes persons on the church staff as:

1. *The doctrinally ordered professional,* who has a theological commitment to the position. Ordination is essential to the one serving in this way.

2. *The commissioned professional* is professionally trained to perform specialized ministerial roles, but ordination is incidental to the office.

3. *The functionaries* include those who perform functional roles such as a secretary, church hostess, or custodian.[12]

Adding a staff person who possesses special abilities can greatly enrich the ministry of a local church. Within most churches there is a wide variety of talent with great potential for ministry, but that potential is often not reached because there is no one to guide and blend those talents into an effective serving unit.

The demand for competent staff people is still great, specifically for service in Christian education-related ministries. The majority of churches are looking for people with experience in their field, but some are willing to give opportunity to recent graduates with a Christian education major. The National Association of Directors of Christian Education has a working relationship with Inter-Cristo, the national information center on Christian work opportunities, whereby individuals seeking a local church staff position or churches looking for such an individual may write for information (Inter-Cristo, P. O. Box 9323, Seattle, Washington 98109). Churches should ask for the "Job Description" form; individuals request the "Intermatch Personal Profile."

Before a pastor and people move to add professionals to the staff, they need to seriously consider the purpose for such action. Herman J. Sweet, in his outstanding volume *The Multiple Staff in the Local Church*, says that the basic question to be asked by a church developing multiple staff is: *"Is it our intention to deepen the ministry of the church or to extend the institution?"*[13] His concern is that if the church does not have clearly in perspective the purpose for which it exists, adding more staff may only perpetuate and compound its weaknesses. Adding a staff member will probably increase activity in church programming. But if that is the sole result, the church may yet fail to see spiritual growth on the part of its people.

The pastor is the key to making a multiple staff function in a harmonious, productive manner. Martin Anderson observes in his book *Multiple Ministries,* "The one-flock-one-shepherd parish has many advantages. It is much simpler. Most of us find it easier to work alone than in a team."[14] A pastor needs to realistically evaluate whether he is a team person and has the capability or even the desire to lead a team. He should seriously consider:

1. Would I find it possible to share my ministry with others?
2. Does it bother me who gets the credit?
3. Am I secure in my leadership role? (Adding staff could place a great strain on that security.)
4. Would I enjoy spending time in staff meetings?
5. Can I deal with the dynamics of change initiated by others?
6. Do I have executive abilities?

It is never weakness to take a good hard look at yourself and honestly evaluate the leadership style for which God has best suited you.

The *Christian Leadership Letter* has devoted an issue to the special situation in which two people, with one having the ultimate authority, share the management of an organization. These suggestions under the caption "How to Be a Good Number One" are helpful:

1. *It takes time.* Just as the Number Two needs to learn about the Chief Executive Officer, so must the Chief Executive Officer learn the skills and limitations of Number Two.

2. *The Chief Executive Officer must be open to change.* A strong Number Two will undoubtedly have suggestions for running the organization more effectively.

3. *Channels of communication must be kept open.* Nothing takes the place of openness and a policy of "no secrets."

4. *Conflict should be expected.* Strong individuals will differ. Iron sharpens iron.[15]

Though the pastor must of necessity accept responsibility for leading a multiple team, every staff member is responsible to function on that team with an unselfish, cooperative spirit. *"Excellence in the relationship of a dual or multiple ministry lies in the realm of the spirit, not in the mechanics of organization."*[16] Unquestionably, the key to effective multiple staff ministry in any church is the interpersonal relationships between the members of that staff as well as their relationships with members of the congregation.

The necessity for dismissing a staff member arises far more frequently because of the inability of the individual to get along with people than because of a lack of competency in his profession. In a study of causes of stress experienced by ministers of education, the overwhelming first cause was found to be conflict with the pastor. Causes, in order of frequency were:

> Conflict with pastor
> Uncertainty about new church/position
> Conflict in staff relations
> Work assignments/responsibilities
> Conflict with parishioners
> Overwork
> Conflict between pastor and congregation
> Financial difficulties[17]

This study substantiates what many in ministry have experienced—conflict with people is the most serious deterrent to effective ministry in the local church.[18]

The experience of a pastor in Long Beach, California, searching for staff members for the church he pastors is helpful. He was seeking people who wanted to put their future in that church and keep their efforts concentrated there over a period of years. He found that individuals of high caliber wanted to know such things as:

1. What is the potential here for using my talents?
2. Does the church offer me an opportunity for growth?
3. What kind of people will I be working with—is the board progressive in its thinking? Are staff relationships open and honest?

The pastor, in turn, believed that a professional staff person should be well paid and should have multiple fringe benefits, including some often-neglected things such as time to further his education.

A study by H. Norman Wright of Talbot Theological Seminary indicated that the average term of an educational staff member in the local church ranged between one and two years.[19] (More recent observation seems to indicate some lengthening of that time.) The critical concern here, of course, is that there can be little long-lasting impact in a church unless the professional staff is willing to devote a substantial number of years in developing a ministry.

The Minister of Education

The second staff person added to a church staff is often a director or minister of Christian education. When one examines the ministry of the average church, a rather large percentage of what takes place would fall into some category of Christian education. An individual to give coordinative direction to this major segment of a church's ministry can be an important key in the effectiveness of any church.

Marvin T. Judy gives a brief history of the professional church staff position of director of Christian education, tracing its origin back to the early years of the twentieth century.[20] It is difficult to determine how many people are engaged in such a ministry today, though they would undoubtedly number in the thousands.

The DCE position in the local church has its occupational hazards, not the least of which is economic. Often a church extends itself financially to add the full-time professional educator. When this eventually proves to be too heavy a financial burden for the church or there are other financial difficulties, the DCE becomes an expendable commodity. The primary answer to such a hazard, however, is an attitude of career permanency on the part of the DCE. The field is greatly in need of individuals who will approach the educational ministry with a commitment to make it a lifetime calling where God so directs. The opportunities are still abundant; churches are looking for people who are committed to the ministry of Christian education.

The question is sometimes asked, "How long can one remain a DCE in the local church?" There really are no limitations if one remains a growing person, both spiritually and professionally. Continuing education is available in many forms, and the growing DCE must make time for reading, attending helpful seminars, and continuing to stay active as a teacher himself. The larger a church becomes, the more demanding is the administrative load for the DCE. Many in large churches discover they are spending a major portion of their time in administrative duties. Though he may be a gifted administrator, his opportunities for ministry need to be varied if he is to find the position a fulfilling and challenging one.

One step that will strengthen the permanency and respectability of the DCE is for the individual to seek and qualify for ordination to the educational ministry. Becoming a duly ordained minister of education, as in the case of ordination to the pastoral ministry, helps to communicate the commitment of the person to the field and aids in achieving the needed response from the people he has been called to lead.

Since interpersonal relationships, particularly with the senior pastor, are a key factor in permanency in the local church ministry of Christian education, the minister of education can be a significant supportive arm for the senior pastor. Some good insight into the matter of functioning as a productive staff member is included in one issue of the *Christian Leadership Letter*. Stressed are such fundamentals as supporting the senior pastor's ministry, understanding his style, being fully loyal, and spending time planning together.[21]

Individuals candidating for a DCE position in a local church need to obtain a description, in writing, of what the church's expectations are for such a position. Many churches have not adequately thought through their needs and expectations, and putting those into writing will cause the church leadership to more accurately evaluate what they are seeking in such an individual. The DCE can assist in that process by sharing his own philosophy of Christian education and the personal strengths he would bring to the particular local church ministry. Joseph Bayly of the David C. Cook Publishing Company recommends that before accepting a new church staff position the individual do a thorough situational analysis and come up with appropriate programs for that particular church, rather than simply suggesting transplanted programs that have been successful in his previous church.[22]

Lois LeBar categorizes the chief responsibilities of the DCE as motivation, evaluation, integration, administration, training, supervision, and counseling.[23] Though fulfilling those responsibilities in the educational area will keep an individual more than busy in the average church, he will be greatly appreciated by both senior pastor and people as he demonstrates an attitude of cooperation toward the total pastoral needs of a church. Specialization does not preclude sensitivity.

THE MINISTER TO YOUTH

Almost every church where youth attend is concerned about "getting someone to work with the young people." That very mindset has some built-in challenges for the prospective youth pastor:

He will be expected to have sufficient energy to attend all of the youth functions.

He must have the maturity to relate to parents of young people in what they consider an adult manner.

He must prove himself a responsible individual to the adult leadership of the church.

Having the qualities of energy, maturity, and responsible conduct is certainly a tremendous asset for a youth director in the local church. But finding a person with such qualities does not automatically discharge a church's responsibility for the youth ministry. *Youth ministry is not a one-man job,* and the ultimate success of a youth pastor in a church will depend on his ability to motivate the lay people to share in ministry to and with young people.

Leading Bible studies, enjoying summer and winter camp experiences, visiting informally on the school campus, counseling young people and their parents, and sharing in evangelistic, athletic, and social activities are rewarding areas of youth ministry.

But the recruitment and training of youth sponsors and teachers is a primary, ongoing task of the youth director.

In most churches the youth director is responsible for junior high, high school, and college-age people. In some areas, it is becoming more common to shift the college youth into the adult department, under the category of young adults. A large church may have a youth pastor for each age division, but normally the youth person will carry the responsibility for at least two age groups. Most youth workers have a personal preference or a natural ability to work with one age group and therefore must be careful not to neglect their ministry to the other groups.

Youth ministry is sometimes regarded as the survival of the fittest. Though most youth pastors are young, there are some who have remained in this ministry for many years (generally in the same church) and continue to be very effective.

MINISTER TO CHILDREN/MINISTER TO FAMILIES

The breakdown of the home has emerged as a major concern within the evangelical church. In seeking to find answers to that growing problem, staff positions to minister to children and to families have emerged in professional church leadership.

A position to supervise and administer childhood education has long existed in churches where there have been a large number of children in attendance. But more recently there has been concern for the family dimension. Here the ministry includes marriage and family education, family camps, church activities involving the entire family, and the small group, body-life ministry that churches are using to bring their families together in meaningful relationships.

A student considering children's work, family ministry, or a combination of the two should obtain a good biblical background, develop a philosophy of family ministry that includes children's ministry, and obtain as much experience as possible with all age levels.

OTHER COMBINATION MINISTRIES

The individual starting out in a local church staff ministry will frequently find that the ability to provide more than one type of leadership will enhance his opportunities for finding a place of service. Most growing churches sense the need to add professional staff leadership, but often struggle with the problem of limited budget.

Where the staff person has the necessary qualifications, possible combination positions such as minister of education and music, minister of education and youth, children's director and church secretary are very workable. It enables the church to benefit from the leadership of a multi-talented person during a time of limited resources. The obvious disadvantage in such an arrangement is the frustration the staff person may experience in trying to give adequate attention to each of his major responsibilities.

It is easy to concentrate on problems involved in professionals working together in local church ministry. But as Sweet has indicated, where we are determined to deepen the ministry rather than merely extend the institutional church, and the professional staff sees its primary task as the equipping of the church to be the people of God, the work becomes a rewarding experience for both church and staff person.[24]

FOR FURTHER STUDY

1. Prepare a staff organizational chart for a church with at least four staff persons. Indicate their primary duties, lines of responsibility, and how they interrelate.
2. Visit a local church and prepare an analysis of the type of church it is, based on the book *All Originality Makes a Dull Church*. Give reasons for your conclusions.
3. Visualizing the church of tomorrow, what "paraministry" positions do you forsee for the local church? Why?

4. Do a study from the gospels of how Jesus equipped His disciples for ministry.
5. Prepare a list of questions you would ask a church that is interviewing you for a staff position. Include a personal profile that would encompass your philosophy of Christian education.
6. Interview a person who is functioning in a combination ministry in the local church. Summarize the advantages and disadvantages of such a role and give your own evaluation of such a ministry.

NOTES

1. Douglas Stave, "Coming Boom: Paraministry," *Christianity Today*, 15 March 1974, pp. 40-42.
2. Ibid., p. 42.
3. Findley B. Edge, *The Greening of the Church* (Waco, Tex.: Word, 1971), p. 31.
4. Ibid., p. 38.
5. Dan Baumann, *All Originality Makes a Dull Church* (Santa Ana, Calif.: Vision House, 1976), chap. 3.
6. Ibid., pp. 50-51.
7. Quoted in Lois E. LeBar, *Focus On People in Church Education* (Westwood, N.J.: Revell, 1968), p. 127.
8. Gaines S. Dobbins, *A Ministering Church* (Nashville: Broadman, 1960), p. 46.
9. Ibid., p. 48.
10. Findley B. Edge, *A Quest for Vitality in Religion* (Nashville: Broadman, 1963), p. 99.
11. Marvin T. Judy, *The Multitple Staff Ministry* (Nashville: Abingdon, 1969), p. 35.
12. Ibid., p. 38.
13. Herman J. Sweet, *The Multiple Staff in the Local Church* (Philadelphia: Westminster, 1963), p. 116.
14. Martin Anderson, *Multiple Ministries* (Minneapolis: Augsburg, 1965), p. 18.
15. "How to Be Number Two," *Christian Leadership Letter*, August 1977, p. 3.
16. Anderson, p. 40.
17. J. Clifford Thorp, Jr., "The Minister of Education and Career Success," *Search* 6, no. 3 (Spring 1976), p. 40.
18. Herman J. Sweet's chapter "Approaches to Better Staff Relationships" is recommended reading for anyone serving or planning to serve on a church staff.
19. H. Norman Wright, "A Report on the Professional Status of Christian Education Directors and Youth Directors." Mimeographed. Fall 1972, p. 3.
20. Judy, p. 143.
21. *Christian Leadership Letter*, p. 2.
22. Joseph Bayly, "Church Tailors," *Eternity*, December 1977, p. 57.
23. LeBar, pp. 127-28.
24. Sweet, p. 104.

SUGGESTED READING

Anderson, Martin. *Multiple Ministries*. Minneapolis: Augsburg, 1965. Gives helpful guidelines to both congregations and pastors in making multiple ministries work.

Baumann, Dan. *All Originality Makes a Dull Church*. Santa Ana, Calif.: Vision House, 1976. An analysis of five types of growing churches with suggestion that you borrow applicable principles.

Dobbins, Gaines S. *A Ministering Church*. Nashville: Broadman, 1960. Follows Southern Baptist educational pattern, but many principles have universal application in the church.

Edge, Findley B. *The Greening of the Church*. Waco, Tex.: Word, 1971. An incisive look at today's church and some challenging suggestions for change.
————. *A Quest for Vitality in Religion*. Nashville: Broadman, 1963. An experienced Christian educator proposes how the goals of religious education must be achieved in the local church.

Engstrom, Ted W. *The Making of a Christian Leader*. Grand Rapids: Zondervan, 1976. A refreshing review of both the principles of management and human relationships. Strong biblical leadership principles..

Gangel, Kenneth O. *Competent to Lead*. Chicago: Moody, 1974. Good biblical basis plus specific procedures for Christian administrators—including youth pastors.

Hakes, J. Edward, ed. *An Introduction to Evangelical Christian Education*. Chicago: Moody, 1964. Predecessor of this volume. Much sound guidance by leading Christian educators.

Judy, Marvin T. *The Multiple Staff Ministry*. Nashville: Abingdon, 1969. A scholarly and exhaustive study involving extensive research.

LeBar, Lois E. *Focus on People in Christian Education*. Westwood, N.J.: Revell, 1968. A fine tool for the local church educator to evaluate and build programs, placing the emphasis properly on people.

McDonough, Reginald M. *Working with Volunteer Leaders in the Church*. Nashville: Broadman, 1976. Sound help for church staffs in dealing with one of their most perplexing problems.

Pioneer Girls Leaders' Handbook. Wheaton, Ill.: Pioneer Girls, 1975. Contains an outstanding section on recruiting, training, and supervising leadership.

Snyder, Howard A. *The Problem of Wine Skins*. Downers Grove, Ill.: InterVarsity, 1975. Snyder is a significant author on the subject of church renewal.

Sweet, Herman J. *The Multiple Staff in the Local Church*. Philadelphia: Westminster, 1963. This book continues to be the basic manual on multiple staff ministries. Written by one with thirty-five years experience as a member of multiple staffs.

The Youth Pastor. Tempe, Az.: Success with Youth (under the direction of the Youth Commission of the National Sunday School Association), 1971.

Zuck, Roy, and Benson, Warren, eds. *Youth Education in the Church*. Chicago: Moody, 1978. A resource book dealing with all aspects of youth ministry. Also enables one to build a biblical philosophy of youth ministry.

19

The Organizational Structure

PAUL L. DIRKS

PLANNING AND ORGANIZATION are vital to the success of any group or program. It is certainly true that "it is better to get set up before you go ahead, and get upset." The church that has careful organization based on thoughtful planning will get more done and will do it in a more efficient and effective manner.

Organization involves people cooperating together to implement their plan. "It is creative union of people and purpose."[1] Or as Ted W. Engstrom puts it, "the manifestation of a shared purpose."[2]

BIBLICAL ORGANIZATION

Our God is a God of order—the universe demonstrates that. There is order and organization in all of creation: stars are in their orbits, plants complete their cycles, animals have complex circulatory and respiratory systems. All show forth God's wondrous design.

The Bible clearly shows that God wants His work done decently and in order (1 Cor. 14:40). We have many examples in His Word of those who were effective organizers.

MOSES

Although he is known as one of the great leaders in the Old Testament, Moses had to learn how to be an effective organizer. God used his father-in-law, Jethro, to teach him the principle of delegation (Exod. 18:13-24).[3] Moses had been giving all his time and energy to judging the people. Jethro said to him, "The thing that you are doing is not good. You will surely wear out . . . you cannot do it alone" (18:17-18).

PAUL L. DIRKS, Ph.D., is dean of the California Graduate School of Theology, Glendale, California.

Moses had the good sense to take Jethro's advice. He organized his work by choosing able men as judges over groups of people, which freed himself to carry on his other duties.

NEHEMIAH

Another Old Testament leader who accomplished much through careful organization was Nehemiah. Organization was the means that enabled Nehemiah, under the hand of God, to effectively combine resources and people in the rebuilding of the walls of Jerusalem (Neh. 3).

CHRIST

The New Testament details how Jesus Christ went systematically about His work. His disciples, for example, were organized and sent forth "two by two" (Mark 6:7). Kenneth O. Gangel, in his book *Competent to Lead* points out four qualities of His efficient leadership: "He focused on his purpose, on individuals, on the scriptures, and on himself as Savior. He was a great example of a competent organizer."[4]

PAUL

The apostle Paul "carefully organized the churches he established."[5] In his first epistle to the Corinthians, he used the human body as an analogy to illustrate how the church should function (1 Cor. 12:12-31) .

ORGANIZATION APPLIED

IN THE TEACHING LESSON

A key factor in the success of any lesson is organization. Sometimes after a lesson pupils can be heard to say, "I just didn't get anything out of that class," or "I couldn't follow what the teacher had to say." Often the problem is that the material has not been logically outlined, and/or the class time has not been carefully organized.

Lesson organization focuses on a thoughtfully written, specifically stated aim—an aim that is based on the needs of the pupils.

Gangel states well that "methodology, curriculum, administration . . . only fall into place after objectives have been clearly defined."[6] The material to be presented is then properly arranged so that it will meet and satisfy the aim. Organization is the means to that end. When lesson material is carefully planned and the class time is properly organized, students will be more likely to leave saying, "I really got a lot from that class," and, "I can use what I have just learned."

IN THE EDUCATIONAL PROGRAM OF THE CHURCH

The great goal of the church of Jesus Christ in this world is to bring people to spiritual maturity (Eph. 4:13). The maturing process begins with evangelism and continues by edification.

Maturity is accomplished through many different programs. Involved in evangelism are children's clubs, home Bible studies, visitation, and similar ministries. The programs of the church that edify the Body are clustered about four elements or emphases: instruction, worship, expression, and fellowship. As people become involved in those programs, they are helped to grow toward maturity.

Two keys to success in the program of the church are proper motivation and careful organization. People must be stimulated to become involved, and they must also be related to each other in efficient and effective ways.

Many churches find it helpful to organize all their activity into divisions, or commissions. A. M. Adams, for example, suggests these commissions: worship, membership, evangelism, Christian education, finance, and stewardship.[7] The commissions operate with equal status, and the leaders of each one together with the pastor and his staff form the ruling body of the church.

A simple chart diagramming the relationships and functions of the various agencies in the church helps identify present and future organizational problems. Gangel in *Leadership for Church Education* provides four examples of charts that cover most church organizations, and he offers these suggestions for the making and using of a chart:

1. Chart the organization as it presently exists.
2. Circulate it among all the teachers and workers.
3. Construct another chart with suggested changes to improve organization and administration.
4. Continually update the chart.[8]

Remember to keep the chart as simple as possible. Too many lines on the chart will only reduce its effectiveness. It is not necessary to show every relationship or function. A good test is this: Does a teacher in a Sunday school department know who is in the line of authority over him and where his class fits into the overall ministry of the church?

USING A BOARD OF CHRISTIAN EDUCATION

The concluding phrase of the Old Testament book of Judges, "Everyone did what was right in his own eyes," sums up the underlying reason for the problems Israel faced at that time. When individuals in a group march to their own drumbeat, chaos can result. Only when Israel repented and then responded properly to God and His designated leader did the nation have His blessing.

With its many agencies and programs, the church today must likewise set up a managing body and then agree to respond to its leadership. Only as each group and individual cooperates with others in the church can the goals that have been established be met.

Gangel points out, therefore, that a board of Christian education is needed for such coordination and organizational unity.[9] Dalton has found in his church education experience that "no church is too small or too limited in leadership to have such a board and to profit from its work."[10] That board can be of great assistance to the pastor of the local church in the administration of educational ministry.

Where the church has a director of Christian education, the director should "work with the board of Christian education to survey the educational needs . . . help the board to set goals, and evaluate its program."[11]

SCRIPTURAL BASIS FOR THE BOARD

We have already noted that God's work should be done decently and in order. For that to be accomplished, authority must be delegated to others. This principle is demonstrated in the book of Acts. The apostles selected those to whom authority would be given in certain areas of the work (Acts 6:1-4). Paul and Barnabas appointed elders to assist them (Acts 14:23). Paul also used Timothy in the process of delegating the teaching of the Word of God to others (2 Tim. 2:2).

FUNCTION OF THE BOARD

The board of Christian education is concerned with administering the educational program of the church. R. K. Bower in his book on church administration gives six basic administrative operations, or general functions, of the board of Christian education. Those are planning, organizing, delegating, staffing, coordinating, and controlling.[12]

Those broad areas need to be spelled out in specific responsibilities. First, the board should *survey the educational needs* of the church. Each church has its own distinctives and needs. The program for a church must be set up to meet that church's needs.

The board of Christian education constantly surveys such areas as curriculum, facilities, equipment, and personnel to determine whether the needs are being met. Most important of all, members of the board must continually be sensitive to the needs of individuals, as well as groups, who make up the church. Our Lord gave us a wonderful example in His dealing with individuals. He spent a great amount of His time with them—a bungling Peter, a disbelieving Philip, a seeking Nicodemus. The success of the program in any church can usually be measured in the lives of individuals.

Another responsibility of the board is to *establish the objectives* of the program. Programs that have no aims or objectives are literally going nowhere. Goals may both be physical and spiritual. Physical goals include attendance, outreach, building, and equipment, while objectives in the spiritual sphere include evangelism, Christian growth, and biblical knowledge. One church printed its educational goals and distributed them to the members of the congregation, who then had a specific understanding of the direction of the church's program.

The board of Christian education has the responsibility of *developing the program*. It looks at needs and sets objectives, then puts in the program to carry out the objectives. The members of the board will ask themselves, "How can we as a church body accomplish the task God has given to us to do in this place? What ministries (agencies) are necessary to reach our objectives?"

A fourth responsibility of a board has to do with the *approval of the curriculum*. The board should know what is being taught in each department of the church, both in terms of truth and in terms of balance and continuity. Board members should visit departments and classes periodically. A good criterion for the curriculum is that it be Christ-centered, Bible-based, and attractively pupil-related.

The board, further, *oversees the staffing* of the program. To do that in the most efficient manner, a personnel committee can be established. The responsibility of the committee is to recruit, train, and place workers.

The board will *recommend a budget* for carrying out the program of Christian education. That budget will include provision for materials and equipment needed for the Sunday school, youth activities, camp, vacation Bible school, and related programs. The careful preparation of such a budget will do much to encourage the efficient operation of the educational ministry.

The *providing of proper facilities* is another responsibility of the board. Learning is considerably influenced by the environment in which it takes place. Airlines and restaurants do much today to make their facilities attractive and functional. The church does well to do likewise.

A major concern of the educational board is to *develop an educational awareness* among the members of the congregation. That is needed so that a climate will be provided where new ideas and innovative concepts may be attempted. Members of the church must be aware not only of what is taking place educationally but also of what is needed for the most effective work to be done in the ministry of the church.

Another basic goal of the board is to *encourage home-church cooperation*. The church may have the child for up to 3 percent of his time, but the home has the child under its direction for up to 80 percent of his time. Therefore the church must work with the home in any Christian education impact.

Finally, the board will *evaluate the progress* being made in the educational ministry. The evaluation should determine what is being done well so that it can be continued and amplified. It should also determine the areas that need improvement and strengthening.

SETTING UP THE BOARD

It is recommended that the board consist of five to ten members, appointed or elected. Smaller churches may have from two to three members. Major educational areas of the program should be represented on the board, with the pastor serving as ex officio member. The board should meet at regular intervals, usually once a month. An agenda should be carefully prepared for each meeting and, if possible, sent ahead of time to each member.

The board of Christian education should serve as a recommending body with major decisions and policies reviewed and approved by the official board of the church. In some cases the church board has a representative on the educational board.

COORDINATION THROUGH ORGANIZATION

A well-functioning Christian education board leads toward an organized, productive, educational church ministry, where the various educational agencies involved will be *coordinated* toward common goals through their use of coordinated materials and efforts. Bower defines coordination as "the act of achieving unity and harmony of effort in the achievement of organizational goals. It is . . . the regulation of activities so that efficiency of operation results."[13] Lack of coordination leads to competition between programs (a contest for the junior high Sunday school department at the same time as another contest for the junior high evening youth group) and duplication in curriculum (the story of Daniel in the lions' den told the same week in the junior Sunday school and at the weekday club meeting). Nor may there be awareness of what is happening spiritually in the lives of individuals active in another group. A coordinating means is essential.

How can a coordinated program be achieved? The various responsibilities of a Christian education board take effect as they view the church's program through the eyes of the individuals for whom the activities are planned, establishing both needs to be met and specific programs to meet them.

Major age divisions should be established. Supervisors or coordinators who would oversee all the activities in an age division should be estab-

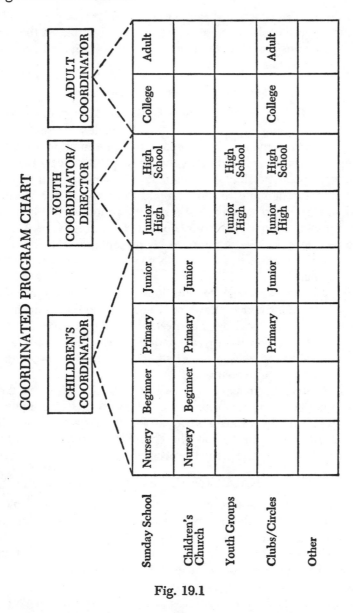

Fig. 19.1

lished as part of a Christian education board responsibility. (See figure 19.1.) All the workers in each division would be ultimately responsible to their coordinator. All plans must be cleared through the coordinator, and all materials and equipment purchases approved by the coordinator.

This plan makes it possible for the pastor or director of Christian education to guide any size program through only three key people: a children's coordinator, a youth coordinator, and an adult coordinator. As the ministry grows, the age divisions may, of course, be further divided and coordinators appointed as needed.

IMPLEMENTING ORGANIZATION

There are several practical suggestions relating to organization. First, when an organizational change or addition is needed, present new programs or concepts convincingly. Prepare the presentation well. W. J. Asper suggests that recommendations should be presented by two means: (1) a tentative plan—possibly as a manual or a handbook stating details showing how the program is to function and (2) resolutions necessary for the board and/or congregation to authorize the program.[14] When the one making the presentation has done his "homework" carefully, he is far more certain to receive a positive response to his presentation. In the planning stages it is also important to involve the people who will be affected by the recommendation.

Second, a practical approach to situations that are in need of change is to know how to adapt and be flexible. Once the ultimate goal has been set and the road to the goal has been established, it is necessary to deal positively and creatively with present conditions. A willingness on the part of a leader to react positively to the existing situation will encourage support when it comes time to change.

A final reminder should be given. All organization must be directed toward spiritual goals. In the organization of the church, the living Body of Christ, we must always keep in mind that "we are dealing with an *organism* and therefore must allow the church's spiritual aspects to constantly permeate the organizational process."[15]

FOR FURTHER STUDY

1. Make a list of principles of organization you can find in the Bible.
2. Write a paragraph explaining why people are the most important ingredient in organization.
3. How would you answer a church leader who objects to organization because "too much organization will push the Lord right out of the church"?
4. Observe the program of educational activities that takes place in your church on Sunday and evaluate the organizational effectiveness.
5. Make organizational charts of two existing churches. Make one chart from a church with less than 150 in Sunday school. Make another chart from a church with more than 500 in Sunday school.

6. Visit a Christian education board meeting. Make a list of the actions taken during the meeting and evaluate what was accomplished.
7. Talk to a youth director and find out how he coordinates all the activities in the youth program. Outline your findings.

NOTES

1. Robert Blake and Jane Morton, *Corporate Excellence Through Grid Organization* (Houston: Gulf, 1968), p. 12.
2. Ted W. Engstrom and Edward R. Dayton, *The Art of Management for Christian Leaders* (Waco, Tex.: Word, 1976), p. 100.
3. Robert N. Gray, *Managing the Church* (Enid, Okla.: Haymaker, 1971), p. 94.
4. Kenneth O. Gangel, *Competent to Lead* (Chicago: Moody, 1970), p. 14.
5. H. W. Byrne, *Christian Education for the Local Church* (Grand Rapids: Zondervan, 1973), p. 33.
6. Kenneth O. Gangel, *Leadership for Church Education* (Chicago: Moody, 1970), p. 45.
7. Arthur M. Adams, *Pastoral Administration* (Philadelphia: Westminster, 1964), p. 42.
8. Gangel, *Leadership for Church Education*, pp. 56-57.
9. Ibid., p. 104.
10. Dean A. Dalton, "'The Board of Christian Education," in *An Introduction to Evangelical Christian Education*, ed. J. Edward Hakes (Chicago: Moody, 1964), p. 232.
11. Vernon R. Kraft, *The Director of Christian Education in the Local Church* (Chicago: Moody, 1957), p. 91.
12. Robert K. Bower, *Administering Christian Education* (Grand Rapids: Eerdmans, 1964), pp. 20-22.
13. Ibid., p. 137 (in an excellent chapter on coordination).
14. Wallace J. Asper, *How to Organize the Educational Program of Your Church* (Minneapolis: Augsburg, 1959), p. 57.
15. Gangel, *Leadership for Church Education*, p. 60.

SUGGESTED READING

Adams, Arthur M. *Pastoral Administration.* Philadelphia: Westminster, 1964.

Asper, Wallace J. *How to Organize the Educational Program of Your Church.* Minneapolis: Augsburg, 1959.

Barnard, Chester I. *The Functions of the Executive.* Cambridge, Mass.: Harvard U., 1956. Helpful sections on formal and informal organizations.

Blake, Robert, and Morton, Jane. *Corporate Excellence Through Grid Organization.* Houston: Gulf, 1968. A rather technical work on organization.

Bower, Robert K. *Administering Christian Education.* Grand Rapids: Eerdmans, 1964. An excellent book on administration.

Byrne, H. W. *Christian Education for the Local Church.* Grand Rapids: Zondervan, 1973. A basic text on Christian education with a good chapter on the board of Christian education.

Engstrom, Ted W., and Dayton, Edward R. *The Art of Management for Christian Leaders.* Waco, Tex.: Word, 1976. A good book on the techniques of personal management.

Gangel, Kenneth O. *Competent to Lead.* Chicago: Moody, 1974. A comprehensive view of church leadership.

————. *Leadership for Church Education*. Chicago: Moody, 1970. Excellent section on organizational plans with charts showing four basic plans into which most churches will fit.

Gray, Robert N. *Managing the Church*. Enid, Okla.: Haymaker, 1971. An excellent book with much practical and useful material.

Kraft, Vernon R. *The Director of Christian Education in the Local Church*. Chicago: Moody, 1957. An old but helpful book that contains practical suggestions for those involved in Christian education ministry.

Person, Peter P. *The Minister in Christian Education*. Grand Rapids: Baker, 1960. Sensible and practical guidelines for church organizations.

20

Educational Administration and Supervision

RONALD P. CHADWICK

OFTEN THE TERMS, *administration, leadership,* and *management,* are used interchangeably. Management, according to *The American Institute of Management,* is "the art of bringing ends and means together . . . the art of purposeful action." Some have referred to it as "getting things done through people," or as R. Alec Mackenzie states, "achieving objectives through others."[1] Management involves the control or guidance of both human and material resources to accomplish a specific end or objective.

Leadership, by definition, implies an impact upon or an influence/control over people. Mackenzie adds, "Leadership is a process of influencing people to achieve desired goals and objectives."[2] A good leader is one who knows where he is going and is capable of taking others along with him. Thus, a leader can be described as one who can generate, communicate, and sustain commonality of purpose. That definition of leadership moves us closer to our understanding of administration.

The term *administration* probably includes both leadership and management. For a working definition, we can conclude that administration is the comprehensive effort to direct, guide, and integrate related human efforts that are focused toward some specific end. The functions of administration can include the following: planning, organizing, staffing, initiating, delegating, directing, overseeing, coordinating, evaluating, and motivating.

BIBLICAL RATIONALE

Does the Scripture speak of administration? The reference to administration found in 1 Corinthians 12:5, "there are differences of administrations, but the same Lord" (KJV), is the word for ministry, or serving. The word is *diakonia,* which comes from *diakonos,* and means to

---

RONALD P. CHADWICK, Ph.D., is director of Christian education, Baptist Seminary, Grand Rapids, Michigan.

run errands or to serve as a waiter at a table or in some other menial duties.[3] It is especially used in the New Testament of "those who are deacons, ministers, or servants." However, in 1 Corinthians 12:28, the word that is translated "government" in the KJV and "administration" in the NASB comes from the Greek word *kubernesis*. The word picture here is that of a helmsman, the captain, or shipmaster, and literally means to "steer, or pilot."[4] This word implies that there are those who have been gifted specifically with the supernatural ability to give direction to the functioning of the Body of Christ.

Two additional points need to be noted concerning biblical administration. First, God Himself is an administrator. That is demonstrated in the biblical concept of order as seen in the account of creation (Gen. 1–2) and in His work by preservation (Psalm 104:19), where we are told that the moon has its seasons by appointment of God. Psalm 147:8-19 emphasizes the scope of God's administrative work in preservation in relationship to the entire spectrum of God's creation. Likewise, God is seen as an effective administrator in relationship to future events in the order of the resurrection (1 Cor. 15:23-24).

Finally, because the church is an organism it must employ organization and utilize effective administration. It is possible to have organization and not have life, but it is impossible to have life without organization. The Scripture clearly teaches us that the church is an organism, a body; and therefore, administration or leadership becomes essential to carry out the workings of that organism.

Acts 6:1-8, for example, demonstrates to us how the early church used good administration to help it concentrate on the primary, not the peripheral, responsibilities.

The results of that administration in the early church are clearly given to us in the passage:

1. The apostles were released to do what God had called them to do to give themselves to the ministry of the Word and to prayer (v. 4).
2. The Word of God increased and the number of the disciples was multiplied (v. 7).
3. The resources of the church were harnessed specifically with men like Stephen and Philip coming into focus (v. 8).

Principles Conceptualized

A good administrator causes others to get involved in the work. Though initially or temporarily he may have to do the job himself, a good administrator is not one who can do the work of ten men, but one who can get ten men to do the work. Actually, the goal of the administrator is not to work himself out of a job, but to work others into the job, so that as an effective leader, he can move into other areas.

There are many types, or styles, of leadership, as expressed in the following contrasts:

Autocratic (boss-centered)	Democratic (subordinate-centered)
Exploitive	Participatory
Authoritarian	Democratic
Task-Oriented	People-Oriented
Nomothetic (institution)	Idiographic (individuals)

Though there are variables in each set of contrasts, basically leadership comes either from the top down or from the bottom up.[5]

It is important to realize that an organization at various stages in its growth may require differing styles of leadership. During the initial growth period of an organization, it may be essential to have an aggressive, visionary, action-oriented leader or administrator, and without that individual, the organization would not grow. However, there may come a period when the administrator begins wearing all of the hats, plays hunches, and disparages a planned approach. The result is that there are no controls, no training, no team work, high turnover of leadership, no delegation, and essentially management by crisis. Thus, as an organization goes through its growth period, so the administrator needs also to be a growing leader. So when the organization passes through critical early periods and moves into more maturing development, there is increasing potential for team work, participative management, management by objectives, planning, control, and a rational decision making process.

Sometimes the "Peter Principle," where a man rises to his own level of incompetence, occurs when the organization actually outgrows the leadership or leadership style of those who are at the top. Certainly, key words in leadership style must be flexibility, adjustability, and adaptability, or as Alvin Toffler in *Future Shock* puts it, "copeability."[6]

A good administrator delegates responsibility. Have you ever heard the expressions: "He's overworked, but he won't let go," "It's a one-man show, but we can't seem to break the pattern"? Psalm 37:5 tells us to "commit your way to the LORD, trust also in Him, and He will do it." The Hebrew concept of committing is to roll the burden onto someone else and is exactly the concept that is given to us in 2 Timothy 2:2. "And the things which you have heard from me in the presence of many witnesses, these entrust to faithful men, who will be able to teach others also." The principle that Paul was giving us is that we are not responsible for doing all the work but are responsible for training and equipping people so that they can more effectively be involved in doing with us the "work of service [ministry]" (Eph. 4:11-12).

There are a number of benefits to be derived from delegation. First, it extends results from what a man is able to do himself to what he can manage. The benefit is that the administrator is released for other work. Further, it helps develop the initiative, skills, knowledge, and competence of the other team members.

Certainly Nehemiah, in the rebuilding of the walls of Jerusalem, did not attempt to do the work himself, nor did he take the approach that it was everyone's responsibility without giving leadership or direction. Thirty-four times in the book of Nehemiah, the phrase "next to him" gives to us the picture of how the priests, princes, and the people were all welded together with the result that the wall was rebuilt in fifty-two days. Effective delegation is carried out when functions, not policy-making, are delegated. Further, delegation must be to qualified people, and it is also the administrator's responsibility to establish controls and to provide for a system of reporting. The key elements in the process of delegation are: responsibility, authority, and accountability.

A good administrator selects the right person for the job. People are like chemicals. They represent potential. Enlistment of leadership is finding the right person for the right place. Jesus Christ, in choosing the twelve disciples, chose not on the basis of the present but on the basis of what those men could become.

First Timothy, chapter 3, describes *leadership qualities* or *qualifications*.[7] Compare those with Ordway Tead's ten essentials of leadership: (1) learning and (2) following. When put together these give to us the picture of true discipleship. A disciple is a follower, who is a learner. (3) Serving. Certainly, the Lord Jesus is an excellent model of the servant concept of leadership, for He Himself declared, "The Son of Man did not come to be served, but to serve, and to give His life . . ." (Matt. 20:28). (4) Dedication, or the concept of total commitment. (5) Integrity or wholeness. This is the picture of consistency in the public as well as the private life of the individual leader. (6) Technical mastery or simple "know-how." (7) Decisiveness or speed in decision-making. It is not that others do not have the ability to make decisions, it is just that an effective leader is able to make the same decisions faster. (8) Intelligence. Here the focus is on *EQ—Efficiency Quotient* (rather than on IQ, Intelligence Quotient) where the individual is utilizing to the full potential his ability. (9) Teaching skill, or the process of communication. This is crucial to one's ability to lead or function as an administrator. (10) Faith. The writer of Hebrews (11:1) tells us that faith gives substance or reality to the things that are not seen. A true Christian leader is a man of faith and vision because he has his eyes fastened on the Lord (Heb. 12:12).[8] It is important in Christian leadership positions to recognize the principle that Paul gives in 2 Corinthians 3:5-6; it is not self-sufficiency or self-competency, but God-given competence.

To improve the level of job performance, it is helpful to provide a job or position description.

Basically, a job description can be summarized in three categories: the requirements for the job, the relationships of the job (to whom and for whom you are responsible), and the responsibilities, or duties, of the specific job.

A good administrator uses committees for planning. First, one must determine the committee's purpose. Although the committee is for the purpose of planning, it is individual men who will carry out the work planned. That, of course, requires that the administrator know the individuals of the committee, both in terms of their dependability as well as their abilities.

Thus, a good administrator will not assign responsibility without accountability.

A.V.O.—avoid verbal orders. Responsibility and accountability effectively carried out requires that directions be written. One practice to follow is to take the minutes of a planning session and underline in red all of the items that apply to a particular member as he is sent his copy of the minutes. That, of course, assumes the keeping of clear minutes.

A good administrator avoids overlapping, overworking, and overlooking team members. Unless a task *requires* that more than one person be assigned, no more than one person should be given the same responsibility. We must also always be careful that we do not spread ourselves or others too thin. A good rule of thumb to follow is that each person within the Christian education program should have only one *major* preparation responsibility. To prevent overlooking, show appreciation for a job well done. People must feel needed and appreciated, and simple expressions of thanks go a long way toward helping to motivate the team members.

THE ADMINISTRATOR AS SUPERVISOR

The art of supervision is teaching how to work with people and getting people to work as a part of the team. At the heart of supervision lies the concept of improvement. It also means acknowledging the presence of the Holy Spirit in the life of the believer and recognizing the provision of spiritual gifts that have been given to each as members of the Body of Christ (1 Cor. 12:7; Eph. 4:7).

The process of supervision includes:

1. Telling the person what you expect—*Responsibility.*

2. Checking at regular intervals the performance by the standards established—*Evaluation*.
3. Developing a list of the goals and corrective actions necessary for growth—*Improvement*.
4. Providing sources from which the individual can obtain help—*Resources*.
5. Keeping the spiritual dynamic as the basic motivation for service—*Spiritual Growth*.

ADMINISTRATIVE PLANNING

Planning is the logical determination of where you want to go and how you are going to get there. It concerns the future impact of present decisions.

Risk is involved in progress, so in planning we do not eliminate risk, but we seek to avoid unnecessary risk by maximizing the use of available resources and time.

ONE MODEL FOR LONG-RANGE PLANNING

Community Analysis   Performance Evaluation—Recycling

Church Resources   Short-Range and Long-Range Plans

Basic Assumptions   Strategy—Plan

Goals—Objectives

Community Analysis: Reliable information about the past, present, and projected economic, social, political, and technological environment.

Church Resources: Past and present performance. Strengths and limitations; financial, human, facilities, uniqueness (denomination, location).

Basic Assumptions: Biblical—beliefs concerning God, man, the church, the Great Commission. Practical—beliefs concerning community, growth, population, economics.

Goals: Quantitative and qualitative statements of goals—clear, specific, measurable, realistic, consistent, time oriented.

Strategy: Short-range planning 6 months-1 year. Long-range planning 2-5 years; 10 years. Must include alternatives. Must be prepared to make adjustments without losing sight of ultimate goal.

Implementation of longe-range plans and the integration of short-range plans.

Performance Evaluation: The need for determining variances between goals and actual performance.

PROCESS OF CHANGE

Change, though inevitable, comes slowly. Suggestions for reducing stress and overcoming resistance to change include:

1. Point out need for change by noting lack of progress in the status quo.
2. Create positive attitude by involving people in the process of change.
3. Be sure people not only understand the what, how, when, who, where, and how much, but very clearly the basic question of *why*.
4. Make known any positive results of small changes already being implemented.
5. Because change begins at the point of control, educate the key people from the top down.
6. Watch your timing. Agreement by the group as to the time and rate of change is crucial to overcoming resistance.
7. Constantly rely on the supernatural dynamic of the Holy Spirit to change people and situations.

FOR FURTHER STUDY

1. Using additional resources from the administrative field, both secular and Christian, analyze the statement "The dominant characteristic of good administration is purpose."
2. Using men like Moses, Abraham, Joshua, and Nehemiah, do a character study of an administrator in action.
3. Determine the leadership style of the man at the top of a growing organization. Has this always been the leadership style for this organization? What style of leadership will be needed in the future?
4. Interview five Christian leaders to determine their three biggest human relations, or people, problems. Summarize your responses, grouping similar ones together, and state any conclusions that might be drawn.
5. Utilizing the items and suggestions given in the chapter, write a job or position description for some area of local church ministry. Especially focus on requirements, relationships, and responsibilities.
6. Assuming you have been asked to give leadership to a new church teaching program, how would you handle the problem of reducing stress in overcoming resistance to change?

NOTES

1. R. Alec Mackenzie, "The Management Process in 3-D," *Harvard Business Reviews*, November-December, 1969, p. 80.
2. Ibid.
3. Gerhard Kittel and Gerhard Friedrich, eds., *Theological Dictionary of the New Testament*, 9 vols. (Grand Rapids: Eerdmans, 1964), 2:88-93.
4. Ibid., 3:1035-37.

5. For an excellent discussion of leadership styles, see chapter 7, "Styles of Leadership," in Ted W. Engstrom, *The Making of a Christian Leader* (Grand Rapids: Zondervan, 1976).
6. Alvin Toffler, *Future Shock* (New York: Random, 1970).
7. An excellent discussion of leadership qualities may be found in Gene Getz, *The Measure of a Man* (Glendale, Calif.: Gospel Light, Regal, 1974).
8. Ordway Tead, *The Art of Leadership* (New York: McGraw-Hill, 1963), chaps. 6-9.

SUGGESTED READING

Alexander, John. *Managing Our Work.* Downers Grove, Ill.: Inter-Varsity, 1974.

Bell, A. Donald. *How to Get Along with People in the Church.* Grand Rapids: Zondervan, 1960.

Bennis, Warren G. *Changing Organizations.* New York: McGraw-Hill, 1966.

Berne, Eric. *Games People Play.* New York: Grove, 1964.

Bower, Robert K. *Administering Christian Education.* Grand Rapids: Eerdmans, 1964. Basic principles of administration for Christian workers applicable to both small and large churches.

Butt, Howard. *The Velvet Covered Brick.* New York: Harper & Row, 1973.

Drucker, Peter F. *The Effective Executive.* New York: Harper & Row, 1966. The author specifies five "talents," weaving them together through the process of effective decision making.

————. *Managing for Results.* New York: Harper & Row, 1964. Secular, but valuable, dealing with the tasks and risks of the administrative decision-maker.

————. *The Practice of Management.* New York: Harper & Row, 1954. The six sections of the book thoroughly cover all phases of management from the nature, considerations, problems, structure, the worker, the means, and the responsibilities of the management.

Eims, Leroy. *Be the Leader You Want to Be.* Wheaton, Ill.: Scripture Press, Victor, 1975. Practical book designed to facilitate effective leadership at the local church level. A leader's guide also available.

Engstrom, Ted W. *The Making of a Christian Leader.* Grand Rapids: Zondervan, 1976. Current adiminstrative theory put into a biblical context and practically presented.

Engstrom, Ted W., and Mackenzie, R. Alec. *Managing Your Time.* Grand Rapids: Zondervan, 1967. Practical principles of time management with a special focus on self management.

Gangel, Kenneth O. *Competent to Lead.* Chicago: Moody, 1974. Excellent practical presentation of the latest administrative theory tied to the very heart of the work of the local church. A must for the serious Christian administrator!

————. *Leadership for Church Education.* Chicago: Moody, 1970. Most complete presentation of the leadership situation at the local church level.

Harris, S. L. *Leadership Unlimited.* Nashville: Convention, 1969.

Hendrix, Olan. *Management and the Christian Worker*. Manila: Living Books for All, 1972. Goes much broader than simply the subject of management. Draws upon the rich background of the author's practical field experience as well as administrative training.

Kilinski, Kenneth K., and Wofford, Jerry C. *Organization and Leadership in the Local Church*. Grand Rapids: Zondervan, 1973. Excellent text drawing upon the biblical and pastoral training and experience of Kenneth Kilinski and the administrative, leadership training, and experience of Jerry Wofford. Deals with the role, prerequisites, and structure of the local church as it attempts to remain relevant in a time of cultural change.

LeTourneau, Richard. *Management Plus*. Grand Rapids: Zondervan, 1973. Adds the spiritual dimension in leadership though it is not always carefully woven into each section.

Lowrie, Roy W., Jr. *Serving God on the Christian School Board*. Whittier, Calif.: Western Association of Christian Schools, 1976. One of a kind. A concise and insightful combination of administrative theory and years of practical experience giving the Christian school board member a wealth of practical wisdom.

Ross, Murray G., and Hendry, Charles L. *New Understanding of Leadership*. New York: Association, 1957. A secular presentation, but certainly an excellent unfolding of current leadership theory. Unfortunately, this volume is out of print.

Sanders, J. Oswald. *Spiritual Leadership*. Rev. ed. Chicago: Moody, 1980. A presentation of a balanced Spirit-filled leadership model using both biblical and extrabiblical examples.

Tead, Ordway. *The Art of Administration*. New York: McGraw-Hill, 1963.

————. *The Art of Leadership*. New York: McGraw-Hill, 1963. Practical presentation of the art of leading as opposed to bossing and how those skills can be developed.

Wolff, Richard. *Man at the Top*. Wheaton, Ill.: Tyndale, 1969. Practical talks on the subject of leadership dealing with the biblical foundation, styles, traits, cost, and techniques the administrative leader must utilize in working with people.

21

Teacher and Leadership Training

LOWELL E. BROWN

TRAINING THE CHURCH'S educational leadership is never a one-time effort. Just as you must continually be recruiting leaders even before the need arises, you must provide continual training for all your leaders. Everything changes constantly—teaching staff, learners, culture, society, methods, organization, and needs. In order for your teaching ministry to be prepared to meet changes, training must be a continuing program.

Several different kinds of training are needed. New teachers and leaders need orientation to your organization, educational philosophy, and training methods. Your current staff members must constantly upgrade their teaching skills and their knowledge. All Sunday school leaders and teachers need training in basic educational philosophy, organizational principles, objectives of the Sunday school, and the basics of how to personalize learning. They also need specific training relating to the age group with which they work.

CHARACTERISTICS OF GOOD TRAINING

A good training program for teachers is marked by five major characteristics:

TRAINING SHOULD BE RELATED TO AGE LEVEL

Although principles of learning are essentially the same for all age groups, it is difficult to make specific applications of those principles when early childhood teachers and youth teachers are together in the same room. Teachers benefit most from training that focuses on the age group they teach.

LOWELL E. BROWN, M.R.E., is vice president of education of Gospel Light Publications and director of the G/L International Center for Learning, Ventura, California.

Four major groupings have proved practical in providing training sessions: early childhood (birth-5 years), children (grades 1-6), youth (grades 7-12), adult (ages 18 and up). Even though there are significant differences between toddlers and five-year-olds, the large number of common factors make it possible to have highly productive training sessions with teachers of all early childhood departments. That is also true of the other three groups.

TRAINING SHOULD BE PRACTICAL

Simply knowing student characteristics or principles of learning will not ensure that the quality of teaching improves. The focus of any training session should always be on a practical application in next week's session.

TRAINING SHOULD BE CURRICULUM-ORIENTED

For example, a training session on meeting children's needs should develop examples from next week's lesson. Teachers should be able to see how their *Teacher's Manual* can help them continue to implement a newly learned procedure. Training and curriculum should go hand in hand, supporting one basic plan that volunteers can implement efficiently.

TRAINING SHOULD BE EXPERIENTIAL

Every session should involve participants in practicing the skills they are being trained to use. It is not enough to explain or even demonstrate the use of learning materials. Teachers need to work with those materials themselves until they feel comfortable. Then they will be likely to try them in their classes.

TRAINING SHOULD BE REGULAR AND SYSTEMATIC

When a teacher is recruited, the church should make clear its plan for equipping that teacher to succeed. All training efforts should be carefully selected to reinforce that plan.

MAJOR TYPES OF TRAINING EXPERIENCES

SPECIAL TRAINING EVENTS

All teachers need opportunities to participate in extensive training workshops in which their total teaching ministry can be evaluated and enriched. Many churches recognize the need that new teachers have for an introductory course to get them started on the right foot. But experienced teachers need similar experiences to help them learn new skills, correct mistakes, and regain a vision for the ministry of teaching.

Every church should plan at least two special training events each year, four to six months apart. More than one such event is needed because (1) not all teachers will be able to attend any single event, (2) new teachers need significant reinforcement during the first two years of service, (3) new staff added during the year need special help, and (4) change is always difficult, thus improvements made during a year need considerable support to avoid misunderstanding and the natural desire to return to the familiar.

One type of special training event is the seminar/clinic program, provided by organizations such as the International Center for Learning.

Since 1970, ICL has conducted seminars and clinics throughout North America. Highly trained age-level specialists lead the sessions, which focus specifically on Bible teaching in the Sunday school. The format is highly participatory with observation, practice, discussion, and evaluation woven through the two-day and three-day sessions. Various denominations and publishing companies likewise conduct training events that focus on helping people use their curriculum materials more effectively.

Sunday school conventions and institutes are also held in many communities as cooperative efforts in training. Conventions generally tend to be more valuable for inspiration and idea sharing than for concentrated training. Although the quality of workshops may vary greatly, most teachers benefit from those opportunities to learn.

LOCAL CHURCH TRAINING COURSES

Churches schedule sessions to best fit local circumstances: Weekend training (Friday night and Saturday morning or all day Saturday); a training week (four successive evenings); or a training month (one session per week for four weeks). Sessions should be provided for each of the four age divisions, dealing with topics such as these:

Early childhood (birth-5 years)
—Child characteristics
—How children learn
—Learning objectives
—Scheduling the teaching time
—Bible learning activities
—Using music learning
—Building storytelling skills
—Guiding conversation with children
—Preventing and resolving behavior problems

Children (grades 1-6)
—The role of the teacher
—Leading a child to Christ

—Building relationships with children
—Behavior challenges
—Scheduling the session
—Bible study for children
—Bible learning activities
—Guided conversation
—Lesson planning

Youth (grades 7-12)
—Experience a model session
—Learning objectives
—Bible learning activities for youth
—Planning a session
—Discipline

Adult (ages 18 and up)
—Principles of adult learning
—Activities for adult involvement
—Planning a session
—Lesson objectives
—Selecting and using learning methods
—Building a caring fellowship

MONTHLY PLANNING/TRAINING MEETINGS

In addition to special events and courses, teachers in each age division should meet together at least once a month, consistently stretching toward excellence. Significant growth and improvement will come only as teachers work together regularly. Teachers need to interact with each other in planning for upcoming lessons. A training emphasis at every meeting will also stimulate interest. Whether a department consists of only two teachers or a large group, planning/training meetings are essential for building and maintaining a quality ministry.

Four crucial items can be dealt with effectively in one two-hour meeting every month. Each segment requires about thirty minutes. (Departments that are new to planning together find items 3 and 4 require more time for the first several meetings.) Here is a sample agenda that works:

1. *7:00—Ministry to each other.* Include Bible Study based on Scripture for next unit. Discuss how that passage relates to individual lives, sharing personal concerns and victories. Conclude with prayer. (*This segment can be done with teachers from all age groups together, with all teachers in one age division together, or with each department meeting separately.*)

2. *7:30—Teacher skill improvement.* Focus on one specific area each month. Involve teachers in activities and discussion to improve that one aspect of teaching. (*This segment can be done with all teachers in one age division together, or with each department meeting separately.*)
3. *8:00—Unit preview.* Survey the next unit of lessons. Compare the unit aims with the aims for each lesson. Check on the Scripture to be studied. Select and practice songs that will help accomplish the unit aims. Choose the Bible learning activities to be used. If more than one lesson is taught in a department, this segment should focus on sharing ideas in areas common to each teacher. (*This segment should be done by teachers from one department meeting together.*)
4. *8:30—Lesson planning.* Work together to complete planning for the first session of the unit. Check on all activities, procedures, and materials needed. If more than one lesson is taught in a department this segment should be completed at home by each teacher. (*This segment should be done by teachers from one department meeting together.*)

If you have less than two hours, it is best to eliminate one or more complete segments rather than to condense everything. Consider these factors in deciding which items are most needed by your staff:

Sharing together in prayer and Bible Study is essential for building spiritual commitment and a sense of shared ministry. This sharing should be included in every staff meeting.

Skill improvement sessions are very helpful in attracting teachers to monthly meetings, especially when such meetings are new to teachers. Departments that do a good job of planning the upcoming unit every month find the skill improvement sessions a continuing encouragement.

Unit planning as a department is usually more necessary than lesson planning. Unit planning is needed every month for coordination of department efforts. However, elimination of lesson planning as a department will reduce opportunity to share ideas and evaluate specific parts of a session.

Churches that follow this plan discover that teaching sessions improve due to:

Better coordination and cooperation among teachers
Increased understanding of teaching procedures
Enhanced confidence and skill in using new ideas
Deepened commitment to teaching and to each other

PREPARATION FOR PLANNING/TRAINING MEETINGS

The success of the planning/training meeting depends on good preparation.

Set the date well in advance. Establish a regular day of the month when other church agencies will not schedule conflicting events and teachers can plan their calendars accordingly.

Notify teachers well in advance, in person. Teachers are busy people and cannot often rearrange schedules to accommodate a hastily announced meeting. Every month the division coordinator or general superintendent should talk personally with each department leader about the next meeting. Department leaders should talk with each teacher.

Explain why each teacher's presence is needed. How will the meeting contribute to each teacher? How can teachers contribute to each other?

Give preparation assignments. When teachers come prepared, the meeting will accomplish a great deal more than if everyone simply arrives. Also, assignments increase each participant's sense of responsibility to attend.

Remind teachers of meeting. The Sunday before the meeting is a good time to check again with each person. A poster is helpful, but a personal word is most effective.

Assist teachers with possible problems. Transporation and baby-sitting are two common factors that interfere with attendance. If those or other problems affect your department, develop a plan to deal with them. Attendance at teacher's meetings should be made as easy as possible.

Prepare a realistic agenda for the meeting. Clearly state items to be included, indicating probable length of time for each. Give the agenda to all teachers so they know where the meeting is going.

Eliminate factors that would detour the meeting from the purpose of planning and training. For example, redoing bulletin boards, cleaning supply shelves or planning the Sunday school picnic are worthwhile. However, those are secondary to the Sunday school's purpose of teaching the Bible and should not be allowed to replace planning and training time. Make a list of nonteaching topics discussed that could have been handled individually or did not really need to be discussed at all.

Start and end on time. Be thankful for those who attend instead of discouraged by those who do not. Write down all decisions and assignments. Serve light refreshments.

WEEKLY PLANNING MEETINGS

Many churches find their planning becomes even more productive when teachers meet each week to plan for next Sunday's session. In such cases, ministry to each other and lesson planning become the most important features in the meeting. Unit preview is included before the start of each new unit. Skill improvement sessions may occasionally be included in response to a specific need in the department.

Remember the story Jesus told in Matthew 25 about the man who was leaving for a far country and gave his servants the responsibility for increasing his wealth while he was away. First he gave each servant, according to his ability, the wherewithal to accomplish the assignment.

OBSERVING AND ASSISTING

Finally, every new leader needs some orientation in the Sunday school before taking on the responsibility for a class or department, even if he has had experience in teaching elsewhere. The best way to orient a new teacher or leader is to let him observe and assist for several weeks in the department in which he will be working. He can simply observe, or he can help with secretarial duties. He should be included in all planning meetings for that department. After observing for a few weeks, he should join with the learners as a participant in the Bible learning activities. When he is comfortable with the procedures, he will be ready for the responsibility of a class or department. In this way you are using your experienced teachers and leaders as your trainers.

Choose the most capable teacher or department in each division of your Sunday school for this training activity. Ask the teacher or department leader to assist in the training ministry by accepting new teachers for observation and assisting assignments.

The church with a vision to grow cannot afford to withhold training for the helping, teaching, leading tasks of the educational ministry. Although costly in time, effort, and money, providing training and learning resources is essential in helping people achieve their leadership potential in the work of Christ.

FOR FURTHER STUDY

1. Observe a local church teacher training program, evaluating how well it meets the five characteristics given in the chapter for a good program.
2. Lay out a weekend leadership training program for a church of 100 members.
3. Develop a promotion program for obtaining maximum registration of the church in a leadership training effort. Include pulpit, bulletins, special flyers, and promotional events.
4. Plan a year of monthly planning/training meetings for a Sunday school, based on the sample agenda shown in chapter.

RESOURCES

Evangelical Teacher Training Association
110 Bridge Street
Wheaton, IL 60187

International Center for Learning
P.O. Box 3875
Ventura, CA 93006

22

Educational Curriculum

WINONA WALWORTH

CLARENCE BENSON, a founder of the All Bible Graded curriculum approach in the early thirties, emphatically stated that next to the teaching staff, *the most important factor in the Sunday school was the curriculum.*[1]

Some fifty years later, contemporary Sunday school authorities like Elmer Towns are still emphasizing that curriculum is one of the critical ingredients in Sunday school success.[2]

It seems clear that a working understanding of educational curriculum is an essential part of the Christian educator's ministry.

DEFINING CURRICULUM

In its simplest form, curriculum is what you are going to teach. It is the course of study, including the manuals and materials of that course.

However, in more contemporary usage, curriculum can be defined as all the resources and experiences within a teaching-learning situation that help achieve educational goals.

As Howard P. Colson and Raymond M. Rigdon point out, it can be considered "the sum of all learning experiences resulting from a curriculum plan."[3]

The word *plan*, of course, suggests that materials and experiences are not merely thrown together in a teaching situation, but are carefully arranged to fulfill goals.

HISTORICAL DEVELOPMENT

From the inception of the Sunday school movement in America to the year 1815, the curriculum in the average school was the catechism—each particular text varied with the denominational connection of the Sunday school leader.

In 1815, there was a wave of interest in the memorization of Scripture verses. Individual children might master as many as a thousand in one

---

WINONA WALWORTH, educator and formerly of Scripture Press Ministries in Wheaton, Illinois, is now retired.

quarter. Interest was stimulated by offering Scripture text cards as quarterly prizes, which in turn could be exchanged for a grand prize—a Bible or a New Testament. The commonly accepted method of learning in the schools of that period was memorizing, and the American Bible Society, formed in 1816, made it possible to procure copies of the Scriptures at greatly reduced prices.

In 1825, Professor James Gill of Scotland arranged what he considered to be the heart of the Scriptures—including narrative, poetry, and doctrine—in a study cycle of five years titled "Limited Lessons." It was soon in use in America.

The American Sunday School Union (now known as the American Missionary Fellowship) was quick to sense the situation and also had issued "Selected Lessons," followed by two supplementary works, "The Union Question Book" and in 1847 the "Union Answer Book."

The various denominations soon awoke to the necessity of instruction in specific denominational doctrine and, accordingly, began issuing still further types of Sunday school materials. Competition of denominational boards, interdenominational unions, and private publishers led to confusion and chaos. In fact, the period from 1840 to 1872 became known as the "Babel" period.

In 1872, during the International Sunday School Convention, the first committee on uniform lessons was appointed and developed a program. The system was widely adopted because it seemed to secure Bible study and unity for the curriculum. Between 1872 and 1914 no radical changes were made.

However, criticism of the Uniform Series developed and led to the preparation of the International Graded Series, used as an alternate to the Uniform Series. Fresh criticism arose because of the use of extrabiblical materials in the Graded Series.

In 1918 a new lesson committee effected a change in the International Uniform Lessons that gave the series a more departmental emphasis.

Dr. Clarence H. Benson of the Moody Bible Institute became concerned in 1922 about the need for adequate evangelical curriculum materials. He objected to the uniform lessons in use since 1872 because they were planned to cover only 35 percent of the Bible. He also objected to the lesson outlines because they "were framed, prepared, and worked out from the adult point of view" and "not adapted to children." Benson began to work with his Christian education students at Moody Bible Institute on the development of a new system of lessons. After eight years of investigation, criticism, and experiment, in 1933 they offered to the evangelical public a new series of Sunday school lessons, which they called the All Bible Graded Series (later developed as Scripture Press).[4]

Meanwhile, the director of Christian education at First Presbyterian Church of Hollywood, California, had begun to develop her own curriculum materials for her Sunday school. Henrietta Mears's concern was for attractive, systematic Bible teaching on a closely graded basis. The interest aroused by those early mimeographed lessons for First Presbyterian led to the founding, also in 1933, of Gospel Light Publications.

In 1944, a meeting was called in Columbus, Ohio by the Church School Commission of the National Association of Evangelicals. It was attended by independent publishers, denominational publishers, and editors and leaders of interdenominational and undenominational organizations. Two proposals were made: first, new uniform Sunday school lesson outlines should be produced for evangelicals desiring to use uniform lessons; second, the task of producing them should be committed to a new national Sunday school association organized on evangelical bases. So urgent was the need felt for evangelical lessons that when the lesson committee, which had done considerable work on the project, made a report to the first NSSA (National Sunday School Association) convention in 1946, that body expressed its unanimous and enthusiastic approval of the uniform lessons proposed. Those lessons were first used in 1948.

CURRICULUM BASICS

BIBLE AS CURRICULUM FOUNDATION

The heart of teaching content for the evangelical Christian is the Bible, God's written revelation of Himself and His plan for man.

As Colson and Rigdon point out, "In Christian education we begin with the Bible as the divine 'given.' It is the basis of all our curriculum. Without it there would be no Christian teaching. The Bible is the indispensable book."[5]

Our curriculum, therefore, is *Bible-based*. All curriculum materials and activities are to be faithful to and based squarely on the foundation of biblical truth. It is the truth to be transmitted to our students.

CHRIST AS CURRICULUM FOCUS

The written Word reveals the living Word, Jesus Christ (John 1:1). He is the Savior, the Lord, the Friend, the Intercessor, the coming King on whom all Scripture is focused. Because Christianity is Christ, Christian teaching must be centered on Him, the goal of Christian living. Pupils are to "grow up in all aspects into Him" (Eph. 4:15), and to be mature in Him (Col. 1:28). Christlikeness is the goal toward which evangelical educators seek to lead their pupils.

Finally, Christ is the source of strength for Christian teachers. They must look to Him for spiritual sustenance, gracious enablement, and divine power. Only in Christ can they know the "exceeding greatness of [God's] power" (Eph. 1:19).

Christ is truly the *center* of evangelical curriculum.

PUPIL AS CURRICULUM OBJECT

The curricuulm is not used in a vacuum. It must be *pupil-related* in the sense that Bible content is to be made relevant and become a part of pupils' experiences. That is accomplished by means of the teaching ministry of the Holy Spirit, in which He illuminates the minds and hearts of pupils and applies the Word to them. Bible teaching should be concerned with helping pupils know, feel, and do God's Word; to learn and live Bible truths; to know and love the Lord Jesus Christ personally and deeply.[6]

Curriculum development is pointed toward meeting teaching goals— guiding materials and experiences toward meeting the needs of pupils at their level of interest and ability.

Curriculum materials, therefore, must be built upon clearly established objectives—what the curriculum seeks to accomplish in making the Bible meaningful to pupils.

CRITERIA FOR CURRICULUM CHOICE

Ronald C. Doll has suggested the following criteria (questions to be asked) about materials:

SOUND BIBLICAL BASIS

1. Are the materials based on the Scriptures as the major instructional source for Christian education?

2. Do they provide faithful record of and a friendly commentary on biblical events and teachings, rather than on interpretation of events and teachings that is actually or potentially negative?

3. Do the materials speak with assurance of God's power and goodness in performing miracles, including the great miracles of Christ's virgin birth and His resurrection?

4. Do they uphold the Bible's validity in helping people solve problems today?

5. Do they emphasize the stable, dependable values that the Scriptures teach?

6. Do the materials encourage the learner to commit himself to Jesus Christ as his personal Savior?

7. Do they make it clear that the learner's right relationship with God is a necessary precondition to his having right relationships with his fellowmen?

8. Do they help those learners who have given themselves to Christ to increase their faith and trust in Him?

GOOD EDUCATIONAL PRINCIPLES

9. Do the materials state understandable and acceptable objectives?

10. Do they contain specific data, main ideas, and key concepts in balanced proportion and arrangement?

11. Do they achieve a focus on main ideas and key concepts to which all other content clearly contributes?

12. Are the materials appropriate to learners' abilities, needs, and interests?

13. Do they cause learners to repeat important experiences and review important ideas?

14. Do the materials increase in difficulty throughout the span of years they cover?

15. Do the materials provide a variety of ways to stimulate learning?

16. Do they contain and suggest supplementary aids to learning?

17. Do they make thrifty use of the time available for learning?

TEACHER HELPS

18. Are inexperienced teachers able to use the materials without difficulty or confusion?

19. Are teachers' guides or teachers' editions of the materials genuinely helpful, suggesting procedures that make teaching easier and more effective?

20. Do they contain suggestions for teacher planning and growth and for ways of evaluating teaching and learning?[7]

CURRICULUM CORRELATION

In Colson and Rigdon's list of seven characteristics of a good curriculum, the final characteristic is *correlation.*

A review of the activities in a total Christian education program today makes clear that curriculum no longer concerns merely the Sunday school. There are a variety of ministries, such as vacation Bible school, children's church, weekday clubs, and camping. Each has its curriculum.

That variety emphasizes the vital place of a board of Christian education in guiding the church's educational ministry.

Usually the board of Christian education and/or designated staff select and provide the proper curriculum materials for each activity. That requires close supervision to avoid unnecessary overlapping of curriculum coverage and also to avoid overlooking content that must be included. It

BASIC TYPES OF CURRICULUM MATERIALS

Type	Definition	Distinctives	Publisher(s)
Uniform	All departments study the same *Scripture* for a particular lesson.	It allows for family discussion, review, and growth together.	Union Gospel Press
Unified	All departments study the same *theme* for a particular lesson.	Can discuss common theme, as families. Is good for church that has an assembly with entire Sunday school together.	David C. Cook
Departmentally Graded	Two or three grades or ages use the same materials.	Can use worship time to prepare students for the lesson. May be better for small churches.	Scripture Press Regular Baptist Press
Group Graded	Several grades or ages use the same materials.	Can be used with a group made up of many ages.	Child Evangelism Fellowship Bible Club Movement
Closely Graded	A separate set of materials are used for each grade or age.	Can be geared to a specific age or grade. Is used most effectively in a larger church.	Gospel Light
Electives and Selectives	Pupils choose topic to be studied. (In selectives they choose from a limited range of topics.)	Allows a topic to be discussed that meets an immediate need of the pupils. Allows topics of special interest to be studied.	Scripture Press (youth and adult —training hour material)

calls for a systematic, progressive teaching plan, preferably avoiding a "smorgasbord" approach to materials.

The need for correlation of curriculum programs and materials from one agency or department to another is a perennial problem in the church. Sunday school teachers should be concerned not only with what *they* are teaching but also with what is being taught the same pupils in club work, vacation Bible school, and each of the other educational programs of the church. It would be well for workers to meet together and share the content and goals of their programs. A curriculum chart indicating what is being studied in each agency and department of the church would be helpful. Long-range planning is also essential. The challenge is to build progressively from one level to another.[8]

Correlation also relates to curriculum unit or module planning. Each unit of study (two or more lessons concerned with a common topic) needs not only its own introduction and culmination activity but also to be integrated into the overall direction of the course of study.

FOR FURTHER STUDY

1. Place the curriculum criteria listed in this chapter in a chart form that can be used as an evaluation guide.
2. Do a comparative study of your church's educational curricula (what is taught in Sunday school, youth programs, clubs, and the other educational ministries being used).
3. Write a short paper comparing the advantages and disadvantages of two of the curriculum types for a small church.
4. Interview several local church Sunday school leaders who have had electives in their church on the advantages and disadvantages of that program.

NOTES

1. Clarence H. Benson, *The Sunday School in Action* (Chicago: Moody, 1969), p. 138.
2. Elmer L. Towns, *How to Grow an Effective Sunday School* (Denver: Accent, 1979), p. 98.
3. Howard P. Colson and Raymond M. Rigdon, *Understanding Your Church's Curriculum* (Nashville: Broadman, 1970), p. 38.
4. Gene Getz, *MBI—The Story of Moody Bible Institute* (Chicago: Moody, 1969), p. 222.
5. Colson and Rigdon, p. 112.
6. Roy B. Zuck, *Spiritual Power in Your Teaching*, rev. ed. (Chicago: Moody, 1972), p. 108.
7. Ronald C. Doll, "Twenty Questions to Ask About Sunday School Materials," *Christianity Today*, 3 March 1972, pp. 7-8.
8. Roy B. Zuck and Robert E. Clark, *Childhood Education in the Church* (Chicago: Moody, 1975), p. 360.

SUGGESTED READING

Colson, Howard P., and Rigdon, Raymond M. *Understanding Your Church's Curriculum*. Nashville: Broadman, 1969.

Edge, Findley B. *Teaching for Results*. Nashville: Broadman, 1956.
Getz, Gene A. *MBI—The Story of Moody Bible Institute*. Chicago: Moody, 1969.
Wyckoff, D. Campbell. *Theory and Design of Christian Education Curriculum*. Philadelphia: Westminster, 1961.
Zuck, Roy B. *Spiritual Power in Your Teaching*. Rev. ed. Chicago: Moody, 1972.
Zuck, Roy B., and Clark, Robert E. *Childhood Education in the Church*. Chicago: Moody, 1975.

23

Educational Facilities and Equipment

GAINES S. DOBBINS

EDITOR'S NOTE:

PRESIDENT JAMES GARFIELD's pronouncement on the comparative value of educational facilities and teachers is well known. That famous choice of a true teacher (Mark Hopkins) on a simple bench over "all the buildings, apparatus and libraries without him" has left its educational mark.

Yet, we do carry on education with the aid of buildings and equipment. It is a major consideration in public education, and it is also a critical factor in Christian education. Most of us would find it difficult to envision a Sunday school without some type of meeting facilities and at least basic shelter from the elements.

As we have become increasingly aware of the relation of physical and psychological comfort to learning, the place of facilities has received increasing attention, from the use of mood colors to the contouring of children's chairs.

Prominent among major contemporary thrusts is the continuing emphasis on multiple use and open space. Another development is the learning center emphasis with its variations of book centers, music centers, and related learning activities.

However, in a day of accentuated change and innovation it becomes especially important to not only *indicate* change, but to provide a broad foundation for considering change. We are therefore making available in this volume Gaines Dobbins's fine study of Christian education building.[1] Contemporary notes and bibliography have been added.

GAINES S. DOBBINS, Th.D., D.D., LL.D., is Distinguished Professor, Golden Gate Baptist Theological Seminary, Mill Valley, California.

"The Building Sets the Pattern"

This statement represents a turning point in the history of those evangelical Christian bodies in the United States that have sought to recover the teaching church. The old-fashioned Sunday school limped along with educational inadequacies that made it almost an absurdity. The adult organized class movement near the beginning of this century broke with the continental tradition that the Sunday school was for children only. The "Baraca" and "Philathea" type of classes for men and women attracted large numbers, and through various promotional means brought phenomenal popularity to the "organized class." Yet by the 1920's that movement had lost its bloom, and the Sunday school as an institution was floundering again. The riddle, "When is a school not a school?" brought the answer, "When it's a Sunday school!"

Educational Church Patterns

Why could the Sunday school not be a school? It had teachers, pupils, curriculum materials, organization, and administration, and obviously met a deep-felt need. The Sunday school had outgrown its original nondescript character and had developed standards and leadership that should have made it a much more effectual educational agency than it was generally found to be. There were those who saw what the Sunday school might become, but they often felt themselves somehow frustrated. Increasingly there was recognized the demand for an educational pattern suitable to the distinctive function of the church school.

An analysis of types of churches to be found in typical American communities indicates a number of distinguishable patterns.

SACRAMENTAL PATTERN

Salvation may be conceived as mediated by the church through the sacraments of baptism, confirmation, the eucharist, penance, extreme unction, holy orders, and matrimony. The church building, whether it be modest chapel or great cathedral, will of necessity reflect that sacramental concept. Teaching and preaching have a minor place in the formal services of such a church. The Roman Catholic Counter-Reformation revived education, but located it in a parochial school.

CEREMONIAL PATTERN

The Protestant revolt from sacramentalism did not involve the repudiation of many of the ceremonies that had been developed through the centuries. Religion in the Old Testament found expression through elaborate ceremonials. Although Jesus was not concerned with the maintenance of Jewish ritual, He approved attendance at the Temple and taught and preached in the synagogues. There is evidence of the use of the ritual in worship in the gospels and throughout the New Testament. It would be difficult to conduct a service of worship wholly devoid of ceremony. In the course of time, ceremonies of worship became more or less standardized. On the calendar of the church year were fixed special days and occasions that were celebrated by the use of appropriate liturgies. Eventually the chief purpose of church attendance came to be the performance of and participation in prescribed ceremonies of worship. If a church is a place where rites are performed, the building and its furnishings will be provided accordingly.

EVANGELICAL PATTERN

Mark records that "Jesus came . . . preaching the gospel of God" (Mark 1:14). Obviously He was more concerned with announcing "good news" than with administering sacraments or performing ceremonies. The first Christians were tremendously concerned with making known the gospel message. When the saving gospel became identified with sacraments and the saving mission of the church became encrusted with the ceremonial, reformers arose who sought to recover the evangelical nature of Christianity. The priest became preacher, the church service a means of winning the lost and strengthening the saved, the primary function that of preaching. In this evangelical view, the church building is mainly a "meeting house." It may be a residence or a store front, a tent or a tabernacle, or a one-room house with pulpit and pews. Where numbers and wealth make it possible, the church building may be a beautiful and impressive auditorium or sanctuary, seating hundreds or even thousands of persons, its principal purpose being to give maximum opportunity to preach and to hear the gospel. There may be other activities of the evangelical church, but they are subordinate to the high hour on Sunday when the pastor preaches and the people listen and respond.

EDUCATIONAL PATTERN

A church may conceive of itself as a school. To be sure, it is more than a school, but its purposes and activities can best be described in terms of teaching and learning. The gospel records picture Jesus as teacher, His immediate followers as disciples or learners, His method that of the teacher, His results those which come from teaching and training. His preaching contained a large element of teaching; His character and His deeds taught even more effectively than His lips. His early followers saw themselves as preachers and teachers, with healing concern for the sick and crippled. The church as a school of Christian living and witnessing, of learning and serving, needs more than a house of worship or a preaching place—it needs buildings and equipment that will enable it most effectually to "make disciples," learners who become faithful and intelligent followers of Jesus Christ.

CORRELATING PREACHING AND TEACHING

In planning the church building, preaching and teaching should be recognized as correlative. The primary purpose of preaching is persuasion; the primary purpose of teaching is instruction. Preaching loses much of its attractiveness and power when it becomes academic; teaching loses much of its distinctiveness and effectiveness when it becomes homiletical. The preacher has a great advantage when he can assume that those whom he addresses have a background of biblical information and understanding. The teacher is made more confident of results if he can assume that his instruction will find its full fruitage in the preacher's persuasion. There is no sharp dividing line between preaching and teaching, for all good preaching has an element of teaching and all good teaching has an element of preaching, but there is a difference, and both are enhanced when the distinction is observed.

The church building should establish and maintain this supplementary relationship of preaching and teaching. Provision for teaching should, wherever possible, be under the same roof as the auditorium or sanctuary. Officers and teachers of the Sunday school should realize their partnership with the preacher and others who gather about him in the conduct of the service of corporate worship. Care should be taken to provide ample and convenient passageways from departments and classes of the Sunday school to the place of worship. The building itself should in every possible way encourage the conviction that the service of preaching and the service of teaching are not separate but two halves of a common whole. The idea of "staying for church" (meaning the preaching service) should give way to the concept that both services are equally "church," and the building should symbolize and implement this concept.

DEFINING CHURCH OBJECTIVES

When a church decides to build, it may go about it in several ways.

The approach may be made from the standpoint of location. What factors determine the site of the church? Sometimes the chief consideration may be economic—the cost of the land as within the limited means of the congregation. The result may be a location that handicaps the church for educational purposes. The lot may be too small, making impossible future expansion of space for teaching and training. Or the location may be too crowded and noisy, thus depriving teachers and pupils of the quiet necessary to educational effectiveness. The location may be too far away from the center of population in the community, thus losing its appeal to many who might attend if the church school were more accessible. One of the first considerations of a church should be both the present and the future desirability of the location for educational purposes.

The approach may be from the standpoint of materials and costs. Many churches must begin modestly. The decision may be to begin with a basement, covered with temporary roof, in the expectation that a second or third story may be built later. Almost invariably this plan involves disappointment. Experience warns against the basement for a church building. Rarely does it prove to be economical as compared with building above ground. A basement is highly undesirable for teaching purposes. The church would be well advised to delay building if necessary in order to obtain enough land to dispense with the basement altogether, except for storage and for heating and cooling apparatus. Cheap building materials and cheap construction prove to be most expensive in the long run. The other extreme is that of a building so expensively constructed as to reduce to a minimum space for teaching and training. It is unfortunate when a church permits costs and materials to be the determining factors in erecting the house of God.

The approach may be from the standpoint of the need of a place of worship. In the Protestant tradition, the house of worship with preaching central has been the first consideration. A church may therefore make the building of the sanctuary its first objective. With no less concern for worship, churches today are discovering that the service of worship must have a supporting service of teaching and training. Where a choice must be made, therefore, it has been found wise procedure to build the educational unit first. Within this unit of course will be made provision for the worship service, avowedly temporarily, yet in the conviction confirmed by experience that an adequate and worthy sanctuary can more assuredly be built if the program of the church is undergirded by a strong program of teaching and training.

The wise approach will therefore be made from the standpoint of the church's immediate and ultimate objectives. The determinative question is, What is this church for? If it is true to its New Testament mission, the answer will be:

To reach the multitudes.

To teach them so as to make disciples.

To bring the saved to baptism, church membership, and conformity to Christ.

To continue to teach and train and inspire the church members that they will so bear their witness as to reach more of the multitudes.

Such a church building, at present and as planned for the long future, will say to the world: "This is our witness to the greatness of God."

It would seem axiomatic that a church should look like a church. True, there is no divinely given design that distinguishes a church from other buildings, but tradition has long established certain distinctive marks of ecclesiastical architecture. A church building should represent a combination of strength, durability, dignity, reality, utility, and beauty. One or more of those qualities may be considered more important than others, but all should be present in such combinations as to leave no doubt that the structure is a church. To the passerby, the building itself should bear the silent witness: This is a house of God. Something precious is lost if a church building looks like a barn, store, apartment house, school building, or theater.

Yet impressiveness of exterior should not be gained at the sacrifice of usefulness of the interior. Not only should the question be raised, How will this building look? but also, What will be its use? Church buildings occupy valuable land and cost hard-earned money. In their appearance they should be assets to the community and in their usefulness they should serve the community. The building committee and the architect may overemphasize one or the other of those aspects of the building. The tendency has generally been to stress exterior appearance to the neglect of interior utility. Occasionally it is the other way around—appearance has been sacrificed to use. Clearly there should be no conflict, for beauty and utility are not contrary to each other.

The educational purposes of the church require a graded building to serve graded teaching and training. That calls for exceeding care in devising the floor plan. A teaching church is one that makes provision for every age group, from the youngest to the oldest. Not only will such provision be made, but the building will implement a sound concept of teaching and learning. If teaching is not to be thought of as telling and learning as listening, classrooms must be provided that give privacy to teacher and pupils. Those classrooms should be small enough that the teacher and his teaching will be person-minded. Educators know that learning cannot be divorced from responding, and that responses may take many forms. Classrooms should therefore be not only separate and sound-proof and small enough to encourage togetherness, but so equipped as to stimulate active participation. The kind and quality of teaching and learning will be in large measure determined by the place in which the experiences occur. Consequently it is of first importance in planning any church building to determine that the interior shall be functional in accordance with the educational aims and goals of those who will use it.

Designing for Education

In achieving this ideal of an impressive place of worship together with a useful place of teaching and training, the committee may run into difficulty with the architect. Church designs have been the concern of architects through the ages. Church architecture has developed noble traditions. Pagan temples and Christian cathedrals alike have been notable for their grandeur. Certain types of architecture have long been established as standard and normative. Qualified architects are students of the history of their profession and are disciplined not only in the techniques of design but also in the great traditions of the master designers of the past. It would be somewhat unusual, therefore, for the typical architect, called on to draw the plans for a church building, to think in terms first of a floor plan for educational purposes. If such provision is to be made, often it will be as an afterthought and subordinate to the sanctuary design.

At this point, the minister and the planning committee must be appreciative but firm. They must make it crystal clear that the educational purposes of the building are of paramount importance, for in vain will they build for worship if they do not at the same time build for teaching. This, they must explain, is not only a New Testament ideal but also a practical necessity in the modern world. With competition for people's time and support at a level never before confronted by the churches, and with media of communication that have taken from the preacher his priority, rarely can a church today hope to attract great throngs of worshipers and audiences if listening is the chief appeal. After all, the architect realizes that he is the servant of his client and has no right to impose a preconceived traditional design contrary to the fundamental need of the church. Almost all denominational bodies have consultative architectural services. That aid should be sought and brought to the attention of the employed architect. If he has the church's best interest at heart, the architect will gladly welcome counsel from such an authoritative source and will bring his resources and those of his office to harmonize the church's educational needs with his ideals as to appropriate design.

Adequate Space for All Age Groups

The Sunday school originated in an effort to do something for the underprivileged children of England. At first it was unrelated to the churches except as church people fostered the movement. Then came tax-supported public schools with their provision of equal educational opportunity for all the children. Gradually the Sunday school was adopted by the churches both of Europe and of America as their chief agency for teaching the Bible. In many parts of the Western world the Sunday school remained an affair for the children. In the United States the Sunday school was extended to include adults, with the development of age-group grading that begins with babies in the nursery and continues successively to the end of life. With variations, the age groups are designated as nursery (birth to 3 years); beginners (4-5 years); primaries (6-8 years); juniors (9-12 years); intermediates (13-16 years); young people (17-24 years); and adults (25 years and above). More recently, the long span of adulthood has been subdivided as young adults, middle adults, and senior adults.

A church building planned for educational purposes will provide adequate and appropriate space and equipment for each age group. Loving attention will be given to the nursery. Ideally, there will be the reception room where the children are separated from their parents; then at least four other well-lighted and attractive rooms—for the bed babies in their little cribs and for children one, two, and three years old respectively. The educational importance of the nursery is being more and more realized. Here life is at its beginning, and much can be done in those first three formative years to determine the child's future religious life.

Beginners, four and five years of age, need a large, attractive room without partitions, arranged so as to permit maximum learning experiences. Everything in the room should remind the child of God's love in Christ expressed through the church.

Primaries likewise do not always need separate classrooms but can be cared for and taught in a room large enough for them to assemble for common activities, and then separate to go to interest centers where teaching and learning will take into account the active nature of children six to eight years of age. In schools with large numbers of primaries, separate rooms for each age or grade have proved to be feasible.

Juniors, by the age of nine, have attained a new level of independence and responsibility. They need a department assembly room where they can gather for directed worship with maximum spontaneity and participation. Adjacent to the assembly room should be the classrooms, just large enough for teacher and eight or ten pupils to sit about a table and engage in purposeful Bible study. The same provision should be made for intermediates, with separate classes for each age group and with boys and girls separated during the Bible study period. Again, where there are sufficient numbers of juniors and intermediates, individual assembly rooms for each age or grade are often used.

Department assembly rooms should likewise be provided for young people and adults. Here brief services of worship and fellowship will be held preceding the teaching of the lesson. Classrooms may be somewhat larger, yet rarely larger than to accommodate more than twenty-five or thirty persons. With increased numbers, there should be multiple departments and additional classes, graded so as to maintain congeniality in accordance with the changing interests and needs that come with maturity.

Many churches are recognizing that the hour of Bible teaching is not enough. To this service they are adding a program of training that follows as exactly as possible the age groupings of the Sunday school. Just as there is a teaching service preceding the morning hour of worship, so there is a training service preceding the evening hour of worship. To this hour of training all members of the family are invited, and for each age group provision is made as in the Sunday school. Since somewhat larger groups than in Bible study will be desirable, folding doors may be placed between two Sunday school classrooms so that the larger space will be available for the training hour. Otherwise the same facilities will be used both morning and evening for both teaching and training.

In addition to use on Sunday, the educational building should provide for weekday activities. Churches are experimenting with a weekday teaching service, utilizing the building after school hours for school children and on week nights for young people and adults. The "family night" midweek service may bring to the church large numbers of its members of all ages for a meal together, and then for group study and activities.

Obviously all this calls for a building carefully designed for educational purposes, a multi-use type of structure, adaptable to the program of each agency of the church.

EDUCATIONAL EQUIPMENT

Every aspect of the building and its equipment should be tested by the question, Will it facilitate teaching and learning? For the little children, there should be educational toys and other play equipment that will engage them in happy activities that constitute an essential part of their learning. Much use should be made of appropriate recorded music and the best obtainable pictures. Window ledges, chairs, tables, and all other furniture and fixtures should be suited to the age of the children. Musical instruments in the departments should be of good quality and kept in tune. Cabinets for materials should be provided and audio-visual teaching aids made available. In teaching the greatest Book for the highest ends, in the noblest of all institutions, the best curriculum materials should be sought.

Sometimes the building committee will make a serious mistake in the matter of equipment. Costs of the building will be determined and the money raised with little account being taken of the necessity for adequate furnishings and facilities. If a church takes seriously its teaching commission, it should be just as concerned to see that the building is provided with adequate equipment as with the finished building itself.

LONG-RANGE PLANNING

A church has to begin where it is and with what it has. In that respect, it is like every other growing thing. Those who plan the building may be confronted with severe limitations. Perhaps a small, modest building is all the church at first can afford. It is of utmost importance that the beginning be made with a view to future growth and expansion. Wise planning of the building calls for an overall design that may require many years to attain. That design will envision successive units to be added as the church grows. Such a long-range master plan will foresee the time when the church school will have an enrollment of three hundred, then five hundred, then a thousand or more. For the realization of that expectation, there must be enough land space, including off-street parking. As each unit is added, it should be with minimum disturbance of the existing building and as a unitary entity. When eventually the total building stands complete, it will have architectural symmetry and maximum functional ability.

Thus will be justified all the time and effort, the thought and planning, the money and life that have gone into the building of the house of God, where the example of Jesus may be fully followed, who "went about . . . preaching . . . teaching. . . ." Thus will be fulfilled the word of the Lord of hosts to the prophet: " 'Consider your ways! Go up to the mountains, bring wood and rebuild the temple, that I may be pleased with it and be glorified,' says the LORD" (Hag. 1:7-8).

CONTEMPORARY CONCERNS

In an era of rapid change it is important to avoid being locked into facilities that dictate program and make adjustments of any kind difficult. A key guideline for the eighties and nineties is, therefore, the concept of *flexibility*—to plan building and space for maximum utilization. Ralph Belknap in *Effective Use of Church Space* expresses it well: "Flexible space can well serve all areas of church life. Rooms designed for single use are costly both initially and throughout their useful life. There is no theological case against multi-use space. The inconveniences are few and the benefits are many. Wise stewardship demands that both new and existing church structures greatly increase their proportion of flexible space."[2]

Flexibility has both *program* and *economic* rationale. As a church considers new directions in its educational ministry, the ability to use facilities with minimum adjustments often makes its improvements and developments feasible.

An integral part of flexibility is, of course, the *long-range planning* that makes it practical. A church involved in building, for example, that recognizes even a dim possibility for a day school as part of its future ministry, will check the building code requirements it needs to follow for such multiple use of its educational facilities. The same applies to day care facilities. If a church plans to grow, it must project the implications of such growth for its facilities.

The economic rationale for flexibility has many implications. Rowland Crowder writes about them in his publication on contemporary building: "The high cost of construction, escalating interest rates, increasing utility rates, and the possibility of a real energy crisis will perhaps make multiple use of more space more desirable, or maybe even necessary."[3]

A second key guideline for educational building and equipment in the future is the impact of *contemporary communication.* The term "electric church," used to designate especially the religious television field (with its listening constituency larger than local church services) is descriptive of this area.[4] The educational implications of audiovisual media touch such facility-related concerns as closed circuit television, individual audio-viewing equipment and cassettes, and the constantly expanding array of space age communication systems and materials.

Indicative of the potential for the church is a view of a modern public school classroom with its electronic teaching equipment.

Along with the guidelines of *flexibility* and *contemporary communication impact,* there is the concern for *educational resources.* The church today has available an overwhelming potential of printed and audiovisual resource material—books, magazines, pictures, slides, films. Essentially, the key to effective use of those materials lies in the facilities the church provides for organized availability and use. This is the function of a library-resource center. Besides providing for the reading of books, this is a teaching resource for also viewing, listening, and experiencing. The contemporary evangelical church has before it a vast opportunity to expand and enrich its educational ministry. An essential tool here is a volume such as Betty McMichael's *Library and Resource Center in Christian Education.*[5]

Finally, as previously noted, such current concerns as energy conservation must be part of the contemporary church's thinking as it seeks to make its facilities and equipment a productive factor in its teaching ministry.

In their challenging volume on contemporary building for Christian education, Mildred C. Widber and Scott Turner Ritenour include these guidelines:

Flexibility and multipurpose use should be primary considerations.

Planning should include consideration of emerging educational trends, such as weekday time and the increasing use of electronic media.

Limit the use of space by building large, imaginatively designed rooms.

Art should be used imaginatively to express the church's message.

Possibly provide space for varied community activities.

Strive for simplicity and harmony in building.[6]

FOR FURTHER STUDY

1. Visit and analyze the facilities of local churches, looking for examples of the four building patterns described in the text.
2. Study the educational facilities of your church and develop a sequential series of improvement steps.
3. Do a color study of the educational facilities of a church in terms of suitability for age groups.
4. Do a study of multiple space use as it is effected by a church using Sunday school facilities for day school classes.
5. Draw up a plan for a small church's educational facilities, which are geared toward growth.

NOTES

1. Gaines S. Dobbins, "Building and Equipment for Christian Education," in *An Introduction to Evangelical Christian Education*, ed. J. Edward Hakes (Chicago: Moody, 1964). Reprinted with certain stylistic changes.
2. Ralph L. Belknap, *Effective Use of Church Space* (Valley Forge, Pa.: Judson, 1978), p. 73.
3. Rowland E. Crowder, *Designing Church Buildings for Southern Baptist Churches* (Nashville: Convention, 1976), p. 40.
4. Ben Armstrong, *The Electric Church* (Nashville: Thomas Nelson, 1979).
5. Betty McMichael, *The Library and Resource Center in Christian Education* (Chicago: Moody, 1977).
6. Mildred C. Widber and Scott Turner Ritenour, *Focus: Building for Christian Education* (Philadelphia: United Church, 1969), p. 12.

SUGGESTED READING

Belknap, Ralph L. *Effective Use of Church Space.* Valley Forge, Pa.: Judson, 1978.

Crowder, Rowland E. *Designing Church Buildings for Southern Baptist Churches.* Nashville: Convention, 1976.

Dobbins, Gaines S. *Building Better Churches.* Nashville: Broadman, 1947.

Harrell, William A. *Planning Better Church Buildings.* Nashville: Broadman, 1947.

Schaller, Lyle E. *Hey, That's Our Church!* Nashville: Abingdon, 1975.

Widber, Mildred C., and Ritenour, Scott Turner. *Focus: Building for Christian Education.* Philadelphia: United Church, 1969.

Part VI

THE SCHOOL IN CHRISTIAN EDUCATION

THE EDUCATIONAL PROCESS in America is still firmly associated with schools. It is vital, therefore, to understand the part schools play, or should play, in the life of the evangelical community.

To introduce this aspect of organized education, chapter 24 provides a useful perspective on American education.

The explosive development of the Christian schools movement is considered next in chapter 25. Finally, the unit moves into an incisive look at higher education and the development of continuing education, both secular and Christian.

This unit of three chapters has particular relevance as a base for the church and parents to evaluate the contemporary meaning and direction of education.

24

Education in Secular and Christian Perspective

GLEN E. HECK *and* ROBERT V. MEYERS

A SUBSTANTIAL SEGMENT of American society has declared itself in favor of private Christian schooling, in contrast to the general acceptance of the secularized schooling provided through public funding. The belief that education should have a Christian focus is certainly not new, but it has taken on new life during the past twenty-five years; and those who hold that belief have been vigorously pursuing the development of Christian schooling as a viable alternative to public education.

The seeds of such pluralistic educational emphasis began to take root early in the formative years of institutionalized education in the United States. The relationship of Christian and secular education must therefore be understood in the light of the historical antecedents, as a context for any meaningful decisions on educational preferences.

POLITICAL DETERMINANTS OF EDUCATION

In the earliest days of colonial America, authority for public education traced back from the colonial governments to the British Parliament and the King of England. But colonial education had its own distinct direction.

Three New England colonies—Massachusetts, Connecticut, and New Hampshire—passed laws in the 1640s requiring parents to see that their children learned to read, understand the capital laws, know the orthodox catechism, and become skilled in a trade. Such laws soon forced communities to appoint teachers and pay them by means of local taxes.

GLEN E. HECK is the vice president for institutional advancement, National College of Education, Evanston, Ill.

ROBERT V. MEYERS is director of admissions and field experience program operations for the school of continuing studies, National College of Education, Evanston, Illinois.

Thus, public education in the United States began with religious and secular values side by side. As the colonial leaders began to consider independence, however, they had to face up to principles that would also demand a reexamination of the practices and priorities of education. Two such principles were the right of people to govern themselves and the right to worship according to the dictates of one's own conscience—the twin accords of *civil* and *religious* freedom.

No responsible study of education—Christian or secular—could proceed without first providing a clear understanding of those cardinal values.

The principle of civil liberty was forcefully spelled out in the Declaration and Resolves of the First Continental Congress on October 14, 1774, which said in part: "That the foundation of English liberty, and all of free government, is a right in the people to participate in their legislative council . . . which the aforesaid deputies, in behalf of themselves and their constituents, do claim, demand, and insist on, as their indubitable rights and liberties. . . ."[1]

The Second Continental Congress approved a declaration clearly setting forth the two principles noted with equal force. Dated July 6, 1775, that declaration read in part: "Our forefathers, inhabitants of the island of Great-Britain, left their native land, to seek on these shores a residence for civil and religious freedom."[2]

Clearly, civil and religious freedom were central to the founding of this nation, and it is the continued zeal for those two liberties that is now reflected in our current conflicts over religious and secular education and schools.

It is important to understand that in the minds of some of the founding fathers the principles were not a single freedom. To them full civil freedom and full religious freedom could be found only when government and religion were free from each other as well as both being free from outside coercion. That is the root of the doctrine of the separation of church and state, and it is the view that began to challenge the all-inclusive educational patterns of the New England states.

The separation between two freedoms was not seen by all. Many political and religious leaders of that day held that an undeniable relationship existed between government, religion, and education, and that it had to be honored. An example of that view is seen in the statement of the Northwest Ordinance of 1787, one of the most famous declarations involving education.

The purpose of the Northwest Ordinance was to establish a government for the territory of the United States northwest of the Ohio River, in what is now the states of Ohio, Indiana, Illinois, Michigan, and Wisconsin. The government thus established was to insure that as those states came into the Union they would be equal in every respect to the original thirteen states. The words of the ordinance clearly show the intent to extend "the fundamental principles of civil and religious liberty, which form the basis whereon these republics, their laws and constitutions are erected; to fix and establish these principles as the basis of all laws, constitutions, and governments, which forever hereafter shall be formed in the said territory. . . ."[3]

In Article 3, the ordinance goes on to state, "Religion, morality, and knowledge, being necessary to good government and the happiness of mankind, schools and the means of education shall forever be encouraged."[4]

While the members of the Continental Congress, meeting in New York, were passing their last significant act, the Northwest Ordinance, fellow citizens were in Philadelphia drafting a new constitution that was ratified on June 21, 1788.

The preamble to the Constitution set forth six aims intended to strengthen the Republic. The first and the last are directly related to education:

> We the People of the United States, in Order to form a more perfect Union, establish Justice, insure domestic Tranquility, provide for the common defence, promote the general Welfare, and secure the Blessings of Liberty to ourselves and our Posterity, do ordain and establish this Constitution for the United States of America.[5]

The Constitution was designed primarily to provide civil liberties through self-government. It reflected the philosophy expressed earlier in the Declaration of Independence, that "all men are created equal, that they are endowed by their Creator with certain inalienable Rights, that among these are Life, Liberty and the pursuit of Happiness. That to secure these rights, Governments are instituted among Men, deriving their just powers from the consent of the governed."[6]

Insofar as religion is concerned, the Constitution was primarily a prohibition to the federal government against any linking between government and religion that might lead to an established church. The First Amendment to the Constitution read: "Congress shall make no law respecting an establishment of religion, or prohibiting the free exercise thereof."[7]

On education, the Constitution says virtually nothing, leaving the whole matter in the hands of state and local governments through the "reserved to the states" clause of the Tenth Amendment.

Within a year after the Declaration of Independence had been signed, ten states had rewritten their constitutions, and the rest of the states followed without much delay. The Massachusetts constitution of 1780 is a prime example of the attention given by most states to education:

Wisdom and knowledge, as well as virtue, diffused generally among the body of the people, being necessary for the preservation of their rights and liberties; and as these depend on spreading the opportunities and advantages of education in the various parts of the country, and among the different orders of the people, it shall be the duty of legislatures and magistrates, in all future periods of this commonwealth, to cherish the interests of literature and the sciences, and all seminaries of them; especially the university at Cambridge, public schools and grammar schools in the towns . . . to countenance and inculcate the principles of humanity and general benevolence, public and private charity, industry and frugality, honesty and punctuality in their dealings; sincerity, good humor, and all social affections, and generous sentiments, among the people.[8]

In the words of R. Freeman Butts, "To specify education as an integral element in so many state constitutions in the 1770s, while the war was being fought, was a considerable achievement. It implied a recognition of the political importance of education long before public education was widely put into practice in the middle of the nineteenth century."[9]

The political foundations for education had thus been laid. Education had been declared a necessity, and the responsibility for education had been given to state and local governments rather than to the federal government. Whatever directions education was to take, both civil and religious liberty had been named as essential values to be preserved for all generations.

INTELLECTUAL DETERMINANTS OF EDUCATION

By the beginning of the nineteenth century, two major intellectual viewpoints related to religious liberty were vying for the allegiance of the nation's leaders. They were Protestant Christianity and secularism.

In this context, *secularism* should not be understood as merely the removal of doctrinal religious teaching from the public classroom, although that did gradually take place. *Secularism* in a broader sense refers to the whole cultural tone of modern societies as they became more analytical, rational, and empirical because of the influence of the scientific method.

The most influential taproot of Christianity in America was the Puritanism of New England. Formed in the European Protestant Reformation, Puritanism followed the lead of John Calvin. In both the Puritan church and school, the Bible was central. This latter point is emphasized by S. Alexander Rippa in *Education in a Free Society*, where he states: "A cardinal principle of Puritan faith was the acceptance of the Bible as the inspired word of God, granting to man a divine rule of conduct and an approved form of worship. Every aspect of the church required authorization of the Scriptures."[10]

However, Puritan thought also included a high regard for all knowledge, and sought to relate that knowledge to Scripture. Rippa summarizes that comprehensive view of life through faith and reason:

> Puritanism was an articulate philosophy, reflecting the intellectual climate of seventeenth-century England. Although man was an inherently evil creature, he was also a rational being, capable of understanding his own actions and accepting responsibility for them. Human life, moreover, had value insofar as man had the freedom to choose between good and evil. Drawing upon the traditions and ideals of the Reformation and the Renaissance, the Puritans stressed the harmony of faith and reason, insisting that one strengthened the other. In the Puritan mind, there was no conflict between the revealed truth of God and the natural world of man. The Puritan could even accept scientific knowledge as an adjunct to faith. The Puritans adopted an intellectual rather than an intuitive approach to life and sought to unify faith and reason into a coherent ideology.[11]

While Puritanism was dominating thought in New England, another intellectual movement came to the fore in Europe and was transmitted to America, especially influencing the intellectual and political leaders of the Revolutionary period. That movement, called the *Enlightenment,* or the *Age or Reason,* "refers to a profound intellectual revolution in world history which rejected theology as the final arbiter and sought instead to interpret the universe in terms of logical analysis. It was a rational movement . . . in which faith in science and human reason was substituted for dogma based on religious belief and supernatural revelation."[12]

Key individuals and their ideas that contributed to that Enlightenment were Nicolaus Copernicus's heliocentric universe, Francis Bacon's scientific method, John Locke's empiricism, and Jean Jacques Rousseau's views of man as good and capable of forming his own social contract, or government. Rationalism found popular expression in America in a form of deism, incorporating a view of religion that rejected anything contrary to reason or scientific verification. Its influential adherents included Thomas Paine, Benjamin Franklin, and Thomas Jefferson. Deism clearly contributed to the advance of secularism.

Virginia may have been the state most influenced by secularism during the latter years of the eighteenth century. At least, it was standing in strong contrast to Puritan New England, where the government was almost theocratic.

Guided by Jefferson's ideas on civil and religious liberty, James Madison built a legal framework in Virginia, and later in the Constitutional Convention, that culminated in the First Amendment doctrine, "Congress shall make no laws respecting an establishment of religion, or prohibiting the free exercise thereof."

Thus, as we saw earlier in the political determinants of education, a rationale of separation between church and state was also being established along intellectual lines, growing out of the broad trend toward the secularization of society.

Jefferson, in particular, chafed under the Virginia pattern in which an established church, the Anglican, transported from England, had certain powers over civil government while, in turn, the government supported the approved church by taxation. He believed that under that system, neither the government nor the church was truly free. Especially onerous to Jefferson was the state statute requiring church membership or affiliation as a prerequisite for civic participation, including membership in the Virginia House of Burgesses. For Jefferson, that meant that he, although a deist, had to certify allegiance to the church before he could hold a political office.

In a larger sense, Jefferson felt that no true liberty, civic or religious, was possible if a single source, such as the church, could control who should be given what information. It is that belief in intellectual liberty that underscores Jefferson's own selection of his three most significant contributions to history: civil liberty was the aim of his contribution to the Declaration of Independence; religious liberty was the aim of his Virginia Bill for Religious Liberty; and his Virginia Plan for Education was his combined strategy for preserving both civil and religious liberty.

"I have sworn upon the altar of God, eternal hostility against every tyranny over the mind of man." Those words of Jefferson, which are enshrined in the memorial to him in the nation's capital, give eloquent expression to his firm belief in the central place of reason and an informed mind as the best guarantee of the continuation of both civil and religious liberty necessary to the growth of the individual citizen and the Republic.

How Jefferson sought to insure freedom from the "tyranny over the mind" can be seen best, perhaps, in the 1786 Virginia Statute of Religious Liberty:

> Whereas Almighty God has created the mind free; that all attempts to influence it by temporal punishments or burthens, or by civil incapacitations, tend only to beget habits of hypocrisy and meanness, and are a departure from the plan of the Holy author of our religion, who being Lord both of body and mind, yet chose not to propagate it by coercions on either, as was in his Almighty power to do. . . .
>
> Be it enacted by the General Assembly, that no man shall be compelled to frequent or support any religious worship, place or ministry whatsoever, nor shall be forced, restrained, molested, or burthened in his body or goods, nor shall otherwise suffer on account of his religious opinions or belief; but that all men shall be free to profess, and by argument to maintain, their opinion in matters of religion, and that the same shall in no wise diminish, enlarge or affect their civil capacities.[13]

This statute was supported by Section 16 of the 1776 Virginia Bill of Rights, a section drafted by Patrick Henry, which states:

> Religion, or the duty which we owe to our Creator, and the manner of discharging it, can be directed only by reason and conviction, not by force or violence; and therefore all men are equally entitled to the free exercise of religion, according to the dictates of conscience; and that it is the mutual duty of all to practise Christian forbearance, love, and charity towards each other.[14]

Both of those statutes contributed directly to the language of the First Amendment to the Constitution.

In short, civil and religious liberty in the United States require a dual system of separate governmental and religious rights and responsibilities. It is the constitutional and legal basis in the United States that mandates that public, or governmental, schools be nonreligious and that religious schools be private and not controlled or supported by governmental agencies.

A dual system of public and religious schools is, therefore, a contemporary expression of support for the historic American view of civil and religious liberty.

CULTURAL DETERMINANTS OF EDUCATION

Forces at work in the first half of the nineteenth century strengthened the case for more schooling. Chief among them was the rise of industrialization. Between the presidencies of Andrew Jackson, starting in 1829, and Abraham Lincoln at the close of the Civil War, manufacturing replaced home and village industries in the New England and Middle states and in the waterfront cities of the Mississippi Valley.

Industrialization fostered urbanization and placed demands on state governments for an increased centralization of their legal systems. The effect of that centralization upon education was the rise of statewide systems of education, led by Pennsylvania in the Middle states, Massachusetts in New England, and Ohio in the Midwest.

Each state found a spokesman for its state system of tax-supported schools. Among those able leaders, the most eloquent was Horace Mann of Massachusetts. Mann spoke effectively of the role of education as a pervasive force for enlightenment and morality in the support of civil liberty and government. As Massachusetts became more pluralistic in its religious bodies, Mann argued that the public schools must be nonsectarian, but not godless. He held that the Bible should be read, but not interpreted from a sectarian viewpoint.

From 1837 until 1848, Mann crusaded tirelessly for a nonsectarian public system of schools in Massachusetts. In 1855, seven years after Mann had resigned as Superintendent of the Massachusetts State Board of Education, Massachusetts passed an amendment to the state constitution excluding direct religious instruction from the schools. By the middle of the nineteenth century, it was clear that public schools were going to be increasingly nonreligious and that religious schools were going to be privately controlled and financed by tuition and tithes.

While Mann was essentially holding that public schools in Massachusetts could be Protestant but nonsectarian, Roman Catholics in New York, Maryland, and other major urban areas were battling to insure that public schools be both nonsectarian and non-Protestant. New York City was the center of that conflict.

Favoring tax-supported city schools, the Catholics wanted either a tax-supported dual system, Catholic and Protestant, or a city system that was truly nonsectarian and non-Protestant. Such was not to be. The result was that the Catholics in New York City and elsewhere chose to establish their own parochial schools and leave the public schools to the increasingly prevailing view that "religious education must be banished from the common schools and consigned to the family and churches."[15]

A pluralistic religious society, with each sectarian group zealous to guard its young from heresy, reluctantly came to the conclusion that religion was too important and too divisive to be entrusted to a common or public school system. Coming to a similar result through a far different rationale were those who saw religious instruction in a public school system as a threat to religious liberty.

Thus, the public school, supported by the majority as a necessary means of civil liberty, was called upon to remain neutral toward religion, lest it diminish religious liberty. The home, the church, and the parochial school were to be the bastions of religious liberty and instruction.

The die was cast. A pluralistic, modernizing nation needed schools that would reflect the aims and values of the varied cultures and groups within that nation. Only a dual system of public tax-supported schools and privately supported and controlled religious schools could meet the demand.

This pattern of dual systems of schools was seriously challenged by the people of Oregon in the early 1920s when a law was passed requiring all children to attend the public schools. The law was challenged in the case of *Pierce* v. *the Society of Sisters of the Holy Names of Jesus and Mary,* and the Supreme Court ruled against the state. Thus, since 1925, public secular and private religious schools have been held equal under the Constitution.

As the United States continued to expand over the years, its culture has grown ever more complex. Drives toward unification or centralization have been met by drives for pluralism and diversity. R. Freeman Butts structures the many sources of diversity into three major themes that continue to shape education policy and practice:

1. The cohesive value claims of a democratic political community summed up in the constitutional ideals of liberty, equality, justice, and an obligation for the public good

2. The pluralistic loyalties that give particular identity and coherence to the different segments of society that arise from diversities of religion, language, culture, ethnicity, race, and locality

3. The long-term worldwide modernization process that has been pushing all Western societies for more than two hundred years toward national centralization, popular participation, industrialization, urbanization, and secularization

"The interaction of these often divergent trends, especially the twin drives to cultural pluralism and to political cohesion, has resulted in chronic conflicts and cleavages over the control and practices of American education."[16]

Every practitioner in the field of Christian education must strive to understand those diversities.

ESTABLISHING A PHILOSOPHY OF SOCIETY AND SCHOOLS

After assessing the factors from the past that called the separate systems of Christian and secular schools into existence, the Christian educator must begin to project schools for the future that will meet the expectations of that segment of society in which he or she chooses to serve. It is the purpose of this section of the chapter to lead the reader through an analytical process by which he may begin to develop a philosophy of society and education that will enable him to determine what kind(s) of schools a given society wants or needs.

Credit for the five-step configuration of this analytical process goes to William Frankena and his introductory essay in *Philosophy of Education*.[17]

An understanding of the schools in a society begins not with the schools themselves but with the fundamental aims of the society and the assumptions underlying those aims. An orderly and logical approach to those aims and assumptions and the resultant schools can be gained by viewing these three elements as a set and visualizing them in a diagrammatic triad. Figure 24.1 shows the elements constituting the "Set of Society." A second set dealing more centrally with schools will follow.

To illustrate the Set of Society from the discussion of the American society that has been developed in this chapter, let us deal first with the secular viewpoint and subsequently with the Christian viewpoint.

The primary secular *aim* of the founding fathers was to establish a republic, a new and more perfect union. Let A represent that aim.

SET OF SOCIETY

Fundamental Aims
of Society

Basic Assumptions
Underlying Aims

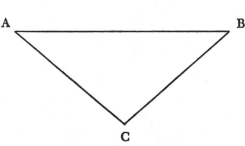

Educational Means for
Achieving Societal Aims

Fig. 24.1

A *basic assumption*, or value, supporting that aim was civil liberty, the maximum amount of political freedom possible. Let *B* represent this assumption.

The *educational means* necessary for insuring a continuing republic with civil liberty was knowledge, the kind and extent of knowledge that could be made available to all only through a formal school system. Therefore, schools that taught the precepts of civil liberty were necessary as a means of fulfilling the aim of establishing an enduring republic of free citizens. Let *C* represent that means.

The segment of society that declared itself Christian certainly shared the values and conclusions represented by *A*, *B*, and *C* as outlined above. However, the Christians held additional essential views that would not have been shared by the secularists.

A fundamental *aim* (*A*) of the Christian segment of society was that man worship and obey God as revealed in Scripture. An *assumption* (*B*) underlying that aim was that revealed and natural truth are complementary and in some way inherently related. The *educational means* (*C*) for reaching that societal aim was a system of schools dedicated to teaching the harmony of Christian faith and reason.

These illustrations underscore vividly the formative effect of societal aims and assumptions on the schools within any given society.

To complete our schematic analysis of American society and schools, we proceed to the second triad, the Set of the Schools. See figure 24.2. In this set, *C* represents the *aims of the schools; D* represents the *basic knowl-*

edge about schooling; and *E* represents the *educational means* necessary to achieve the aims of the school (*C*) that are in harmony with *D*.

SET OF THE SCHOOLS

Aims of the   Basic Knowledge
Schools   About Schooling

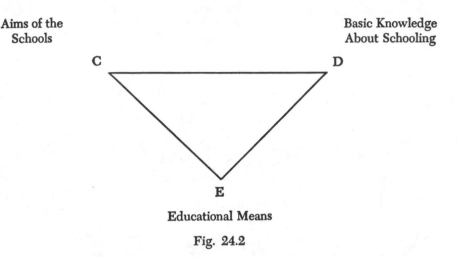

Educational Means

Fig. 24.2

The secular *aim of the schools* (*C*) was a public school system available to all providing knowledge necessary for free men. This aim was supported by *basic knowledge about schooling* (*D*) that was to become increasingly scientific and empirical, favoring the use of inquiry and verifiable proof for acceptance. The *educational means* (*E*) for secular schools were highlighted by nonreligious curricula and materials taught by teachers approved by the state without regard for religious affiliation or commitments.

The Christian *aim of the schools* (*C*) was knowledge in harmony with Scripture. The *basic knowledge about schooling* (*D*) included biblical and general knowledge consistent with both faith and reason. The *educational means* (*E*) was a curriculum true to the Bible and integrating all other valid knowledge conveyed through appropriate materials by Christian teachers. Those teachers were to have a knowledge of, and a personal commitment to, Christianity and the special talents and training that would enable them to both share that knowledge and model its implications before their students.

It has been the view of this chapter that schools largely reflect the aims and assumptions of the society of which they are a part. Figure 24.3 illustrates that relationship. The Set of Society—*A, B, C*—is the dominant set. The Set of the Schools—*C, D, E*—is the subordinate set.

RELATIONSHIP BETWEEN SETS

Aims of
Society

Basic Assumptions

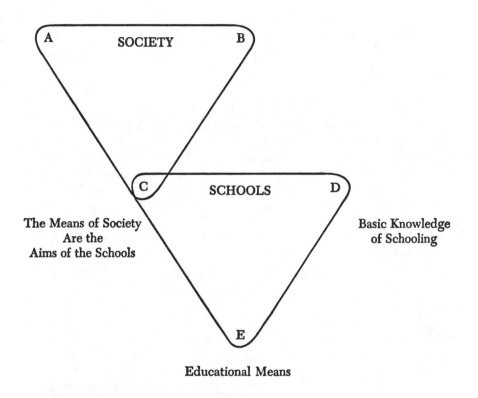

Educational Means

Fig. 24.3

A crucial point in this analysis is that step *C* serves *two* major functions. It is the *educational means* for the Set of Society to achieve its aims. It is also the *aims of the schools* in the Set of the Schools. In the language of modern set theory, *C* is the *intersection* of the two sets, the Set of Society and the Set of the Schools. It is that step in our analytical scheme that links the two sets and illustrates the manner in which schools reflect society. The means of society *are* the aims of its schools.

The five-step analytical model just described is a valuable tool for assisting a person in developing a comprehensive philosophy of society and schools. It provides through steps *A*, *C*, and *E* a clear way of linking the aims of society to the aims of the schools and of insuring appropriate

means of accomplishing those aims. In turn, it encourages the more difficult tasks of examining the underlying assumptions of society (*B*) and of
reviewing the basic knowledge of schooling (*D*) that justifies choices in
C and *E*.

IMPLICATIONS OF THE TWO-SYSTEMS APPROACH TO EDUCATION

We now turn our attention from the political basis for private religious
and public secular schools to the personal decisions involved in choosing
one over the other.

ENVIRONMENT

A parent may choose a Christian school for his child out of the belief
that the enviroment of a Christian school is healthier for learning and
growing than a secular school environment. If the philosophical goals of
the Christian school are met, Christian perspectives and dogma will be a
natural part of the curriculum and the activities of the school. Teachers
will model mature Christian behavior and express Christian thought, both
of which are highly important forms of indirect education. When those
goals are reached, the Christian school is clearly an extension of the teaching efforts of the church, and it does produce a special environment.

Some Christian parents choose against the Christian school precisely
because they do not want their children so totally enveloped in a church-
controlled environment. They consider that artificial and too sheltered. One
hears the argument that a hothouse plant often wilts or even dies when it
is placed into a natural setting and that, similarly, the child who has been
sheltered in a Christian school may not cope well in the "real world"
later on.

The authors' personal observation indicates that the "hothouse syndrome" is largely a needless worry in the majority of Christian schools.
Although the school administration strives to maintain the most wholesome
atmosphere possible, most children, nevertheless, go through the same
stages of mischievous behavior, struggles with dishonesty, body jokes, experimentation with profanity, and boy-girl temptations as students in
secular schools. The Christian school reacts more overtly with negative
controls on inappropriate behavior and with positive teaching on avoiding
such pitfalls, but the students are not actually sheltered from exposure as
the "hothouse theory" proponents would have us think.

VALUES

Related to indoctrination and behavior patterns is the matter of relative
versus absolute values. As implied earlier in this chapter, Christians hold

that some values are absolute because God has revealed His will in Scripture. Secularists tend to hold that values are relative and that choices should be made on pragmatic grounds.

As in most alternatives, each of those positions has both advantages and disadvantages. For the Christian, omitting the direct teaching of biblical values is unthinkable. But human traditions sometimes take on the weight of absolute values and are taught as such. That, of course, violates the very philosophy the Christian school is dedicated to support; namely, that there is a distinction between human and divine wisdom and that the divine is to be preferred. If students later on conclude that they have been taught a human tradition as if it were divine revelation, they may feel somewhat betrayed, and some may begin to hold all teaching by Christians as slightly suspect. That places a grave responsibility upon the Christian school to not teach presumptuously.

Secularists try to avoid that danger by focusing on the process of valuing rather than on the support of specific values, and that process focus fits better with relativism. But, students who learn to think clearly about how and why they make value choices are better off than students who adopt a belief system or a behavior regimen without understanding the rationale behind it.

Of course, the Christian school can and should include the process of valuing in its curriculum. Sometimes it does not because administrators fear the process itself or because they do not understand it. Sometimes administrators do not want to risk having students question the validity of teachings they have been given, believing that such questioning undermines respect for authority. Those views may be shortsighted, because life ultimately forces people to test ideas, values, and beliefs to see whether they are true and worthy of allegiance.

The contrast in value systems can be summarized in the idea that Christian schools tend toward the teaching of faith whereas secular schools tend toward teaching one to doubt. Healthy Christians evidence faith, but they are not afraid of doubt, knowing that doubt resolved can lead to even deeper faith. It is unresolved doubt that weakens faith. The process of questioning is important to spiritual growth, and it should not be excluded from Christian schools.

QUALITY EDUCATION

Some parents choose Christian schools specifically because the Christian school offers better academic quality than the secular school in their district. They may be Christian or merely tolerant of their children receiving Christian teaching in order to reach their priority of academic excellence. Conversely, some parents may prefer a Christian school but choose a public school because they have little confidence that Christian schools deliver comparable quality.

Some of the associations of Christian schools and many individual schools have made quality a priority and can cite test scores that exceed national averages. One must question, however, whether such excellence exists consistently throughout the Christian school movement. No one should fault a parent who chooses on these grounds.

If quality in education is disdained in favor of Christian theology, one must ask whether the lifelong benefit to the student truly measures up to the loss he or she may sustain through weak academic training. The Christian school is not, after all, the only source of religious training the child will have in most instances. The church and the home will be primary sources of spiritual guidance, too. But basic academic knowledge and skills are not going to be taught by the home or the church, except through a church-sponsored school. In those areas, the school legally provides the primary and possibly the only source of such instruction. Providing anything less than a first-rate educational experience is not fair to the student and should not be acceptable as a fulfillment of Christian responsibility.

FINANCE

Sending a child to a Christian school represents a heavy financial commitment on the part of most parents. Administrating or teaching in a Christian school represents a heavy financial commitment, too. Such professional positions usually pay better in public schools. This factor is accepted by all who decide in favor of a Christian school. Unfortunately, sometimes the willingness to pay tuition as well as taxes causes uninformed people to think Christians are merely caught up in a sense of elitism. That attitude may be partly a carryover from public feelings toward the prestige private schools that are used predominantly by the wealthy.

In contrast, some people will react to those attending a Christian school as if they are willing to accept second-rate education. That attitude is even more distressing to students, and they should be helped to handle such situations.

Another aspect of finance should be mentioned in light of the strong argument noted in this chapter on the separation of church and state. Is any form of federal or state financial assistance to the Christian school legitimate or wise? Even tax credits to parents must be considered very carefully in terms of whether or not they would threaten the political basis for and freedom of Christian schools.

SEGREGATION/INTEGRATION

The charge has been leveled that some Christian schools are little more than evasions of federal guidelines on integration. Admissions policies and screening practices of the school in question help a person understand that school's philosophy on the subject. More often, however, one must discover the prevailing attitude of the sponsoring agency. Certainly, the public school continues to struggle with the problems of racism, and no full solutions have been found. Anyone considering a Christian school— whether as a parent, teacher, pupil, administrator, or sponsor—must determine for himself if his motives and the school's practices are indeed Christian.

CONCLUSION

Education is vital to the well-being of this nation as a free society. The twin goals of civil and religious liberty form a basis for alternative systems of publicly funded secular and privately funded and controlled religious schools, which stand equal under the Constitution. It is only through such alternatives that education can be truly responsive to the pluralistic society it must serve.

During the last decades of the twentieth century, quality will certainly be a major emphasis in educational progress. As that quality is built into both public and private schools, education will come to meet more fully the personal and societal aims set before it.

The choice between Christian and secular schooling must remain an individual choice, but it is essential to the continued freedom of the United States that the choice be there for each person to make.

FOR FURTHER STUDY

1. Let the class (or study groups) assume the role of a local church task force and, in the light of philosophical and financial considerations, determine whether to recommend that the church (1) open a Christian day school, (2) encourage parents to use the public schools but double the church's budget and programming in Christian education, or (3) _____ (an alternative of your choosing).

2. List five aims you believe are appropriate to the Christian school, rank them by importance, and discuss with one other person your reasons for choosing and ranking as you did.

3. In order to get firsthand experience in observing the philosophies by which schools operate, visit a range of both secular and Christian schools and outline the similarities and differences noted.

4. To personalize the analytical system explained in this chapter, state briefly and diagram your own:
   A—major aim in life

     C—educational aim as a means of achieving *A*

     E—educational means for achieving *C*

Those wishing to develop this further may delineate their underlying assumptions (*B*) and basic knowledge about schooling (*D*) to complete a more comprehensive analysis of their personal philosophy of education.

5. Apply this analytical system to the catalog of the school you are attending in order to ascertain the school's distinctive philosophy of education.

6. As of now, if you had to choose whether to teach in a Christian school or a public school, which would you choose and why?

7. Assuming the role of a Christian parent, and also assuming that no Christian school was available to your child, how might you seek to provide optimum Christian growth to your child through the home and church?

NOTES

1. "Declaration and Resolves of the First Continental Congress," October 14, 1774. See Henry Steele Commager, ed., *Documents of American History* (New York: Appleton-Century-Crofts, 1949), pp. 83-84.
2. "Declaration of the Causes and Necessity of Taking Up Arms," July 6, 1775, ibid., pp. 92-93.
3. "The Northwest Ordinance," July 13, 1787, ibid., p. 130.
4. Ibid., p. 131.
5. *United States Constitution*, ibid., p. 139.
6. "The Declaration of Independence," July 4, 1776, ibid., p. 100.
7. *United States Constitution*, ibid., p. 146.
8. Francis Newton Thorpe, comp., *The Federal and State Constitutions, Colonial Charters, and Other Organic Laws of the States, Territories, and Colonies Now or Heretofore Forming the United States of America* (Washington, D.C.: Government Printing Office, 1909) 3:1907-8.
9. R. Freeman Butts, *Public Education in the United States* (New York: Holt, Rinehart & Winston, 1978), p. 15.
10. S. Alexander Rippa, *Education in a Free Society*, 2d ed. (New York: McKay, 1974), p. 19.
11. Rippa, p. 20.
12. Ibid., p. 47.
13. "Virginia Statute of Religious Liberty," January 16, 1786, Commager, pp. 125-126.
14. "The Virginia Bill of Rights," June 12, 1776, ibid., p. 104.
15. Earle H. West, *The Black American and Education* (Columbus, Ohio: Merrill, 1972), pp. 77-78.
16. Butts, pp. vi-vii.
17. William Frankena, *Philosophy of Education* (New York: Macmillan, 1965).

SUGGESTED READING

Butts, R. Freeman. *Public Education in the United States.* New York: Holt, Rinehart & Winston, 1978.

Byrnes, Lawrence. *Religion and Public Education.* New York: Harper & Row, 1975.

Commager, Henry Steele, ed. *Documents of American History*. New York: Appleton-Century-Crofts, 1949.

Frankena, William K. *Philosophy of Education*. New York: Macmillan, 1965.

Maston, T. B. *The Christian, The Church, and Contemporary Problems*. Waco, Tex.: Word, 1968.

Rippa, S. Alexander. *Education in a Free Society*. 2d ed. New York: McKay, 1971.

Strout, Cushing. *The New Heavens and New Earth, Political Religion in America*. New York: Harper & Row, 1974.

Thorpe, Francis Newton, comp. *The Federal and State Constitutions, Colonial Charters, and Other Organic Laws of the States, Territories, and Colonies Now or Heretofore Forming the United States of America*. Vol. 3. Washington, D.C.: Government Printing Office, 1909.

West, Earle H. *The Black American and Education*. Columbus, Ohio: Merrill, 1972.

25

Christian (Day) Schools

PAUL A. KIENEL

THE MODERN Christian school movement had its beginning soon after World War II. The schools are sometimes still referred to as Christian *day* schools. They were "day schools" during their development years to identify them as different from the boarding schools that had been popular in the twenties and thirties. Since there are now relatively few boarding schools, the term "day school" has been dropped for simply "Christian school."

Indicative of the movement's growth, various Christian school associations came into existence in the late forties and early fifties—associations such as the Mid-Atlantic Association of Christian Schools, the Midwest Association of Teachers of Christian Schools, the National Association of Christian Schools, and the California Association of Christian Schools.

The growth of the California group is typical of Christian school increases throughout America. In 1950 there were eight Christian schools in the newly formed California Association of Christian Schools (CACS). The first CACS convention for teachers was held in a single classroom at a Christian school in Paramount, California. By 1977 the combined attendance of the two California Christian school teacher conventions, held in two convention centers, was 4,885.

From 1950 to 1966 the number of Christian Schools in CACS grew steadily; but the number did not exceed one hundred schools. Between 1967 and 1978 the association grew from 102 to 627 schools and colleges, or a 515 percent increase! During the same period, student enrollment leaped from 14,659 to 77,984. In 1978 Christian schools in California increased at the rate of 1.9 new schools per week and 1,003 students per month.

PAUL A. KIENEL is executive director, Association of Christian Schools International, Whittier, California.

RATE OF GROWTH OF CALIFORNIA CHRISTIAN SCHOOLS
AT SIX-YEAR INTERVALS

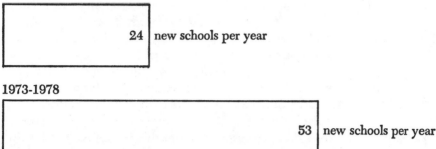

1967-1972

24 | new schools per year

1973-1978

53 | new schools per year

Fig. 25.1

The rapid proliferation of Christian schools is not a California phenomenon. There has been steady growth throughout America. In the late 1970s Christian schools were coming into existence across the United States at the rate of two new schools a day.

PROFILE OF CHRISTIAN SCHOOL DEVELOPMENT

The average size of a typical Christian school that has been in existence three years or more is 250 students. It began with a kindergarten and grades one through four, employing three teachers: a kindergarten teacher, a first-and-second-grade combination teacher, and a third-and-fourth-grade combination teacher. One of the teachers served as lead teacher or acting principal. It also hired at least a part-time school secretary.

The average starting enrollment was seventy-five students. Most Christian schools double in size their second year of operation. This phenomenon occurs because there is the inevitable "wait and see" of parents in the first year of operation, until they know the school will succeed. During the second year the first-and-second and the third-and-fourth-grade combination classes usually divide into single grade classes and a fifth-and-sixth-grade combination class is added. The fifth-and-sixth-grade class divides and a seventh grade is added.

Experience has shown that gradual growth in the upper grades is advisable. It is usually best when the majority of upper level students come up through the lower grades of a Christian school. This is equally true at the high school level. The support base of one or more Christian elementary schools feeding in students that are spiritually and academically mature, helps minimize excessive strain on staff and administration.

Although the average size of a Christian school in existence three years is 250 students, there are a sizable number with 1,000 or more students, even going as high as 5,000.

A new trend in Christian school education is the development of Christian school systems such as *Christian Unified Schools of San Diego, Valley Christian Schools,* and *Whittier Christian Schools* in California. Those are characterized by several schools under one board with a superintendent, and a principal for each school, in a multi-campus situation.[1] Within such a system there are most often several elementary schools, one or more junior high schools, and a Christian high school. In addition to the normal school staff of teachers, these systems often provide specialized teachers and support personnel that are not always possible for individual institutions.

Another interesting development currently characterizing Christian school education is a growing tie between Christian schools and Christian colleges and universities. More than fifty Christian colleges belong to the Association of Christian Schools International. Those ties are mutually beneficial. For Christian colleges, Christian high schools represent a major source of students. One Christian college president reported that a full third of his student body came from Christian high schools.[2] Because Christian school educators feel strongly about Christian education, they normally urge their students to go on to Christian colleges and Christian universities if at all possible.

For the Christian school, on the other hand, the tie between Christian schools and colleges represents an important potential supply of teachers and principals. Many Christian colleges report a high percentage of their graduates in education going on to a teaching ministry in Christian schools. A number of Christian colleges and graduate schools now offer a Master of Arts degree in Christian school administration.[3]

TYPES OF CHRISTIAN SCHOOLS

There are four types of Christian schools: church-sponsored, board-sponsored, parent-sponsored, and boarding schools.

THE CHURCH-SPONSORED SCHOOL

The embryo idea for establishing a Christian school usually begins in the heart and mind of an individual who is concerned about the education of his own children. Consequently, a large percentage of church-sponsored schools are started by young church pastors who have their own children to educate. Because of their pastoral training they have strong biblical convictions and often sense that the educational philosophy of the local public school is in conflict with biblical teaching. Some church-sponsored schools are begun by older pastors who have monitored over the years the effect of public school education on their own children or on the children of their church families.

An immediate advantage a church can give to the establishment of a Christian school ministry is land and buildings. Thousands of church facilities throughout America are used but a few hours each week. Often churches have built costly classroom complexes for their Sunday schools and use them little more than fifty-two hours a year. Many church leaders, seeing this as poor stewardship, have established a Christian school ministry as a part of their church ministry.

There are, of course, the potential problems of conflict between Sunday school and Christian school in the use of the same facilities, as well as related church-school differences. Tim LaHaye, pastor of Scott Memorial Baptist Church in San Diego (sponsors of the Christian Unified School System of San Diego) has spoken to this:

> The primary long range risk, as I see it, is the possibility that conflict could generate with multiple use of the same facility by a church organization on weekends and a school organization between Sundays. Occasionally we hear of pastors who tyrannically dominate the school administration, or the school that tries to manipulate or control the church's destiny. The solution to that problem is personnel. The pastoral leadership of the church and the leadership of the Christian school must be spiritually motivated men who can work together compatibly. They must respect each other's integrity, capability and motivation. They must be willing to sacrifice some personal liberty and get used to longer range planning to avoid conflicts. The head of the church and the school must be good friends who work closely together. This sets an example for the staffs of both organizations to work in harmony. Anything short of this can destroy what otherwise would be an effective tool in the cause of Christ.[4]

THE BOARD-SPONSORED SCHOOL

Under the corporate structure of an independent board-sponsored school, the school board is not accountable to a church board or a church corporation for its decisions.

Independent board-sponsored schools also tend to attract more contributions because contributors know their gifts are not accruing to the net worth of a church that may or may not be of their particular faith.

Church pastors from a variety of churches often more readily promote the ministry of an independent board-sponsored school, although a nonparochial approach by a church-sponsored school will be a considerable factor here.

On the other hand, independent school board members are more indi-

vidually responsible for their decisions and can be held financially accountable if the school should get into extreme financial difficulty.

Also, tuition is sometimes higher in an independent school, especially if
the school has the financial burden of purchasing its own property and
educational buildings, or if the school is paying heavy lease payments on a
former public school facility.

THE PARENT-SPONSORED SCHOOL

A parent-sponsored school is created by a group of parents who corporately come together to provide a Christian school education for their children. They form a nonprofit educational corporation similar in nature to a
board-sponsored school. The parents who make up the corporation elect
from among themselves a board of directors. The board of directors makes
school policies within the framework of corporate bylaws established by
the parents. Properties and assets acquired by the school are in the name
of the parents or "parent society," as some are called.

Not all the parents who send their children to a parent-sponsored school
are members of the school corporation. Parents must sign a statement of
faith to be eligible to join. Because Christian schools draw on a rather wide
cross section of the community, some parents cannot sign the statement or
do not choose to become involved. Normally about one fourth of the
parents who send their youngsters to a local parent-sponsored school are
members of the school's parent corporation.

A strong feature of a parent-sponsored school is the potential for closer
parent cooperation and involvement in school activity because of their personal tie with the school corporation.

THE BOARDING SCHOOL

Boarding schools were popular the first half of this century. Christian
boarding schools preceded the modern Christian school movement. Among
the remaining schools, with their founding dates, are:

Ben Lippen School	Asheville, N.C.	1940
Canyonville Bible Academy	Canyonville, Ore.	1935
Houghton Academy	Houghton, N.Y.	1883
Linfield School	Temecula, Calif.	1936
Monte Vista Christian School	Watsonville, Calif.	1926
Prairie Bible Institute	Three Hills, Alberta	1922
Stoney Brook School	Long Island, N.Y.	1922

The advantages of a boarding school are similar in nature to the advantages of a Christian college. Students can concentrate more intensely on
their studies because their time is better regulated. The environment is

more controlled. The curriculum is often more diversified. Lasting friendships develop because of the extended exposure to their student colleagues.

The disadvantages include the fact that young people are away from their parents when they need the support of their families.

INFLUENCES BEHIND THE CHRISTIAN SCHOOL MOVEMENT

A God-centered person "thinks Christianly" only after he learns to interpret life in a Christian way. Christians can have a secular mind if they have not trained their minds to see the world through the eyes of God, as revealed in the Bible. Harry Blemires in his book *The Christian Mind* writes,

> There is no longer a Christian mind . . . the modern Christian has succumbed to secularization. He accepts religion—its morality, its worship, its spiritual culture; but he rejects the religious view of life, the view which sets all earthly issues within the context of the eternal, the view which relates all human problems—social, political, cultural—to the doctrinal foundations of the Christian faith, the view which sees all things here below in terms of God's supremacy and earth's transitoriness, in terms of Heaven and Hell.[5]

For generations, the minds of Americans have been bombarded with the secular philosophy of an essentially secular public school system, a secular news media, and secular radio and television. In the process we have developed a secular nonbiblical mind. Paul writing to the Romans said, ". . . the mind set on the flesh [carnal] is death; but the mind set on the Spirit is life and peace" (Rom. 8:6).

A major influence behind the Christian school movement is the intended ministry of bringing into focus for children and young people the spiritual discipline of thinking "Christianly."

A second influence behind Christian school education is the declining enthusiasm for public schools. Sidney P. Marland, Jr., former Assistant Secretary for Education, US Department of Health, Education, and Welfare, summed up public attitude toward public schools. "There is manifest in the country—to my knowledge, for the first time in our history—an active loss of enchantment with our schools . . . from kindergarten through graduate school. For the first time, Americans in significant numbers are questioning the purpose of education, the competence of educators, and the usefulness of the system in preparing young minds for life in these turbulent times."[6]

In 1969 the California Association of Christian Schools conducted a statewide survey of its members regarding the occupations of parents sending students to their Christian schools. The largest single professional group was public school teachers and principals.[7]

There are at least three reasons for the decline of enthusiasm for public education, especially among Christians:

1. Public schools no longer represent the views of many parents. Christians believe that if you are a parent you are accountable to God for the education of your children and for what your children are taught in school. Proverbs 22:6 is a direct command to parents: "Train up a child in the way he should go. . . ." What your children are taught in school should be a direct extension of your parental views. The teachers under whom your children are taught should be the kind of teachers you would personally hire if your children were being educated in your home. Many Christian parents believe that the supremacy-of-man-over-the-supremacy-of-God philosophy of the public school disqualifies the public school as an acceptable training institution for their children. Although they may have a concern for the future of public schools if they take their children out, their greater concern is for the future of their children.[8]

2. Parents are concerned about the fact that there is a decline in discipline in public schools. According to the *Eighth Annual Gallup Poll of Public Attitudes Towards Education,* lack of discipline in the public schools continued to head the list of problems cited most often by survey respondents.

3. Public education has suffered steady academic declines since the mid 1960s.

> There is little doubt anymore that the 1960's on into the early 1970's was a period of eroding academic standards in the nation's schools. Requirements were relaxed. Courses once considered basic to a child's education began to appear on an ever-expanding list of electives. Students who previously would have been required to study literature or a foreign language often chose to enroll in something less demanding.[9]

The *Los Angeles Times,* beginning August 15, 1976, ran a three-part series on the academic decline of public schools with an opening headline: "Drop in Student Skills Unequaled in History" and a subheadline that read, "Test Results Show Downward Spiral in Reading, Writing, Mathematics Continues.[10]

An Associated Press story appearing in Oregon's largest newspaper, the *Oregonian,* regarding reading declines said, "The inability of many youngsters to read even the simplest sentence far into their grade school years has become a national disgrace."[11]

In contrast, test scores in Christian school education have been on a steady increase.[12] In 1975, for example, the Western Association of Christian Schools administered the Stanford Achievement Test to first through eighth grade Christian school students in the western states. Results showed those students to be five to nine months ahead of the national norm in all subject areas. In 1978 those figures jumped to seven to thirteen months ahead of the national norm.

QUESTIONS AND ANSWERS ABOUT CHRISTIAN SCHOOLS

IN A CHRISTIAN SCHOOL DO PARENTS SHELTER THEIR CHILDREN FROM THE REAL WORLD?

The "real" world is a God-centered world, not a humanistic, man-centered world. Dr. Roy Lowrie, president of the Association of Christian Schools International, writes, "An introduction to the real world begins with an introduction to God. God is, and He can be known. But public school children are not taught this, and they miss the real world in their education."[13]

WHAT IS THE PLACE OF THE BIBLE IN THE CHRISTIAN SCHOOL?

The late Mark Fakkema, in the foreword of his *Christian Philosophy* lecture series, said, "Truth is not necessarily truth because it is regarded as such by contemporary scholarship. By way of verifying His statements, our Lord did not appeal to the recognized leadership of His day. Our Lord constantly quoted Scripture as His authority. God's Word is the test of all truth. All teaching that is expressive of God's Word is true. Teaching that is not expository of the Word is falsehood."[14]

Therefore, the Christian philosophy of education calls for an educational process that puts the Bible at the center and asks the student and the teacher to evaluate all they see in the world through the eyes of God— because God is Truth. All must conform to Him or it is not truth. Jesus said, "I am the way, and the truth, and the life" (John 14:6). In true Christian education, students learn to use the Bible to evaluate all of life. The Bible is Life—it is the living Word—it is above every other book.[15]

IS THE CHRISTIAN SCHOOL A RACIALLY SEGREGATED ACADEMY?

Roy Lowrie again answers:

> The Christian school falls within the command of Jesus Christ to His disciples that they should teach all nations. This Great Commission is recorded at the end of Matthew 28. Since "all nations" refers to all races of the world, any taint of racial prejudice in the school is not biblical, but is a perversion of Christ's desire and order. The Christian school is not a segregation academy. It does not exist to avoid integration in education.

> To see students and teachers of varied racial heritage working harmoniously in the school is an example of the functioning of the body of Christ. It is universal, made up of all races. The message of Christ's love is for the

entire world, not for a particular race. The Christian school shows race relations at their best, demonstrating that God enables children, young people, parents and teachers to work well together with acceptance and concern for each other.[16]

FOR FURTHER STUDY

1. Prepare a comparative study of the philosophic objectives of the public school and the Christian school.
2. Lead a course discussion on the four types of Christian schools as set forth in this chapter.
3. Prepare to lead a discussion on what public school educators could do to change the declining enthusiasm for public schools.
4. Write a brief analysis of Harry Blemire's statement that "there is no longer a Christian mind" as discussed in this chapter.
5. Analyze the reasons for the rapid growth of the Christian school movement.

NOTES

1. Helpful reading here is Bill Kelly, *A Guide for Principals and Board Members on Christian School Growth* (Whittier, Calif.: Western Association of Christian Schools, 1976), especially chapter 8.
2. Paul A. Kienel, *The Christian School: Why It Is Right for Your Child* (Wheaton, Ill.: Scripture Press, Victor, 1974), p. 83.
3. Henry M. Morris, *Education for the Real World* (San Diego: Creation Life, 1977), especially chapter 6, is helpful here.
4. Tim LaHaye, in Foreword to *A Guide for Principals and Board Members on Christian School Growth*, by Bill Kelly.
5. Harry Blemires, *The Christian Mind* (London: S.P.C.K., 1966), pp. 3-4.
6. S. P. Marland, Jr., "Education and Public Confidence," *American Education*, May 1973, p. 5.
7. Kienel, p. 43.
8. Helpful reading here is Paul A. Kienel, *Reasons for Sending Your Child to a Christian School* (LaHabra, Calif.: P. K. Books, 1978), especially chapters 1 and 2.
9. "Why Our Schools Went Wrong," *Changing Times*, May 1978.
10. Jack McCurdy and Don Speich, *Los Angeles Times*, 15 August 1976.
11. Kathryn Diehl and G. K. Hodenfield, "Johnny Still Can't Read," *Portland Oregonian*, 4 September, 1976.
12. Paul A. Kienel, *What This Country Needs* (San Diego: Beta Books, 1976), especially chapter 10.
13. Roy W. Lowrie, Jr., *Sheltered from the Real World in the Public School System* (Whittier, Calif.: Association of Christian Schools International).
14. Mark Fakkema, Foreword to *Christian Philosophy and Its Educational Implications*, 3 vols. (Chicago: National Association of Christian Schools, 1952), vol. 1.
15. Helpful reading here is Roy W. Lowrie, Jr., *To Those Who Teach in Christian Schools* (Whittier, Calif.: Association of Christian Schools International, 1978), especially chapters 1 and 6. Also see Paul A. Kienel, ed., *The Philosophy of Christian School Education* (Whittier, Calif.: Western Association of Christian Schools, 1977), especially chapter 2 by Kenneth O. Gangel and chapter 5 by James W. Braley.
16. Lowrie, *To Those Who Teach*, pp. 89-90.

SUGGESTED READING

Blemires, Harry. *The Christian Mind.* London: S.P.C.K., 1966.

Kelly, Bill. *A Guide for Principals and Board Members on Christian School Growth.* Whittier, Calif.: Western Association of Christian Schools, 1976. The writings of a successful Christian school administrator on Christian school growth. A "how to" book.

Kienel, Paul A. *The Christian School: Why It Is Right For Your Child.* Wheaton, Ill.: Scripture Press, Victor, 1974. This book explains the forces behind the Christian school movement.

————. *Reasons for Sending Your Child to a Christian School.* La Habra, Calif: P. K. Books, 1978. Establishes rationale for sending children to Christian schools and colleges.

————. *What This Country Needs.* San Diego: Beta Books, 1976. An emphasis on Christian families and Christian schools as the most valuable sources of training children and young people.

Kienel, Paul A., ed. *The Philosophy of Christian School Education.* Whittier, Calif.: Western Association of Christian Schools, 1977. A basic text on the subject.

Lowrie, Roy W., Jr. *To Those Who Teach in Christian Schools.* Whittier, Calif.: Association of Christian Schools International, 1978. An extremely valuable contribution on applied Christian school education.

Morris, Henry M. *Education for the Real World.* San Diego: Creation Life, 1977. A solid presentation of the Christian philosophy of education. Somewhat slanted, however, to the Christian college level.

Marland, S. P., "Education and Public Confidence." *American Education,* May 1973, p. 5.

26

Christian Higher Education and Lifelong Learning

Kenneth O. Gangel

THE DISTINCTIVE PURPOSE of America's first institution of higher learning is well known. The earliest printed rules of Harvard College announced that the chief aim should be that "everyone shall consider the mayne End of his life & studyes, to know God & Jesus Christ, which is Eternal life."[1]

The pattern of secularization set in quickly in the colonies, however, and was well on its way a hundred years after the founding of the nation's first college. John Brubacher and Willis Rudy make these observations about the ministerial productivity of our early institutions: "The percentage of college graduates going into the ministry was 50 during the first half of the 18th century. By 1761, however, this had fallen to 37 per cent and by 1801 to 22 per cent. Revivalism brought the figure back to 30 per cent by 1836, but then a steady decline set in, and it was 20 per cent in 1861, 11 per cent in 1881, and 6.5 per cent in 1900."[2]

Today Christian colleges represent only a small segment of the private sector, but never in the history of the church has the impact of Christian higher education on the total ministry of the evangelical community been greater. Every aspect of Christian work is affected by Christian higher education. The Bible colleges and Bible institutes have virtually kept the twentieth-century missions movement in operation. Seminary graduates carry out educational responsibilities in local churches as pastors and ministers of education and in parachurch organizations focus on evangelism and missions.

Definitions are important at the outset of the chapter. The term *higher education* is used to refer to that vast network of postsecondary schools of

---

KENNETH O. GANGEL, Ph.D., is professor of Christian Education, Miami Christian College, Miami, Florida.

learning without specification as to whether they are public or private, proprietary or nonprofit, two-year or four-year colleges, graduate or undergraduate, Christian or non-Christian.

The primary focus of this chapter, of course, is on Christian higher education, notably schools of three kinds—Bible institutes and colleges, Christian liberal arts colleges, and seminaries. This kind of school is more specifically defined as *a postsecondary institution of learning that takes seriously an evangelical doctrinal statement, classes in Bible and Christian ministry, a distinctively Christian philosophy of education and life, and the quality of spiritual life on campus.*

HISTORICAL PERSPECTIVE

Although concentrating on the present and the future, it is important to recognize the lessons of the past. There is certainly no question that the earliest colleges in America were Christian institutions. The colonial Anglicans and Calvinists wanted a highly literate and college-trained clergy functioning in their churches, and established their colleges with that educational goal in mind. As Brubacher and Rudy point out, "The Christian tradition was the foundation stone of the whole intellectual structure which was brought to the New World."[3]

To the early American church leaders the *advancement of learning* and the *service of the church* were merely two sides of the same coin. Piety was not to be separated from intellect, and religious faith was to be taught in a rational and systematic manner not only to clergymen but also to the potential professional men in other fields.

In the early years, educational institutions set the pattern for society and were largely governed by the influence of the churches. Slowly, however, as secularization spread throughout the growing young nation, it also strengthened its grip on educational institutions. The size of the country, its heterogeneous makeup, and the increasing geographical spread of its population fostered a pluralistic trend in both theology and style of educational institutions.

William Warren Sweet, noted church historian, suggests that the principle dynamic behind the college-founding enthusiasms of American Christians was the spirit of revivalism and missionary thrust in such movements as the Great Awakening in the mid-eighteenth century. Yet the mortality rate of colleges founded in the eighteenth and nineteenth centuries amounted to nearly 80 percent by the end of the Civil War!

Writing in 1852, John Henry Cardinal Newman in his *The Idea of a University*, saw the tremendous vacuum and emptiness of modern culture and how education even a century ago was failing to speak to the problems. Newman argued that a university could not profess universal knowledge without the presence of a faculty of theology. He affirmed that "faith [is] an intellectual act, its object truth, and its result knowledge."[4]

CONTEMPORARY STATUS

The contemporary scene in Christian higher education is almost as confusing as the society that forms its backdrop. College president David McKenna suggests that the Christian college, having passed through "the church era, the alumni era, the accreditation era, and the business era" is now in the government era. He adds,

> This new identity is still being developed. Yet it seems safe to say that the government era will give the Christian college its most severe test in both identity and exposure. It may imply a broader base of student enrollments. It could give the curriculum a public service thrust. It will certainly require a redefinition of the purpose of the Christian college when "service in the public interest" is added to the traditional statements about "Christian service," "institutional loyalty," "academic quality," and "community participation."[5]

Few people realize how massive the educational enterprise is in America. For example, over $144 billion were spent in the educational year 1977-78 in America. Such figures make education the largest single economic enterprise in America. In the spring of 1978 more bachelors and graduate degrees were awarded than in any previous year in the nation's history—almost one million baccalaureate degrees, over 350 thousand master's degrees, and some 35 thousand doctorates. Almost 11.5 million people were enrolled in formal programs of higher education in America in the fall of 1977, representing a 3.3 percent increase over the previous year.

On the other hand, the general trend is toward a declining applicant market. In 1974 first-time enrollees for degree credit were expected to fall by over a half-million students by 1991. That is a 28 percent reduction in the current level, as estimated by the US Bureau of Census in cooperation with the Department of Health, Education, and Welfare. Three other factors that also affect the present status of Christian education are the *consumer protection movement, declining aptitudes,* and *governmental interference. Finance,* a fourth factor, will be dealt with in a later portion of the chapter.

CONSUMER PROTECTION MOVEMENT

There are specifically four areas in which consumer protection agencies are concerned with higher education.

1. Protection from fraud and abuse, where the minimum requirement would be to comply with the distinct state and federal laws and regulations.

2. Information disclosure, in which a minimal response might consist of a disclaimer in official catalogs in compliance with the consumer information provisions of the 1976 Education Amendments.

3. Fair practices, in which the path of least resistance for postsecondary institutions would be to assume that joint procedures are, by and large, quite fair and that particular problems can be dealt with on a case by case basis.

4. Program quality, in which consumer protection agencies (most frequently called licensing boards) rely on accreditation status instead of subjective claims to an institution's "reputation," "distinguished alumni," or "dedicated and talented faculty."

The most important question for the Christian institution has to do with integrity, the accuracy with which an institution describes itself. A rejection of established checks and balances in educational quality leads to a superseparatism that produces intellectual and academic inbreeding, stagnation of educational quality, and a smug complacency. A diploma mill by any other name is still a diploma mill even though it may have the name "Christian" or "Bible" on its catalog.

DECLINING APTITUDES

Christian colleges today are also having to grapple with declining aptitudes on the part of entering students. Sixty percent of the students who entered America's colleges in the fall of 1977, for example, indicated that their high school educations had been deficient.

A special advisory panel appointed by the national college entrance examination board rejected these four popular theories as explanation for the declining scores:
1. Cultural bias in the tests
2. Predictable wide variation among ethnic groups
3. Changes in the difficulty of the test or the ways of scoring it
4. Ineffective correlation between S.A.T. scores and student high school grades.

What has happened obviously is not a problem with the tests themselves, but rather that the tests have somehow gotten out of line with either the practices of secondary or postsecondary education or, more likely, the *quality* of secondary education. The advisory panel cited four reasons for the declining scores, which they believe were genuinely representative of the declining abilities:
1. Television. We are all familiar with the statistics that by age sixteen young people have spent between 10 thousand and 15 thousand hours watching television.
2. Broken homes. Although these statistics have not been specifically

identified, the panel suggests that "there is probably more than coincidence between the decline in the S.A.T. scores and the drop in the number of children living in two-parent homes."

3. Student motivation. What with the open admissions of the community college movement and the pressure on all of us to recruit and admit, there would seem to be less emphasis on trying to achieve.

4. National turmoil. The early seventies produced a great national trauma of war, political assassinations, crime, and drug abuse. There is simply no way to measure the impact of those kinds of things on high school students in the country.[8]

GOVERNMENTAL INTERFERENCE

The marriage between the federal government and the higher educational establishment in the United States, arranged shortly after the Second World War, and developed during the 1960s is in severe trouble. Government interference in the form of sheer paperwork (to say nothing of regulations) threatens to undo us all. The package now includes race quotas, sex quotas, sexual preference questionnaires, what one can ask, what one cannot ask, whom one can hire and whom one cannot hire, discrimination, and reverse discrimination.

Most Christian institutions of higher education are involved in government programs even though they may have never taken direct federal funds for the instituiton. The usual government aid and college work study programs are more than sufficient to warrant government interference in the institution.

LEGITIMATE RECOGNITION

A Christian college must be both Christian and college. Serious Christian educators believe in professional and objective recognition of an institution by appropriate agencies. In short, an institution of Christian higher education ought to be accredited. It is impossible for parents or local churches to check all the variables in an attempt to establish educational quality—faculty credentials, library holdings, curriculum design, instructional patterns, facilities and equipment, and transferability of credits. But those can all be measured under the broad banner of accreditation, either regional or professional.

The Council of Postsecondary Accreditation (COPA) contains professional and regional associations, both program and institutional associations. A Bible college, for example, is appropriately accredited by the American Association of Bible Colleges, the only COPA Member officially recognized to accredit professional programs of theological undergraduate education. Of course, Bible colleges might also seek regional accreditation with one of six regional agencies representing the traditional patterns of accreditation in America.

Likewise, a seminary could hold dual accreditation in the professional Association of Theological Schools and the appropriate regional association. Even though it is the ultimate goal of COPA that accreditation by an institution on the part of any one of its members should be recognized by all members, increasing numbers of colleges and seminaries have found it desirable to seek dual accreditation to establish the credibility and viability of Christian higher education in the broader world of college and university activity.

Licensing and accreditation certify an institution as having met acceptable standards. They do not necessarily affirm its spiritual viability, but they do suggest an honest effort toward doing the work of God in an acceptable manner. The ultimate goal, of course, is excellence marked not only by a visible commitment to the authority of the Bible and its activity in the lives of students as well as the curriculum, but also by such things as a clear concept of purpose, a clear articulation of uniqueness, quality, and competence in the teaching-learning process, willingness to innovate in order to meet contemporary needs, adequate and careful long-range planning, and sufficient financial support.

DIAGNOSTIC PROJECTIONS

A decreasing birthrate leads most prophets of higher education to prognosticate a *decreasing enrollment* in the future college market. Generally, a 10 percent drop in enrollment is expected in colleges and universities between the early 1980s and mid 1990s. But birthrate is only one of the many factors affecting college enrollment, particularly in Christian schools. For example, denominational schools are greatly influenced by the growth or decline of that denomination, probably the most significant factor affecting its school's enrollment. The burgeoning evangelical private elementary and secondary school movement will be of some benefit to Christian colleges. Likewise, the rank permissiveness in state colleges and universities may eventually turn parents and pastors toward Christian higher education much in the way they have turned from public education to Christian elementary and secondary schools in this decade.

A helpful volume entitled *A Digest of Trends in Higher Education Within the Christian Perspective*, compiled by Ben Wood and Associates of Wheaton, Illinois, has pinpointed the crucial factor: "Generally, Christian schools of the future will attract a larger percentage of the market if they retain and revitalize their distinctive integration of Christian faith and learning."[7] After treating the enrollment issue from various perspectives, the editors of that report offer this concluding paragraph:

The interplay of these many factors, while complex, indicates hope for the continuation of education in Christian oriented schools. The key for future stability is twofold. First, it is necessary that schools increase their sensitivity to a student's needs and goals. This is especially important as we see more students desiring a practical educational experience. Second, reaffirmation of the Christian world view in all aspects of the Christian college training is vital. Again, an integration of faith and learning applicable both inside and outside of an academic setting is highly desirable.[8]

Probably the most positive current phenomenon in evangelical higher education is the health of seminaries in this last quarter of the twentieth century. An 11 percent increase was reported in seminary enrollments between the fall of 1974 and the opening of the 1975-76 academic year. Since that time they have continued to climb until by 1979 there were well over five thousand students in graduate theological schools in the United States and Canada. A revival of interest in evangelical theological institutions and the creation of the Doctor of Ministries degree contributed most significantly to seminary growth in the seventies.

A second area of projection is the matter of *curriculum.* The clearcut trend in the area of curriculum across higher education in America is vocationalism. Students are seeking marketable skills rather than the general refinement of the cultured personality.

Still a third area in which projection is essential is the area of *finance.* Institutions are caught between effectiveness and economy as the two polarities on a continuum line of financial practice. *Effectiveness* can enjoy the luxury of concerning itself only with the institution's goals and objectives, with full emphasis on results instead of resources. *Economy,* on the other hand, simply aims at managing without waste and constantly guards the resources. It is a belt-tightening procedure that talks a lot about survival rather than growth.

There is a middle ground, of course, and we can call it *efficiency,* an emphasis on the maximum return for the dollar. Its key ideas are caution and management to produce the greatest outputs with minimum inputs.

The danger, of course, is for the Christian institution to somehow consider itself immune from the problems of finance that plague higher education in general. President Paul Reinert of St. Louis University reminds us:

> Today, as never before in modern times, the entire private sector of U. S. higher education is unsure of its future. The latest figures in a continuing study by the Association of American Colleges reveal that some 365 of the nation's private colleges and universities may be ready to close their doors in 1981 unless immediate aid is forthcoming. Two hundred institutions will be exhausting their liquid assets within a year. Within ten years, forty percent of all private Ph.D. granting institutions will be out of business.[9]

Christian schools dare not be passive toward the sources of financial support for their institutions. The previously noted report prepared by Ben Wood Associates concludes:

> To thrive in the next two decades, Christian schools will have to continually be open to new sources of revenue, reducing the portion now brought in by the student. Technology will play an increasingly important role which will require creative, open thinking on the part of Christian schools. Careful planning in these and other areas mentioned in this section will result in a positive financial picture for the foreseeable future.[10]

One other trend that we might well see in higher education in this last quarter of the twentieth century is a return to more conservative thinking regarding *educational standards.* Pass-fail (in which no one ever fails), admission of undergraduate students who cannot write a coherent sentence, and so-called free universities and open education, may eventually be demonstrated as folly.

Nontraditional Options

Because of the declining applicant pool among traditionally aged college students, higher education is looking for new populations. We have become aware that in the eighties the number of twenty-five to thirty-four-year-olds in the national population will increase substantially. One can therefore predict that by the mid 1980s higher education will focus considerably more of its attention on that adult age group.

According to the National Center of Educational Statistics, in 1977 there were 17 million students engaged in "adult education" outside the formal college and university setting. A more recent report by the Conference Board indicates that the nation's largest companies spend more than $1.6 billion annually for in-house education of their employees.[11]

The church also has been aware of the necessity of continuing education, and it has focused largely upon the various aspects of adult church education at the lay level. It is important to note here the difference between *adult education* and *continuing education* as those terms are understood in the academic community. *Adult education* has to do with lay level experiences in lieu of formal degree programs. *Continuing education,* to borrow a definition used by Connolly C. Gamble, is "that part of a learner's planned education that has its point of beginning where formal education ceases to be his primary occupation of life."[12] In other words, *continuing education* is for professional church workers whose responsibility it is to provide *adult education* for the laity.

It is also important to note that Gamble's definition does not preclude formal schooling as a part of continuing education, but merely indicates that continuing education must go on after formal schooling is no longer the primary occupation of life. Graves broadens the concept when he says, "Continuing education involves a planned program of systematic sustained learning for ministers in service, whether conducted on seminary or college campuses, through guided study on the church field, whether in short term conferences, seminars and workshops or in more extended periods of study in the classroom, conference room, or laboratory settings."[13]

Though evening schools have long been a part of traditional programs in Christian higher education, only lately have our institutions caught on to the tremendous importance of being a part of what Theodore M. Hesburgh, Paul A. Miller, and Clifton R. Wharton, Jr., have called "Patterns for Lifelong Learning."[14]

Christian colleges and seminaries are now recognizing the legitimacy and value of placing extension classes and centers in strategic locations to "take the learning to the people."

The most dramatic demonstration of theological education by extension in America has been the creation of Doctor of Ministry programs by dozens of seminaries. With minimal on-campus residence requirements, these programs build on a combination of the Master of Divinity degree and ministerial experience to provide a new degree program closely integrated with the professional church worker's field responsibilities. Extension classes are often taught hundreds of miles away from the main campus.

The matter of lifelong learning was well presented in a chapter entitled, "Cyclic Life Patterns" from *Relating Work and Education,* edited by Dyckman W. Vermilye. The chapter decries the common commitment to a "linear life plan."

"The tremendous growth of economic productivity brought about by industrialization has allowed tremendous increases of non-work time as a proportion of total lifetime. . . . Only 13.5 percent of a person's total lifetime during the industrial era is spent on work, compared to 28.6 percent of a person's lifetime during the agricultural era and 33 percent of a person's life during the primitive era.[15]

The concern, of course, is to relate the increased available time to educational opportunities.

> Until recently, our society thought it proper to administer education—from elementary through advanced graduate levels—in one massive dose. Education was for young people—and beyond a certain point for just certain young people. And the whole process was best accomplished with little or no interruption. . . . It was not until the massive democratization of education during the 1960s that educational research and the political

pressures fostered by a larger and more diverse educational constituency forced a widespread recognition that different individuals learn best under varying methods and time frames. The result has been a wave of educational innovations such as student-initiated courses, non-graded studies, academic credit for work and other experiences, vouchers and learning contracts, residential colleges, decentralized campuses, ethnic curriculums, programs for the elderly, and equivalency examinations. In terms of future life patterns, these "non-traditional" approaches to education will be generally conducive to more cyclic patterns. Then continuance and likely growth will tend to increase the scheduling flexibility of schooling and therefore to foster increasing departures from current linear life patterns.[16]

If the evangelical community is going to take advantage of this wave of commitment to lifelong learning, it must research and experiment with new programs of cooperation between church and educational institutions. The local church itself cannot provide the kind of *adult education* that will have cutting-edge credibility, or *continuing education* at a professional level. By the same token, the college or seminary cannot expect everyone to rush to its halls of learning each time learning is to take place. A cooperative endeavor, therefore, is essential, and there are already some models worthy of study. Moody Bible Institute enrolls almost 1500 students in evening school programs on its Chicago campus and in extension programs in eight other midwest locations aimed primarily at noncredit adult education. Miami Christian College now enrolls more students in extension classes than on the main campus, and almost all of those extension classes offer courses for credit, transferable to any degree program in the college. Most of the extension classes are housed in local churches. The Grace Community Church of Panorama City, California, is operating a Bible institute on its premises aimed largely at adult education, and, in cooperation with Talbot Theological Seminary, offers an extension center for continuing education.

Of course, there will always be some who are not able to make it to a resident center for formal learning experiences, or who have no such opportunities in their areas.

For them, learning by mail is an alternative, using the correspondence programs of schools such as the Moody Bible Institute in Chicago or Fort Wayne Bible College in Indiana.

The absolute importance of Christian higher education to the church of Jesus Christ in the late twentieth century cannot be overemphasized. *The church desperately needs the Christian college,* though too often it forgets that need amidst its other problems and pressures.

FOR FURTHER STUDY

1. Analyze a college that you are acquainted with in the matter of educational quality, as measured by experience and preparation of the faculty, by relationship with an accrediting association, and by library resources.
2. Review ten Christian college catalogs from the registrar's office or other source. Compare their doctrinal statements in terms of historic evangelical Christianity.
3. Interview the registrar or director of admissions at your institution as to how he is handling the problems of decreasing registration and availability of students at the traditional college attendance ages.
4. Write to one of the organizations listed at the end of this chapter, requesting information. Prepare a report describing the activities of that organization and how it serves the cause of Christian higher education.
5. Using the bibliography at the end of the chapter, study further in the matter of a distinctively Christian philosophy of Christian higher education. Write your own statement of mission or purpose for a Christian college.
6. Research the availability of schools in your area that provide either continuing education or adult education.

GLOSSARY OF TERMS

Credit unit: Official certification of a course completed satisfactorily, statements of competence, and other increment of verified educational accomplishments (theses, oral and written examinations, internships, etc.) accepted toward completion of requirements for certificates and degrees. Credit units are most often assigned semester or quarter hour values.

Degree: An honor bestowed by an educational institution for meeting its requirements through the satisfactory completion of a program of study or other verified educational accomplishment.

Educational credential: A certificate, diploma, or degree document (associate, baccalaureate, or graduate) certifying that the requirements therefor have been met through satisfactory completion of a program of study or other verified educational accomplishment.

External degree: An academic award earned through one or more of the following means: extra-institutional learning, credit by examination, specially devised experiential learning programs, self-directed study, and satisfactory completion of campus or noncampus courses. In some programs, the learning is attained in circumstances outside the sponsorship or supervision of the awarding agency.

Extra-institutional learning: Learning that is attained outside the sponsorship of legally authorized and accredited postsecondary institutions The term applies to learning acquired from work and life experiences, independent reading and study, the mass media, and participation in formal courses sponsored by associations, business, government, industry, the military, unions, and other social institutions such as hospitals.

Higher education: The part of postsecondary education that leads to the award of a degree.

Postsecondary education: The array of educational opportunities available to post-high-school age adults, including educational programs of postsecondary education institutions and extra-institutional learning experiences defined above.

(From the Task Force on Educational Credit and Credentials of the American Council on Education, endorsed by the Council's Board of Directors on January 30, 1978.)

NOTES

1. *Colonial Society of Massachusetts, Collections,* Harvard College Records I, 15:24.
2. John S. Brubacher and Willis Rudy, *Higher Education in Transition* (New York: Harper & Row, 1958), p. 10.
3. Ibid., p. 6.
4. Frank T. Rhodes, "A Continuing Vision of Truth, Faith, and Knowledge," *Chronicle of Higher Education,* 6 February 1978.
5. David McKenna, "Changing Partnerships in Christian Higher Education," *Christianity Today,* 21 August 1970, p. 7.
6. *Chronicle of Higher Education,* 6 September 1977, p. 12.
7. *A Digest of Trends in Higher Education Within the Christian Perspective* (Wheaton, Ill.: Ben Wood and Associates, 1976), p. 12.
8. Ibid.
9. "Rescue Begins at Home," (Management Division, Academy for Education, 1972), pp. 7-8.
10. *A Digest of Trends,* p. 32.
11. Harold L. Hodgkinson, "Truth and Consequences on Enrollment," *AGB Reports* 20 (January-February 1978): 10.
12. Connolly C. Gamble, Jr., "Theological School and the Minister's Continuing Education," *Theological Education* 1 (Summer 1965): 198.
13. Allen W. Graves, "Continuing Theological Education," *Review and Expositor,* Winter 1973, pp. 63-64.
14. Theodore M. Hesburgh, Paul A. Miller, and Clifton R. Wharton, Jr., *Patterns for Lifelong Learning* (San Francisco: Jossey-Bass, 1973).
15. Dyckman W. Vermilye, ed., *Relating Work and Education* (San Francisco: Jossey-Bass, 1977), p. 251.
16. Barry Stern and Fred Best, "Cyclic Life Patterns," in *Relating Work and Education.*

SUGGESTED READING

BOOKS

Averill, Lloyd J. *A Strategy for the Protestant College.* Philadelphia: Westminster, 1966.

Brubacher, John S., and Rudy, Willis. *Higher Education in Transition.* New York: Harper & Row, 1958.

Byrne, Herbert W. *A Christian Approach to Education.* Grand Rapids: Zondervan, 1961.

Doescher, Waldemar O. *The Church College in Today's Culture*. Minneapolis: Augsburg, 1963.

Erickson, Donald A., ed. *Public Controls for Non-Public Schools*. Chicago: U. of Chicago, 1961.

Gaebelein, Frank E. *A Varied Harvest*. Grand Rapids: Eerdmans, 1967.

————. *The Pattern of God's Truth*. Chicago: Moody, 1968.

————. *Christian Education in a Democracy*. New York: Oxford U., 1951.

Hesburgh, Theodore; Miller, Paul A.; and Wharton, Clifton R., Jr. *Patterns for Lifelong Learning*. San Francisco: Jossey-Bass, 1973.

Holmes, Arthur F. *The Idea of a Christian College*. Grand Rapids: Eerdmans, 1975.

Jahsmann, Allan Hart. *What's Lutheran in Education?* St. Louis: Concordia, 1960.

Lewis, C. S. *The Abolition of Man*. New York: Macmillan, 1947.

Lockerbie, D. Bruce. *The Way They Should Go*. New York: Oxford U., 1972.

May, Phillip. *Which Way to Educate?* Chicago: Moody, 1975.

Mayers, Marvin K.; Richards, Lawrence O.; and Webber, Robert. *Reshaping Evangelical Higher Education*. Grand Rapids: Zondervan, 1972.

Miller, Alexander S. *Faith and Learning: Christian Faith and Higher Education in 20th-Century America*. New York: Association, 1960.

Newman, John Henry Cardinal. *The Idea of a University*. London: Longmans, Green and Company, 1925.

Pattillo, Manning M., Jr., and Mackenzie, Donald M. *Church-Sponsored Higher Education in the United States*. Washington: American Council on Education, 1966.

Pinnock, Clark H. *Set Forth Your Case*. Chicago: Moody, 1971.

Ramm, Bernard. *The Christian College in the Twentieth Century*. Grand Rapids: Eerdmans, 1963.

St. Olaf College Self-Study Committee, *Integration in the Christian Liberal Arts College*. Northfield, Minn.: St. Olaf College, 1956.

Sauer, Erick. *The King of the Earth*. Grand Rapids: Eerdmans, 1962.

Schaeffer, Francis A. *How Should We Then Live?* Old Tappan, N.J.: Revell, 1976.

Sire, James W. *The Universe Next Door*. Downers Grove Ill.: Inter-Varsity, 1976.

Trueblood, Elton. *The Idea of a College*. New York: Harper, Publishers, 1959.

Vermilye, Dyckman W., ed. *Lifelong Learners—A New Clientele for Higher Education*. (Current issues in Higher Education, 1974.) San Francisco: Jossey-Bass, 1974.

Webber, Robert. *How to Choose a Christian College*. Carol Stream, Ill.: Creation House, 1973.

Witmer, Safara A. *Education with Dimension*. Manhasset, N.Y.· Channel, 1962.

Zylstra, Henry. *Testament of Vision*. Grand Rapids: Eerdmans, 1961.

PERIODICALS

"Academic Freedom in Evangelical Perspective." *Christianity Today*, 3 July 1970, p. 20.

Cattell, Everett L. "The Grim Alternatives in Christian Higher Education." *Christianity Today*, 3 July 1970, p. 4.

Chapman, James. "Christian Colleges Need to Shape Up." *Eternity*, June 1970, p. 30.

Frankel, Charles. "Piercing the Veil of the Commonplace." *The Chronicle of Higher Education*, 3 May 1976, p. 32.

Gaebelein, Frank E. "Christian Education in Relation to Teacher and Student." *Grace Journal*, Fall 1962, pp. 27-34.

———. "The Major Premise of Christian Education." *Grace Journal*, Fall 1962. pp. 12-18.

———. "The Need and Nature of a Christian Philosophy of Education." *Grace Journal*, Fall 1962, pp. 3-11.

———. "Towards a Christian Philosophy of Education." *Grace Journal*, Fall 1962.

Gangel, Kenneth O. "Behavioral Objectives: Curse or Cure." *The Christian School Administrator*, Fall 1976, p. 5.

———. "The Bible College Then and Now." *Communicare*, Fall 1976.

———. "The Christian College in the Volatile World of Higher Education," *Communicare*, Fall 1975.

———. "The Local College and the Local Church." *Communicare*, Winter 1976.

———. "The Meaning and Ministry of Christian Higher Education." *Communicare*, Spring 1978.

Grant, Daniel R. "Moral Relativism and Christian Absolutes: Problems and Opportunities for the Christian College." *Search*, Spring 1977, p. 40.

Groves, Allen W. "Continuing Theological Education." *Review and Expositor*, Winter 1974, pp. 63-74.

Highet, Gilbert. "The Need to 'Make it New.'" *The Chronicle of Higher Education*, 21 June 1977, p. 40.

Holmes, Arthur F. "Academic Freedom in the Christian College." *Bulletin of Wheaton College*, February 1964, p. 2.

Jellema, William W. "Campus Deities." *Christianity Today*, 17 February 1962, pp. 15-17.

McKenna, David. "Changing Partnerships in Christian Higher Education." *Christianity Today*, 21 August 1970, p. 7.

Reid, W. Stanford. "Jesus Christ: Focal Point of Knowledge." *Christianity Today*, 10 May 1968, pp. 3-4.

Rhodes, Frank H. T. "A Continuing Vision of Truth, Faith, and Knowledge." *The Chronicle of Higher Education*, 6 February 1978.

Trueblood, Elton. "Colleges Can Be Redeemed!" *Southern Baptist Educator*, July-Angust 1976, p. 43.

PERIODICALS HELPFUL IN THE STUDY OF CHRISTIAN HIGHER EDUCATION

AABC Newsletter. Published by the Accrediting Association of Bible Colleges, Box 543, Wheaton, IL 60187. Appears quarterly for member institutions.

AAUP Bulletin. Published by the American Association of University Professors, 1785 Massachusetts Ave., N.W., Washington, D.C. 20036. Appears quarterly. Circulation 65,000.

Chronicle of Higher Education. 1717 Massachusetts Avenue, N.W., Washington, D.C. 20036. Appears weekly.

College and University Bulletin. Published by the American Association for Higher Education, One Dupont Circle, Washington, D.C. 20036. Appears semimonthly October 1 through June 1 (except Jan. 1) with a combined issue on April 1-15.

Improving College and University Teaching. Published by the Graduate School of Oregon State University, 101 Waldo Hall, Corvallis, OR 97331. Appears quarterly.

Journal of Higher Education. Published by the AAHE and the Ohio State University Press, 2070 Neil Ave., Columbus, OH 43210. Appears monthly except July, August, and September.

Theological Education. Published by the American Association of Theological Schools, 534 Third National Building, Dayton, OH 45402. Appears quarterly.

Trustee. Published by the Division of Higher Education, Board of Higher Education and Ministry, United Methodist Church, P. O. Box 871, Nashville, TN 37202.

Part VII

CONTEMPORARY PERSPECTIVES IN
CHRISTIAN EDUCATION

Every day brings new opportunities for exciting, meaningful service for Christ in the field of Christian education. Churches, schools, children's and youth ministry organizations, publishing companies, and mission boards are seeking qualified persons to fill Christian education vocational positions across America and around the world. This unit introduces such ministry.

Chapter 27 details the growing variety of professional vocations available to both men and women for Christian education ministry in the areas of children, youth, and adults. Requirements and qualifications are presented for the parachurch ministries.

A relatively recent concern in Christian education is the need for church sponsored special education programs for the emotionally and/or mentally handicapped. Chapter 28 addresses the potential outreach and impact of Christian special education programming.

With many churches abandoning inner city areas to build in the suburbs, a crisis has developed in ministering to the masses within the cities of the United States—a melting pot of peoples representing wide differences in cultural, racial, social and economic backgrounds. Inner city Christian education is the focus of chapter 29.

Many mission fields are now seeking help as national churches become ready to develop teaching and training ministries for their own congregations. Ministry in Bible colleges and seminaries on the mission field is expanding, as well as in the writing and publishing of suitable Christian education curriculum materials. Christian education on the mission field is the subject of the closing chapter of the book.

27

Parachurch Vocations in Christian Education

Warren S. Benson

One of the major developments in Christian education this century has been the growth of organizations and movements having origin and continuing life outside the official church. C. B. Eavey's *History of Christian Education* identified them as *extrachurch*. Today they are usually designated as *parachurch*—alongside of the church.

The place of parachurch ministries is a subject of continuing debate between strong supporters and those who question any program not an integral part of the church per se.

Regardless of position, programs such as Campus Crusade, Awana, and Youth For Christ are a major influence in Christian education ministry in our day. They must be recognized. Vic Glavach and Milford S. Sholund have expressed it well:

> Parachurch youth movements are an evidence that God is no respecter of churches per se. These organizations are an effort of individuals and groups of individuals to express the will of God, to desire to witness and work in response to God's call and the needs of others. Some have often sensed a vacuum in the vitality and vision of churches. Others have recognized the limitations of the institution and have sought to overcome these limitations. The parachurch youth movement is, in a sense, a phenomenon among churches in a nation that has provided a congenial setting for religious freedom. It is not meant to rival the institution but to be an extension into fields where the institution cannot go or has not gone, much as the missionary is an extension of the domestic institutional church.[1]

Evangelical parachurch organizations should not be seen as appendages to the church. Although they may operate outside the local church organ-

---

Warren S. Benson, Ph.D., is vice president of academic administration and professor of Christian education at Trinity Evangelical Divinity School, Deerfield, Illinois.

izational structure, they are not outside the Body of Christ. Certainly they need to work with the local church and provide dynamic vision and implemental skills when at all possible. Indeed, many parachurch organizations increasingly have blended their ministries with local churches. Mutual growth, power, and fellowship have been the result. A relationship of appreciation and respect among organizations and churches is mandatory if the evangelical movement is to maximize its mission.

The major thrust of this chapter is to give a broad perspective of parachurch Christian education ministries with particular reference to the vocational opportunities they afford and the type of preparation they require.

The parachurch field is broadly presented in six major divisions, with selected representative organizations for each division:

Children/Youth Organizations Not Under Local Church Sponsorship
Children/Youth Organizations Operating Under Local Church Sponsorship
Christian Day Schools
Mission Boards
Christian Publishers
Camping Organizations

It is to be understood that all of the selected evangelical organizations presented require a commitment to their doctrinal statement (whether detailed or broad) and to the basic philosophy of ministry and operation of that ministry, and that all organizations desire to recruit women and minorities for their staff.

CHRISTIAN DAY SCHOOLS*

The radical growth of the evangelical elementary and secondary day school movement in the late seventies was phenomenal. On the other hand, the Roman Catholic school system entered into a period of unprecedented decline between 1965 and 1971, when enrollment fell by 900,000 and one thousand schools were closed.[2] Entering the eighties the Catholic slide appeared to be bottoming out with 3.4 million enrolled.[3]

While the Roman Catholic Church was in its period of flux and apathy and public schools were declining from the record high of 1971 due to the decreasing birth rates, the Protestant school enrollment approached 900,000.[4]

An interesting prospect is eventuating from the public school situation for the future of Christian day schools. With the number of teachers

*See also chapter 25.

SELECTED CHILDREN/YOUTH ORGANIZATIONS NOT UNDER LOCAL CHURCH SPONSORSHIP

Type of Ministry	Educational Background	Experience Preferred	Opportunities
CHILD EVANGELISM FELLOWSHIP			
Evangelistic and growth-centered. Good News Clubs held in homes; five-day backyard Bible clubs during summer; film and tract presentations at state fairs and other public meetings; weekly training classes of adults and seminars in churches. Striving to work with and through church-sponsored ministries. Curriculum materials available. National television program.	Bible college, liberal arts, or seminary training preferred, but not required. Fifteen-week and twelve-week training programs provided. Annual in-service training.	Full-time staff generally comes out of the volunteer ranks. Teaching skills with children and adults (training programs) must be demonstrated. Young talent desired for staff.	Regional and country leaders needed in US. Expanding overseas ministry (in 72 countries aiming toward an indigenous basis for support and direction). Need writers for materials and magazine and specialists in TV ministry. Greatest needs overseas.
YOUNG LIFE			
Evangelistic and "whole man" ministry with high school people. "Campaigners" is their Bible study discipling arm with Christians. Club sessions consist of singing, skits, and a brief talk about an aspect of the Christian life. Significant camping ministry in North America. Inner-city work. Heavily relational in theological orientation.	Full-time staff expected to work on an M.A. degree from Young Life Institute (degree granted by Fuller Seminary) or at Gordon-Conwell, North Park, Luther/Northwestern Theological, or Bethel Seminary.	Staff generally come out of volunteer ranks. Proved ability to relate to teenagers, have potential in leading other adults in ministry, be able to motivate local area committee that supports staff.	Number of staff members needed is limited by the areas able to support staff. Need for volunteer staff unlimited. 900 paid staff, both full and part-time workers.

Type of Ministry	Educational Background	Experience Preferred	Opportunities
YOUTH FOR CHRIST, INTERNATIONAL			
Evangelism and edification given balanced emphasis. Aggressive guidance ministry to delinquents, drug addicts, and troubled youth. "Whole man" thrust. Utilize large fun events and smaller group studies / meetings. Attempt ministry to families. Outstanding *Campus Life* magazine. Extensive overseas ministry. Inner-city work.	Bachelors degree in Bible, sociology, or psychology. Those who have earned fewer than 20 hours in undergraduate required to attend School of Theological Studies. Four-week training provided in youth evangelism and 90 hours of in-service classroom training during initial year on staff.	Leadership skills and sufficient maturity to work with youth, adult community, and a board. Looking for people with a solid self-image, pleasant personality, well-organized, who live in light of priorities, preferable from a family that will provide moral support. Must care deeply about people and be able to develop relationships.	Need between 175 to 300 new full-time men and women in future. Ratios: 35% women, 15% minorities, 60% from within their alumni, 40% college recruitment.
WORD OF LIFE			
Began as youth rally movement. Although evangelism is always predominant, Bible teaching has grown in all areas of its work. Bible Institute and camp at Schroon Lake, New York, remains central. Now have five camps and four Bible Institutes overseas. Lately, church sponsored club program has developed.	Enrollment in WOL Bible Institute required only of those with inadequate Bible training. Thorough Bible Institute level doctrinal education mandatory for staff.	Agreement with WOL's positions. Very cautious about choice of staff people. Clear, concise, and conservative staff positional papers on subjects such as "cooperative evangelism," "dress standards," and "speaking in tongues" provide guidance and tone of organization.	Need field people for motivation and training of lay leadership working with clubs in local churches. Graduate training preferred for Bible Institute faculties.

Type of Ministry	Educational Background	Experience Preferred	Opportunities
NAVIGATORS Evangelistic and edification emphasis. They work quietly, patiently, and demandingly in discipleship. Strong emphasis on Scripture memory and Bible study.	College preferred, but not mandatory, depending on kind of ministry. Training processes are informal and cumulative. They emphasize experiential faith grounded in the promises of God and centered in the person of Christ.	They grow their own staff. Stress large number of "laborers," who are actively teaming with them in local disciple-making ministries.	As of 1978, 1400 persons on staff in 34 countries. They work with key individuals at least 5-6 years before they invite them to join their staff. Foster a deep commitment to their movement. Will not advertise for candidates or recruit staff directly from the Christian community.
CAMPUS CRUSADE FOR CHRIST Over 5300 staff members in 84 countries in diversified ministries. Campus work remains its primary thrust. Campus staff conducts discipleship training, evangelistic appointments, Bible studies, and work with faculty and local churches. Lay training institutes and pastors' conferences are conducted. Other ministries: Agape (2-year Christian "Peace Corps"); Athletes in Action (play best college teams and present a witness); recently began high school ministry; recently began its own theological seminary.	Bachelors degree for assignment with college or high school work. All applicants expected to attend the Institute of Biblical Studies and/or staff training annually. Staff raise their own support.	A concern for others and evidence of past fruitfulness. Knowledge of Scripture and its application to life crucial. Leadership potential and attractiveness to others in personality, character, and appearance.	Needs: (1) primarily campus workers; (2) people to work with pastors and laymen in churches; (3) overseas personnel; (4) people for support roles such as administrators, secretaries, tradesmen; (5) nationals from various countries for all phases of ministry; and (6) people trained beyond college for special assignments.

Type of Ministry	Educational Background	Experience Preferred	Opportunities

INTER-VARSITY CHRISTIAN FELLOWSHIP

Ministry to United States (Canada has separate organization) collegians and student nurses (Nurses Christian Fellowship). An adjunct work (Theological Students Fellowship) promotes an evangelical witness on secular college campuses and at nonevangelical Protestant denominational and ecumenical seminaries in North America. Distinguished book publisher. Logos bookstores associated with but not organizationally part of IVCF. Biannual missionary convention at Urbana, Ill., and *His* magazine outstanding contributons to evangelicalism. Over 800 chapters on United States campuses.

Bachelors degree and graduate work desired, but most have not attended seminary. Staff training provided both initially and on a continuing educational basis. Staff raise their own support.

Full-time staff most often come from volunteer leaders on campuses. Spiritually alert and analytically perceptive in advising groups, skillful in motivating and training student leaders.

Needs: primarily field staff and people for support roles such as editors and clerical workers.

SELECTED CHURCH-SPONSORED CHILDREN AND YOUTH ORGANIZATIONS

AWANA

Clubs for boys and girls, grades K-12. Objectives: salvation, education, leaders modeling Christian character, outreach programs; 175,000 boys and girls involved weekly in the US. Strong emphasis on Bible knowledge personally applied. Program emphases on Scripture memory, athletics, and awards.

Qualifications: called of God to this position. No other formal requirements. Headquarters staff: 50, including part-time. Appropriate training programs available.

Staff generally comes through the local church ministries. Proved workers with children and youth desired.

Presently 24 field men totally, two in Canada, one in Australia. The international aspects growing. Looking for field people plus home office staff such as writers, artists, clerical, etc.

Type of Ministry	Educational Background	Experience Preferred	Opportunities
PIONEER GIRLS Clubs for girls, grades 2-12. Objectives: salvation, lordship of Christ, Bible study, relationships with other girls and women, development of the whole person, involvement in the local church, equip girls to reach others and serve. Weekday and camp ministry. Five-day club programs, grades 2-12; 19 camps in the US, 6 in Canada. Handbook and programming aids designed to be useful with or apart from achievement program.	Bachelors degree in: sociology, education, recreation, business, camping, journalism, or curriculum. Training program provided.	(1) Able to meet and deal with people, (2) work harmoniously, (3) willingness to improve skills and knowledge through formal or informal study.	Presently 30 home office staff, 25 field staff, including secretaries. Additional field staff personnel needed to train 25,000 volunteers in churches. Need: marketing managers, curriculum writers, media production personnel, office workers, camp directors, and support staff. Unusually skillful management and perceptive approach to ministry with girls and women.
CHRISTIAN SERVICE BRIGADE Clubs for boys, ages 8-18. Objectives: start with a church where it is in its ministry with boys, lead that church to develop a plan that will include the training of men and the discipling of boys. 70,000 boys plus involved weekly; 16,000 volunteer leaders. Outstanding materials and magazines available for boys and men.	Qualifications: dedication of life to God for Christian service and a call from God to a ministry for Christ. Liberal arts education or equivalent is basic. Graduate study or other practical experience is encouraged. Some formal Bible training is preferred. Informal and formal training recommended to staff. Excellent set of guidelines available for those in undergraduate study for choosing best majors and courses.	Experience in some phase of Brigade activity important for those involved in the field ministry. In that field men are "men's workers", rather than "boy's workers"; they must be competent to lead, motivate, and train men. Ability to work as part of a missionary team and raise part of their support.	Presently 22 field representatives, 50 home office personnel, 15 on Canadian staff. Greatest need: field representatives throughout the US and Canada; occasional need for home office support staff.

needed in the public schools decreasing and the number of available teachers who are university trained with state certification, the Christian day school may be able to choose a higher caliber of faculty.

A college degree (possibly, a master's degree as well), teaching certificate, training in Bible, and a major in the area in which the teacher will spend the majority of teaching time may well become standard.

The richer one's background is in theology and Bible, the greater the possibility of achieving the all-important goal of Christian education—the integration of truth in natural (general) and special revelation. Kenneth O. Gangel states, "The graduate of a state university with purely secular courses in education, no matter how highly esteemed his degree and training, is no more qualified to teach in a Christian school than is the graduate of a three-year Bible institute who has focused for ninety semester hours on only biblical studies."[5] Obviously, preparation as a Christian school teacher is not adequate unless one is qualified both academically and theologically. The integration of Scripture with academic instruction is crucial.

Potential teachers must know Jesus Christ as Savior and Lord, evidence spiritual maturity, have teaching ability, be skillful in establishing relationships with students, and understand curriculum development.

One director of an association criticizes teacher candidates who "appear in very youth-oriented attire after having introduced themselves by a letter written sloppily on lined paper that has been torn out of a notebook. Professionalism is a necessary part of training."[6]

Teaching at the Bible college, college of liberal arts, or theological seminary levels demands a minimum of a master's degree in the field of specialization. A doctoral degree is basic for seminary teaching, and a Ph.D. is clearly preferred over the Th.D.

MISSION BOARDS

The missionary opportunities in the seventies were overwhelming. At one point (April 1978), Intercristo, the international Christian placement organization, had "21,000 openings with about 400 Christian mission agencies, organizations, churches, schools, ministries, businesses and individuals world-wide."[7] Most of those were overseas. The prospects for ministry abroad have been overwhelming in church planting, direct evangelism, teaching in Bible colleges and seminaries, radio-television, and numerous other specialist roles.

Yet some changes are imminent. The indigenous principle of the people doing the work of the ministry (Eph. 4:11-16) and the evolution of international societies has altered the strategy of and the demands on today's missionary. Following World War II the missionary conformed reasonably well to the stereotype of the calling—a Bible institute or college graduate who went out to preach. Later, in the 1960s, the call was for specialists, particularly educators and medical and technical personnel—people who had a needed skill that could open doors to countries where traditional evangelism/church-planting missionaries were not permitted.[8]

Dave Carlstrom of Intercristo, after interviewing some of the participants at the Independent Foreign Missions Association and the Evangelical Foreign Missions Association joint personnel seminar in 1977, stated:

> These days many missionary receiving countries are overtechnicianed, so unemployment among their trained nationals is a problem and there is a reluctance to allow foreigners to fill nationals' jobs. Fifteen years ago North Americans quite frequently went overseas calling themselves missionaries and with a primary assignment to operate a mimeograph or to drive a truck. Now such assignments are frowned on—if not prohibited—by national governments, and most missions consider them a poor use of personnel and financial resources. So today there is renewed demand for "missionary missionaries"—mature Christians committed to the church and to the training of nationals in evangelism and discipleship. Where technology yet unlocks doors into emerging countries the keys have been changed. For example, in the Sudan visas were once granted for work in education and curative medicine—work which now has been assumed by the government. But visas are available in the Sudan today for work in rural development (e.g. agriculture and water resources) and preventive medicine (e.g. public health), provided the foreigner is also able and willing to train nationals to assume responsibility for the work themselves.[9]

There is a resurgence of "missionary missionaries," yet also a definite place for the specialist whose work may be short-lived. Therefore, attitudes of flexibility and adaptability are seen as essential traits for prospective missionaries. Inability to adapt to a new culture, language, and life-style account for a high number of casualties. Many missions are looking for candidates who are 27-29 years of age, with more life experience than the college graduate of only 22. One missionary leader believes that a pastorate or associate pastoral stint is important for work abroad because of the experience gained in teaching and training.[10]

The richer the academic and experiential preparation, the greater the tendency toward high level achievement. Missions are not looking for people who receive many "average" checks on reference forms. First-quality people meet their requirements. A missions executive's statement is typical of the type of candidates for which they are looking:

> CAM is looking for above average people to meet our goal. Never before in the history of CAM have we so carefully screened our applicants. It

does not take a college or seminary education to lead a person to Christ, however, we are interested in reproducing in kind. That means that if we expect a person to develop into the type of Christian that is doctrinally sound and spiritually mature, our personnel has to meet that same requirement. Thirty hours of Bible is the minimum, and if a person is going into the field of education, we require much more. For church planters and evangelists, an applicant must have had not only formal training in Bible and theology, but also experience here in the homelands as well. For someone wanting to teach in the seminary, a master's degree is required. For those desiring to teach on the Bible school level, a college degree with an emphasis on Bible is required. Even our MK teachers are required to have at least 30 hours of Bible.[11]

In Europe, requirements are very high due to the intellectual climate. Instructors in the Bible institutes have the minimum of a master's degree in their field of specialization and doctorates are required in the seminaries. Short-term or degree programs for continuing education during furloughs are encouraged.[12]

Some missions have eight-week practical missionary training courses in addition to the traditional two-week candidate school as they enter missionary ministry. In some cases, internships in North America are required.

Bible translation work affords outstanding opportunities for ministry. The *Ethnologue* (8th edition, 1974) states that there are 5,687 known languages of the world.[13] At least 2,000 languages have yet to have any translated portion of Scripture. Generally it takes two linguist-translators per language to do the linguistic and translation work. Therefore at least 4,000 people are needed. The board of directors of the Wycliffe Bible Translators affirmed in 1977 the need for recruits in all aspects of their work, with some 500 new members looked for.[14]

A fine contribution to personnel placement for Bible college, liberal arts college, and seminary students is Intercristo's computerized Futures Intermatch process. Conference and seminar attendees (e.g., at Inter-Varsity Christian Fellowship's giant biannual missionary convention at Urbana, Illinois) are encouraged to discover their gifts and abilities and develop them in preparation for the investment of their lives in short-term or career ministries. Intercristo's *Directory of Christian Work Opportunities*, which lists over 20,000 job openings, provides additional guidance. The type of opportunities range from summer camping positions for high schoolers through short-term stints for retired people. Included are both paid and "raise-your-support" openings; short-term, long-term, and career ministries; for people just out of college; for career missionaries; for people wanting to take six months leave from their secular jobs to serve in missions; and for people who have retired from paying jobs and are looking for volunteer work where they can put their years of experience to work in Christian service.[15]

In turning to the domestic scene, many organizations and ministries considered earlier in this chapter, such as Youth For Christ and Christian Service Brigade, could legitimately be termed home missions, However, there are several organizations that are representative of home missions in the field of Christian education. The Canadian Sunday School Mission and the American Missionary Fellowship have distinguished themselves in going to some of the forgotten pockets of people in North America.

The A.M.F., founded as the American Sunday School Union in 1816, has lost little of its vigor in its goal of reaching areas where there are no well-established local churches. Their work now includes evangelism, medical work, and education in rural and, recently, inner-city United States. Its outreach extends to 2,700 churches each year.[16] A.M.F. is another evidence that a parachurch organization can become an asset to the churches and that such an organization can be useful for more than one generation. The Sunday school itself, considered a parachurch organization during A.M.F.'s first seventy-five years, has now been successfully integrated into the life of the local church.[17]

The Canadian Sunday School Mission, though relatively unknown in the United States, celebrated fifty years of ministry in 1977. C.S.S.M. has given itself not only to the rural areas of the prairie provinces, but to eastern Canada as well. In Ontario, eight Bible teachers typically enter 390 classrooms twice a month and teach nearly 12,000 children during schooltime. One hundred fifty full-time missionaries are augmented by over one thousand summer staff workers each year across the Dominion of Canada.[18] A.M.F. and C.S.S.M. are key representatives of the summer and full-time ministries available for those who feel the call to work with the rural people of North America. Some of the personnel needs are camp managers and directors, pioneer missionaries and church planters, pastors, released time teachers, and office workers. Bible college and seminary graduates are sought.

CHRISTIAN PUBLISHERS

Evangelical publishing includes: Sunday school and Christian education publishers, Christian magazines, Christian day school curriculum houses, and book publishers.

Evangelical publishing houses see themselves as part of the mass media team that may be salt and light in a desperately needy world. One leader in this field said, "I am convinced [that print media] is one of the means which the Lord is using today to present His plan of redemption in astonishing ways. Indeed, this well could be identified as a day of communication—unlike any other period in history."[19] It is that kind of conviction and sense of urgency that most all of the publishers conveyed in answer to my request for data. Business it is, but first and foremost it is God's business. And the keenness of competition among them has not dulled the edge of why they are in this ministry.

Here are typical responses regarding the type of people for whom publishers are looking:

- *Biblical commitment:* "To fulfill this mission, we need Christian men and women committed to Jesus Christ, to the Scriptures, and to excellence in their specialized areas. In most instances college and graduate school are necessary, with seminary or journalism as the best graduate preparation."[20]
- *The right attitude:* "We look for people with professional expertise and an enthusiasm for their work. Of special concern to us at Scripture Press is finding team-players—professionally sharpened skills (through education and experience) with a servant-leader attitude."[21]
- *A willingness to work:* "We need very conscientious hard-working personnel who may or may not have had college educations. We are certainly not against education, but many people come from schools not being able to do anything because they have not had practical training along the way and this is most important."[22]
- *A teachable spirit:* "We would be delighted to find staff who were already trained in the publication field who also had the educational philosophy and experiential involvement in the local church along with their communication skills. Because these kinds of Christian educators are practically non-existent, we are selecting Christians who are educators first and have basic oral and written communication skills second. We then spend a year or two training in mechanics on the job."[23]

The power of print is obvious. A wide variety of ministry options are available within the field of Christian journalism.

CAMPING ORGANIZATIONS

When discussing parachurch vocational possibilities one cannot forget the impact of camping. The versatility of the camping experience makes it unique in the ministry of Christian education. Leaders modeling the message influence the Christian experience of thousands each year. Christian Camping International is an interdenominational fellowship that represents over one thousand camps and conferences in over fifty countries. C.C.I. encourages the setting of standards of excellence that enhance the establishing of quality facilities and programs. C.C.I. affiliated camps and conferences have a strong commitment to recruiting outstanding young people who are competent and well-trained to assure the continued growth of the movement. Many are developing programs of staff internships, in some cases as a part of a master's or a doctoral camping program.[24]

CONCLUSION

The opportunities of serving Jesus Christ through parachurch ministries in the field of Christian education in our day have never been greater and more extensive. Each organization considered should be evaluated on the basis of biblical criteria. If parachurch movements stray from biblical principles, they have lost their reason for and right to exist.

FOR FURTHER STUDY

1. Develop vocational resource files for the six major parachurch divisions, based on books and materials noted in the chapter. Add your own resources.
2. Do an in-depth study of one of the organizations listed. Obtain materials, interview representatives/participants.
3. Write a five-page essay on the history of the parachurch movement, with a concluding evaluation of its potential in future Christian education ministry.
4. Participate in a panel discussion on the biblical relationship of parachurch ministry to the local church.

NOTES

1. Glavach, Vic, and Sholund, Milford S., "Parachurch Youth Movements and Organizations," in *Youth Education in the Church*, ed. Roy B. Zuck and Warren S. Benson (Chicago: Moody, 1978), p. 374.
2. Gabert, Glen, *In Hoc Signo?: A Brief History of Catholic Parochial Education in America* (Port Washington, N.Y.: Kennikat, 1973), p. VII.
3. Ibid., p. 44.
4. Ostling, Richard N., "Why Protestant Schools Are Booming," *Christian Herald*, July-August 1977, p. 45.
5. Gangel, Kenneth O., "Christian School Explosion: Be Careful of the Fallout!" *Guide*, January 1977, p. 3. See Gangel's chapter "Integrating Faith and Learning: Principles and Process," in *The Philosophy of Christian School Education*, ed. Paul A. Kienel (Whittier, Calif.: Western Association of Christian Schools, 1977).
6. Correspondence from Herman Van Schuyver, director, National Association of Christian Schools, Wheaton, Illinois, 5 April 1978.
7. Correspondence, Dawn Cone, Intercristo Public Relations, Seattle, Washington, 12 April 1978.
8. Dave Carlstrom, "The Reverend Paul, Apostle and Today's Missions: What the Evangelical Missions Are Looking for in an Overseas Missions Candidate Today,"
9. Ibid.
10. Dr. George W. Peters, Dallas, Tex., 30 May 1978: personal communication.
11. Correspondence from Donald C. Rutledge, vice president of home ministries, CAM International, Dallas, Tex., 5 April 1978.
12. Correspondence from Donald Brugmann, executive director, Greater Europe Mission, Wheaton, Ill., 21 April 1978.
13. Grimes, Barbara F.; Pittman, Richard S.; and Grimes, Joseph E., *Ethnologue*, 8th ed. (Huntington Beach, Calif.: Wycliffe Bible Translators, 1974).

14. Correspondence from Jacqueline Bernhardt, Academic Affairs, Special Projects, Summer Institute of Linguistics, Dallas, Tex., 20 June 1978.
15. Correspondence from Dawn Cone.
16. Margaret Fisk, ed., *Encyclopedia of Associations* (Detroit: Gale Research, 1975), p. 7.
17. Glavach and Sholund, p. 376.
18. Data and statistics gathered from materials provided by the Canadian Sunday School Mission headquarters, Winnipeg, Manitoba.
19. Correspondence from Robert Walker, editor, *Christian Life* magazine, Wheaton, Ill., 4 April 1978.
20. Correspondence from Joseph Bayly, vice president, David C. Cook Publishing Company, Elgin, Ill., 13 April 1978.
21. Correspondence from James E. Lemon, Jr., vice president of Marketing, Scripture Press, Wheaton, Ill., 13 April 1978.
22. Correspondence from Robert Hawkins, president, Harvest House Publishers, Irvine, Calif., 10 April 1978.
23. Correspondence from Lois L. Curley, executive editor, Education Division, Gospel Light Publications, Glendale, Calif., 18 April 1978.
24. Correspondence from Edward Oulund, executive director, Christian Camping International, Somonauk, Ill., 10 April 1978.

SUGGESTED READING

VOCATIONAL CHOICE

Adams, James F. *Understanding Adolescence: Current Developments in Adolescent Psychology.* 3d ed. Boston: Allyn and Bacon, 1976.

Ahlem, Lloyd II. *Do I Have to Be Me?* Glendale, Calif.: Gospel Light, Regal, 1973.

Anderson, Robert H., ed. *Education in Anticipation of Tomorrow.* Worthington, Ohio: Jones, 1973.

Augsburger, A. Don. *Creating Christian Personality.* Scottdale, Pa.: Herald, 1966.

Augsburger, David. *Caring Enough to Confront.* Glendale, Calif.: Gospel Light, Regal, 1973.

Barnette, Henlee H. *Christian Calling and Vocation.* Grand Rapids: Baker, 1965.

Bruner, Jerome S. *Social Change in Human Behavior.* Rockville, Md.: National Institute of Mental Health, 1972.

Conger, John Janeway. *Adolescence and Youth: Psychological Development in a Changing World.* 2d ed. New York: Harper & Row, 1977.

David, Thomas G., and Wright, Benjamin D. *Learning Environments.* Chicago: U. of Chicago, 1975.

Dobson, James. *Dare to Discipline.* Wheaton, Ill.: Tyndale, 1970.

————. *Hide and Seek.* Old Tappan, N.J.: Revell, 1974.

————. *The Strong-Willed Child.* Wheaton, Ill.: Tyndale, 1978.

Elkind, David. "The Development of Religious Understanding in Children and Adolescents." In *Research on Religious Development.* Edited by Merton P. Strommen. New York: Hawthorn, 1971.

Elizey, W. Clark. *Preparing Your Children for Marriage.* New York: Association, 1964.

Erikson, Erik H. *Identity, Youth and Crisis.* New York: Norton, 1968.

Gangel, Kenneth O. "Vocational Counseling." In *Youth Education in the Church,* edited by Roy B. Zuck and Warren S. Benson. Chicago: Moody, 1978.

Griffiths, Michael C. *Give Up Your Small Ambitions.* Chicago: Moody, 1971.

Havighurst, Robert J. *Developmental Tasks and Education.* 3d ed. New York: McKay, 1972.

————. "Objectives for Youth Development." In *Youth: The Seventy Fourth Yearbook of the National Society for the Study of Education.* Chicago: National Society for the Study of Education, 1975.

Havighurst, Robert J., and Gottlieb, David. "Youth and the Meaning of Work." In *Youth: The Seventy Fourth Yearbook of the National Society for the Study of Education.* Chicago: National Society for the Study of Education, 1975.

Hendricks, Howard G. *Heaven Help the Home.* Wheaton, Ill.: Scripture Press, Victor, 1975.

Kennedy, Robert L. "A Psychological Study of the Development Through the Christian Family and Church of Values Which Lead to a Christian Vocational Career Commitment in the Adolescent." Master's thesis, Dallas Theological Seminary, 1978.

Lawhead, Steve, ed. *After You Graduate.* Grand Rapids: Zondervan, 1978.

Lidz, Theodore. *The Person.* Rev. ed. New York: Basic Books, 1976.

Meier, Paul D. *Christian Child-Rearing and Personality Development.* Grand Rapids: Baker, 1977.

Miller, Donald E. *The Wing-Footed Wanderer: Conscience and Transcendence.* Nashville: Abingdon, 1977.

Proctor, Robert A., Jr. "Relating Developmental Tasks to Religious Education." In *Vital Principles in Religious Education,* edited by John T. Sisemore. Nashville: Broadman, 1966.

Skoglund, Elizabeth. *Can I Talk to You?* Glendale, Calif.: Gospel Light, Regal, 1977.

————. *Where Do I Go to Buy Happiness?* Downers Grove, Ill.: Inter-Varsity, 1972.

Snyder, Ross A. *Young People and Their Culture.* Nashville: Abingdon, 1969.

Sparkman, G. Temp, ed. *Knowing and Helping Youth.* Nashville: Broadman, 1977.

Strommen, Merton P. *Research on Religious Development.* New York: Hawthorn, 1971.

VinKemulder, Yvonne. *Enrich Your Life.* Downers Grove, Ill.: Inter-Varsity, 1972.

Welter, Paul. *Family Problems and Predicaments: How to Respond.* Wheaton, Ill.: Tyndale, 1977.

Zuck, Roy B., and Getz, Gene A. *Christian Youth—An In-Depth Study.* Chicago: Moody, 1968.

CHILDREN AND YOUTH MINISTRIES

Bollback, Harry. *The House That Jack God Built.* Schroon Lake, N.Y.: Word of Life, 1972.

Bolton, Barbara J. *Ways to Help Them Learn: Children, Grades 1 to 6.* Glendale, Calif.: Gospel Light, Regal, 1972.

Bronfenbrenner, Urie. *Two Worlds of Childhood.* New York: Russel Sage, 1969.

Duska, Ronald, and Whelan, Mariellen. *Moral Development: A Guide to Piaget and Kohlberg.* New York: Paulist, 1975.

Gleason, John F., Jr. *Growing Up to God.* Nashville: Abingdon, 1975.

Goldman, Ronald. *Religious Thinking from Childhood to Adolescence.* New York: Seabury, 1968.

Ingle, Clifford, ed. *Children and Conversion.* Nashville: Broadman, 1970.

Joy, Donald A. *Meaningful Learning in the Church.* Winona Lake, Ind.: Light and Life, 1969.

Kohlberg, Lawrence. "The Child As a Moral Philosopher." *Pyschology Today* 1 (Sept., 1968): 25-30.

Little, Sara. *Youth, World and the Church.* Richmond: John Knox, 1972.

Louthan, Sheldon, and Martin, Grant. *Family Ministries in Your Church.* Glendale, Calif.: Gospel Light, Regal, 1977.

Meredith, Char. *It's a Sin to Bore a Kid: The Story of Young Life.* Waco, Tex.: Word, 1978.

Powell, John. *Why Am I Afraid to Tell You Who I Am?* Niles, Ill.: Argus, 1969.

Richards, Lawrence O. *Youth Ministry: Its Renewal in the Local Church.* Grand Rapids: Zondervan, 1972.

Sigsworth, John W. *Careers for Christian Youth.* Chicago: Moody, 1958.

Southard, Samuel. *Counseling for Church Vocations.* Nashville: Broadman, 1957.

Strommen, Merton P. *Five Cries of Youth.* New York: Harper & Row, 1974.

Towns, Elmer. *Successful Biblical Youth Work.* Nashville: Impact, 1973.

Vocational Guidance Series. Nashville: Sunday School Board, Southern Baptist Convention.

Vocational Series. Fort Worth, Tex.: Radio and Television Commission, Southern Baptist Convention.

Warren, Michael, ed. *Resources for Youth Ministry.* New York: Paulist, 1978.

Westerhoff, John H., and Neville, Gwen Kennedy. *Generation to Generation.* Philadelphia: Pilgrim, 1974.

Wilson, Carl W. *With Christ in the School of Disciple Building.* Grand Rapids: Zondervan, 1976.

Zuck, Roy B., and Clark, Robert E., eds. *Childhood Education in the Church.* Chicago: Moody, 1975.

Zuck, Roy B., and Benson, Warren S., eds. *Youth Education in the Church.* Chicago: Moody, 1978.

CHRISTIAN DAY SCHOOLS AND CHRISTIAN COLLEGES

Benson, Warren S. "A History of the National Association of Christian Schools: 1947-1972." Ph.D. dissertation, Loyola University of Chicago, 1975.

Beversluis, N. H. *Christian Philosophy of Education.* Grand Rapids: National Union of Christian Schools, 1971.

Byrne, Herbert W. *A Christian Approach to Education.* Grand Rapids: Zondervan, 1961.

DeJong, Norman. *Education in the Truth.* Phillipsburg, N.J.: Presbyterian & Reformed, 1969.

Gaebelein, Frank E. *The Pattern of God's Truth.* Chicago: Moody, 1968.

————. "Towards a Christian Philosophy of Education." *Grace Journal,* Fall 1962, p. 3.

Gutek, Gerald Lee. *Philosophical Alternatives in Education.* Columbus, Ohio: Merrill, 1974.

Henkel, Milford Franklin. "A History of the Christian Day Schools Affiliated with the National Union of Christian Schools." Ph.D. dissertation, University of Pittsburgh, 1958.

Holmes, Arthur F. *All Truth Is God's Truth.* Grand Rapids: Eerdmans, 1977.

————. The Idea of a Christian College. Grand Rapids: Eerdmans, 1975.

Kienel, Paul A., ed. *The Philosophy of Christian School Education.* Whittier, Calif.: Western Association of Christian Schools, 1977.

Kneller, George F. *Introduction to the Philosophy of Education.* 2d ed. New York: John Wiley, 1971.

Krauschaar, Otto. *American Nonpublic Schools.* Baltimore: Johns Hopkins U., 1972.

LeBar, Lois E. *Education That Is Christian.* Old Tappan, N.J.: Revell, 1958.

Lockerbie, D. Bruce. *The Way They Should Go.* New York: Oxford U., 1972.

Marshall, John P. *The Teacher and His Philosophy.* Lincoln, Neb.: Professional Educators, 1974.

May, Philip. *Which Way to Educate?* Chicago: Moody, 1975.

Meyers, Marvin K.; Richards, Lawrence O.; and Webber, Robert E. *Reshaping Evangelical Higher Education.* Grand Rapids: Zondervan, 1972.

Morris, Van Cleve, and Pai, Young. *Philosophy and the American School.* Boston: Houghton Mifflin, 1976.

Rushdoony, Rousas J. *The Messianic Character of American Education.* Nutley, N.J.: Craig, 1972.

————. *Intellectual Schizophrenia.* Phillipsburg, N.J.: Presbyterian & Reformed, 1966.

Schaeffer, Francis A. *How Should We Then Live?* Old Tappan, N.J.: Revell, 1976.

Webber, Robert E. *How to Choose a Christian College.* Carol Stream, Ill.: Creation House, 1973

MISSIONS

Adeney, David H. *The Unchanging Commission.* Chicago: Inter-Varsity, 1956.

Anderson, Virginia. *Making Missions Meaningful.* Wheaton, Ill.: Pioneer Girls, 1966.

Bartlett, Margaret. "Teaching Missions to Primaries." *Key* 9 (Fall, 1969)· 29-32.

Engel, James F., and Norton, H. Wilbert. *What's Gone Wrong with the Harvest?* Grand Rapids: Zondervan, 1975.

Gilleo, Alma. *How to Teach Missions.* Elgin, Ill.: David C. Cook, 1964.

Haskin, Dorothy C. "How You Can Teach Missions to Children." *World Vision* 16 (February 1972): 12-13.

Peters, George W. *A Biblical Theology of Missions.* Chicago: Moody, 1972.

Stott, John R. W. *Christian Mission in the Modern World.* Downers Grove, Ill.: Inter-Varsity, 1975.

Voelkel, Jack. *Student Evangelism in a World of Revolution.* Grand Rapids: Zondervan, 1974.

Wagner, C. Peter, ed. *Church/Mission Tensions Today.* Chicago: Moody, 1972.

CAMPING

Bynum, Bill. "Missionary Education of Youth." In *Youth Education in the Church,* edited by Roy B. Zuck and Warren S. Benson. Chicago: Moody, 1978.

Camp Directors Handbook. Wheaton, Ill.: Scripture Press, 1959.

Ensign, John, and Ensign, Ruth. *Camping Together as Christians.* Richmond: John Knox, 1958.

Graendorf, Werner, and Crosby, Jerry. *Christian Camp Counseling.* (Correspondence Course.) Chicago: Moody Correspondence School, 1979.

Graendorf, Werner, and Mattson, Lloyd. *An Introduction to Christian Camping.* Chicago: Moody, 1979.

Journal of Christian Camping. Somanauk, Ill.: Christian Camping International.

Mackay, Joy. *Creative Camping.* Wheaton, Ill.: Scripture Press, Victor, 1972.

Mattson, Lloyd. *Camping Guideposts.* Chicago: Moody, 1972.

Nelson, Virgil, and Nelson, Lynn. *Retreat Handbook.* Valley Forge, Pa.: Judson, 1976.

Todd, Floyd, and Todd, Pauline. *Camping for Christian Youth.* New York: Harper & Row, 1963.

Troup, Richard E. "Recreation and Camps." In *Childhood Education in the Church,* edited by Roy B. Zuck and Robert E. Clark. Chicago: Moody, 1975.

SELECTED CHILDREN-YOUTH ORGANIZATIONS NOT UNDER LOCAL CHURCH SPONSORSHIP

Campus Crusade for Christ
Arrowhead Springs
San Bernardino, CA 92414

Young Life
720 W. Monument Street/P. O. Box 520
Colorado Springs, CO 80901

Child Evangelism Fellowship
P. O. Box 348
Warrenton, MO 63383

Youth For Christ, International
P. O. Box 419
Wheaton, IL 60187

Inter-Varsity Christian Fellowship
233 Langdon Street
Madison, WI 53703

Word of Life Fellowship
Schroon Lake, NY 12870

Navigators
P. O. Box 20
Colorado Springs, CO 80901

SELECTED CHURCH-SPONSORED CHILDREN AND YOUTH ORGANIZATIONS

Awana
3215 Algonquin Rd.
Rolling Meadows, IL 60008

Pioneer Girls
P. O. Box 788
Wheaton, IL 60187

Christian Service Brigade
P. O. Box 150
Wheaton, IL 60187

SELECTED CHRISTIAN DAY SCHOOL ASSOCIATIONS

American Association of Christian Schools
1017 N. School Street
Normal, IL 61761

Association of Christian Schools, International
P. O. Box 4097
Whittier, CA 90607

National Christian School Education Association
464 Malin Road
Newtown Square, PA 19073

Ohio Association of Christian Schools
1960 Fay Meadow Avenue
Columbus, OH 43229

Western Association of Christian Schools
P. O. Box 4097
Whittier, CA 90607

Intercristo
P. O. Box 9323
Seattle, WA 98109. (Although not an association, it has listings of placement
opportunities in North America, but particularly of missionary day schools.)

National Association of Christian Schools
P. O. Box 550
Wheaton, IL 60187

National Union of Christian Schools
865 28th Street, S.E.
Grand Rapids, MI 49508

SELECTED CHRISTIAN DAY SCHOOL CURRICULUM PUBLISHERS

A Beka Book Publications
125 E. St. John Street
Pensacola, FL 23503

Accelerated Christian Education
2700 Oakland Avenue
Garland, TX 75041

Alpha Omega Publications
P. O. Box 3153
Tempe, AZ 85281

Baptist Day School Association
9845 Woodley Avenue
Sepulveda, CA 91343

Concordia Publishing House
3558 S. Jefferson Avenue
St. Louis, MO 63118

Bob Jones University Press
Greenville, SC 29614

Association for Bible Curriculum Development
1515 N. Los Robles
Pasadena, CA 91104
    (being published by:)
        Lifeway Bible Curriculum
        1825 College Avenue
        Wheaton, IL 60187

28

Christian Education and Special Education

Leslie A. Grammer, Jr.

A SUBSTANTIAL NUMBER of our population is composed of persons variously identified as "handicapped," "exceptional," or "retarded."[*1] They are provided for educationally in a program generally called "special education."

The broad category of physical handicaps concerns such areas as impaired hearing or vision, disorders in motor abilities, and other impairments to physical movement.

Another broad area is sometimes identified as learning disabilities or behavior disorders. That could include difficulties such as hyperkineticism and autism.

The third category is in relation to mental handicaps—retardation.

In all areas of the handicapped there are increasing concerns and programs for their education.

In the United States the first form of education for the mentally handicapped was through the residential schools. Unfortunately, students with handicaps were often placed in such private or state schools and promptly forgotten. The schools became, in effect, places where frustrated families and society in general could relieve themselves of an overwhelming burden.

After World War I, however, there were so many disabled veterans returning home that society was forced to assume a new attitude toward the handicapped. Parents with handicapped children now began to form local groups where those having similar concerns could come and share their mutual problems. Eventually, state and national associations were formed. They began to lobby and pressure for government intervention. As a

[*]Roberta L. Groff, for example, indicates that 3% of the population is retarded.

LESLIE A. GRAMMER, Jr., M.A. Special Education, is the assistant director of Treasury Operations at the Moody Bible Institute, Chicago, Illinois.

result research for work with the handicapped began to develop in medicine, chemistry, psychology, and related fields.

Parent organizations meanwhile began their own special education programs, allowing their children the opportunity to learn and remain in the family unit.

Before 1920 there were very few educational institutions that offered any courses in the area of special education (education for the physically or mentally disabled). There was nothing in organized curriculum.

By 1950, however, more than seventy institutions of higher education reported having a sequence of courses relating to special education.

Today federal and state governments have made it mandatory that school districts make provisions for the education and instruction of all those with handicaps.[2]

It is estimated that there are over eight million young people under the age of twenty-one having handicaps to the extent that they need a special program of education to help them achieve their potential. Without those special programs, many handicapped young people would never learn to function in and contribute to our present society. They would eventually become a burden and a recipient of welfare, adding to the problems of our social structure. However, with special education, they have the possibility of eventually becoming self-supporting and functional.

CHURCH OPPORTUNITY

The church has a basic directive for concern for the handicapped in the life of Jesus Christ, who in His earthly ministry met the handicapped of His day with love and compassion. He healed the leper, cast out demons, and made the blind to see. He taught His disciples to likewise have concern and compassion and to follow His example (Matt. 8-10).

Thus Peter, Paul, and the others followed Jesus in working with handicapped, and in some cases they saw God demonstrate His power to heal through them (Acts 3, 19, 28). Clearly, Christianity has provided the base for contemporary concern for special education.

There is also concern for the families of the retarded. Many parents caring for handicapped persons remain home from religious services because there are no church programs to meet the needs of the handicapped. Where special programs are available, they not only provide care and instruction for the handicapped but they also make it possible for the instruction and refreshing of parents.

Jesus said, "To the extent that you did it to one of these brothers of mine, even the least of them, you did it to Me" (Matt. 25:40).

Roberta Groff has expressed it well:

The church can help meet the spiritual needs of retarded children in a way that no community program can possibly do. A concerned parent has suggested two specific ways in which local churches can minister to retardates. First, churches, realizing that the retarded are individuals for whom Christ died, can provide classes in Sunday school and vacation Bible school and boys' and girls' weekday activities for the retarded. Second, churches can show concern for each retardate's family members. Brothers, sisters, grandparents, and other relatives are deeply affected by the discovery that a child in their family has mental retardation. The parents of the mentally retarded have heavy burdens. The church can share in these burdens through the gift of understanding.[3]

CLASSIFICATION OF RETARDATION

Mental retardation is usually defined in terms of subaverage mental functioning and impairment of ability to cope adequately socially. A broad division in relation to education is the *educable retarded* (IQ 50-75) and *trainable retarded* (IQ 30-50). The educable have limited vocabulary but can achieve social adjustment and be somewhat self-directive. The trainable have a low concentration level and lack of motivation.

TRAINING FOR SPECIAL EDUCATION

"Not everyone can teach exceptional children. The teacher of exceptional children should have all the qualities of the best in the teaching profession, plus some additional competencies."[4]

The type and amount of training required for the teacher depends largely upon the program provided and its purposes.

Teaching a Sunday school class, for example, would not require the same expertise necessary for one teaching in a day school program. Administrators and supervisors of special programs would have to be knowledgeable in additional areas.

SUNDAY SCHOOL TEACHER

Even though the Sunday school or Bible school teacher would have the handicapped for a relatively short time, he must have some basic knowledge of the handicap represented by the student. That would include awareness of medical problems such as the influence of medication on the behavior and response of children under treatment. The teacher should be equipped to handle seizures, choking, hyperventilation, and similar incidents.

It is well to have a nurse or doctor approved by the church readily accessible in cases of emergencies.

Some children may need special assistance and handling with their personal care and toileting. Teachers must be alert and sensitive to those needs. For that reason, it is wise to have an assistant in each special class.

Each teacher must have a working knowledge of the basic laws of teaching and be creative enough to adapt the curriculum to meet the needs of the pupil. Love, patience, and perseverance are the key words for these teachers—it is the quality and not quantity of work that is important.

Some Bible colleges and Christian publishers offer courses and curricula for work with the handicapped. (See Resource section.)

DAY SCHOOL TEACHER

This teacher should have at least a bachelor's degree in education and a minimum of nine to twelve hours in special education.

There are three main areas of concentration:

1. A study of the emotional, physical, and mental characteristics of the handicapped.

2. A study of teaching methods and curricula for working with the handicapped.

3. Observation and student teaching.

The day school teacher, as a professional, must continue to upgrade his level of knowledge and competence. A growing personal knowledge of the Bible and basic Bible doctrine is, of course, a prerequisite.

ADMINISTRATIVE TRAINING

The administrator of a special education program should have at least a master's degree in education with an emphasis on special education.

It will also be necessary to be well informed of federal and state laws as they relate to special education and the operation of special education facilities.

The administrator will be in regular contact with parents, parent organizations, and medical personnel. It is important for this person to be well informed of community resources and services available to his staff and constituents.

Related course work could concern personnel management and business administration.

METHODS FOR SPECIAL EDUCATION

Elmer L. Towns and Roberta L. Groff, in *Successful Ministry to the Retarded,* suggest these basic methods:

> Storytelling
> Creative Play-Acting
> Pantomime
> Role-Playing
> Puppetry

Visual Aids
Creative Art
Creative Music Activities[5]

PLANNING FOR SPECIAL EDUCATION

There must be research and consideration of the cost before venturing into a special education program.

In the endeavor to provide special education, it is not necessary to begin with a total special program. The first step may be to alter the physical structure by adding ramps to the building, hearing aids and sound amplification to selected pews or rooms, or braille instructions in certain locations.

It is also important as a first step to survey the church and the community to ascertain the number and types of handicapped in the area and what is presently being done.

There may be other programs already in existence to serve certain areas of the handicapped. If so, it may be wise not to duplicate service but rather to form a joint effort or cooperate in forming a ministry in a different area.

When planning a facility for handicapped persons, it is necessary to consider very carefully the needs of each handicap represented. Wide halls, ramps, and washroom stalls are necessary for those on crutches or in wheelchairs. Chalkboards recessed from the wall and equipped with rails are also a must for such a ministry. For the blind, one must consider a classroom with as few obstacles as possible.

The room used will be determined by the age of the pupils, type of handicap, activity to be done in the room, and number of students.

Other areas to consider in developing a ministry for handicapped people are: special buses with a lift, buildings with ramps, special hearing devices, braille curriculum materials, specialized medical and professional consultants, and a properly trained staff.

New programs are costly. Start in the Sunday school with a simple ministry, either with some physical handicapped or a few mentally handicapped. Then grow with the programs.

WORKING IN SPECIAL EDUCATION

It is important to emphasize that the worth of a program depends to a large extent on the quality of the teaching staff.

Along with teaching skills, the teacher and administrator of a special program must have a sensitivity to the entire family unit and their interactions one with another. The parent and teacher should form a strong cooperating relationship and complement each other's instructions.

It is necessary for the teacher to recognize and work with the parents' knowledge of their child's special need. Most parents of handicapped children, though not professionally trained, are usually basically informed about the medical and educational needs of their child.

There will be occasions when the teacher will be a counselor and educator to the parents, as some parents may have guilt feelings concerning a handicapped child. There may have been drug problems, missing a doctor's instructions, or even a feeling that God is punishing for sins.

Some parents may become overprotective and concerned for the handicapped individual and may neglect other members of the family. Others refuse to accept the fact that their child has a handicap.

The effective administration and supervision of special education programs requires skilled and knowledgeable guidance. Because of the complexity of the problems in the field, it is important to be able to adapt and cooperate with other professional and nonprofessional persons in developing a program suited to each exceptional child's needs and abilities.

FOR FURTHER STUDY

1. Visit a school, workshop, or rehabilitation program serving the handicapped, and record observations for class discussion.
2. Invite a family with a handicapped person to dinner or a picnic.
3. Contact state and federal organizations and ask for copies of laws pertaining to the handicapped.
4. Volunteer to care for a handicapped person to free the family for a day.
5. Contact an organization for the handicapped and ask for a special speaker to come and present their services to your group.
6. Include films and curricula for the handicapped in your teacher-training program for church.
7. Start a special education library and file for your church.
8. Write a research paper about a particular handicap.
9. Interview parents of several handicapped children and see how the special child has affected the family unit.
10. Develop a resource file of organizations in your area that serve the handicapped.

NOTES

1. Roberta L. Groff, "Teaching Mentally Retarded Children," in *Childhood Education in the Church*, ed. Roy B. Zuck and Robert E. Clark (Chicago: Moody, 1975), p. 426.
2. The Education for All Handicapped Children Act, Public Law 94-142, was signed by President Gerald Ford on November 29, 1975. It requires a free appropriate public education for all handicapped children in the United States.
3. Roberta L. Groff, pp. 426-27.
4. William M. Cruickshank and Orville Johnson, *Education of Exceptional Children and Youth* (Englewood Cliffs, N.J.: Prentice-Hall, 1958), p. 28.
5. Elmer L. Towns and Roberta L. Groff, *Successful Ministry to the Retarded* (Chicago: Moody, 1972), pp. 77-91.

SUGGESTED READING

Axline, Virginia M. *Dibs: In Search of Self.* New York: Random, Ballantine, 1976.

Bogardus, LaDonna. *Christian Education of Retarded Children and Youth.* Nashville: Abingdon, 1963.

Carlson, Bernice W., and Ginglend, David R. *Play Activities for the Retarded Child.* Nashville: Abingdon, 1961.

Carpenter, Robert D. *Why Can't I Learn?* Glendale, Calif.: Gospel Light, 1972.

Clark, Dorothy; Dahl, Jane; and Ganzenback, Lois. *Look At Me, Please Look At Me.* Elgin, Ill.: Cook, 1973.

————. *Teach Me, Please Teach Me.* Elgin, Ill.: Cook, 1974.

Cruikshank, William M., and Johnson, Orville. *Education of Exceptional Children and Youth.* Englewood Cliffs, N.J.: Prentice-Hall, 1958.

Eareckson, Joni, and Musser, Joe. *Joni.* New York: Bantam, 1978.

Hahn, Hans R., and Raasch, Werner H. *Helping the Retarded to Know God.* St. Louis: Concordia, 1969.

Macracken, Mary. *A Circle of Children.* Philadelphia: Lippincott, 1973.

Nelson, Marion H. *Why Christians Crack Up.* Chicago: Moody, 1974.

Rogers, Dale Evans. *Angel Unaware.* New York: Harcourt Brace Jovanovich, Pillar, 1975.

Schultz, Edna Moore. *Kathy.* Chicago: Moody, 1972.

Stubblefield, Harold W. *The Church's Ministry in Mental Retardation.* Nashville: Broadman, 1965.

Towns, Elmer L., and Groff, Roberta L. *Successful Ministry to the Retarded.* Chicago: Moody, 1972.

Zuck, Roy B., and Clark, Robert E., eds. *Childhood Education in the Church.* Chicago: Moody, 1975.

RESOURCES

Abingdon Press, 201 Eighth Ave. South, Nashville, TN 37203.

Bible Club Movement, 237 Fairfield Ave., Upper Darby, PA 19082. Has a program known as "Handi-Vangelism," which offers training in local churches to help those interested in organizing new programs.

Closer Look, Box 1492, Washington, D.C. 20013.

Concordia Publishing House, 3558 S. Jefferson St., St. Louis, MO 63118. Filmstrips, cassettes, and lessons for the handicapped and their teachers.

Council for Exceptional Children, 1499 Jefferson Davis Highway, Suite 900, Arlington, VA 22202. Ask for a price list of material.

John Knox Press, 801 E. Main St., Richmond, VA 22309.

The National Special Education Information Center, US Department of Health Education and Welfare, P. O. Box 1492, Washington, D.C. 20013. Ask for free publications, practical advice to parents and parent organizations and other groups concerned with children who have special needs (for your state).

Porter Sargent Publishers, 11 Beacon Street, Boston, MA 02108. Guide to summer schools and summer camps including those for handicapped.

"A Resource Guide for the Physically Handicapped" and "Access Chicago" (free), from Rehabilitation Institute of Chicago, 345 E. Superior, Chicago, IL 60610.

Shepherds, Inc. P. O. Box 1261, Union Grove, WI 53182.

Sunday School Board, Southern Baptist Convention, 127 Ninth Ave., North, Nashville, TN 37203.

US Department of Health, Education and Welfare, Office of Education, US Government Printing Office, Washington, D.C. 20402.

29

Urban Christian Education

MELVIN E. BANKS

WHY SHOULD WE CONCERN OURSELVES with *urban* (city) Christian education? Perhaps the most obvious answer to that question is that there are people in urban areas. Why they are there has a wide variety of reasons, but there are three that stand out.

Some came to the city seeking survival. They have heard that cities offer the best opportunities for financial security. Whether one is a pauper looking for a job, a student seeking educational opportunities, or an entrepreneur looking for a chance to succeed in business, cities have a reputation for sustaining persons economically.

Some came seeking excitement. Tiring of small towns and country living where there's "nothing to see and do," many come to the big city looking for new sounds, new sights, and new experiences. Furthermore, cities offer anonymity where people can do what they please with little fear of being detected or condemned.

Some are trapped. A significant group of the urban population is made up of the offspring of parents who migrated to the city for either of the above reasons, but who now find themselves without the resources, and in some instances the inclination, to change their environment.

For whatever reasons they came or remain, people are jammed into cities—people of diverse classes, cultures, ethnic groups, religions, and philosophies.

Finding reasons to avoid working with city dwellers is easy. Who craves an environment of crime, overcrowdedness, and pollution? Yet, when the purpose of God is taken into account, one cannot bypass the city. To do so is to ignore the clear indication of Scripture that God wants

MELVIN E. BANKS, is the president of Urban Ministries, Chicago, Illinois.

the gospel to be proclaimed to every creature. And because so many of those "creatures" are located in the urban areas, cities offer a golden opportunity for implementing Christ's commission for making disciples (Matt. 28:19-20).

THE URBAN ENVIRONMENT

POPULATION

America is a nation of cities. Seventy percent of the country's population lives on about 1 percent of the total land.[1] More than 66 percent of its people live in areas containing 2,500 people or more.[2] So steady and intense has been the migration from rural toward urban areas (in 1800 only 5 percent of the population lived in areas 2,500 or more), sociologists have had to search for new terms to describe this urbanization. To speak of metropolitan areas is no longer adequate. Social scientists are today devising strategies for dealing with *megalopolises*—that is, large urban sprawls extending from one metropolitan area to another. The specific focus of our interest in this chapter, however, is on a segment of the total urban environment variously termed "ghetto," "central city," or "inner city." Those terms generally refer to that segment of city dwellers other than the white middle class.

Who are these "other than white middle class," who form a significant portion of most central cities? Although whites still constitute the highest percentage of the *urban* population as defined by the Census Bureau (2,500 or more), central cities have substantially higher percentages of blacks and other minority groups. At the time of the 1970 census, blacks made up 92 percent of the nonwhite population in the United States.[3] Chicanos, Indians, and Japanese accounted for most of the remaining 8 percent. At that time (1970) nineteen of the fifty biggest American cities were more than 30 percent black. Four of the fifty cities were more than 50 percent black.

According to Senator Fred Harris and New York mayor John V. Lindsay, "The trend shows no sign of abating."[4] They estimated that by the mid 1980s thirteen cities will have black populations of 50 percent or more. "It does appear that by the end of the decade, most of our biggest cities will be predominately black, and brown. . . ."[5] The Council of Great Cities found in 1972 that nine of the twenty-two big-city school systems had school enrollments in which half or more of the students were black. Projections are that by the mid 1980s twenty-three cities will have predominately black public school systems.[6]

PROBLEMS OF THE INNER CITY

After the riots of the 1960s, President Lyndon B. Johnson appointed a commission to study the causes of unrest. The report of the National Advisory Commission on Civil Disorders documented several major problems:

1. *Unemployment and underemployment.* Blacks earn only 58 percent of the median income of the white population. The gap was seen to be growing instead of decreasing, even though income for all persons is increasing. Unemployment within the black community often runs as high as 24 percent among employable men and up to 46 percent among employable *young* men and women.

2. *Poverty.* Using the Social Security Administration's definition of poverty, in 1966, 11.9 of the nation's whites were living in poverty whereas 40.6 of the nation's nonwhites were below the poverty level.

3. *Crime and insecurity.* "The majority of the law abiding citizens who live in disadvantaged black areas face much higher probabilities of being victimized than residents of most higher income areas, including almost all suburbs. For non-whites, the probability of suffering from any index crime except larceny in 78 percent higher than for whites."[7]

4. *Health.* People in central cities are not as healthy as those in other parts of the country. There are higher mortality rates, more disease, and fewer medical services.[8] Jack Geiger, of the School of Medicine at the State University of New York says, "The poor are sick more often, get less care, and die sooner (in all age groups and from almost all causes) than the more affluent." He goes on to say that the "primary cause of these burdens of ill health, increased disability, and excess death must lie in the physical, biological, and social environments."[9]

URBAN MINISTRIES

Given the magnitude and complexity of urban problems, outsiders might wonder if anything of consequence can be done by way of ministry in the inner cities. Despite the fact that the majority of existing ministries struggle with meager resources, in many instances they do a commendable job. A brief survey of types of ministries follows:

BLACK DENOMINATIONAL CHURCHES

Practically every one of the more than thirty black denominations[10] has some plan for the establishment of local churches. Experience has demonstrated that although many churches and church groups do not speak the traditional "evangelical" language, a significant number regard Jesus as Lord.

The overall results of such church planting—even the storefront variety— cannot be minimized.

RADIO

Radio has been utilized in a number of evangelistic efforts with varying degrees of success. For the most part such efforts have been essentially a "sowing" type of ministry with little success in follow-up and in-depth discipleship. Despite that handicap, well-known figures like Tom Skinner, Howard Jones, and Clay Evans, along with a good number of lesser known personalities, have used this medium to reach inner-city residents with the gospel.

CAMPS

Summer camps located in states such as Michigan, Mississippi, Tennessee, South Carolina, New York, and California reach thousands of inner-city children and teens each year. Those outdoor ministries are essentially evangelistic in nature, but provide fair amounts of Bible teaching. Despite the understaffing and centralized type of camping that frequently exists, these volunteer efforts are productive.

PRISON MINISTRIES

One of the most innovative approaches to meeting both spiritual as well as the educational needs of prisoners is that of the PACE* Institute located
*Programmed Activities for Correctional Education.
in Chicago. John Irwin, who for a number of years was a chaplain at Cook County, Illinois, jail pioneered a program to train and educate men during their incarceration. As a result of that program the number of persons who return to jail has been so dramatically reduced that other out-of-state institutions are using PACE as a model for their programs.

NATIONAL BLACK EVANGELISTIC ASSOCIATION

Sensing the need for fellowship and the call of God to minister to the needs of black people, the NBEA was organized in 1963 in Los Angeles. At its annual convention various commissions deal with current issues affecting the life and life-style of black evangelicals. Out of this fellowship has grown a number of smaller evangelistic efforts.

BLACK CHRISTIAN STUDENT CONFERENCE

Black Christian students who attended the NBEA for a number of years eventually felt the need for a fellowship where they could deal in greater detail with problems affecting them as students. As a result, the BCSC fellowship was established a few years ago, with Drs. William and Ruth Bentley serving as leaders.

BIBLE SCHOOLS AND HIGHER EDUCATION

A number of community Bible schools have existed from time to time in various parts of the country, including those in Harlem, New York; Washington, D.C.; Philadelphia; Chicago; Los Angeles; San Francisco; and Spring City, Tennessee. One example, the Manna Bible Institute on the north side of Philadelphia, has developed from a small evening school meeting twice per week to an accredited day and evening school.

Moody Bible Institute and Wheaton College Graduate School have added cross-cultural majors to their curriculum.

North Park College, located on the north side of Chicago, has in conjunction with Young Life instituted a master's degree program in youth ministries with an urban black concentration.

CHURCHES WITH A TOTAL MINISTRY PERSPECTIVE

Many inner-city churches have for years recognized the need to minister to the total man. In many instances it was simply a matter of survival. It is refreshing, however, to observe in recent years a few predominately white inner-city evangelical churches ministering to the total needs of people. The LaSalle Street Church in Chicago has established a legal aid service for poor people.

The Voice of Calvary Ministries under the direction of John Perkins has instituted in Mississippi a spiritual and economic development project. The objective is to enable poor people to know Christ and to become self-sufficient in meeting their physical needs.

CHRISTIAN LITERATURE

Recognizing the inadequacy of available literature, an independent publisher called Urban Ministries, Incorporated (UMI) came into being in 1970. Assisted in its initial stages by Scripture Press, Zondervan, and several other publishing organizations, UMI became the first predominately black-owned independent publisher of Sunday school literature.

UMI's purpose is to develop and distribute literature more relevant to the needs of urban youth in general and black urban youth in particular. Chicago-based UMI writes Sunday school lessons, based on the international uniform outlines, in the idiom of black experience and life-style. Its ultimate goal is to lead young people into meaningful relationships with Jesus Christ.

Objectives for an Urban Christian Education Curriculum

The destructive conditions within inner cities demand that any curriculum or program for ministry take into account not only the cultural characteristics of the inhabitants but also the need for improving the life-style and living conditions.

The overall purpose of an urban or inner city church curriculum is adequately summarized by Jesus in His Great Commission. Indeed the purpose of an inner city ministry is no different from the purpose of the church as a whole, even though specific strategies may vary.

Jesus instructed the disciples, "Go, therefore, and make disciples of all the nations, baptizing them in the name of the Father and the Son and the Holy Spirit, teaching them to observe all that I commanded you . . ." (Matt. 28:19-20). The church is commanded to present the message of salvation to all people.

In addition to evangelism, the church is instructed to teach those who respond in faith to obey *all* that Jesus taught His disciples—and He dealt with all essential areas of life.

Based on Jesus' words, we conclude first that an adequate inner-city/ urban curriculum must guide persons toward *a proper relationship with God through Jesus Christ*. Such a relationship comes as a result of people's responding to the truth of God as presented in the Scriptures. That truth, however, must be presented in a way inner city and urban people can understand and respond to it. The gospel must be presented through the use of symbols and illustrations that communicate to inner-city people.

For example, to proclaim, "God is love," to a poor inner-city resident and to illustrate it with a picture of a person living in an affluent suburban home conveys a totally different "message" to the destitute mother struggling to provide for her family. Despite the verbal message that God loves her, what she really *hears* and *sees* is that God loves rich folks.

God must be presented as one who fully understands the nature and needs of those who live in inner-city areas. He must be presented as a God who does not approve of the desperate plight of the exploited poor in those areas. He must be shown to be a God who is interested in their total human situation.

Second, an inner-city/urban curriculum must show people how to cope with their inner frustrations and develop into *totally mature individuals*— spiritually, socially, psychologically, and physically. Such a goal recognizes that one cannot mature properly without the inner presence and working of the Holy Spirit of God.

Such people must be helped to deal with the frustrations of overcrowdedness and the fears and insecurities brought on by unemployment and crime. They must learn to cope with the defeatist syndrome related to lack of achievement in poor schools.

Whereas theologians can and should systematize the truth of God as revealed in the Scriptures, and whereas maturing believers need a good grasp of the total revelation of God, the man on the street, the frustrated person in the ghetto, wants to know how God relates to *his* situation. The distressed father wants to know what God has to say to him now—the rat just bit his baby! When one examines the Scriptures, one discovers that that is essentially how the Scriptures were revealed to us: God telling us and showing us Himself in relationship to our need.

Having enabled people to come to grips with God and themselves, an inner-city/urban curriculum should help persons cope with the most immediate interpersonal relationships—*the family and the extended family*. The program should include elements to help people deal with the complexities of their *urban ethnic* family life.

Much has been made over the matriarchal nature of many black families. According to the Census Bureau, in 1972 about 60 percent of all black families were headed by husband and wife. About 35 percent of black families were headed by a woman, a 3 percent increase from five years earlier.[11] Such percentages are closely related to income and education. Those black men, for example, who have completed high school are more likely than those without a high school education to have their first wife living with them.[12]

Marriage in our country as a whole is in serious difficulty, and there is no question that it is also a problem in inner cities. Certainly, if a curriculum aims to develop people into the likeness of Jesus Christ, it must include elements that enable individuals to cope with the pressure of urban family living.

Fourth, moving out from the family, the urban *believer's* next "world" is the *local church fellowship*. He is a member of the Body of Christ, and the inner-city/urban curriculum must deal with the scriptural teaching concerning the church, showing believers how to find their places and how to function in the Body for the benefit of themselves, other believers, and the world as a whole.

Finally, the *wider world* of the urban believer includes his immediate community, the city, state, national, and international community. In each of those spheres the Scriptures have something to teach us about our attitude and conduct, either directly or indirectly in principle form. But what does it say? And how should the principles be applied to the myriad circumstances confronting the urban Christian believer? The inner-city curriculum should provide some answers.

Jesus relieved the total needs of people, and the gospels are profuse with such accounts (e.g. Matthew 8-9). Jesus expressed unequivocable concern for the total needs of people (Matthew 9:36; 15:32-39), and He clearly commissioned the church to teach people to observe *"everything"* He taught (Matthew 28:20). We cannot, therefore, dismiss our responsibility for the total needs of people. Certainly we must guard against any attempt to equate good works with salvation, but we cannot biblically withdraw ourselves from the very world for which we are called to be lights and salt.

STRATEGIES FOR THE URBAN CHRISTIAN EDUCATION MINISTRY

The pattern or strategy for an inner-city/urban curriculum that deals with the total needs of individuals is outlined for us in the book of Acts (2:42-47), where we find the early church engaging in activities that met all the needs of the people who were so involved. Luke records that the believers were "continually devoting themselves to the apostles' *teaching* and to *fellowship* to the *breaking of bread* and to *prayer.*" The subsequent records (Acts 2:43-46; 3:1-10; 4:32-35; 6:1-4; 11:27-30) describe the believers busily engaged in meeting the *physical* needs of fellow believers, as they were taught by the apostles and controlled by the Holy Spirit.

MEETING INTELLECTUAL NEEDS

The local church focuses its intellectual attention on that which only the church can provide. The church encourages and supports other agencies in the community to do its best in teaching general subjects, although in some inner city communities, churches find they must teach reading before they can teach the Bible.

The urban church's main concerns include origins and coping with present existence.

1. *Studies for understanding our origins.* People need to know where they came from. The nature of God, His creative activity, the patriarchs, the development of Israel, and the plan of redemption are all parts of our origins. Because of the lack of affirmation and identity on the part of blacks in this country, it is essential that they know where black people crossed the pages of biblical history. All that the Scriptures teach in terms of origins needs to be known.

In addition, when the family or other instructional institutions fail to provide some knowledge of ethnic history, the church in a supplementary fashion may need to provide this kind of teaching for its constituency.

2. *Studies for coping with our present existence.* Church teaching must deal with the *life situations* faced by people living in inner-city/urban areas. The Christian's one infallible source of knowledge is the Bible. People need and want to know what *God* has to say about the difficult situations with which they have to cope every day. Through time-honored agencies like the Sunday school, vacation Bible school, and home Bible classes, the church can systematically teach the Word of God, showing how the truths relate to the *personal* needs of urban dwellers. Program-

ming and scheduling for meeting those needs must also take into account the varied life-styles of inner-city/urban people.

Family life studies can help young people and adults come to grips with love, courtship, and marriage. This could be an elective series taught at the Sunday school hour or at the designated Sunday afternoon learning session. Children need principles for growing up in the city, and family members must learn to cope with the realities of living together.

Church life studies are a must if members of the fellowship are to have meaningful relationships within the church. What is the church? Why does it exist? How does it carry out its functions? Training in the *what* and *how* of church life is one of the crucial concerns of inner-city church leaders.

Community life series will vary depending on the community and the needs in that community. Certainly believers need to know how to vote, how their government operates, and how they can communicate with their government representatives. Members need to know how to look for a job, where to apply for government-sponsored food and medical services. In some communities other agencies or the people themselves are sufficiently knowledgeable to deal with their social needs, but since the church must be concerned with the total person, where other agencies are inadequate the church must be sensitive and supply the needed information.

MEETING EMOTIONAL NEEDS

1. *Worship.* The church fellowship has been established as the meeting place for collective worship of believers. The desirability of worship needs no elaboration. What is needed, however, is the recognition that various ethnic groups that attend inner-city churches need not sacrifice their culture in order to genuinely worship. One form of worship should not be regarded as "emotional" or "cold" because it does not conform to the established custom of another group. What is important is that worship be carried on "in spirit and truth" (John 4:24).

If worship is our response to God for Who He is and what He has done, then we must use God's Word to increase our knowledge of Him. Knowledge, in turn, helps to deepen our response to Him. But truth as revealed in the Scriptures must become truth known from experience. For example, we can praise God for His promise never to leave us (Heb. 13:5). When through some test we have *experienced* His presence, our worship of Him and our appreciation for that promise is deeper. That is why oppressed minority groups can become quite emotional when they think about the goodness of God. Many, historically, have been through so much that had it not been for God they never would have made it. Their worship often reflects their gratitude.

2. *Fellowship.* The pressures and frustrations of city living dictate that the church must not neglect providing opportunities for genuine fellowship if it is to meet the total needs of people.

The early church recognized that need and provided for it. The loving concern that prompted the sharing of their resources undoubtedly was the result of relating to each other. Larger churches especially need to group people into smaller cells for more intimate sharing. The Progressive Baptist Church pastored by the late Dr. T. E. Brown in Chicago had five thousand members, but each person was also a member of a small "club" established for the very purpose of providing small-group fellowship. Urban inner-city people need a chance to fellowship.

MEETING EXPRESSIONAL NEEDS

Participation and involvement are generally recognized by Christian educators as vital ingredients for effective spiritual growth.[13] What should be emphasized is the special need among people in urban and inner-city fellowships. Historically, black people were shut out of most social environments, so that the church was the only place they could be somebody. To a large extent that condition still prevails. Those who cannot stand tall in the larger society need to do so within the church fellowship. Recognition, appreciation, and participation are important in urban churches.

Leaders must be especially sensitive to the expressional needs of the younger people. Frequently older people feel insecure and are unwilling to allow youth to assume leadership. Since the Scriptures indicate that all members of the Body have been given gifts to enhance the Body, everyone should be given the chance to exercise his gift.

Each person should be encouraged to achieve his best. A pastor in Chicago has made it his personal responsibility to see that every high school graduate in his church enrolls in a higher educational institution. Achievement is important for all, but it is critical in inner-city churches.

LEADERSHIP FOR URBAN CHRISTIAN EDUCATION

DESCRIPTION OF URBAN LEADERSHIP

1. *Models.* Examples of what a mature believer should look like head the list of leadership characteristics. Jesus, of course, is the supreme example, but the average person does not identify sufficiently with Jesus as a model. Inner-city ministries need people whose lives match their profession. Young models are especially important to young people. They need to see *how* the principles of Christianity work in their communities.

2. *Working knowledge of the Word of God.* Leaders who have studied the Bible with the needs of the urban and black people in mind are especially needed. Often recognized scholars outside the inner-city milieu

have little appreciation for the needs of urban people and how the Word of God can be brought to bear on the issues of urban living.

3. *Adequate understanding of the psychological, social, and behavioral patterns of inner-city people.* Just living in the community gives one some understanding of the needs, but a systematic understanding is vital in planning ministries.

4. *Working knowledge of communicative methods.* Methods that *best* communicate to the urban person must be employed.

5. *Understanding the dynamics of cross-cultural communication for the group involved.*

    a. Develop an adequate understanding of the life-style, the way of living as practiced by the group.

    b. Develop a healthy identity *with* the group. In the case of whites communicating with blacks, whites who have been effective appreciated that the black person's struggle for justice and equality is a just struggle.

    c. Learn to respect the culture and cultural attainments of the group. While knowing that the lordship of Christ demands that all aspects of a life-style fall under His purview, the effective communicator, in urging Christian maturity, distinguishes between scriptural principles and his own cultural traditions.

    d. The communicator, knowing he cannot completely forgo his own need for personal fulfillment, nevertheless suppresses his own desire for fulfillment in order that the group might be ministered to. The effective missionaries have been those who, like Christ, lost themselves—gave up their right to be—for the well-being of the community.

STRATEGIES FOR LEADERSHIP DEVELOPMENT

Those who have concern for ministering in urban communities today must recognize their responsibility to serve as models of leadership for those who follow. They will encourage younger people to aspire, encouraging even the very youngest to participate and do his best at his level of competency.

Potential leaders must be selected and given concentrated training. Care must be taken to encourage students to matriculate in those institutions that will be most sensitive to their ethnic and urban needs. The training black students receive must not alienate them from the very community to which they desire to minister.

Predominantly white institutions must recognize their responsibility to guide the young people in retaining their own cultural identity while gaining the tools they need to serve their community. Mature ethnic counselors who can help do this are critically needed in such institutions.

FOR FURTHER STUDY

1. The human personality is composed of *intellect, emotions,* and *volition,* housed in a physical *body.* Go through any one of the gospel records, categorizing the miracles and teachings of Jesus under one or more of the aspects of personality to see how He ministered to the total needs of individuals.
2. Racism, with its concomitants of segregation and exploitation, is viewed by many inner-city residents as the greatest obstacle to an effective ministry by the white majority. Draw up a list of recommendations on how a white inner-city worker can identify subtle and overt racism, and how it can be overcome.
3. Visit an inner city mission, settlement house, prison, or school to observe how the leaders deal with the needs of persons under their care. Write a report on the findings.
4. Visit an inner-city Sunday school. Do a comparative study on a suburban and an inner-city Christian education program. How are they similar? How are they dissimilar? How does one explain the dissimilarities?
5. Select a curriculum published by a predominantly white publisher. Evaluate the materials for an inner-city church, comparing content, teaching methods, and illustrations.
6. Prepare a lesson plan for an inner-city Sunday school class. Gather illustrations, teaching tools, and so on, in anticipation of conducting the class.
7. Prepare a job description for a director of Christian education in a large inner-city church.

NOTES

1. Robert L. Branyan and Lawrence H. Larsen, *Urban Crisis in Modern America* (Lexington, Mass.: Heath, 1972), p. vii.
2. *World Book Encyclopedia,* 20 vols. (Chicago: Field Enterprises, 1970): 598.
3. US Bureau of the Census, *The Social and Economic Status of the Black Population in the United States,* Current Population Reports (Washington, D.C.: US Government Printing Office, 1973), series P-23, no. 46, p. iii.
4. Fred R. Harris and John V. Lindsay, *The State of the Cities* (New York: Praegar, 1972), p. 36.
5. Ibid.
6. *Report of the National Advisory Commission on Civil Disorders* (New York: Bantam, 1968), pp. 266-74.
7. Ibid., p. 268.
8. Ibid., p. 269.
9. James F. Blumstein and Eddie J. Martin, *The Urban Scene in the Seventies* (Nashville: Vanderbuilt, 1974), p. 156.

10. Constant H. Jacquet, Jr., ed., *Yearbook of American and Canadian Churches* (New York: Abingdon, 1978).
11. *Social and Economic Status of Black Population*, p. 3.
12. Ibid.
13. H. W. Byrne, *Christian Education for the Local Church* (Grand Rapids: Zondervan, 1973), pp. 26-28.

SUGGESTED READING

Blumstein, James F., and Martin, Eddie J. *The Urban Scene in the Seventies.* Nashville, Tenn.: Vanderbilt, 1975. A compilation of papers by professionals outlining what they foresaw in that decade.

Branyan, Robert L., and Larsen, Lawrence H. *Urban Crisis in Modern America.* Lexington, Mass.: D. C. Heath, 1971. A study of the transformation of the urban areas since World War I.

Byrne, H. W. *Christian Education for the Local Church.* Grand Rapids: Zondervan, 1973. An evangelical and functional approach to Christian education in the local church.

Dunston, Bishop Alfred G. *The Black Man in the Old Testament and Its World.* Philadelphia: Dorrance, 1974. Research and analysis of texts where blacks cross the pages of the Old Testament.

Harris, Fred, and Lindsay, John V. *The State of the Cities.* New York: Praeger, 1972. A follow-up report to the National Advisory Commission on Civil Disorders.

Henry, Carl F. H. *Christian Personal Ethics.* Grand Rapids: Eerdmans, 1957. A survey of philosophical views on ethics followed by an analysis of biblical texts, aimed at arriving at ethics for evangelicals.

Jacquet, Constant H., Jr., ed. *Yearbook of American Churches.* New York: Abingdon, 1978.

McNeil, Jesse Jai. *Mission in Metropolis.* Grand Rapids: Eerdmans, 1966. An analysis of forces at work in the city and how thoughtful churches can minister to the urban populations.

Report of the National Advisory Commission on Civil Disorders. New York: Bantam, 1968. An authoritative edition of this commission's report in response to President Lyndon Johnson's authorization.

Samkange, Stanlake. *African Saga.* Nashville: Abingdon, 1971. A brief introduction to African history. Despite the author's acceptance of the evolutionary origin of man, the book has helpful data concerning the history of black people in Africa.

Strong, A. H. *Systematic Theology.* Philadelphia: Judson, 1907. A classic book on theology.

US Department of the Census. *Social and Economic Status of the Black Population in the United States.* Washington, D.C.: US Government Printing Office, 1973. Series P-23, No. 46.

Washington, Joseph R. *Black Religion.* Boston: Beacon, 1964. A study of the religion of black people in the United States.

World Book Encyclopedia. 20 vols. Chicago: Field Enterprises, 1970.

30

Christian Education and Missions

ROGER E. COON

THE INTEGRAL RELATIONSHIP of missions and Christian education has never been more clearly focused than in Christ's own words in Matthew 28:19, "Go therefore and make disciples . . . ," and in 28:20, ". . . teaching them to observe all that I commanded you."

Cross-cultural missionary enterprise in the modern world is faced with two major challenges, both of which call for *theological knowledge combined with educational skills.* One challenge lies in those lands where there has been a great response to the gospel. It is the challenge of helping a young church become more firmly rooted in Christian truth. The second challenge lies in those lands where the people have resisted the gospel, whether because of religious antagonism or ideological antipathy. This is the challenge of leading them to a realization of the basic truth of the Christian redemptive message.

The work of the missionary in both situations involves communicating new concepts and helping people acquire a new understanding. Evangelism and discipling are based on instruction. The response involves learning in its total sense—a learning that can only be fully achieved through the new birth and the enabling of God's Spirit. Needed are those who understand what makes people want to learn and how they learn in Christ.

Research is showing a growing realization in "evangelized" lands that the level of biblical understanding in the new churches is lower than it ought to be.[1] Only half of the answers given by church members surveyed in four countries represented an evangelical understanding of Christian belief. To correct that, churches must be helped to understand the nature of true life-changing learning. They must be helped to create indigenous

ROGER E. COON is coordinator for Christian education with the Association of Evangelicals of Africa and Madagascar, Nairobi, Kenya.

structures to facilitate teaching at all levels. It is an essential area of study for every well-trained missionary and national church leader.

Missionaries face other problems in their ministries that require sound Christian education. One example can be found in catechetical courses prepared for indigenous churches to use with new believers. Some of those courses are based on purely rote memorization of Bible verses. Catechumens often simply do not understand the significance of the questions and answers that have been memorized.

Missionaries were often good disciplers themselves but did not succeed in training their followers to be disciple-trainers. Perhaps they did not identify what enabled discipling to take place. Missionaries must be able to pass on that capability in circumstances where classical western instructional methods are not effective.

The great need is for missionaries, trained in the basic principles and philosophy of biblical Christian education, who are able to apply those principles to any culture.[2] New churches in other lands may use different methods for instruction and training, but the basic educational principles will be the same. Concrete illustrations rather than abstract reasoning may characterize the logical process; songs rather than paper work may help the learner apply the lesson to life. But the need for instruction aided by learning activities and principles such as understanding and perceiving personal practical relevance are universal.

CHRISTIAN EDUCATION AND THE GOAL OF MISSIONS

Students in seminaries, Christian colleges, and Bible institutes sometimes think of Christian education and theology as areas of study for ministry only in America. But in today's climate of theological syncretism, those are the exact areas of preparation most needed for overseas mission service. Christianity is most vigorously attacked in the area of religious education in schools and universities overseas. To counter that, Christian educators must be theologians. And the growth of nationalism reinforces biblical principles calling for self-maturity and local leadership—the objectives of Christian education. Missionaries, when asked to list what they consider to be the greatest need in missions for new recruits, almost always include the area of Christian education and training.

As noted, Jesus explicitly involved Christian education with missionary outreach in His mandate to the disciples. "Teaching them to observe all that I command you" (Matt. 28:20) is both part of the disciple-making process and the goal to be provided for before the task can be considered fulfilled.[3] This total ministry is amply illustrated in New Testament missionary practice. Prolonged and profound instruction was always provided for the new churches. Although the apostle Paul moved on after establishing churches and providing basic (sometimes extended) follow-up training, he continued to carry a responsibility for the success of their Christian growth. That is evident in his letters and repeated visits (cf. 1 Thess. 3:1-2, 5).

The Christian Education Department of the Evangelical Churches of West Africa in Nigeria (Sudan Interior Mission) offers a program called "Planned Group and Family Evangelism."[4] This is a program designed particularly for African evangelistic teams among Islamic African peoples. Teams of two evangelists meet weekly for six months on an agreed schedule with all the members of an extended family in a village to relate a series of Bible stories. Each story presents a truth basic to the understanding of God and His redemption. When the series is complete, the family is invited to discuss among themselves what they have learned and to act on it.

Such educational evangelism is valid for more advanced countries as well. A staff member of Inter-Varsity in France (Groupes Bibliques Universitaires) testifies that they organized two types of student camps or conferences. One was for evangelism and one for Christian instruction. They were surprised to discover that as many university students were converted in their instructional camps intended for believers as in their evangelistic camps.

Christian education, then, is vitally linked with mission enterprise, both in evangelism and nurture. A biblical expertise in missionary Christian education methods as well as biblical knowledge of the missionary message is needed if we are to realize our goal: the creation of the church—a redeemed people of God united by the Holy Spirit into a functioning Body of Christ. It is to be a maturing church in which the believers grow together into Christ's image, live according to His intended pattern, and carry out His mission.

The Need for Missionaries Trained in Christian Education

Brief descriptions of the situation in various parts of the world offer an idea of the needs for Christian-education-based ministries. The following is a series of extracts from correspondence and reports. All illustrate the need for missionaries trained in Christian education, although the role of such missionaries may vary from country to country.

AFRICA

A key African evangelical spokesman reported:

> The Church in East Africa is growing at an alarming rate. I say "alarming" because the increase numerically is not matched, in my judgement, by a comparable increase in depth. I am concerned that unless we find

some way of discipling and instructing the new Christians, we might be in
danger in a generation or two when we have a large body of interested
people who call themselves Christians but who have not been taught. . . .
The Church is virile in many Third World countries today. The churches
are alive. They lack very much in the area of teaching, and this is an area
where they will still need help for a long time to come from the larger established churches.[5]

A study conducted in Nigerian churches for a Christian education publishers' consultation noted that there is a basic knowledge of the gospel
and of Bible stories. There is a simple understanding of the nature of
God, of Christ, of sin, and of the second coming. And there is a warm
fellowship and witness through the church. But there is little theological
understanding by which nonbiblical beliefs can be evaluated. The grounds
of our redemption are only vaguely perceived. Christian living is generally
governed by external conformity to a few legalistic standards, while underlying pre-Christian attitudes and patterns of life rest undisturbed. And
family living in particular lacks much of biblical character.[6]

In another study surveying French-speaking west Africa, the following
points appeared:

A. Trained leadership is essential to training constituencies.
 1. Deeper knowledge of the Bible as related to daily living.
 2. How to teach group Bible studies (emphasis on group dynamics,
    inductive studies, etc.)
 3. Training in how to train lay people.
 4. Basic management principles for organisation. . . .

B. Discipleship of new Christians.
 1. Basic follow-up of new believers on assurance, prayer, church
    membership, baptism, witnessing, etc.
 2. Simple doctrine.
 3. Helps to establish regular devotional life.
 4. Church relationships (responsibilities to children, role of each
    person in the church, etc.).
 5. The Christian life (in relation to cultural practices, fruits of the
    Spirit, prayer life, persecution, etc.). . . .

A brief survey of agencies being used in teaching ministries, training
and local Christian education ministries is rather discouraging. In most
instances it has been *too few people for too many jobs.* Although several
missions have Christian Education committees, they have mainly been
slow to transmit the right concepts to churches. Local Christian education
programs are rarely developed under lay leadership and participation.[7]

A growing Christian education department of an African denomination
in Kenya reported an increasing realization in the churches of the need

for systematic study and personal application of God's Word. But at the same time a lack of expository Bible preaching, a lack of discipling for believer development, and a *lack of planning in the churches to meet the needs.*[8]

The Christian Education Commission of the Association of Evangelicals of Africa and Madagascar set three priorities for cooperative endeavor in Africa: (1) the need for strengthening the Christian education training for pastoral leadership of the churches; pastors need to learn to provide effective life-related biblical training and instruction for all their people, (2) the need for helping Christian parents fulfill the role in Christian education that God has given to them, and (3) the need in the local churches for adequate teaching materials for a total program of Christian education suitable for their local African contexts.[9] Although those three needs are seen as priorities for cooperative action, there remain also many other aspects of Christian education ministry in Africa needing attention.

ASIA

In the January 1978 issue of the journal of the Asia Theological Association, Dr. Bong Rin Ro, the ATA Executive Secretary, led off with an editorial under banner headlines. WANTED: CHRISTIAN EDUCATION.

> Recently ATA surveyed some 50 Christian education and church leaders in Asia of the conditions of C.E. in their own countries. Their answers repeatedly stressed the need for teacher training (32 out of 50), Sunday School literature (25) and promulgation of C.E. to pastors and seminarians (13). The words of a Taiwan church leader summarize the feelings of many other leaders today:
>
>> "Few understand the full extent of Christian Education in the local church. Sunday School is generally only for children. Mostly girls teach in Sunday School, few adults with gifts are recruited. Sunday School curriculum is still written to a large extent by missionaries in English and then translated.[10]

Comments reprinted in the magazine included:

> (Sunderaraj, India) The church has not yet seriously recognized the fact that C.E. is for the whole church. Here the theological schools must impress upon their students that C.E. is a *must* for the edification and effectiveness of the church. . . .
>
> (Chang, Taiwan) Most people think C.E. is only Sunday School for children and don't care about training work. . . .
>
> (Singapore) The ideas are fairly widely disseminated in this city of book-gobblers. And a number of them are working at implementation, but without proper guidance they wither and die on the vine. . . .

(Korea) The Korean church emphasizes evangelism and bringing others to church, but does not always plan well for the growth of those who are brought in. . . . The curricula in Korea are generally content and lecture centered. Suggested activities for pupils are not well coordinated with the purpose and are often impractical. . . .

(Taiwan) The cultural difference between the authors of translated materials and Taiwan make these materials hard to teach.[11]

When church leaders were asked to list ways to improve Christian education in their countries, certain responses appeared repeatedly. They give a good indication of the kind of help the churches in those lands would appreciate.

(Taiwan) Give a sound concept of C.E. to church leaders—what it can do, how it works. . . . (India) Impress the importance of C.E. on church leaders and seminarians. . . . (Hong Kong) Educate local churches about C.E. through media. . . . (Korea) Seminars to give church leaders concepts of learner-participation education methods. . . . (Singapore) Get away from the blurring of church programs in which all meetings are similar to each other, with little demarcation of functions.

(Taiwan) Train good Bible teachers. . . . (Singapore) Teacher training, maybe with a mobile van, area-wide workshops, follow-up. . . . (Hong Kong) In-service training for C.E. workers. . . . (Philippines) Teacher Training camps and advanced program for trainers all over the country.

(Taiwan) Write own materials. . . . (India) More use of traditional cultural media. Simpler, up-to-date material with more application activities. . . . (Korea) Writers' conferences for preparing more adequate curriculum.[12]

When asked what questions they would like to put to Christian educators from other countries, their responses focused on how to meet the need for writers of Christian education materials, how to promote Christian education in the churches, and how to make Christian education culturally indigenous.

A letter from the Christian Education Department of the Evangelical Fellowship of India (Ruth Warner) notes that the emphasis in general education is on memorization rather than thinking and understanding, and this is reflected in Christian education as well. Students must learn to think about spiritual truth and then make it their own experience. And *then* learn how to teach others to teach. "Teachers in Christian education must know basic philosophies of C.E. . . . and be able to simplify things to basics." In order to improve teaching, much practical experience is necessary, both in a learning situation and in a teaching situation. "In India we need teachers who are able to train others, who can bring others forward. Teachers who can bring out the potential in others and not just teach facts."

A missionary writing from Japan says, "Interest on the part of the Japanese clergy in C.E. is awakening, but knowledge is little. They are slow to accept suggestions which they consider too western, very committed to higher education, and are a part of their very masculine-oriented culture. Therefore any C.E. personnel who plan to work in Japan should have graduate training in that field, be much stronger on philosophy than on 'gimmicks', have a good basic orientation in theology, and preferably come in the masculine gender."[13]

Those recommendations for missionaries planning to work in Christian education are valid worldwide, with less emphasis on the masculine gender in some countries, depending upon the role of the missionary. The female Christian education specialist, however, even in Japan, can have a significant influence working behind the scene and in an advisory role, particularly with regard to textbooks and Christian education curriculum.

An Australian educator writes:

> As in the rest of the British world, and much of Europe, C.E. is a very different "animal" from that in the U.S., or even from C.E. in countries where there is a lot of American missionary influence. Usually there is quite a need in this area. Sunday Schools have traditionally been strictly for children. Then there is a youth group and perhaps adult study groups of some kind (many churches lack these). All-age Sunday Schools are appearing here in some churches but they are rare.
>
> There are rarely any full-time job opportunities in C.E. except at the denominational level. Church directors of C.E. are almost unheard of, and there would not normally be funds to pay even a church secretary, much less any other full-time or even part-time workers. This does have the advantage that most church work apart from the pastor's work is done on the basis of voluntary effort, and this in my experience, often leads to good motivation. . . .
>
> The problem is that we have a dearth of people trained in C.E. Seminaries rarely give much attention to Christian education, even though virtually all clergy are expected (with lay people too) to take regular classes on religion in state schools, a job usually done very poorly indeed. . . .
>
> So we have considerable need for better training in Christian education at all levels, and for greater recognition of its importance. This does not necessarily mean following the U.S. pattern, but developing a pattern more suited to our needs.[14]

MIDDLE EAST

An instructor at Damavand College in Iran writes:

> Half the population of Iran is under age 15. There is a great need for Christian education of the children and young people, not to mention

adults! The church is very small, a sometimes fearful minority, who would be only encouraged by sound Christian education. There are active young people's groups in most of the protestant churches, for early teens to around age 30. But there is little foundation teaching before that.

It is difficult to list specific kinds of vocational possibilities. Better to come, get involved with the church, learn the language, and then see. There are unlimited opportunities for follow-up of Bible correspondence students. . . . The Child Evangelism Fellowship has workers as far east as Pakistan and as far west as Beirut and North Africa.[15]

EUROPE

The role of the Christian education missionary in Europe is different from that expected in American churches, and yet the skills needed are the same. A missionary in France wrote, "Christian education is so different from the highly organized programs for which young people are trained in the States that I find it hard to draw parallels. The French mentality shies away from highly organized, well-coordinated programs."[16]

Similar ministries exist, but they depend more heavily upon the ability of the individual leaders and less upon program materials and supervision. Missionaries play an important role in offering training, but only after long experience at working directly with various groups within the churches, parachurch ministries and camps.

Churches are small and isolated. "C.E. majors need to acquaint themselves before coming to France with the situation as it exists in order to judge whether they would be comfortable working under these conditions. . . . The majority of jobs require not only a good speaking knowledge of French, but an ever-increasing understanding of the French people. . . . All the jobs require flexibility and creativity—the more the better. American ideas must be modified to fit France or they die a rapid death."[17]

"American" Christian education training does not exist in Europe, yet that training is all the more important in such an unstructured situation. There is an awareness in European Bible schools of the need for educational understanding. Ideas will be valued, but it is unlikely that structures will be transplanted into the churches. An exception is the popularity of Flambeaux/Claire Flamme, a church program for boys and girls. It was modified and transplanted by a Frenchman from a program modified and launched by American missionaries in Africa. The missionaries based their program upon the principles of Christian Service Brigade and Pioneer Girls. Parachurch organizations such as the Bible Club Movement, Young Life, Campus Crusade and Inter-Varsity would welcome Christian-education oriented missionaries.

The cultural caution voiced from France is repeated again from England with a typical British understatement, "There is some resistance to

'American methods'!"[18] This is a caution that Christian education missionaries would do well to heed in any cross-cultural situation, but in some lands it is more pronounced than in others.

At the same time, Martyn J. White, the managing director for a publications ministry in Great Britain, says:

> Many churches are taking Christian education seriously. . . . There is a growing demand for our Bible based teaching aids. Our training conferences are well attended. . . . But progress is slow. . . . All age Sunday School is still a rather new concept and ministers are extremely cautious to move from their traditional programs. (The traditional pattern is for children of all ages to come together for a half-hour joint service followed by a 15 or 20 minute lesson.) . . .
>
> It is not commonplace for Bible Colleges to have a full course on Christian education, although I, and several others do take lectures from time to time. Perhaps this is the major area where there would be a vocational possibility. My dream is to get a good course of Christian education study into every Bible College.[19]

LATIN AMERICA

In a list of missionary personnel needs in Latin America, one mission typically includes: consultants to churches; disciplers of high-school and university students; workers for day-care centers, church schools, and camps; teachers in seminaries, Bible institutes, and Christian day schools; teachers of pastoral studies by extension; and persons for Christian radio and literature.[20] All of those are avenues for utilizing training in Christian education.

A seminary teacher of Christian education in Latin America describes the situation thus:

> Until recently the majority of missionaries and pastors had very little or no training in Christian education. As a result Sunday Schools, young people's societies, etc. have lacked leaders, organization and administration, materials, and teacher training. There has been a gradual change in the last fifteen years or so.
>
> As far as I know, no church in Latin America has a salaried Christian education director. Some churches have Christian education committees. In most of the countries there are committees on a national level composed of missionaries and/or nationals. These committees very often co-ordinate Vacation Bible Schools in the whole country or in a certain area, especially in rural sections, hold workshops, short-term institutes for leadership and maybe organize a Sunday School convention.
>
> Bible Institutes and Seminaries have Christian education courses. Every church has at least one young people's society, but there is a dearth of materials. Camps are beginning to come into their own. There has been

an improvement in grading and organization of Sunday Schools. Workshops, teacher training courses and even a few Sunday School Conventions have been held. But Sunday Schools are still in need of much help.[2]

One significant development of Christian education in missions that originated in Latin America has spread throughout the world. Theological Education by Extension (TEE) was born in Central America. It is generally thought of in the category of pastoral training, but in much of the undeveloped world TEE is helping fill the need for productive adult Bible study for key lay people. This lay application of the principles and materials of TEE is likely to increase. Its wide use of the techniques of programmed instruction with systematic study, involving several local church groups and outside seminar leaders, is particularly effective in semiliterate societies.

VOCATIONAL OPPORTUNITIES AND ADJUSTMENTS

It is not surprising that churches and missions around the world are eager for help with Christian education. Rightly understood, biblical Christian education is not an optional avenue of service for some church members. It is the *basic ministry* of the church. It must lay the foundation for reasonable evangelism, just as God's revelation to the Jews served as the basis for the New Testament mission ("to the Jews first" provided a core in most churches). It is the avenue for making disciples—and thus all consequent witness and service of the church.

Most of what is said in the reports from various countries applies equally to all. The kaleidescope of images forms a total picture that is general and valid for Christian education and missions worldwide.

We must challenge students in American Bible schools and seminaries and make them see the unlimited possibilities of how God can use them and the talents and creativity He has given them for Christian education *on the mission field.*

Missionaries trained in Christian education are needed—for research in indigenous patterns of education and for developing new but culturally relevant instructional practices for families and churches, in emergent realigned life-styles, that have no useable traditional pattern to fall back on.*[22] They are needed as Christian education teachers in Bible schools

---

*Dr. Larry Richards, for example, identified three cultural settings in contemporary Africa that call for distinct Christian educational systems for family life. At a consultation organized by the AEAM Christian Education Commission for African theological students in America, Dr. Richards identified: the rural cohesive nearly traditional family, the rural family with an absent husband who is employed elsewhere, and the much changed city family situation. "Report and Recommendations of a Consultation on the Christian Family in Africa," p. 2 (mimeographed).

and seminaries, for ministries in local churches, for short-term seminars, for teacher-training institutes and workshops. There is place for curriculum development (including programmed instruction for TEE and for use in cassette ministries) and the training and guidance of indigenous writing teams, as field workers for various youth programs, for camps, evangelism, and in church advisement.

The Christian education missionary must be alert to recognize how his insights fit non-American categories and to communicate in those categories. "Young people," for example, is generally a much broader class than in America, reaching often to the thirties but not including many adolescents. The Christian education missionary must tread lightly until he finds out the different standards for interpersonal relationships (especially between the sexes and age groups) and understands the reasons for them. The Christian education missionary must separate American culture (including values) and ways of doing things from biblical principles and ideals. Yet he must realize that people need ways for doing things and that a function of the Christian educator is to help formulate workable patterns of learning and to train people for using them.

The Christian education missionary is needed and challenged to be a unique instrument in the hands of God for the task of creating teaching churches in obedience to the commission of our Lord Jesus Christ.

FOR FURTHER STUDY

1. Interact with Bible references that indicate the place of teaching in the New Testament missionary task.
2. Interview a foreign student regarding the Christian education ministries he grew up in at his local church. What were they like? What problems being faced by Christians there might be helped by improving the Christian education ministries of the church?
3. Plan a study program for equiping a missionary to work with Christian education. Specify undergraduate and graduate courses, and practical experience. Note the emphases in this chapter on theology (including third-world theological trends). How helpful is it for the missionary to be familiar with secular viewpoints such as those of Piaget and Kohlberg on moral development and with trends in nonformal education?
4. Read the sections of *Let the Earth Hear His Voice* specified in the bibliography. Relate those reports from the Lausanne Congress on World Evangelization to the concerns of this chapter.
5. Write to one or more mission boards asking about opportunities for service by missionaries trained in Christian education. Prepare a list

of the qualifications (academic and practical experience) that would be most beneficial for a candidate for one of these opportunities.

6. Write a paper defining the attitudes that a Christian education missionary needs to guard against and those that he ought to cultivate. What types of self-discipline may be necessary in missionary Christian education work?

NOTES

1. Roger E. Coon, "Research Report on Biblical Knowledge and Christian Beliefs in Evangelical Churches in Africa," mimeographed (Association of Evangelicals of Africa and Madagascar, January 1973).
2. See James E. Pleuddeman, "The Coming Crisis in Africa," *The Other Side,* May-June 1972.
3. George W. Peters, *A Biblical Theology of Missions* (Chicago: Moody, 1972), p. 184, says, "May it not be true that the Christian church at home and abroad is betraying weakness because she has neglected the heart of the commission of Christ? We evangelize, make converts and church members, but we fail to make disciples." In this and on following pages Dr. Peters has an excellent treatment of the meaning and making of disciples. See particularly p. 189.
4. "Planned Group and Family Evangelism," mimeographed (Jos, Nigeria: Christian Education Department of the Evangelical Churches of West Africa).
5. Gottfried Osei-Mensah, "The Church in Africa: From Adolescence to Maturity," *Christianity Today,* 7 January 1977, p. 17. Mr. Osei-Mensah was the Executive Secretary of the Lausanne Committee for World Evangelization.
6. Study paper #1 for the AEAM (Association of Evangelicals of Africa and Madagascar) Christian Education Publishers Consultation, submitted by the Christian Education Department of the Evangelical Churches of West Africa, Nigeria, November 1976.
7. Study papers #2 and #3 for the AEAM Christian Education Publishers Consultation, submitted by the Centre de Publications Evangeliques, Ivory Coast, November 1976.
8. Study paper #1 for the AEAM Christian Education Publishers Consultation, submitted by the Christian Education Department of the Africa Inland Church, Kenya, November 1976.
9. As reported to the AEAM Executive Committee, April 1978, and noted also earlier in *Edification,* the newsletter of the AEAM Christian Education Commission.
10. Bong Rin Ro, "Wanted: Christian Education," *Asia Theological News,* January 1978, p. 2.
11. Ibid., pp. 3-6.
12. Ibid.
13. Mrs. Jack Davidson, Christian education instructor at the Alliance Bible College, Hiroshima, Japan, in a letter to the author.
14. P. J. Harrison, secretary for theological education with the Theological Commission of the World Evangelical Fellowship, in a letter to the author.
15. M. Sayre, Bible and Medical Missionary Fellowship, Tehran, Iran, in a letter to the author.
16. S. Page, The Evangelical Alliance Mission, France, in a letter to the author.
17. Ibid.
18. Martyn J. White, London, in a letter to the author.
19. Ibid.
20. From a brochure of the Latin America Mission.
21. D. A. McCullough, Central American Mission, Guatemala, in a letter to the author.
22. Lawrence O. Richards, "Report and Recommendations of a Seminar/Consultation on the Christian Family in Africa," mimeographed (Association of Evangelicals of Africa and Madagascar, June 1976).

SUGGESTED READING

BOOKS

Douglas, J. D., ed. *Let the Earth Hear His Voice.* Minneapolis: World Wide, 1975. Note the following sections:
  p. 152—J. Allen Thompson's chart on aspects of the goal of missions.
  p. 533—James F. Engel. "The Audience for Christian Communication."
  p. 574—Theodore Williams. "Nurturing and Discipling New Converts."
  p 580—John Peters. "Training Believers to Evangelize Their Community."
  p. 588—Marge Alcala Isidro. "Christian Education for Evangelization in the Local Church."
  p. 1216—Byang Kato. "The Gospel, Cultural Contextualization, and Religious Syncretism."
  cf. also pp. 1224, 1229, 1251, 1267.
Engel, James F., and Norton, H. Wilbert. *What's Gone Wrong with the Harvest?* Grand Rapids: Zondervan, 1975. Interesting reading with a paragraph every once in a while that rings a bell relevant for Christian education in missions.
Peters, George W. *A Biblical Theology of Missions.* Chicago: Moody, 1972. Christian education in missions found in a missiological context.
Richards, Lawrence O. *A Theology of Christian Education.* Grand Rapids: Zondervan, 1975. Encourages creative biblical thinking for Christian education as needed in missionary ministries.

PERIODICALS

C. E. Survey of Asia. *Asia Theological News,* January, 1978. P.O. Box 73-119 Shihlin, Taipei, Taiwan, ROC 111.
Coon, Roger E. "Biblical Knowledge and Christian Beliefs in Evangelical Churches in Africa." Mimeographed report. Association of Evangelicals of Africa and Madagascar, January, 1973.
ECWA Journal of Research in Church Education. Irregularly mimeographed. Box 63, Jos, Nigeria.
Edification, Newsletter of the AEAM Christian Education Commission. P. O. Box 49332, Nairobi, Kenya.
Engel, James F. "Church Growth Strategies Plus . . ." *Evangelical Missions Quarterly,* April 1976, p. 97.
————. "Our Readers' opinion." *Evangelical Missions Quarterly,* July 1976, p. 179.
Osei-Mensah, Gottfried. "The Church in Africa: From Adolescence to Maturity." *Christianity Today,* 7 January 1977, p. 17.
Pleuddemann, James E. "The Coming Crisis in Africa." *The Other Side,* May-June, 1972.
————. "Indigenous African Education." Mimeographed dissertation. Association of Evangelicals of Africa and Madagascar, January, 1973.
Report of the CHRISTIAN EDUCATION STRATEGY CONFERENCE. Association of Evangelicals of Africa and Madagascar, January 1973.

Richards, Lawrence O. "Report and Recommendations of a Seminar/Consultation on the Christian Family in Africa." Mimeographed report. Association of Evangelicals of Africa and Madagascar, June 1976.

Ro, Bong Rin. "Wanted: Christian Education." *Asia Theological News,* January 1978.

The Christian Education Bulletin. Christian Education Department of the Evangelical Fellowship of India (CEEFI). 6-3-609/172, Anandnagar, Hyderabad —500 004, India.

Theological Education Today. World Evangelical Fellowship Theological Commission, quarterly. J. Longlois, Les Emrais, Castel, Guernsey, C.I., UK.

Wagner, C. Peter. "Our Readers' Opinions." *Evangelical Missions Quarterly* July 1976, p. 178.

RESOURCES

Information Gathering and Contact Organizations

Specific information on ministries and opportunities can best be secured from individual missions. Departments of missions at Christian colleges and Bible institutes should also be consulted. In addition, the following organizations have access to much useful information.

AEAM Christian Education Commission
P. O. Box 49332
Nairobi, Kenya. AEAM is an alliance of evangelical churches and missions throughout Africa. The C.E. Commission was created to inform and assist member bodies in cooperative action.

Asia Theological Association
P. O. Box 73-119
Shihlin, Taipei, Taiwan, ROC. ATA has a directory of Christian education workers in Asia.

CAMEO (Committee to Assist Missionary Education Overseas)
c/o IFMA, Box 395
Wheaton, IL 60187. Dr. Lois McKinney, the executive director, is especially experienced in South America. CAMEO is particularly concerned with pastoral training.

CEEFI (Christian Education Department of the Evangelical Fellowship of India)
6-3-609/172, Anandnagar, Hyderabad—500 004, India.

Dr. P. Harrison, Editor, *Theological Education Today*
11 Garibaldi Street
Armidale, N.S.W. 2350 Australia. Dr. Harrison is an educational specialist serving with the World Evangelical Fellowship and thus has world-wide contacts.

INTERCRISTO
Box 9323
Seattle, WA 98109. Offers a computerized listing of job opportunities with
missions.

TEMA-INTERSERVICE
1032 Romanel
Switzerland. A catalog listing of workers needed in evangelical Christian work
in Europe.

Dr. Ted Ward
College of Education
Michigan State University
East Lansing, MI 48823. An evangelical educator who specializes in educational technology for third-world missions. Opportunities for graduate studies.

Index